January 4, 2013

For
Jim Mann —

The New Continentalism

From whom
I have learned much
across the years —

With
Highest
Regards —

Kent E. Calder

The New Continentalism

Energy and Twenty-First-Century

Eurasian Geopolitics

Kent E. Calder

Yale UNIVERSITY PRESS

NEW HAVEN AND LONDON

Published under the auspices of the Johns Hopkins University/SAIS Reischauer
Center for East Asian Studies.

Illustrations by Bill Nelson and Yukie Yoshikawa.

Yale University Press books may be purchased in quantity for educational,
business, or promotional use. For information, please e-mail sales.press@yale.edu
(U.S. office) or sales@yaleup.co.uk (U.K. office).

ISBN: 978-0-300-17102-0 (pbk.)

Library of Congress Control Number: 2011940944

A catalogue record for this book is available from the British Library.

This paper meets the requirements of ANSI/NISO Z39.48–1992 (Permanence of
Paper).

10 9 8 7 6 5 4 3 2 1

To the Memory of
Grant H. and Rose E. Calder

Who first showed me the nuance, and the beauty
Of the Silk Road

"In Asia, the oldest inhabited continent, there has always been a strong, instinctive aversion to fixed boundaries."

—*Lord George Curzon, "Frontiers"—
The 1907 Romanes Lecture, Oxford University*

———————————

"Although the entire policy of a state does not derive from its geography, it cannot escape that geography. Size, shape, location, topography, and climate posit conditions from which there is no escape, however skilled the Foreign Office, and however resourceful the General Staff."

— *Nicholas Spykman (1938)*

Contents

Tables

Figures

Abbreviations

AIOC	Anglo-Iranian Oil Company
AMED	Asia-Middle East Dialogue
ASEAN	Association of Southeast Asian Nations
ASEM	Asia-Europe Meeting
BTC	Baku-Tbilisi-Ceyhan (pipeline)
CBM	Confidence-Building Measure
CBN	chemical, biological, and nuclear
CCP	Chinese Communist Party
CICA	Conference on Interaction and Confidence Building Measures in Asia
CJ	Critical Juncture
CNPC	China National Petroleum Corporation
CPSU	Communist Party of the Soviet Union
CSTO	Collective Security Treaty Organization
DPRK	Democratic People's Republic of Korea (North Korea)
EAS	East Asian Summit
ESPO	East Siberia Pacific Ocean (pipeline)
GCC	Gulf Cooperation Council

GDP	Gross Domestic Product
GNPOC	Greater Nile Petroleum Operating Company
GECF	Gas Exporting Countries Forum
IEA	International Energy Agency
IEF	International Energy Forum (Riyadh)
IMF	International Monetary Fund
IMT	Islamic Movement of Turkestan
IMU	Islamic Movement of Uzbekistan
IPI	Iran-Pakistan-India (pipeline)
LNG	liquefied natural gas
METI	Ministry of Economics, Trade and Industry (Japan)
MITI	Ministry of International Trade and Industry (Japan)
MOFA	Ministry of Foreign Affairs (Japan)
MOFAT	Ministry of Foreign Affairs and Trade (Korea)
MOU	Memorandum of Understanding
NATO	North Atlantic Treaty Organization
NOC	National Oil Company
OAPEC	Organization of Arab Petroleum Exporting Countries
ODA	Official Development Assistance
OECD	Organization for Economic Cooperation and Development
OIC	Organization of the Islamic Conference
ONGC	Oil and Natural Gas Corporation (India)
OPEC	Organization of Petroleum Exporting Countries
ROK	Republic of Korea (South Korea)
PRC	People's Republic of China
SABIC	Saudi Basic Industries Corporation
SAMA	Saudi Arabia Monetary Authority
SCO	Shanghai Cooperation Organization
SCPMA	Supreme Council for Petroleum and Mineral Affairs (Saudi Arabia)
SODECO	Sakhalin Oil Development Corporation
SWF	sovereign wealth fund
TAPI	Turkmenistan-Afghanistan-Pakistan-India (pipeline)
TOE	Tons/Oil Equivalent
UAE	United Arab Emirates
WMD	weapons of mass destruction
WTO	World Trade Organization

A Note on Conventions

Asian names throughout the text are presented in their traditional form—that is, with the surname followed by the given name, in reversal of standard Western practice. Macron marks have been used where relevant in all cases except where the word in question appears so commonly in English discourse without macrons that such usage has become relatively standard. "Korea" denotes the Republic of Korea (South Korea), unless otherwise noted. The term "Eurasia" is used when both "Asia" and "Russia" are implied.

Preface

Political-economic transformation has been a hallmark of world affairs over the past three decades—nowhere more so than on the Eurasian continent. China and India have emerged into the global economy, even as the Cold War has ended and Russia has taken on a new incarnation. Fundamentalist Islam has emerged as a global force, and the global energy economy, ever more intimately linked to Asia, has been radically re-structured. Beyond the Bin Laden era, with the American presence in Iraq at an end, and that in Afghanistan receding, a new world is emerging. Yet we fail fully to understand or to adequately cope with the fateful consequences that are quietly falling upon us.

Ever since I was a boy, growing up in Burma and Ethiopia, I have been fascinated with the future of the developing world, and the role that it would ultimately play on the global stage. I can remember, at the age of eight, gazing from the New Territories out into mainland China, then *terra incognita* to virtually all Westerners of my generation, and wondering when it might awake, and move the world. A decade later, as a student traveler, I remember watching the dawn over the imposing ruins of Persepolis, and wondering when and how Iran, together with the Islamic world of which it was such a formidable if complex part, would once again emerge to re-configure the international scene.

A decade later still, from the dawn of my academic career, I began trying to make intellectual sense of the Asian transition and its global implications. That effort has consumed the better part of thirty years, even as the transformation itself unfolds, and is still continuing. In *The Eastasia Edge*, published in 1982 on the basis of seminars that Roy Hofheinz and I taught in the Harvard University Government Department during 1979–1981, Roy and I predicted an era of prolonged growth across Asia, and the possible twilight of the long era of Western global dominance that had begun with the Industrial Revolution. Over a decade later still, in *Pacific Defense* and in *Foreign Affairs*, I focused on the catalytic role of energy in bringing the East and West of Asia together. And in research for *The Making of Northeast Asia*, I began to see the deepening integration that was beginning to transpire across continental Eurasia, driven in part—although less exclusively than often claimed—by the rise of China.

This book, which chronicles and explains the gradual emergence of a more integrated Eurasia, has thus been in many ways thirty years and more in the making. It has been inspired by a broad range of personal experiences and intellectual stimuli. I have also been blessed by an able, loyal series of research assistants, and the continuing support of friends and family.

Special thanks must go to the researchers who have worked with me closely, over more than four years, as I have puzzled out the details of this book, whose broad logic I have intuitively sensed for so long. A unique place in the genesis of this work goes to Serene Hung, an insightful young scholar from Singapore and one of my last students at Princeton, who spent more than a year at the Reischauer Center, and contributed much to this work in its early stages. Yukie Yoshikawa also contributed significantly, especially in the graphic and statistical dimensions, over several years. I had the good fortune to re-connect with Mariko de Freytas, another former student at Princeton with whom I had lost contact, in the spring of 2008, leading to Mariko's joining the Reischauer Center as a senior researcher; Mariko's precision and sensitive insights made this a deeper and more accurate book. Michael Boyd, Mika Brooks, Jonathan Brooks, Ichiyama Shin-ichiro, Viktoriya Kim, Haillee Lee, Li Yimian, Samia Khoury, and Wang Yanan have all likewise contributed to the research presented here.

The SAIS Reischauer Center for East Asian Studies, where I make my intellectual home, has generously contributed financially to the research presented here, for which I am grateful. I also thank my academic colleagues, including Jessica Einhorn, John Harrington, Zbigniew Brzezinski, Francis Fukuyama, Mike Lampton, Carla Freeman, Karl Jackson, Mike Mandelbaum, Fred Starr, Rust Deming, and Bill Brooks for their support and encouragement. Ryan Calder, Chang Boo-seung, John Garver, Flynt Leverett, Skipp Orr, Alexander Panov, Saito Hirokazu, Konstantin Sarkisov, and Zhao Quangsheng have all contributed important insights. Bill Frucht of Yale University Press has been a delightful and empathetic interlocutor, who has deepened my conception of this book's intellectual role, while his colleagues at the Press and its affiliates, including especially Jaya Chatterjee, Michael Haggett, and Bill Nelson, have sensitively and efficiently nudged this book into production. Lastly, but not least, my family, with its roots in East Asia and deep interest in the Middle East, has inspired me throughout. To all, I am most grateful, while recognizing, in scholarship, that the inevitable remaining shortcomings are my own.

There is in my mind no higher task, for both scholarship and policy, than to understand the forces that drive the future, in a manageable empirical context. Eurasia is such a context, and the forces at work there are fatefully reshaping our world, as three decades of experience and research have suggested to me, and as the reader will hopefully come to see in the pages that follow.

Kent Calder
Washington, D.C.
November, 2011

Introduction

A generation ago, as the Berlin Wall went down, the world stood on the cusp of a new era. The Soviet Union was collapsing, while global market forces and Western democracy waxed triumphant. For a brief, shining moment, we seemed to stand at the end of history—with challenging dialectics no more.

Two decades on, the world confronts palpably more complex challenges. Powerful new engines of growth have arisen in China and India, the great beneficiaries of globalization, lifting hundreds of millions from poverty. Yet that same liberating growth has also brought new shadows, including resource shortages and new leverage for authoritarian petrostates in the global system.

Out of the liberating post–Cold War changes, in short, has emerged an unsettling if unremarked new dialectic that now quietly challenges the very unipolar Pax Americana that many so recently acclaimed as enduring. The collapse of communism produced a global world that has begotten growth; growth, in turn, has led to resource shortages, notably in energy. Tightening energy markets, in response, have provoked the rise of new forces—many authoritarian—that now challenge the unipolar democratic world order itself. Many once-promising democratic experiments, from the Ukraine's Orange Revolution to the Arab Spring of 2011, have likewise struggled with and often fallen to those new forces.

This book chronicles the historic political-economic changes that have transformed global affairs since the late 1970s, bringing down the bipolar, military-centric Cold War system and opening the way to new configurations. It then outlines and assesses the new world order finally emerging in the Cold War's wake, after two decades of transition. The book focuses on the two variables most central to the historic changes underway—energy and geopolitics.

Traditional social science classically considers these two unrelated—energy is freely available through market processes, while geopolitics is a product of political-military interaction. Quiet yet sweeping global changes since China's Four Modernizations began in 1978, however, have fused the inter-relationship between those critical drivers of the future—not just for Americans, but for all the world. Driven by surging new demand in developing nations—compounding the costs of our own extravagant energy-consuming lifestyle—hydrocarbons have become an increasingly scarce and valued resource, even as the major consuming nations grow increasingly dependent on imports.[1] They must also increasingly be drawn from the copious reserves remaining in the Middle East and the former Soviet Union, giving those petro-states enhanced influence in global affairs.[2] And fateful changes sweeping the Eurasian continent over the past generation—nationalization of Western energy firms, the Iranian Revolution, the collapse of the Soviet Union, and the advent of Vladimir Putin—have together unleashed forces of Islamic fundamentalism and Russian geostrategy that politicize energy and world affairs still further.

Back in 1970 the United States remained the world's largest oil producer, supplying virtually all its own needs. Since then, domestic production has steadily declined, and America today imports over three-fifths of its consumption. It must do so in a world where Europe, Japan, Korea, and now China and India are importing heavily as well. Meanwhile, OPEC's embargoes and arbitrary price increases of the 1970s, not to mention the recent pressure tactics of Ahmadinejad, Putin, and Chavez, have taught us that such import dependence can breed political challenge also, especially in the tight energy markets of the twenty-first century.

These epic changes in the world of energy have profound implications for global political economy. Most fatefully, they erode the virtually unlimited discretion that the United States has enjoyed in international affairs for a full generation since the Berlin Wall went down. For all America's global geo-political weight, its soft power, and the dynamism of its leadership, not to mention the far-flung and formidable transnational networks of its people,[3] the United States controls the levers of neither global energy demand nor supply. Eurasia, instead, is the nexus in energy matters, both as producer and consumer.[4] And it is to that volatile, growing, pivotal, and increasingly integrated continent that this book directs its focus.

As we shall see, East and South Asia together increasingly configure world energy demand. Indeed, over 42 percent of global primary energy consumption increases since 1990 are attributable to China and India alone, and the International Energy Agency forecasts that share to rise to an average of over 49 percent for the coming two decades.[5] Similarly, it is Eurasia—the Middle East and also the successor states of the Soviet Union, once America's preeminent Cold War competitor—that determines long-term hydrocarbon supply. Together, these countries hold almost 66 percent of proven oil, and nearly 71 percent of proven gas reserves.[6] As in the days of the classic Silk Road, Eurasia—not America—once again stands as the central actor on the stage of global energy affairs, although its supply and demand decisions will fatefully shape our own futures as well.

AN ANALYTICAL GAP

Energy geopolitics has become a fashionable subject of late,[7] and deepening intra-Asian energy ties are clearly drawing increased notice.[8] Yet much remains to be explained. Why have trans-Asian relationships, after centuries of mutual isolation among the nations of the continent, gained such sudden dynamism? Why have they grown so geopolitical? What political and economic forces, in particular, are giving birth to this new Eurasian political-economic configuration? How and why do critical junctures matter? How are emerging intra-Asian energy ties shaped by politics—domestic and transnational—in the component nations, and what do the resulting ententes portend for future years? How does the deepening energy interdependence across Eurasia transform perceptions, policies, and politics in the nations of the region? What do the emerging energy ties among China, India, the Middle East, and the former Soviet Union—fated to deepen steadily over the next generation—portend for both their continent and the broader world? Finally, what should be done, concretely—both in policy terms and by the private sector—to respond to the historic changes in energy geopolitics now underway in Eurasia?

THE PROBLEM FOR ANALYSIS:
THEORETICAL CONTEXT

This book addresses the paradox of Eurasian continent's sudden energy supply-demand transformation and the geopolitical implications thereof, at two levels: comparative politics and international political economy. In doing so, it also brings geography—a long-neglected discipline—back in. That hybrid approach itself is distinctive.

This research proceeds in three stages, designed to test the utility of our central tools for explaining political-economic continuity and change. First, I outline the fragmented, static, paternalistic, and largely secular Cold War structure of Eurasia before this remarkable transcontinental integration began—a rigid political-economic straitjacket that inhibited many regional ties and oriented at least the capitalist states on the rim of Asia across the seas, to the broader world beyond. After outlining the preexisting Cold War structure, I introduce the concept of critical juncture, heretofore applied largely in the field of domestic political development,[9] to deepen understanding of structural change in the very different field of international relations.

To gain insights into the international impact of critical junctures, I explore historic national political transformations across Eurasia that took place from the late 1970s onward, and the systemic changes at the regional and global levels that followed. I hypothesize that these domestic changes in key nations first stimulated local economic growth, then opened the way to regional political-economic interdependence, and finally configured deeply the profile of emerging international relationships across the Eurasian continent as a whole, with fateful global implications. I attempt both to describe the changes at the national level and to assess their international implications, especially in deepening transcontinental ties within Eurasia, using both path tracing and counterfactual analysis.

This book contends that Deng Xiaoping's Four Modernizations (1978) and Narasimha Rao's parallel Indian economic reforms (1991), to be more specific, ignited the growth engines in Asia's two new economic giants. The collapse of the USSR (1991) then opened the way to broader regional energy integration, including new infrastructure, trade, and investment among neighbors, across old Cold War lines. The continental proximity of China, India, and the former Soviet Union, in particular, offered fateful new prospects, which could be amplified with the addition of new infrastructure. The nationalization of Aramco in Saudi Arabia (1974), the Iranian Revolution (1979), and the advent of Vladimir Putin in Russia (1999)—all tumults in major petrostates—gave the New Silk Road definition.[10] They decisively configured, in short, the geopolitical challenges and religiously driven uncertainties that now shape emerging Eurasia's volatile profile, in energy matters and beyond, at both the international and domestic levels.

To give additional depth to the assessment of critical junctures and their role in political-economic development, I also consider parallel instances, where critical junctures did not occur. Japan and Korea are the major cases considered. The hypothesis is that these countries play largely technical roles in Eurasian continentalist political economy, in contrast to the transformational impact of nations where CJs occur. The technical roles of the Northeast Asian democracies, however, have served important stabilizing functions by providing construction services, bridge financing, and aid to energy efficiency, to accelerate the convergence of petrostate incentives with those of consuming nations. There is thus a functional differentiation between CJ and non–CJ states, which aids the stable evolution of Eurasian continentalism as a whole.

Beyond the problem of system transformation—an issue in international relations approached here in substantial part through comparative analysis—this research also asks another IR question: why Eurasian energy producers and consumers so easily fall into symbiotic economic relations with one another, once external constraints are removed, even as their political ties remain more distant. Gaining insights on that question once again requires comparative analysis of receptivity toward interdependence that is sensitive to geography as well. That subtle interdisciplinary challenge is approached here by considering comparatively the domestic political economies of four large petrostate producers (Russia, Kazakhstan, Saudi Arabia, and Iran), as well as four major consumers (China, India, Japan, and South Korea). Detailed subnational analysis, both macro- and micropolitical, is used to identify the distinctive national biases of these nations in their energy policies, foreign and domestic, and thereby reasons for transcontinental synergy, amid continuing tension. This sort of comparative analysis, as a vehicle for understanding international ties, is, as I have noted, methodologically unusual in the political science literature, as is introducing a geographic dimension.

CONCEPTUAL AMBITIONS

In terms of international political economy, this research strives to break fresh theoretical ground in three respects. First, it brings geography back into international political analysis. Geopolitics was a fashionable study from the late nineteenth century until World War II, and in the hands of masters like Yale University professor Nicholas Spykman brilliantly foreshadowed emerging conflicts of the post–World War II world.[11] Yet geopolitics has been largely dormant as a field of study in international relations since the advent of the Cold War, even as political geography has emerged as a dynamic topic in other applications,[12] and as statesmen themselves have regained geopolitical consciousness in the post–Cold War world.[13] The research undertaken here shows clearly how policy options and political leverage in energy policy are influenced by geography, and why, in that area, the world is by no means "flat," as some prominent journalists have provocatively maintained.[14] It also shows how political barriers to natural geoeconomic expressions—in this case an energy Silk Road linking East Asian and South Asian consumers with large Middle Eastern and former Soviet petrostate producers—can progressively be overcome, through the interplay of political change at critical junctures, with economic logic.

This work likewise probes the impact of energy in structurally configuring the international political economy. It does so, as in other respects, through a distinctive hybrid approach that integrates comparative and international levels of analysis. One specific contribution is the concept of a stabilizing petrostate—a nation, as defined here, that helps to sustain price and macroeconomic equilibrium in the global political economy through its domestic actions. Contemporary Saudi Arabia is identified as one such state, with Russia and Iran—much more populous political economies confronting stronger populist political pressures as well as political-military constraints—identified as potentially destabilizing. The structural antecedents differentiating "stabilizing" and "destabilizing," including subnational mechanisms for insulating energy decision making from parochial pressures or for magnifying such influences are, of course, laid out in the context of the analysis.

In international political economy, this work makes a third intellectual contribution, in elucidating and empirically verifying the notion of continentalism. The term has been casually used for nearly three centuries, particularly in Britain, Canada, and the United States.[15] It is employed here more specifically to refer to "social and economic policies that encourage and advance economic and political integration of territorially contiguous nations on a continental scale."[16] The concept has not, however, been used extensively in academic literature so far, or applied to Eurasia.

Considerable attention has been given in the scholarly literature to how and why economic regions evolve and begin to take on political and social identities.[17] Much work has also been done recently on already formalized relationships among established trade blocs below the global level, especially between the European Union and analogous regional entities emerging elsewhere.[18] Very little analysis, however, has so far considered the evolution of systematic yet less formal ties at a transcontinental level, between culturally and economically heterogeneous areas that nevertheless enjoy sectoral complementarity in such areas as energy.

Over the past thirty years, as we shall see, a remarkable continentalist transformation, as yet obviously incomplete, has begun quietly occurring in Eurasia. Open state-to-state warfare has largely ceased. Political barriers and historical antagonisms have been eroding, especially since the end of the Cold War, among such diverse nations as Russia, Turkey, China, and Korea. Transcontinental trade, driven by energy interdependence, has intensified, and interpersonal networks have deepened. Most recently, a transcontinental oil and gas pipeline network has begun to emerge, with potentially significant geopolitical implications.

Journalists have begun to note and document this emerging continentalist reality,[19] but scholars have yet to examine the phenomenon or to seriously consider its implications. These phenomena might be called "protocontinental," in that they precede full-fledged formal transcontinental arrangements yet encourage them by reducing transaction costs, facilitating cross-border transactions, and rendering such activities more predictable. With the coming of transcontinental pipelines, security dialogues, and summit conferences, the way is opening for more geopolitically significant collaboration as well, contrasting sharply with the mutual isolation of the Cold War past.

What continentalism is, how it emerges, and what it implies for broader patterns of international affairs are clearly questions of substantial importance for international political economy that are not as yet well explored.[20] There is theoretically inclined literature examining relations between Europe and Northeast Asia,[21] but that relationship is transregional, without the geographical contiguity that one finds in continentalism. Virtually no scholarship has considered in theoretical terms how and why such "halfway house" transnational relationships, between the regional and the global level, emerge across Eurasia, despite their manifest importance to understanding the evolution of international political economy in the post–Cold War world.

To clarify how and why continentalism develops, I propose three simple hypotheses: (1) protocontinental political-economic relationships are expected to develop readily in the energy area, where fixed costs and transaction costs are high, making risk reduction and the fostering of stable political-economic ties a high priority; (2) protocontinental relationships will be strengthened by resource complementarities; and (3) protocontinental relationships are strengthened by functional complementarities at the domestic level, in areas like energy efficiency. We explore continentalist phenomena in the energy area, including pipelines, extensively in chapters 7 and 8, addressing the foregoing conceptual issues.

Such nascent, protocontinental, energy-related interactions can be observed vividly on the Eurasian continent, stretching from Northeast Asia to the Middle East and the gates of Europe, including Russia. Interactions within the Shanghai Cooperation Organization, Asia-Middle East Dialogue and Gas Exporting Countries Forum, for example, often have this flavor, although they are but early signs of a potentially deepening trend that has both formal dimensions and less formal network-centric aspects. The countries involved—spread across the Middle East, Russia, Central Asia, South Asia, and East Asia—are geographically contiguous, as indicated in Figure I.1, share a common history several times more venerable than that of the United States itself, and are drawn together today by energy interdependence.

The nations of Eurasia, however culturally distinct, share commonalities and complementarities that can readily support deeper ties at least in some geographically related sectors such as energy, nonenergy resource extraction, and transportation.[22] During the 1980s this meant deeper maritime ties, especially between the Middle East, on the one hand, and the advanced Japanese and Korean economies on the other. Since the collapse of the Soviet Union and the acceleration of Chindian growth during the early 1990s, overland ties across Eurasia have also grown progressively more intimate, as indicated in Figure I.2. Yet continental integration still remains at an early stage, due to lingering political-economic constraints. The genesis and evolution from protocontinentalism to deeper, more institutionalized ties across the incipient region, as well as the ultimate configuration of continentalism itself, are both analytically interesting and potentially of broader geopolitical significance. They are literally at the still poorly examined interface between geography and politics.

Eurasian continentalism is being driven not only by underlying resource complementarities but also by historic shifts in the locus of economic growth

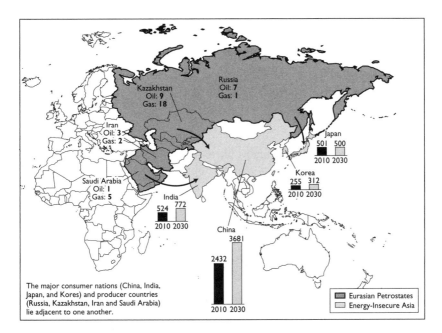

Figure I.1: The energy foundation for Eurasian continentalism.
Sources: BP, *Statistical Review of World Energy*, 2011 edition; U.S. Department of Energy, Energy Information Administration, *International Energy Outlook*, 2010 edition, http://www.eia.doe.gov/oiaf/ieo/pdf/ieoefcase.pdf.
Notes: The major consumer nations (China, India, Japan, and Korea) and producer countries (Russia, Kazakhstan, Iran, and Saudi Arabia) lie adjacent to one another. Figures for China, India, Japan, and Korea indicate energy consumption (million tons oil equivalent). Consumer-nation figures represent energy consumption (2010 vs. 2030 DOE projections). Numbers associated with producer nations indicate global reserve ranking.

and resource demand within key nations, most conspicuously China—since 2009 the largest energy consumer in the world. For the first two decades following the advent of the Four Modernizations in 1978, Chinese growth and energy demand were largely concentrated along the east coast of the People's Republic of China (PRC). Over the past decade, however, new inland growth poles, such as Chengdu, Xian, Chongqing, and even Urumqi and Kashgar in Xinjiang Province have emerged, creating new overland-access energy imperatives as well. The expansion of energy demand in China's inland areas is still in its early stages, but this geopolitically important broadening of demand can be graphically seen in Figure I.3. This growth-inspired development, together with geopolitical aversion to dependence on sea lanes dominated by

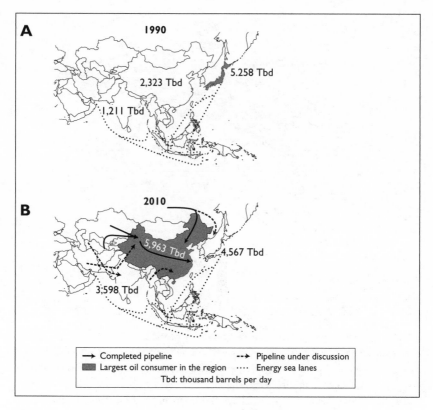

Figure I.2: The changing geography of Asian energy demand (1990–2010).
Notes: (A) With Japan being by far the largest oil consumer in the region, the primary transportation route for oil was by sea from the Middle East. (B) With China and India increasing their oil appetite, and with Cold War barriers eroding, alternatives for oil sourcing emerged: Russia and Central Asia. Alternative overland transportation routes via pipelines, rail, and long-distance electricity grids came to make economic sense as well. This economic change induced a change in geopolitical dynamics: continentalism.

the U.S. Navy, is motivating the PRC to seek international pipeline access to its overland borders to the west, south, and north—intensifying pressures for Eurasian continental interdependence still further.

Also analytically important to understanding the geopolitics of Eurasian energy is the prospective profile of conflict and conciliation in this volatile part of the world, as transcontinental integration proceeds. The conflict in Afghanistan and its relation to regional cooperation, with regard to pipelines, electric power grids, and transportation systems, is just one illustration of the concrete issues at stake. Understanding through the prism of energy geopolitics

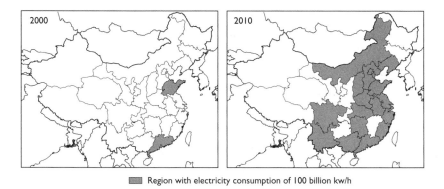

Figure I.3: The continentalist shift in China's domestic energy demand (2000–2010). *Source:* State Statistical Bureau of the PRC, *China Statistical Yearbook*, 2011 (Beijing: State Statistical Bureau of the PRC, 2011).

the profile of rising political-economic interdependence across Eurasia, largely still operating outside formal institutions, thus provides a useful vehicle for examining clearly emerging, if still inchoate, features of the post–Cold War world. These features include the revival of balancing in international relations; reemerging multipolarity; and signs that the long era of interstate warfare on the continent may be drawing to a close, supplanted increasingly by new forms of geoeconomic conflict.[23]

ABOUT THIS BOOK

This volume chronicles the deepening role that Eurasians—both producers and consumers—are coming to play in global energy geopolitics and considers why that role has deepened over the past decade so profoundly. The heart of the book explores the political-economic forces now bringing the rising consumers of East and South Asia and the well-endowed petrostates of the Middle East and the former Soviet Union into such dramatic symbiosis: the geographical proximity, long disrupted by Cold War politics; the sustained long-term economic growth of Asia; the continent's low level of initial energy consumption; and the rapid subsequent rise in its energy demand. The book also considers the simultaneous quest of both Asia and Russia for new geopolitical roles in global affairs and the complex synergy between the deep yearnings of the Islamic world for change, as well as the rising aspirations elsewhere on the continent kindled by Asia's dramatic ascent. Islamic disaffection with the global status quo has been aggravated, as we shall see, by the fervent strivings of Russia since the advent of Putin to re-vive Moscow's Cold War global prominence through the new lever of energy. The book concludes with a searching assessment of what the novel and dy-namic prospect of a New Silk Road based on growing, long-term continental Eurasian energy interdependence in fact means for global affairs, and how the broader world should respond to a resulting incipient Eurasian continen-talism. The book's findings have important theoretical as well as practical implications for both comparative politics and international political econ-omy, as we shall see.

Chapter 1 The Challenge of a New World Emerging

Energy is to the New Silk Road what silk was to its ancestors. Along that long and winding road, stretching in our figurative definition from the Persian Gulf to China, Korea, and Japan, traversing Central Asia and Russia along the way, with a spur to India, lie the largest energy producers, and the most ravenous consumers, on earth. The Gulf alone produces more than 30 percent of the world's oil. Its role can only grow in future, with just three countries—Saudi Arabia, Iran, and Iraq—cornering nearly half the world's entire proven reserves of oil. Meanwhile, Russia, with nearly a quarter of global reserves, may well hold the key in natural gas.

And it is not the producers alone. The road also snakes among teeming masses of the world's most numerous and aspiring energy consumers. The people of China and India—the two most populous nations on earth—are prominent among them. These countries are prospectively large, globally important consumers for three reasons: they are growing rapidly; they are passing through a stage of development when their energy consumption is highly intensive; and they have huge populations. Indeed, nearly half of the world's people live in the New Silk Road nations. Yet they still have among the lowest levels of per-capita energy consumption on earth.

What gives the New Silk Road its prospective cohesion, albeit one fraught with inevitable, concomitant tension, is precisely that delicate complementarity. The Middle East and the rest of Eurasia are fated to be enmeshed in an ever-tightening mutual energy embrace—one destined to cast a deepening shadow over world affairs. Their deepening ties are not a matter of intellectual choice, nor cultural preference, although some scholars talk of "Islamic-Confucian entente."[1] These continental neighbors are mutually entwined prisoners of economic necessity. The forces of supply and demand are binding these two pillars of the pre-Columbian world into deepening interdependence, whether they like it or not—and regardless of what their highly contrasting political systems may nominally decree.

Asia, after all, is the world's ultimate prospective energy importer. Demand is already high, in aggregate terms. Yet it is fated to rise far higher, fueled by extraordinary rates of sustained economic growth, underlying long-term competitiveness, large populations, and per-capita consumption levels far below those of the industrialized world. The per-capita energy consumption of China (thirteen barrels oil equivalent) and India (three) are far lower than those for Japan (twenty-nine) and the United States (fifty-four).[2] Meanwhile, local regional supply remains inevitably limited, with the powerful industrial economies of Northeast Asia notably devoid of local oil and gas reserves.

The Middle East, conversely, is the world's ultimate energy supplier. Its reserves are massive—over half of all the proven oil deposits on earth, and nearly a one-third share of natural gas. Meanwhile, local consumption is limited, and production costs are low, leaving large quantities of product for export. Russia complements this situation with its own massive reserves, particularly in natural gas.

There are, of course, short-term alternatives to the Asia–Middle East energy entente. Africa is one, and Latin America, particularly Brazil and Venezuela, could be another. There are also functional alternatives to hydrocarbons—nuclear or solar power, and, of course, coal. Yet the fierce uncertainties of the global economy—including volatile energy prices—make it difficult to systematically develop these alternatives. In the end one is left with the cold logic of massive emerging Asian demand balanced against substantial, low-production-cost Middle Eastern and former Soviet reserves, in a pattern that could grow markedly more pronounced over the coming generation. The contrasting yet complementary positions of these key regions in the most strategically important segment of the current global energy constellation—worldwide petroleum supply and demand—are presented succinctly in Figure 1.1. It also shows clearly how substantially the globally dominant pattern of Asian demand and Middle Eastern supply, complemented by hydrocarbon resources from the former Soviet Union, will intensify over the coming generation.

Energy markets are of course global, and no patterns of short-run geographical interdependence are foreordained. Yet energy complementarities matter, in the deepening of Eurasian interdependence, because they occur among nations that are so close to one another. Propinquity provides, once political obstacles are removed, a dynamic basis for deepening—and synergistic—economic and strategic interaction among the nations of Eurasia, especially through physical channeling mechanisms such as pipelines, which simultaneously create a distinctive geopolitical intimacy. That is almost unprecedented for Asia, in contrast to circumstances elsewhere in the industrialized world, where extensive trans-continental pipeline grids have existed for some time.

Energy is a vital commodity, to producers and consumers alike, as well as one for which Asia stands in a profoundly complementary relationship with

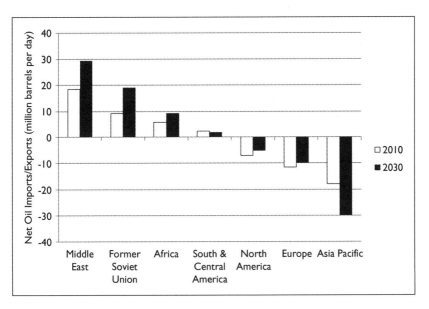

Figure 1.1: The Middle East and Asia: contrasting oil export and import poles (2010 –2030).
Sources: BP, *Statistical Review of World Energy*, 2011 edition; and International Energy Agency, *World Energy Outlook*, 2011 edition.
Note: The historical statistics are figures for 2010 , and the projections are for 2030.

Russia, Central Asia, and the Middle East that is distinct from other inter-regional dependencies and of unique global importance. The more rapidly Asia grows, and the larger it looms on the global economic scene, the more it is likely to need the energy producers along the New Silk Road, with energy price volatility inhibiting other higher-cost alternatives. In this sense, energy, particularly when being conveyed via pipelines, is truly the foundation for a new geopolitical relationship that could, in the world beyond the Iraq and Afghanistan conflicts, profoundly transform the face of global affairs over the coming two decades.

Many configurations of supply and demand are historically embedded, re-flecting not future prospects, or even current complementarities, but decisions of the distant past. This is especially true in North America and Europe, as suggested above. There, much energy infrastructure, especially pipelines, was built in earlier days of energy history, when domestic reserves were larger, and foreign reserves—even in the Persian Gulf—were relatively unknown. That the United States, with a mere 2.4 percent of global reserves, should be pump-ing over three times that share of the world's oil is clearly such a reflection of long-exhausted capabilities. Existing refineries, pipelines, and commercial con-nections make inertia simpler—until the wells run dry—than moving to a more global operating plan.

The trade-offs are somewhat different in Asia than in the West. Established infrastructure is generally not so substantial, and existing standard operating procedures exert much less of a constraint. At the margin, demand is generally rising faster than elsewhere in the world, offering Asian consumers latitude to choose more attractive partners than their Atlantic counterparts enjoy.

Asians tend to think for the long term. And with respect to oil, long-term supply calculations lead—when extenuating circumstances such as embed-ded costs or political risk do not intrude—almost inevitably to the Middle East, and secondarily to the former USSR. This is particularly true for Asian energy firms when they have the opportunity to drill for themselves, as pro-duction costs are extraordinarily low in the Gulf and its environs. Even when East Asian firms cannot enjoy such access, as is typically true, the Middle East can flexibly provide large increments of energy supply, a particular attraction to a region like Asia, where demand is growing so rapidly. Russia is similarly attractive for natural gas.

For many years the range of supply alternatives provided to Asian energy consumers was constrained by the operation of Western multinational inter-mediaries with global access opportunities that the Asians did not enjoy. In the markets themselves, this access differential led to the so-called Asian premium of higher prices for Asian consumers. With globalization, rising competition, and the declining clout of the "Seven Sisters" in the Middle East and elsewhere, however, these price distortions have been eroding, leaving increasingly transparent, market-oriented choices for all.

THE EMERGENCE OF EURASIAN
ENERGY-DRIVEN INTERDEPENDENCE

Emerging synergies across the Eurasian continent, from west to east, extend far beyond energy. Quietly, in the world beyond Baghdad, Kabul, and their fragile links to Washington, a New Silk Road has been emerging, linking East Asia with the Middle East and destinations between. The explosive growth of China and India, coupled with the collapse of the Soviet Union and other historic political changes, have driven the transformation, in response initially to Western consumer demand, to be sure. Yet Atlantic Basin purchases of Asian electronics, textiles, and machine tools have fueled not so much reciprocal prosperity in the West as a historic revival of long-dormant intra-Asian ties, with fateful implications for the future. It is the story of that New Silk Road, and its implications for the world beyond the Iraqi and Afghan conflicts now waning, which concerns us here.

In the new setting of that post-conflict world, East, West, and South Asia—the heart of the original Silk Road itself—are growing into an ever-deeper long-term interdependence, driven by energy, yet transcending it. High-growth East and South Asia need more and more oil and gas. Meanwhile, the Middle East and Russia, hungry for Asia's high-quality industrial goods, are ineluctably becoming the ultimate source.

The rising recent interdependence of these two great pillars of the pre-Columbian world can be seen graphically in the trade figures. The driver, to reiterate, is clearly energy, whose high prices are in turn profoundly animated by Asian growth. Energy generates fully three-quarters of exports from the Middle East and the former Soviet Union on average.[3] Energy also helps create, when oil and gas prices are high, a lucrative, expanding market in those booming petrostates for Asian products and services as well.

Eurasian energy interdependence, it should be noted, has proceeded in two stages. The first, beginning in the 1950s and peaking in relative importance less than a decade ago, was maritime interdependence, with the Middle East and Northeast Asia—principally Japan and South Korea—at the antipodes. The second pattern, making its debut after the Cold War and gaining momentum following the 2008 global financial crisis, involved overland interdependence. Both have promoted Eurasian continentalism in different ways, but we will consider the earlier variant—"maritime continentalism"—first of all.

The Middle East's Growing Asian Markets

As indicated in Figure 1.2, the Middle East—with which East and South Asia's energy relationships are most advanced—now exports substantially more to East Asia than to either Europe or America. This commerce, which flows mainly over energy sea lanes across the Indian Ocean and through the Strait of Malacca to the South China Sea, is a dramatic reversal of patterns prevailing only a decade ago. For more than thirty years—since before the first great oil shock of the 1970s—Asia's share of Middle Eastern exports has been steadily rising—from 20 percent in 1980 to nearly half by 2010, with the vast bulk of mutual commerce between Eurasian partners conducted by sea.[4]

Energy, of course, has been the great driver of this deepening Middle Eastern tilt toward the rest of Asia, as we will see later in great detail. East and South Asia lack adequate domestic energy supplies and have been growing rapidly. The Middle East, conversely, holds massive energy reserves that can accommodate a steady expansion of demand more easily than many other potential suppliers.

Yet the deepening Middle Eastern economic reorientation toward Asia is clearly something more. Oil prices have risen and fallen over the past thirty years, with relatively low prices in the 1980s and 1990s following high prices in the previous decade, and prices resurging again after 2000, until the financial crisis of 2008–2009. They did lead to slight declines in Middle Eastern trade reliance on Asia during the late 1980s and late 1990s. Middle Eastern market gains and economic stakes in Asia, however, have been remarkably steady and sustained over the long run, short-term price volatility notwithstanding. Deepening transcontinental interdependence has transcended energy to include agriculture, arms, and some manufacturing as well.

Nearly as striking, and as unremarked, as the steady Middle Eastern rediscovery of Asian neighbors is the relative decline of the West in Middle Eastern trade. This has been sharpest, as Figure 1.2 makes clear, in the case of the European Union. In 1980 Europe was the dominant destination of Middle Eastern exports, with nearly 30 percent of the region's total exports going there.[5] Yet less than three decades later, in 2008, this ratio had fallen nearly half, to around 15 percent. Exports to the United States, as a share of Middle Eastern

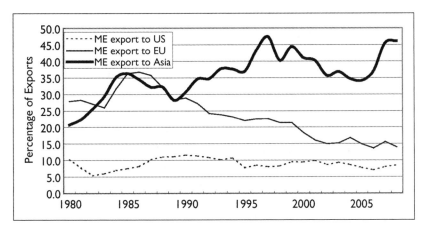

Figure 1.2: Middle East exports to Asia, the United States, and the European Union as a percentage of total Middle East exports.
Source: International Monetary Fund, *Direction of Trade Statistics*, annual.
Note: The IMF defines Asia as consisting of Afghanistan, American Samoa, Bangladesh, Bhutan, Brunei, Darussalam, Cambodia, PRC China, Hong Kong, Macao, Fiji, French Polynesia, Guam, India, Indonesia, Japan, Kiribati, South Korea, Laos, Malaysia, Maldives, Marshall Islands, Micronesia, Mongolia, Myanmar, Nauru, Nepal, New Caledonia, Pakistan, Palau, Papua New Guinea, Philippines, Samoa, Singapore, Solomon Islands, Sri Lanka, Thailand, Tonga, Tuvalu, Vanuatu, and Vietnam. The IMF defines the Middle East as consisting of Bahrain, Egypt, Iran, Iraq, Israel, Jordan, Kuwait, Lebanon, Libya, Oman, Qatar, Saudi Arabia, Syria, United Arab Emirates, West Bank/Gaza, and Yemen.

exports, have been flat or declining for three decades, and are currently lower than in 1980. Currently the United States is less than one-seventh as important a market for the Middle East as Asia is, in overall quantitative terms, and one-eighth as consequential in oil, although the ratios for both parameters were close to equal as late as 1990.

The driver is energy. Middle Eastern exports to Europe have been declining mainly because Europe has become much more self-sufficient in energy than it used to be. Norwegian and British oil, as well as Dutch and Russian gas, have come to supply much of the European market formerly filled by Middle Eastern producers. The declining share of Middle Eastern exports flowing to the United States, even in a period of rising energy prices, has geo-economic logic, but contrasts sharply to the substantial American political-military commitments of the past decade. It may have political as well as economic origins, including modifications in long-standing Saudi political determination to be the largest foreign oil supplier to the United States. Currently both Japan and China import significantly more Saudi oil than the United States does.[6]

Geopolitical shifts as the American military presence in the Islamic world winds down are also, ironically, correlating with an enhanced Asian energy role. In Iraq, where the International Energy Agency projects that the largest oil production increases in the world will occur over the next generation,[7] China garnered the first contract awarded to foreigners in 2008. It also received the largest national share of contracts awarded during 2009–2011, on the eve of the December, 2011 U.S. withdrawal.[8] China also played the central role during 2010–2011 in energy, as well as mineral extraction projects, in Afghanistan.[9]

From Land Rover to Land Cruiser: Asia's Rising Middle Eastern Presence

The converse pattern in Eurasia's "maritime continentalism"—trends in Middle Eastern imports from the rest of Asia—is also striking, especially in comparison with Middle Eastern imports from other major regions of the world. As is shown in Figure 1.3, Middle Eastern imports from Asia—in which motor vehicles play a substantial role—have been steadily rising, from under 20 percent of Middle Eastern imports in 1980 to nearly double that by 2010. With respect to imports from both Europe and the United States, the post–Gulf War period marked an important point of transition. In 1992 fully 44 percent

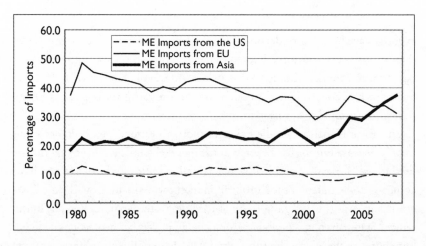

Figure 1.3: Middle East imports from Asia, the United States, and the European Union as a percentage of total Middle East imports.
Source: International Monetary Fund, *Direction of Trade Statistics,* annual.

of the Middle East's imports still came from Europe; by 2006 this ratio had fallen to 31 percent, as Middle Easterners increasingly forsook British Land Rovers for Toyota Land Cruisers as their desert-crossing vehicles. Similarly, America's share of the Middle Eastern market had fallen from 13 to less than 10 percent—massive American arms exports to the region notwithstanding.

Eurasian maritime continentalism, with its foundation in energy trading patterns, shows promise of producing an entirely new sort of global political-economic equation, with transformative implications for world affairs. Significantly, this configuration marginalizes the United States, the largest oil producer on earth for three-quarters of the twentieth century. Indeed, the United States today trades relatively little with Eurasia, even in energy, and finds itself a substantial importer, but largely from elsewhere.[10] The rise of Eurasian continental interdependence, whether by sea or land, similarly erodes the economic role of Western Europe, which trades increasingly with itself.

Both domestic political restrictions and a parallel lack of overarching transnational governance greatly limited economic interchange along the traditional Silk Road byways—"overland continentalism"—across most of the twentieth century. Most conspicuous and geopolitically important, of course, were the commercial and informational controls imposed by the Soviet Union between 1917 and 1991, many of them internal to the USSR itself, and the complementary Cold War restrictions imposed by the United States and its allies, preeminently the trade embargo of China between 1950 and 1971.[11] Together, these constraints led to a virtual collapse of trade and communication between Central Asia and the outside world, including contiguous Islamic neighbors, for nearly three-quarters of a century. Between the early 1960s and the late 1980s, following the Sino-Soviet split, economic interchange between China and the entire Soviet Union nearly ceased as well.[12] And until the 1990s domestic travel, and even commerce within China and Russia themselves, were highly restricted for many local citizens, as well as foreigners.

A GENERATION OF POLITICAL-ECONOMIC REALIGNMENT (1973–1999)

All these embedded political controls and constraints long crippled the expression of the otherwise powerful underlying complementarities of land, labor, and capital prevailing within Eurasia, leading to relative stagnation along the classical course of the old Silk Road. Yet six momentous if largely unrelated developments in diverse parts of the continent fatefully transformed that static equation, to give birth to a more integrated Eurasia and a resurgence of over-land continentalism. These changes aligned the Silk Road nations—backdoor geographic neighbors, after all—synergistically toward one another again, through their complementary roles in energy production and consumption, inspired by the historic economic transformations of the period. Within little more than a decade of the Cold War's denouement, these seismic changes began leading to unprecedented new political-economic ties, including a nascent continental oil and gas grid.

These six fateful critical junctures, considered in detail in Chapter 3, were: (a) widespread nationalization of Western multinational energy holdings in the Arab world, during and after the 1973 Yom Kippur War; (b) Deng Xiaoping's Four Modernizations in China, inaugurated in late 1978, which inspired China's remarkable subsequent growth; (c) the Iranian Revolution of 1979, which reoriented Teheran from the Atlantic nations back toward the non-Western world; (d) India's financial crisis and subsequent economic reforms of 1991, which brought that giant, previously isolated sub-continental nation actively back into Asia, as well as the broader world; (e) the 1991–1992 collapse of the Soviet Union, which opened Central Asia to its Silk Road neighbors; and (f) the ascent of Vladimir Putin, beginning in 1999, which transformed

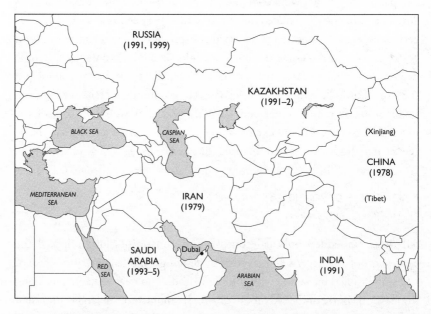

Figure 1.4: A generation of transition in the Eurasian giants: critical junctures, 1973–1999.

Russia into an aggressive, strategic petrostate player in global energy affairs, and a catalyst for deepening Eurasian energy interrelationships. The geographical locale of these fateful developments is noted in Figure 1.4.

Economic growth, energy complementarity, geographical propinquity, and the erosion of old political constraints during the turbulent 1980s and 1990s naturally brought increased economic interdependence, and a growing degree of diplomatic coordination among many of the nations involved, with complementary energy profiles as a critical driver. Yet interdependence did not bring stability. Weapons of mass destruction and their delivery systems proliferated, with India and Pakistan going nuclear in 1999, and North Korea testing in 2006. Terrorism increased, followed by fateful, persistent international conflicts in both Afghanistan (from 2001) and Iraq (from 2003). The emerging Eurasian continentalism has thus become a troubling amalgam of prosperity, energy interdependence, and volatile, dangerous politics, across porous boundaries, driven by growth—with momentous, potentially disturbing implications for all the world. Appendix A surveys the contours of that powerful stimulus to Eurasian energy demand in greater detail, while Appendix B enumerates the new regional institutions striving to integrate the region.

EMERGING POLITICAL-MILITARY CHALLENGES

Eurasian energy interdependence can, as it grows and attains greater intensity, across both its maritime and overland dimensions, potentially pose geopolitical challenges to the broader world in two respects. It could, on one hand, possibly gain such mass and cohesion that it begins to provide an alternative, either institutionally or in the realm of values, to the Pax Americana that has reigned as a global paradigm since the end of the Cold War. Alternatively, this Eurasian continental agglomeration could also, due precisely to the domestic instability or ungovernability of its weaker members, or their mutual rivalries, pose a diffuse, unstructured political-military challenge, with a terrorist dimension that could prove troubling in a very different way.

Internationally, Eurasia has no doubt grown more interconnected than is commonly understood in the West, as energy interdependence has deepened, while key members like China, Russia, and even Turkey have grown more proactive in promoting regional political-economic interdependence. Eurasian nations have already created several growing transregional institutions, for example, that omit the United States. The Asia-Middle East Dialogue (AMED), the Shanghai Cooperation Organization (SCO) and, before 2011, the East

Asia Summit (EAS) are three significant cases in point. The SCO, originally established to formally define borders between China and the successor states of the Soviet Union, has grown and prospered, especially in the security realm, holding annual joint antiterrorist exercises since 2006, and broadening member coordination into the energy and trade policy areas as well. The six formal members of the SCO, including Russia, China, and the Central Asian states, minus Turkmenistan, have also attracted other Eurasian regional powers, including Iran, India, and Pakistan, to participate as observers, while the SCO maintains an ongoing contact dialogue with Afghanistan.

Turning to the domestic side, growth along the New Silk Road has clearly meant affluence. Yet it has also, in country after country, meant social change. The peoples of China and India, Uzbekistan, and even Saudi Arabia have moved from farming and nomadic life to the cities, where many have become educated and entered new professions. Social expectations have generally risen yet often remain unsatisfied. Inequality has deepened, leading to growing disaffection and often political instability.

Across the Islamic segment of the New Silk Road, extending in a great arc from Xinjiang, Rajastan, and the Hindu Kush westward to the Persian Gulf and beyond, fundamentalist sentiment has been rising, inspired by the Iranian Revolution and the Afghan Islamic resistance to Soviet invasion during the late 1970s and the 1980s. This sentiment has often expressed itself perversely in the form of terrorist movements. Apart from the infamous al-Qaeda, Uzbekistan's IMU, Egypt's Muslim Brotherhood, Xinjiang's East Turkestan Front, Kashmir's Lashkar-e-Taiba, and Indonesia's Jamal al-Islamiah, among others, have ironically fed on the social disaffection in the growing societies of the New Silk Road.

Deepening Eurasian interdependence has also given birth to more explicit military challenges, including intraregional tensions. Several growing nations, such as Russia and China, have been emboldened by rising affluence to expand military spending and develop more sophisticated armaments. At times they have turned militarily belligerent, as Russia did against Georgia in August 2008. Several of the more isolated and parochial states, including Iran, Syria, Pakistan, and North Korea, have sought chemical, biological, and nuclear weapons. Proliferation by one or two, as in the Indo-Pakistani rivalry, has led to broader paranoia and a vicious cycle of proliferation to others also.

Where nations depend heavily on trade, some have argued, the impulse to militarization, and especially to attain nuclear-weapons capacity, is muted.[13] This does not appear to be nearly as true across Eurasia as elsewhere in the world, particularly with regard to energy exporters. Trade interdependence is substantial and rising, but heavily energy related. The elites of energy-producing nations, as the petrostate literature clearly suggests, tend to be autistic toward both domestic and international constituencies, while possessing the resources to devote to weapons development and acquisition, even in the face of international disapproval.

Economic growth, in short, has counterintuitively spawned violence, instability, and turmoil across Eurasia, rather than fostering the democracy and stability that have so often felicitously followed in its wake elsewhere. The region's energy dependencies could well be part of the problem. Since energy is such a strategic, universally desired commodity, energy exporters typically do not face the need to accommodate the global community in the same way as their counterparts elsewhere in the developing world, especially in sellers' markets. Energy-demand growth throughout the first post–Asian financial crisis decade (1998–2008) may have encouraged efforts at proliferating weapons of mass destruction, as in the case of Iran. A precipitous short-term fall in energy prices during late 2008 may have conversely leveraged international pressure, but subsequent recovery within less than a year, driven by "Chindian" demand, released that constraint once again.

CONCLUSION

Across the vast expanse from the Yellow Sea to the Persian Gulf and the Suez Canal, a new, transcontinental dynamic is thus arising in the post–Cold War world. Eurasia is becoming a vast interactive political-economic entity, under the powerful, deepening impact of energy interdependence, as Cold War political barriers fall. And Eurasia is growing explosively, with its forward progress driven by the dual engines of Chinese and Indian demand. A distinctive, steadily broadening, and accelerating pattern of continental economic expansion, ever less reliant on the American market, is clearly coming into prospect.

Japan was the growth pioneer, across the turbulent half century in which it emerged from feudal isolation to ultimately vanquish Czarist Russia, at Mukden, Hill 203, and ultimately the Straits of Tsushima, in May 1905. It was followed by the Four Tigers, during the 1960s and 1970s. And then China, whose Four Modernizations of 1978 unleashed a remarkable, historic, and still-continuing expansion that is today profoundly transforming the face of world affairs.

Yet China's expansion, we have discovered, is not the end or even the heart of our story. The key reality is a more complex continental synergy among many nations. Beginning in the early 1990s, the pattern of Asian growth began to broaden beyond East Asia itself, extending to the south and west, gaining added momentum, and becoming linked with increasing intimacy to the Middle East, India, and points in between. An integrated Eurasia, at last, is slowly being born, even as lingering geopolitical and subnational tensions persist.

Simultaneous growth in East, South, and Central Asia, combined with a waning of traditional geopolitical antagonisms, has naturally led to deepened transcontinental interdependence, with both a maritime and an overland dimension. The labor-intensive economies of China and India, on the one hand, and the resource-intensive economies of Central Asia, Russia, and the Middle East, on the other, naturally complement one another. Trade relations, based on energy but transcending that vital resource, have steadily expanded, both by land and by sea, providing a deepening economic basis for a Eurasian energy interrelationship that could potentially change the face of international affairs.

Yet the western rim of Asia, we have found, has experienced volatile and uneven growth over the past two decades, contrasting to the explosive yet sustained expansion of China, India, and much of Central Asia. Western Asia's instability and propensity to become enmeshed in global geopolitical conflicts presents a major challenge to the coherence of the continent as a whole, simultaneously breeding chaos and abetting totalitarianism. This challenge has been deepened and complicated over the past decade by the resurgence and increasing geopolitical activism of Russia in world affairs. Yet the latent importance of the Middle East and Russia to their Eurasian neighbors goes without saying, despite their volatility and unsavory domestic politics, since those strategic energy producers together hold two-thirds of world oil reserves, and two-thirds of global gas as well.

Despite political-economic uncertainties in the large West Asian nations, such as Iran, Turkey, and Saudi Arabia, as well as the changing role of Russia, flexible, entrepreneurial global cities like Singapore and Dubai, complementing catalytic domestic centers like Urumqi, are helping to knit the political economies of Eurasia together, building on an ineluctable underlying economic logic. The challenge of stability, however, is enduring, given the powerful currents of social mobilization and incessant geopolitical rivalry. And the rising political-economic interdependence of the Eurasian nations, as we have seen, has given urgency to new political-military challenges also, both for these countries individually and for the broader world, particularly given the catalytic role that Moscow and Beijing, once and future super-power capitals, could potentially play.

Chapter 2 Where
Geography Still Matters

Geography, and particularly the study of interrelationships among people, the state, and territory, was for centuries an avidly studied and debated subject in both the academy and the realm of practical affairs. Creative faculty like Nicholas John Spykman of Yale taught large and enthusiastic courses at major universities and wielded personal influence in international relations. Geographers and geostrategists were a fixture in diplomatic and military institutes throughout the major nations of the world. And geographical considerations cast a long shadow over world politics for three full centuries, from the Peace of Westphalia (1648) and Vienna (1814) to the Treaty of Versailles (1919) and on to the Cairo, Teheran, Yalta, and Potsdam conferences that reconfigured both Europe and Asia at the turbulent end of World War II.

Given the intellectual prominence that the study of geography enjoyed even seventy years ago, it commands remarkably little attention today. Commentators tell us confidently that "The world is flat," with globalization rendering physical location of marginal concern,[1] and they assert that we live in a "borderless world."[2] International relations theory speaks of "sovereignty at bay"[3] and focuses aridly on the abstract architecture of international regimes, constitutional order, transition processes, and the general qualities and motivations of nation-states in their international dealings, or occasionally on how subnational actors influence patterns of power and interdependence. Yet remarkably little attention has been given lately to the impact of location or local resource endowments on either domestic or international politics, in part due to the prevailing perception that all resources are fungible and mobile.

The physical world itself, of course, has not been fundamentally altered by the recent revolutionary changes in transportation and communications. Beijing remains closer to Tokyo, Seoul, and Teheran than it is to Washington, DC, just as it was a century or a millennium ago. Iran still lies astride the Straits of Hormuz, and Russia continues to be situated between Turkmenistan and Western Europe. The question is not whether these immutable geological truths are in question, but how, when, and why they still matter.

Given the pervasive recent skepticism, in this mobile, global age, that location really does make a differerence and that it could actually grow more important in coming years, it is incumbent on us here to begin making the case. In this chapter, I first review the rise and decline of geographically conditioned thinking, with a special focus on the concept of the heartland in Western, Russian, Turkish, and East Asian geopolitical thought. I then explore the contemporary relevance of such thinking in today's world. I show that, while geography may be of declining relevance in manufacturing and finance, it still retains special utility in the world of energy, and especially in explaining energy relations among Asia, Russia, and the Middle East. In conclusion, I consider just how geography influences transnational energy flows, both directly and mediated through changing political structures, as well as how energy thereby shapes the profile of world affairs.

THE RISE AND FALL OF
GEOGRAPHIC DETERMINISM

The notion that political-military strategy is influenced by the geographic setting of actors has a venerable pedigree, dating back at least to Herodotus.[4] In *The History*, Herodotus chronicled a clash of civilization among Persians,

Egyptians, Scythians, and Greeks—all of whom he believed to be powerfully influenced by their respective geographic settings. The early modern German geostrategist Dietrich Heinrich von Bulow developed a purportedly scientific approach to strategy in his 1799 classic, *The Spirit of the Modern System of War.*[5] Yet it was ultimately late in the nineteenth century, as the world came to be starkly bifurcated between imperial powers and colonies, with no new frontiers for the great powers to explore and the struggle for primacy among major nations escalating, that geostrategic thinking assumed special salience.

During this period, two strains of geopolitical thinking came into particular prominence, epitomized in the work of Alfred Thayer Mahan, the American strategist, and Halford Mackinder, prominent British geographer. Mahan emphasized the importance of sea power to global dominance, while Mackinder stressed the strategic centrality of the vast Eurasian heartland. The two saw geography as important for sharply different reasons. Yet both agreed that location conferred pronounced advantages and disadvantages on individual political-military actors, and of necessity exercised profound influence on national strategy as well.

For Mahan, the decisive geopolitical benefit conveyed by proximity to the sea was mobility. Maritime nations, such as Britain and the United States, had cosmopolitan access and strategic invulnerability that was difficult for land powers to emulate. Sea powers were also able to benefit disproportionately from international trade and to maintain overseas possessions, while conversely capable of blockading their enemies, and thereby consigning them to economic stagnation. By amassing forces in decisive battles, such as Trafalgar, Tsushima, and Jutland, maritime powers could confidently control the course of world affairs and vanquish even potent land powers like Napoleonic France.[6]

Mahan saw some factors apart from geography, notably personal traits such as loyalty, courage, and service to the state, as likewise important in shaping history. He stressed such considerations in his well-regarded two-volume biography of Admiral Horatio Nelson, the victor of Trafalgar.[7] Mahan was also something of a climatic determinist. In his classic assessment of Asia's geostrategic circumstances, for example, he argued that land powers such as imperial Russia were unavoidably dominant in Asia above the fortieth parallel, for climatic reasons, with portions of Asia below the thirtieth parallel conversely subject to the effective control of sea powers like Britain and the United States.[8]

Mackinder, like Mahan, believed profoundly in the importance of physical location. His vision was especially powerful because it distilled from geography a central principle of international politics: that the key to world power is control of the "geographical pivot of history."[9] In gauging this pivot point, he stressed the superior geopolitical benefits of continental over maritime provenance—particularly central location on the Eurasian landmass, far removed from the sea and large navigable rivers emptying into it. The central part of Eurasia, highlighted in Figure 2.1, was a crucial pivot area for Mackinder, from which pressure could be flexibly exerted on both Europe and Asia.

In Mackinder's view, central, continental location provided many advantages—efficient inside lines of communication; proximity to natural resources, food supplies, and industrial centers; and invulnerability to adversarial naval power. These strengths contrasted with what he viewed as the much more exposed circumstances of the maritime nations. Mackinder's notion of geopolitics was epitomized in his oft-quoted maxim: "Who rules East Europe commands the Heartland. Who rules the Heartland commands the World-Island, and who rules the World-Island commands the World."[10] Not surprisingly, his continentalist geopolitics were enthusiastically subscribed to by a long line of German, Russian, and even Japanese theorists,

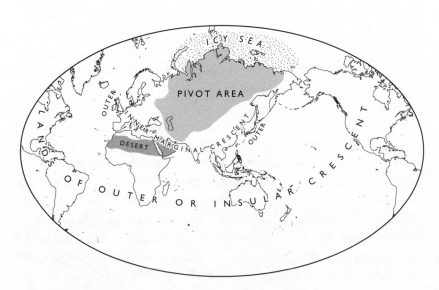

Figure 2.1: Mackinder's geographical pivot.
Source: Mackinder, "The Geographical Pivot of History," 435.

especially in the pre-1945 years. The specter of Napoleon's invasion of Russia and abject defeat, followed by that of Hitler, seemed to confirm both the attraction of the heartland and the near invulnerability of those who held it.

Continental European Perspectives

Kaiser Wilhelm II of Germany, and his chancellor, Theobald von Bethmann Hollweg, while impressed by Mahan, relied intellectually and politically in the first decades of the twentieth century on a version of land power–based geopolitics parallel to that of Mackinder.[11] Emphasizing the importance of centrality, epitomized in the concept of "Mitteleuropa," they forged an alliance with Austro-Hungary and the Ottoman Empire, striving for continental European economic autarky through initiatives such as a customs union with the Austro-Hungarian Empire. Another central piece of Germany's Mitteleuropa concept was the desire for economic domination of the eastern Slavic countries, with Poland being the strategic key.

Following World War I, German geostrategic concerns did not disappear—they only moved further east and became more explicitly focused on Eurasia. Diplomatically, these aspirations were expressed in the Treaty of Rapallo, as well as the covert collaboration between Weimar Germany and newly Soviet Russia that followed.[12] Intellectually, heartland theory found its expression in the works of Karl Haushofer, professor of geography at the University of Munich. For Haushofer, the existence and prosperity of a nation-state depended on *lebensraum* (living space), the pursuit of which necessarily served as the basis for all policies. Germany had a high population density, whereas the old colonial powers, such as the British Empire, had a much lower concentration, making it important for Germany to expand into resource-rich and underpopulated areas. Haushofer's belief in the importance of autarky and living space was strengthened by his neo-Malthusian conception that the earth was becoming progressively saturated with people and was reaching the limits of its ability to provide food for all. Apart from the clear economic imperative for Germany of dominating open spaces to the east in Eurasia, Haushofer also subscribed for geostrategic reasons to Mackinder's belief in the importance of the Eurasian heartland. He viewed the open spaces to Germany's east as the key to the "World Island" and ultimately to global dominance, in a Darwinian world of ceaseless political-military struggle.

Haushofer used Mackinder's heartland concept as a point of departure for his own continental bloc theory, although adding elements affirming the value of alliance among non-Anglo-Saxon nations, including Germany, Austria-

Hungary, Russia, and Japan. Such a Eurasian coalition, he argued, could effectively counter the Anglo-Saxon nations and France. Haushofer's first trips to Japan, both by sea, via British-held ports such as Hong Kong and Singapore, and later overland on the Trans-Siberian Railway, appear to have influenced his thinking. By the mid-1920s, Haushofer had also adapted the "have-not" theory to rationalize placing China and India on the German side, thus further amplifying his proposed non-Anglo-Saxon coalition.[13]

German Geopolitical Concerns Echo to the East

Although the Germans, despite their racialist ideology, were arguably the most persistent European advocates of "Eurasianist" diplomacy prior to 1941, the Soviets were intermittently interested in this concept as well. Like the Germans, the Soviets were outsiders in the geopolitics of the 1920s and 1930s—have-not nations, in Haushofer's phrase—who stood potentially to gain from an alliance with the East, just as Weimar Germany had at Rapallo. Lenin himself appears to have been intrigued, in the shadow of 1917, with the revolutionary potential of the "toilers of the East" and even that of the Chinese peasantry.[14] In the early 1920s, the fledgling Soviet Union also reached out diplomatically to China, Iran, and Turkey, in a zealous effort to secure their neutrality and prevent capitalist encirclement in the ongoing civil war. Leninist internationalism, in its repudiation of racial distinctions, also provided a convenient ideological vehicle for building Silk Road bridges to the East, transcending the discriminatory stance that even Woodrow Wilson condoned at Versailles, in his refusal to support a racial equality clause in the 1919 peace treaty.[15]

Russian Post-Soviet Conceptions

Post-Soviet Russia has continued to prioritize Moscow's relations within Eurasia, even more explicitly and theoretically than before the collapse of the Soviet Union. Although banned in Soviet times as an imperialist-fascist "false science," due to its popularity with the Nazis, geopolitics gained substantial currency in Russia after 1991.[16] The State Duma created a permanent Committee on Geopolitical Affairs—the only body of its kind in the world—and several prominent political figures, including Communist Party leader Gennady Zyuganov and Liberal Democratic Party leader Vladimir Zhirinovsky, wrote major books emphasizing the importance of geopolitics to Russia's political and diplomatic future.[17]

Contemporary Russian geopolitical analysts have followed in the Mackinder tradition. They have invariably concluded from their geopolitical inquiries, ironically as pre–World War II German geostrategists also tended to do, that Russia is the pivot of world politics, as a result of its central location on the Eurasian landmass and its massive size.[18] They see the imperatives involved in maintaining global order and stability, from a Russian strategic standpoint, as twofold: establishing a clear boundary between Western sea power and Eurasian land power in Europe; and preserving the unity of the Eurasian heartland. The latter, in their view, inevitably involves stable, positive, and where possible dominant relations with East, South, and Central Asia, including particularly India and China. Given Russia's massive oil and gas reserves, complementing Asia's great and intensifying deficiencies of the same, born of hypergrowth, energy is inevitably Moscow's tool of choice for sustaining that Eurasian unity and deepening political-economic ties across the continent.[19]

Ottoman and Turkish Thinking

Central geographical positioning has long been a matter of concern for the peoples inhabiting Asia Minor and surrounding areas, although specific priorities and geopolitical strategies have changed over the years. The Ottomans, for example, placed priority in their early days on achieving exclusive control over land trade routes from Europe across Asia, and thereby over resources that could not be replaced, during the Middle Ages at least, by a market.[20] By the late nineteenth century, they had developed another geopolitical obsession: control of the Islamic holy places—Mecca and Medina—thus legitimating their sultan's politically important claims as caliph, or Defender of the Faithful.[21]

Leaders of the secular Turkish republic, established by Ataturk in 1923, continued to be highly conscious of Turkey's pivotal location between East and West—primarily as a bulwark of Western civilization against more parochial Asianist concerns. With the advent of the Justice and Development Party Islamist administration in 2002, however, this Western orientation began to shift and grow more Eurasian-continental. Intellectual inspiration came in the work of Ahmet Davutoglu, a creative political science professor at Marmara and Beykent universities who became Turkish foreign minister in May 2009.

Davutoglu argued that a nation's value is predicated on its geopolitical location and historical depth—dimensions along which, he contended,

Turkey is uniquely endowed.[22] Geopolitically, Turkey lies astride the Bosporus, and historically it stands heir to the Ottoman Empire. Through control of the Balkans, the Middle East, and Central Asia, as Defender of the Faithful, the Ottomans unified the Muslim world. Davutoglu argued that Turkey should similarly build on its Ottoman and Islamic heritage to build a regional economic bloc, encompassing the Middle East and Central Asia, and create a Muslim security mechanism based on the Organization of the Islamic Conference, thus unifying the worldwide community of Muslim believers (*ummah*).[23]

Davutoglu also argued, in the interest of "strategic depth," for the normalization of Turkish relations not only with Islamic neighbors like Syria, Iran, Iraq, or even Indonesia and Malaysia, but also with other major Eurasian powers, including Russia and China.[24] Vehicles for achieving broader legitimacy in the non-Muslim world included an unprecedented effort to establish diplomatic relations with Armenia and deepened ties with Russia, using energy as a driver. Capitalizing on this approach, Russia has, after decades of enmity, become Turkey's largest trading partner, supplying virtually all of the country's natural gas through the Blue Stream pipeline project under the Black Sea. Meanwhile Turkey, with Davutoglu's tacit support, in 2010 concluded its first nuclear power contract, with a Russian-led consortium.[25] Turkey, operationalizing the geopolitical thought of Davutoglu, has thus become a principal catalyst for emergent Eurasian continentalism.

Chinese Conceptions

Chinese thinkers and policymakers over the centuries have persistently held an unassailable sense of cultural self-confidence that has tended to make them inward looking rather than externally oriented.[26] Confucianism has reinforced the defensive and relatively passive orientation of Chinese strategic thinking, with its emphasis on the persuasive powers of governing by moral force.[27] A range of Chinese strategists have also emphasized the value of caution, nonmilitary factors, and long-term orientation, even in military strategy.[28] These cultural and tactical traits have culminated in a paradoxical approach to geopolitics, suggested by Matteo Ricci more than four hundred years ago: "in a kingdom of almost limitless expanse, an innumerable population, and abounding in copious supplies of every description, though they have a well-equipped army and navy that could easily conquer the neighboring nations, neither the king nor his people ever think of waging a war of aggression. They are quite content with what they have, and not ambitious of conquest. In this they are much different from the people of Europe."[29]

Chinese strategic thought has, to be sure, had a significant realist sub-text over the ages. Much of it was stimulated originally by the incessant conflicts among fragmented principalities that ultimately formed a unified China in 221 BC.[30] This strain of thinking, contending that the PRC needed to assert itself more proactively in world affairs, in contrast to the "peaceful rise" and "harmonious world" doctrines of the mid-2000s, became more pronounced during and after the global financial crisis of 2008.[31] The crisis undermined the mystique of Western economic prowess, and encouraged an increasingly nationalist view of the PRC's foreign-policy imperatives.

The dominant recent strain in Chinese strategic thinking, however, has been more cautious and circumspect. As Dai Bingguo pointed out in late 2010, China continues to face enormous changes domestically, including bringing over a tenth of its population above the poverty line—hence it is "not in a position to be arrogant and boastful."[32] Its interests are increasingly interdependent with those of the broader world, he maintains. This emphasis on harmony, however, does not preclude the pursuit of strategic advantage. Whether this sort of diffidence will persist as China rises, PRC fifth-generation leaders consolidate power, and Eurasian continental integration proceeds, however, is an open question, as Henry Kissinger points out.[33]

The Chinese have traditionally been somewhat less clearly and consistently expansionist than the Germans and the Russians, in particular. China's physical circumstances inevitably force policy trade-offs that are often analyzed, and policies that are articulated, in geopolitical terms. China's two central geographic realities, which often intrude into political-military thinking, are (1) the country's central location in continental East Asia, bordered by fourteen other countries; and (2) its possession of both extensive land borders and substantial maritime frontiers. These circumstances inevitably orient Chinese thinkers and policymakers to thinking about the relative merits of continental and maritime strategy, as alternate but related tools for ensuring a national security that, in recent years, has seemed to them perpetually under challenge.

For well over a millennium, China has oscillated between an emphasis on continental and on maritime strategy. The Tang Dynasty (618–907) focused primarily on the land. The early Ming Dynasty, by contrast, focused heavily on the sea, before recalling its ambitious exploration and trading fleets in the mid-fifteenth century, due to resource depletion and concern over land-based threats from northern continental barbarians.[34] The Ching Dynasty (1644–1912) focused again—rather successfully—on continental expansion at first, only to be blindsided by Western inroads from the sea that in the nineteenth century seriously constrained Chinese autonomy.

Postrevolutionary China (1949–) was preoccupied first and foremost with the classic threat of land invasion from the north. The PRC under Mao Zedong thus concentrated its defense budget on the army and largely neglected the seas. Under Deng Xiaoping and Jiang Zemin, China settled numerous land border disputes and turned seaward. Over the past decade, under Hu Jintao, Wen Jiabao, and Xi Jinping—and especially since the global financial crisis of 2008—the pendulum appears to have been shifting back once again toward continentalism, in both theory and policy, as we shall see in the coming pages.

Japanese Perspectives

As Japanese strategists expanded the ambit of their geographical concerns across Asia during the late 1930s and the early 1940s, they also became more geopolitical—influenced heavily by the thinking of Haushofer, in particular. Indeed, most of that German geostrategist's writings were translated into Japanese, and his thought was broadly debated in Tokyo.[35] Kawanishi Masaaki, for example, employed Haushofer's reasoning that have-not empires were justified in expanding their territories to gain dominant critical mass; indeed, he used Haushofer's thought as a rationale for legitimizing Tokyo's Greater East Asia Co-Prosperity Sphere. Kawanishi argued that China and India, with large populations but substantially lower levels of economic development than Japan, could become major markets for Japanese products. Indonesia and Brunei could supply raw materials for Japanese heavy industry, while Thailand's grain could help feed even India, not to mention Japan itself.[36]

Inspired by Haushofer's *Der Kontinentalblock*, stressing the geopolitical strength of a heartland critical mass, Asano Risaburō contended that a vulnerable Soviet Union, flanked by Germany and Japan, would be compelled to tacitly support the emerging global Axis political-economic order. He further argued that the continentalist combination of the Soviet Union, the new German order in Europe, and Japan's Greater East Asia Co-Prosperity Sphere could effectively compete on the world stage with the Anglo-Saxon maritime bloc.[37] Needless to say, this Eurasianist aspiration was thoroughly discredited in the wake of Hitler's attack on the Soviet Union, Stalin's attack on Japan, and the ultimate Axis defeat in 1945. Yet the dream of continental activism and reconciliation with continental Eurasian powers to form a dominant global coalition, avoiding undue dependence on Anglo-Americans, did continue to resonate with some important postwar Japanese political figures and intellectuals. The concept of *rikuheisen*, or "land horizon," continued to have a romantic attraction in Tokyo, even into the twenty-first century.

The Oscillating Influence of Geopolitics

After 1945, a range of developments—political, intellectual, and technological—conspired to discredit geographically based thinking in many parts of the world. On the political and intellectual side, the strong initial embrace of geopolitics by Nazi German theorists such as Haushofer, with their organic theories, involving a Darwinian emphasis on lebensraum and expansionist control of the heartland, naturally provoked a postwar backlash among thinkers worldwide. There had, in reality, been significant tension between geographically grounded "Geopolitik" notions propounded by thinkers like Ratzel and Haushofer, on the one hand, and racist Nazi dogma on the other.[38] Yet this divergence was not widely understood, with the consequence that German geopolitics generally was discredited by the perverse ends to which the Nazis applied it.

Some influential postwar American policy intellectuals such as George Kennan, John Foster Dulles, Henry Kissinger, and Zbigniew Brzezinski were in fact influenced substantially in their strategic thinking by geography.[39] Several of them were familiar, in particular, with the visionary, yet brilliantly insightful political geography of Spykman.[40] That farsighted academic provided key rationales for American transoceanic involvement in Europe and offshore Asia, by stressing the geopolitical importance of "rimland."[41]

This interest in geopolitics did not lead, however, to the sort of systematic examination of geographical factors in international affairs by post–World War II American academia that had been so common in both Europe and America during the first half of the twentieth century. One reason was a paucity of advocates, especially in the early Cold War years. Spykman himself, sadly, did not live to see the postwar world whose geopolitical dynamics he had so insightfully forecast. No doubt Nazi enthusiasm for geopolitics inhibited serious study of the subject after the Axis defeat. An additional reason was dramatic change in the real world. The static character of U.S. and Soviet spheres of influence, as the Cold War deepened after 1950, narrowed fields of inquiry for political geographers and geostrategists, contributing to declining scholarly interest in those two fields, even as their latent policy relevance continued.

Evolution in social-science theory also inhibited geopolitical analysis among scholars.[42] A desire for parsimony in theoretically oriented studies prompted academics during the postwar years to abandon geography, due to its contingency and the difficulty of categorizing it; the increasing abstraction of international relations theory compounded this devaluation of geography.[43] Additionally, geographically informed studies of the early twentieth century had often been marred by determinism, which left no room for the human volition that postwar social science stressed so strongly.

Changing technology, which began radically transforming conceptions of time and space by the mid-twentieth century, also had something to do with this post–World War II intellectual depreciation of geography and physical circumstance. Aviation, after all, made it possible to circumnavigate the globe in a matter of days, and then hours, allowing militaries of the world to become immensely more maneuverable and less territorially bound than in earlier days. The space age accelerated this revolutionary transformation of time and distance. Telecommunications—telegraph, telephone, facsimile, and ultimately the Internet—also rendered space less crucial in that sphere, having major implications as well for spatial location in finance.

These technical revolutions, coupled with the globalization of manufacturing production, made possible the rise of influential "virtual states" like Singapore, with almost no physical expression and little military power, but with powerful managerial, financial, and creative skills to control assets elsewhere.[44] These virtual states were the very antithesis of the geographically expansive, militarily oriented powers that both Mahan and Mackinder had seen as iconic actors in international affairs only half a century before. The virtual states, and the globalized age in which they were embedded, seemed to call clearly into question the relevance to international affairs in the twenty-first century of physical location, resource endowments, and even geography.

Changes in the structure of international politics also operated to reduce interest in geopolitics. Under the pre-1945 multipolar system, political-military alliances and ententes were fluid and often changed in sudden, dramatic fashion. From the late 1940s through the end of the Cold War, by contrast, international fault lines of conflict and cooperation in the strategically important parts of the world grew relatively predictable, and the study of geographic fault lines correspondingly less rewarding and less consequential in policy terms. There has been a modest revival of geopolitical analysis since the end of the Cold War, particularly in Europe.[45] Much of the new work on geopolitics, however, is peripheral to traditional concerns like security policy.[46] The locus of concern has shifted toward subjective attempts to deconstruct the geographically related pronouncements of policymakers, so as to discover their underlying motivations and intentions.[47]

THE ENERGY SECTOR: WHERE GEOGRAPHY STILL CLEARLY MATTERS

Location may well be of declining relevance in many political-economic spheres, ranging from finance and academic inquiry to manufacturing, causing much of the world to grow increasingly "flat" as globalization proceeds. Yet that trend is far less pronounced in the energy sector. Indeed, if anything the converse pattern—of a rising precedence for geography—in fact prevails in the energy realm. As we shall see, globalization is setting in motion powerful forces—notably the integration of over 2 billion heretofore largely impoverished Chinese and Indians into the world economy—that are provoking long-term increases in global energy demand. And that demand must inevitably be met from a fixed range of locations, many of which are remarkably close, overland, to major sources of supply. Natural resources, unlike service or manufacturing industries in this global age, remain immobile. Demand for them will inevitably rise, as the very low levels of per-capita energy demand in China and India (1.8 and 0.4 tons of oil equivalent per year) steadily increase, with rising affluence, toward world-average levels.[48] American per-capita energy consumption, for example, is over four times China's level, and seventeen times India's.[49]

Resources, in contrast to services or light manufactures, are physically weighty and bulky. That physical quality eliminates the air transport option that would otherwise reduce the dependence of both producers and consumers on geography. Hydro-carbon resources cannot avoid flowing to their destinations by rail, ship, or pipeline, often in transit across the territory of others, thus deepening the geopolitical cast of energy still further. Such overland transport is facilitated, in the Eurasian case, by the surprisingly close overland proximity of supplier and consumer.

Increasingly, as demand from rising powers like China and India so ravenously grows, these resources need to be traded across international boundaries, often through pipelines with geographically specified routing. And they need to be sourced from highly concentrated reserves in a small number of fixed, immobile locations, notably the Persian Gulf and the Caspian Basin.

Many of these supply locales, like both the Gulf and the Caspian, are situated in volatile, militarized corners of the globe. Geography thus conditions both the production and the transportation of these ever more valued hydrocarbons. They are increasingly the lifeblood not only of advanced nations but even more urgently of developing countries as well.

Geography has special relevance to the political economy of natural resource issues, due to the physical immobility of resource deposits and the exacting transportation requirements they involve. The strategic significance of these problems is particularly great with respect to energy, especially petroleum, because that resource plays such a central—and often inflexible—role in industrial societies. Neither the civilian economies nor the military forces of such nations can operate without it, and the short-run price elasticity of hydrocarbon demand tends to be low.

HOW GEOGRAPHY MATTERS WITH RESPECT TO
EURASIAN ENERGY

Physical energy deposits, to be sure, may be immobile, while energy transportation is complex and often difficult. Yet energy supplies themselves remain to a substantial degree fungible, and energy markets are, as market fundamentalists often remind us, ultimately global. Why then does geography still matter, in the realm of Eurasian energy that is our special interest here? If it does matter, in what ways does it matter? Before venturing to speak grandly of an emerging Asian energy geopolitics, it is vital to address these important questions, which establish the rationale for seriously examining energy relations among Northeast Asia, Russia, and the Middle East at all.

Geography matters inordinately in Eurasian energy today for four basic reasons:

1. The global supply of hydrocarbon resources available to resource-short regions is highly concentrated in a small number of locations.
2. Asia perceives itself as perilously short of oil and gas, relative to its reserves, prospective demand levels, and geopolitical capacity to ensure adequate supplies.
3. The major sources of hydrocarbon supply and the major emerging centers of demand within the continent are remarkably close to one another geographically, although political and cultural constraints have long kept the countries in question apart.

4. Pipelines are of rising importance in supplying those hydrocarbons, as political barriers erode and as energy demand expands steadily in the interior of the continent.

These geographically related concerns translate ever more directly into policy imperatives in the post–Cold War world, as we shall see in later chapters, because superpower conflicts no longer inhibit geographically rational supply patterns to the degree they did before the collapse of the Soviet Union. Pipelines and cross-border capital investment mandated by geographic and economic logic are becoming increasingly feasible, especially among China, Southwest Asia, and the former Soviet Union, as political barriers fall and economic interdependence rises.

Adequate supply, of course, is a general concern for nations throughout the world, but especially so for Asia because it is growing so rapidly and is an energy-deficit region itself. North America, Europe, South America, and Africa, by contrast, are both growing more slowly and are traditionally more regionally self-sufficient. They consequently face less need to rely on the restricted group of energy swing producers, with discretionary capacity to raise or lower production, outside their regions, concentrated mainly around the Persian Gulf and the Caspian.

If we accept that Eurasia does have a distinctive set of geopolitical concerns with respect to energy, rooted in its own growth pattern, institutions, and marginal global political-military role, in what specific ways does geography shape the energy calculations and behavior of the continent's producers and consumers? This research identifies nine distinctive aspects of geography that shape local energy behavior, contributing to the emergence of the Eurasian continental energy interdependence linking East and South Asia ever more intimately with the Middle East and the former Soviet Union. These energy-relevant geographical dimensions are summarized in Figure 2.2. They are collectively bringing continental overland relationships back to a prominence they have not enjoyed since the arrival of Vasco da Gama at Calicut in 1498.

High Geographical Concentration
of Hydrocarbon Reserves

The first and most important geographic reality shaping Asian energy behavior is of course the intense concentration of overall global hydrocarbon reserves—for both oil and gas—in the Persian Gulf and Russia. As Figure 2.3

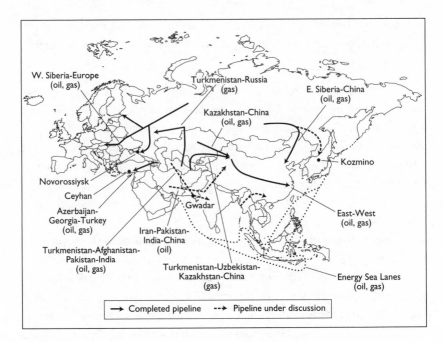

W. Siberia-Europe
(oil, gas)

Turkmenistan-Russia
(gas)

E. Siberia-China
(oil, gas)

Kazakhstan-China
(oil, gas)

Kozmino

Novorossiysk

Ceyhan

Azerbaijan-
Georgia-Turkey
(oil, gas)

Gwadar

East-West
(oil, gas)

Iran-Pakistan-
India-China
(oil)

Turkmenistan-Afghanistan-
Pakistan-India
(oil, gas)

Turkmenistan-Uzbekistan-
Kazakhstan-China
(gas)

Energy Sea Lanes
(oil, gas)

→ Completed pipeline   --→ Pipeline under discussion

Figure 2.2: Energy access options in continental Eurasia.

suggests, Russia and the Gulf together hold nearly two-thirds of both proven oil and proven gas reserves in the world. Saudi Arabia, Iran, and Iraq alone hold well over one-third of proved global oil reserves, while Russia, Iran, and Qatar together have over half of the world's natural gas. Together, this small group of neighboring countries has the potential, in the long run, and with sufficient cohesion, to exercise controlling influence over hydrocarbon resources of vital global importance. With time, oil and gas consumers will need to come back to these producers, if only due to the massive scale of their reserves.

The former Soviet "near abroad"—primarily fledgling Central Asian states over whose energy access to the broader world Russia continues to hold substantial sway—contributes another 23.9 percent to world gas, and 5.6 percent to the world oil equation, thus compounding New Silk Road dominance of the global energy supply.[50] The United States, as Figure 2.3 also makes painfully clear, is quite marginal by comparison. It holds only half the volume of Central Asia's reserves and a small fraction of the massive conventional oil and gas supplies lying beneath Russia and the Persian Gulf, with America's limited domestic reserves contrasting to its massive domestic hydrocarbon demand.

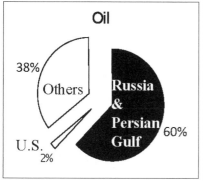
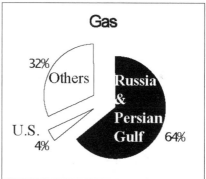

Figure 2.3: Strategic energy reservoirs: proven hydrocarbon reserves of the Persian Gulf and Russia.
Source: BP, *Statistical Review of World Energy,* 2011 edition.

Shale gas may help to reduce America's own import dependence, but it does not fundamentally change the broader international equation, since most Asian nations appear to lack major shale gas potential, and the really substantial hydrocarbon export capacity continues to lie in the Middle East and the former Soviet Union.[51]

The Geopolitics of the Two Seas

The strategic cast of energy for Asian nations is compounded by the unsettling reality that the largest energy reserves in the world are not only close to them physically, as discussed above, but also remarkably close geographically to one another, on the continent of Eurasia. Indeed, Iran and Russia—perhaps the two most strategic nations in the global energy equation—are actually neighbors across the Caspian Sea, as indicated in Figure 2.4. And less than 1,000 miles from the southern shores of the Caspian, just a short journey across Iran, lies the Persian Gulf, whose littoral nations hold over half of the proven oil and close to 40 percent of the proven gas reserves on earth.

Three decades ago, following the Iranian Revolution, it was fashionable to speak of a political "arc of crisis" surrounding the Persian Gulf.[52] Today it is still useful to conceptualize the emerging geopolitics of Eurasian energy in similar terms. Developments around the Persian Gulf—economic, diplomatic, military, and political—remain important, and the politics of the region are still volatile. Yet events further north, around the Caspian, have also grown crucial to the global energy future, following collapse of the Soviet Union and

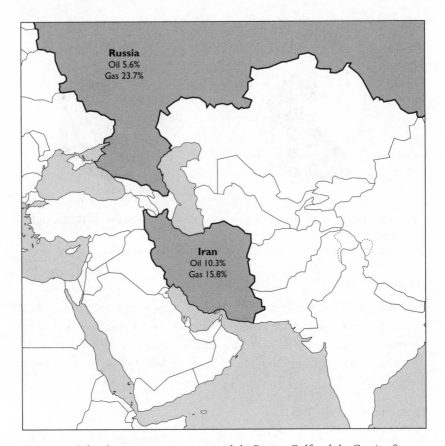

Figure 2.4: Oil and gas concentrations around the Persian Gulf and the Caspian Sea.
Source: BP, *Statistical Review of World Energy*, 2011 edition.
Note: Percentages are shares of global proven reserves at the end of 2010.

the subsequent rise, since 1999, of an assertive, albeit more geographically constrained, Russian petrostate.[53] Thus our analytical focus here on the geopolitics of the Two Seas, which flank Iran on the north and the south, as indicated in Figure 2.3.

In energy, as we have noted, the nations of the Gulf, led by Saudi Arabia, Iran, and Iraq, hold half of the proven oil reserves on earth, while the countries of the former Soviet Union hold an additional tenth. In natural gas, Russia and the Caspian states are slightly more prominent than in oil, with around 30 percent to the Persian Gulf's 40 percent. So collectively, in the world's two most strategic hydrocarbon fuels, the Land of the Two Seas holds well over three-fifths of global reserves.

Whether these Eurasian countries compete or cohere, whether they apply economic or geopolitical criteria in allocating their resources, and whether they remain domestically stable thus become issues of first-rank importance, both for the future of Eurasian continental energy geopolitics and for the global future as well. The aftermath of the 1973 Yom Kippur War and the 1979 Iranian Revolution, when in both cases oil prices rose sharply due to producer cohesion, illustrate the gravity of the issues at stake.[54] The implications of energy interdependence for broader geopolitical relationships are increasingly vital for Eurasia, as energy links across the continent progressively deepen.

High Concentration of Energy-Insecure
Political Economies in Northeast Asia

Several of the largest economies in Northeast Asia, including Japan, Korea, and Taiwan, have virtually no onshore hydrocarbon reserves, in a pattern that contrasts sharply to other industrialized regions, such as Europe and North America. Their giant neighbor, mainland China, has some significant oil and gas deposits at home, but infrastructural problems prevent the efficient and timely exploitation of those reserves. Conflicting political claims, as between Japan and China, or Japan and Korea, prevent the exploitation of apparently substantial offshore reserves—not only of oil and gas but of potentially significant alternative energy resources such as methane hydrates. To make matters worse, Northeast Asia has traditionally had no well-developed transnational oil and gas pipeline grid, to offset domestic insufficiency—again in sharp contrast to Europe and North America.

Across the East Asian region as a whole, energy demand is rising much more rapidly than in most Western industrial nations, despite inadequate reserves at home to supply that demand. Furthermore, the East Asian nations, with China, Japan, and South Korea prominent among them, lack the powerful, domestically based multinational energy firms to ensure reliable access to international markets beyond their region. Additionally, they lack the political-military leverage in global affairs that the major Western powers have traditionally enjoyed. Given the difficulties that the East Asians face in dominating international regimes, or even in ensuring what they consider equitable access arrangements mediated by Western firms, as epitomized in the persistent "Asia premium," many Asians see attraction from a variety of perspectives in deepened energy ties that omit the West, or at least its multinationals.

A Perilous Yet Highly Direct Sea-Lane Link

Among the most important geographic realities of Eurasian energy geopolitics is the extraordinary directness of sea-lane access from the Persian Gulf to
the major consuming markets of Asia. This is particularly true of India—
Mumbai, India's largest city, lies only 1,100 miles from the Straits of Hormuz.
The sea lanes to Europe and America, by contrast, are much, much longer—5,000 miles to Atlantic Europe and 8,000 miles to the United States
around the Cape of Good Hope by supertanker.

The directness of geographic access to the Persian Gulf, as suggested in
Figure 2.5, is also important for Northeast Asia. Although the distance from
the Gulf, across the Arabian Sea, Indian Ocean, and South China Sea to
Northeast Asia, is much farther than in the case of India—more than 6,000
miles from Saudi or United Arab Emirate ports to Yokohama—supertankers
still need not circumnavigate a major continent, as they must do in sailing
from the Gulf to Europe and America. And there is no need for vulnerable
pipelines. Crude oil can be easily loaded at Ras Tanura in Saudi Arabia's Eastern Province and unloaded untouched at the refineries of Ulsan and Yeosu in
South Korea. For the massive, automated supertankers that have been standard

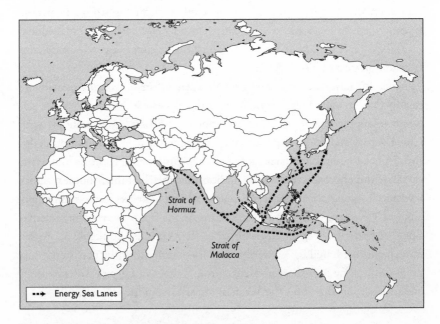

Figure 2.5: Sea lanes from the Persian Gulf to East Asia.

since the 1980s, this operational simplicity, routed in straightforward geography, is a major advantage and a major incentive to deepened commercial ties between the Gulf and the growing markets of Asia.

Although Asian maritime access to the Persian Gulf is geographically direct—much more so than that of Europe or America—it is not without its political-military complexities. Supertankers bound from Ras Tanura or Ras Laffan for Shanghai, Yokohama, or Pusan must first navigate the narrow, twenty-one-mile-wide Strait of Hormuz at the entrance to the Persian Gulf. That in a sense is unexceptional: half of global oil trade—to Europe, America, and elsewhere, as well as to Asia—must pass that way. Yet well over half of Asia's entire oil consumption, or more than 12 million barrels, must also pass through the three-mile-wide Strait of Malacca every single day.[55] Given the rising capacity of Stingers and other precision handheld weaponry, as well as persistent governability issues, especially along Indonesian shores, terrorism is an ever-present danger. There are also the uncertainties of conventional politics within the Gulf itself. And for some consuming nations, most conspicuously China, there is an uncomfortable strategic uncertainty in heavy reliance on sea lanes dominated by a potential rival such as the United States. Yet many of the most obvious alternatives to the Persian Gulf for China, such as oil fields in Angola, Nigeria, or the Sudan, lie even further afield, along the same insecure sea lanes as the energy sea routes to the Persian Gulf, which are also dominated by the U.S. Navy.

Surprising Overland Proximity

For both China and India, in particular, persuasive arguments favor overland access to Middle Eastern and Central Asian oil and gas supplies, especially given the scale of those nations' prospective future energy demand and the surprising geographical proximity of their rapidly growing frontier regions to the Persian Gulf. Gujarat and Mumbai, as we have mentioned, lie only around 1,000 miles from the entrance to the Gulf, while Kashgar and other western Xinjiang cities are within 1,200 miles of the Iranian border, across Pakistan. China directly borders Kazakhstan and lies close to the massive gas fields of Turkmenistan as well. The surprising geographic proximity of Asia's emerging giant energy consumers to the massive reserves of the Gulf and Central Asia, which provides a powerful stimulus to nascent yet rapidly deepening Eurasian continentalism, is shown clearly in Figure 2.6.

This counterintuitive geographic proximity raises the clear prospect of eastward and southward pipeline access for Middle Eastern and Central Asian producers to growing Asian markets. Energy economists generally

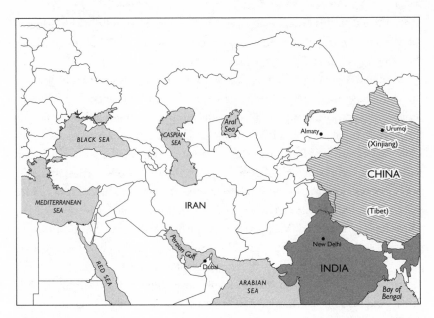

Figure 2.6: Surprising proximity of Asia's giant consumers and Middle Eastern–Central Asian energy reserves.

contend that pipelines of up to 1,500 miles between supply source and market can be clearly economical. Thus, as Chinese and Indian domestic growth extends westward and northward, pipelines connecting the western growth centers of those countries with Persian Gulf and Caspian suppliers become increasingly attractive business propositions, political risk issues aside. These issues are considered in greater detail in Chapter 5.

Geostrategic concerns about trouble-free accessibility of sea lanes enhance the attractiveness of such overland access still further, especially for China. Not surprisingly, the PRC in 2004 completed its first west-east pipeline, a $6 billion effort linking Xinjiang and Shanghai. A second trunk line, a $10 billion, 4,000-mile project to extend a pipeline from Turkmenistan to western China that was completed in December 2009 all the way to Guangzhou in southern China, will be online by the end of 2012.[56] A third west-east pipeline, a $14.6 billion project running parallel to the others and terminating in the PRC's far southern province of Guizhou, is being planned, while fourth and fifth west-east pipelines are in the pre-feasibility stages.[57] Since late 2009 there has also been a continuous, 200,000-barrel-per-day oil pipeline from Atasu, near the shores of the Caspian, running all the way to China's east coast, whose capacity will soon be doubled.[58] China is also completing a pipeline from the rapidly growing central and southwestern provinces of Szechuan and Yunnan, across Myanmar, to the Bay of Bengal.

The Strategic Yet Landlocked Position of Central Asia

The Central Asian states stand in a crucial intermediate geographical position among the major players in the Asian energy equation: China to their east, India to their southeast, Iran and the Persian Gulf to their southwest, and Russia to their northwest. The Central Asians are also sizable geographically and resource rich in their own right. Kazakhstan, after all, is one of the few nations outside the Middle East clearly capable of increasing hydrocarbon production throughout the 2010s, with its still unexploited Kashagan field at the northern end of the Caspian Sea being one of the largest energy finds worldwide over the past thirty years. Uzbekistan and Turkmenistan stand heir to major unexploited natural gas reserves as well.

Since 2005 the BTC (Baku-Tbilisi-Ceyhan) pipeline has been pumping oil from Azeri offshore fields in the Caspian across Georgia to Turkey's Mediterranean coast, as indicated in Figure 2.7, and hence to Western markets. Turkmen and other Central Asian gas also flows through Russia's natural gas pipeline grid to Western Europe. With China and India growing rapidly close by, the economic rationale for pipelines extending east and south from Central Asia to supply those ravenous, growing giants is strong, as also suggested in Figure 2.7. This dynamic enhances the natural, geographically rooted interest of Central Asian states in cooperative projects with their neighbors, although the logic of energy economics can at times run into political complications, as the Afghan conflict and the Indo-Pakistani dispute show all too well. The more activist and important these landlocked nations become in Eurasian energy geopolitics, the more emerging continentalist political-economic linkages are intensified.

Central Asian states have a natural commercial interest in transit access for their resources to world markets, and particularly in pipelines that terminate in ports, to facilitate their access to broader international markets. Kazakhstan, for example, uses the Caspian Pipeline Consortium's pipeline to access Russia's Black Sea port of Novorossiysk. Azerbaijan similarly has the BTC pipeline, which connects Baku, via Georgia, with the Turkish port of Ceyhan on the Mediterranean.

Given their landlocked geographical position, historically embedded infrastructural dependence from Soviet days on access routes through Russia,

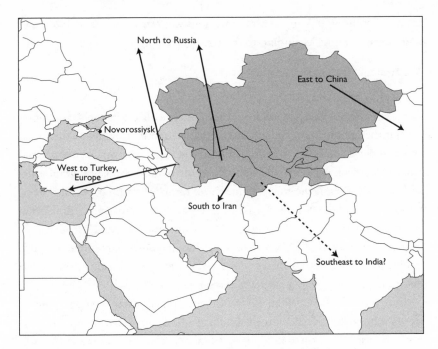

Figure 2.7: Central Asian pipeline prospects extend west, south, and east.

and limited geopolitical leverage in world affairs, the Central Asian states find it difficult to enhance their autonomy in energy matters, especially with Russia itself. Azerbaijan did succeed, however, in defying Moscow by completing the BTC pipeline, with its terminus outside the former USSR, at Ceyhan on Turkey's Mediterranean coast. Kazakhstan and Uzbekistan are similarly finding that relatively large deposits of uranium, potentially transportable by air in refined form, are helping them forge important new ties with Japan and South Korea that also help reduce their dependence on Russia.

Central Asia's location in the midst of the continent does yield some geographical advantages. Sharply rising Chinese energy demand and the manifest willingness of the PRC government to subsidize long-distance pipelines for strategic reasons are also spurring the completion of major pipelines from Turkmenistan, via Kazakhstan, onward to China. These pipelines are creating an important new eastern option for Central Asian energy producers that will likely be of rising importance in future years. The eastern option will also help to reduce geographically and historically conditioned dependence on Moscow still further.

Pivotal Transit Countries:
Pakistan and Turkey

The physical locus of energy production is obviously a key geographical issue with universal importance for energy politics. It matters greatly for Eurasian energy geopolitics, in particular, that so much hydrocarbon production is concentrated in the Gulf, and conversely that littoral Northeast Asia—Japan, Korea, and Taiwan—has so little oil and gas output of its own. It also matters that the locus of Asian growth and energy demand is increasingly in large continental nations—China and India—that are physically close to large producers in Russia, Central Asia, and the Middle East. Yet the energy transport profile, itself necessarily rooted in geography, also has major strategic significance.

Oil and gas inevitably must flow from the energy-rich Land of the Two Seas—the Persian Gulf and the Caspian Sea—outward to the broader world. To flow to Europe in the west, Central Asian resources need to move overland through Russia, or alternatively through Georgia and Turkey. En route southward to India, they could potentially pass through Iran or Afghanistan, and then through Pakistan. To the east, Central Asian resources could flow directly to China, although Middle Eastern oil and gas would need to flow either over the sea lanes, outward from the Persian Gulf and through the Malacca Straits, or at least overland through Iran and Pakistan.

Several countries thus potentially play a dual role, as both producers and transit nations, with the intrinsic interests and rigidities that this duality implies. There is also, however, another category—the pure transit nations, without substantial domestic resources of their own. These countries have special strategic significance in the geopolitics of energy, due to the potential flexibility—as well as volatility and duplicity—in their transit policy stance.

In the world of Eurasian energy, the two most important pure transit countries are Pakistan and Turkey. Pakistan's geographic location gives it fateful significance for both Chinese and Indian energy ambitions, since it lies across both nations' overland access routes to the Persian Gulf and also New Delhi's access to the large natural gas fields of Central Asia, particularly those of Turkmenistan. Since the 1970s, Pakistan has played a crucial role in mediating China's broader relationships with the Islamic world and the Middle East. Yet rising Chinese energy demand over the past decade, together with deepened Sino-Pakistani political ties and the more complicated U.S. South Asian presence since the May, 2011 death of Osama Bin Laden, have been making that geographically ordained position between Xinjiang and the Persian Gulf ever more consequential in global geopolitical terms than ever.

The strategic importance of Pakistan as a transit country in China's deepening, geographically mandated energy relations with the Middle East is enhanced by the evolution of the Gwadar deep-water port project on the Arabian Sea in Balochistan, less than fifty miles east of the Iranian border, as indicated in Figure 2.8. In 2001, after Japan had offered aid the previous year for the port project, on condition of Pakistan's signing the Comprehensive Nuclear Test Ban Treaty,[59] Pakistan turned instead to China, following strong Chinese entreaties, reportedly offering the PRC access for its naval vessels to the port in return for major financial assistance.[60]

In 2002 Pakistan and China signed a loan agreement covering the first phase of construction. China was to finance 80 percent of an initial $248 million in construction costs, while supplying five hundred Chinese workers, who kept the project underway almost around the clock.[61] Despite Balochi

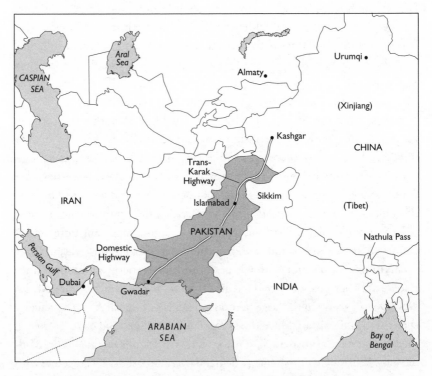

Figure 2.8: China's emerging transport links to the south and west.

separatist violence that killed three Chinese engineers in 2004,[62] the first phase of the Gwadar project was completed in 2005, including three berths capable of potentially accommodating large naval vessels. In 2008 the port began commercial operations, operated by the Singapore Port Authority. Meanwhile, an additional Asian Development Bank loan was announced, as part of the National Trade Corridor Highway Investment Program, to link Gwadar with the north of Pakistan and ultimately with Xinjiang.[63] A pipeline, as well as enhanced power and telecommunications grids, are also being constructed northeast toward China, parallel to the transnational Sino-Pakistani Friendship Highway across the Korakorum Mountains.

Further west, Turkey is also playing the pivotal transit role that it is fated by geography to perform, commanding both overland and maritime access transportation routes. Since 2004, it has hosted the now-functioning BTC pipeline, whose terminus from Azerbaijan is at Ceyhan, on the Mediterranean coast, near the Syrian border. Kazakh oil piped into Russia's Black Sea port of Novorossiysk also flows out to world markets by sea, through the Bosporus and the Dardanelles. Russia provides piped gas to Turkey under the Black Sea through the Blue Stream project and is proposing onward supply to Bulgaria and points westward. An Iran-Turkey gas pipeline has been operating since 2001,[64] and Iran has approached Turkey about selling Iranian gas to Europe.[65] Meanwhile, a Western consortium presses for Turkish participation in the Nabucco project, to bring Middle Eastern gas and oil westward from Iraq to Central Europe. Islamist Turkey's multidirectional diplomacy, driven by the activist geopolitical thinking of Foreign Minister Ahmet Davutoglu discussed above, is capitalizing on this pivotal energy transit role to enhance Turkey's catalytic position in the emergence of a broader Eurasian continentalism in the post–Cold War world. Russia, Greece, Bulgaria, Syria, Iran, Georgia, Azerbaijan, Iraq, and even Israel figure in Turkey's recent energy-transit negotiations, neatly complementing its multidirectional diplomacy as well. In late 2010 and thereafter, Turkey moved to deepen relations with China also, including joint air and ground exercises between their militaries.[66]

The Central Geopolitical Position of Russia

In the geography and geopolitics of Eurasian energy, there is simply no avoiding the central position of Russia. It is, after all, the largest nation on earth, stretching across nine time zones, in the heart of continental Eurasia. Russia borders on both large and growing energy consumers like China, and also on several of the largest exporters, including Kazakhstan, Azerbaijan, and, across the Caspian, on Iran as well.

Russia is also a critically important transit country, especially for Central Asian producers, with whom it is intimately and indeed coercively linked by extensive Soviet-era pipelines. The dependence of Central Asian producers on Russia's pipeline network, and on broader Russian economic and geopolitical support, allowed Gazprom to sell Turkmen gas in Europe during 2008, for example, at nearly triple the wellhead price in Ashgabat.[67] The vast bulk of the difference was accounted for by Gazprom transit fees. Russia has traditionally used the revenue generated by controlling Central Asian gas access to the world to cross-subsidize extremely low domestic gas prices within Russia, thus creating strong political-economic incentives in Moscow to preserve the status quo.[68]

One important aspect of Russia's geographical positioning, of major consequence both for energy economics and for geopolitics, is its central location astride major, established European energy supply routes. Russia is also a dominant natural gas supplier to many Western European nations in its own right. Given Europe's traditional geopolitical importance in world affairs, and the concentration of major Russian political and economic centers in that nation's European segment, Russia tends to have a strong domestic preoccupation with the geopolitics of energy in Europe. It has thus historically tended to neglect opportunities to influence Asia, with whom it shares long borders and deep, rising complementarities of interest in the energy sphere. Thus, geography creates an as yet unresolved dilemma: will Russia orient itself westward toward Europe, or turn eastward toward Asia? At the same time, Russia's central geographical position also creates the basis and the rationale for Moscow's highly strategic use of energy as a diplomatic tool in dealing with both Europe and Asia, as we shall see.

Due to Russia's geographical location and its traditional international standing, that sprawling nation is more central to the global geopolitics of energy than any of its Eurasian partners. It also holds almost a quarter of world proven natural gas reserves, concentrated in the Arctic and Siberia. And the Russian Federation is the one energy exporter that is also a member of the G8. In a post–Cold War world where it has lost much of its former political-military clout, Moscow is relying increasingly on its centrality in the world of energy, suggested in Figure 2.9, to sustain a major role in international affairs—a point I shall explore further in coming pages.

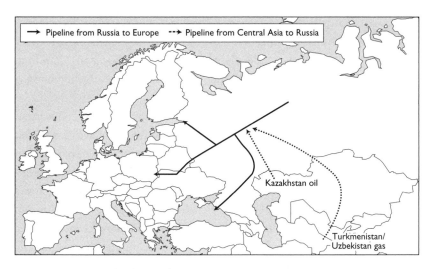

Figure 2.9: Russia's oil and gas infrastructure.

The Unavoidable Geoeconomic Attractions
of Iran

Most Asian nations, like their counterparts in the West, have misgivings about both Iran's nuclear program and its parochial, undemocratic leadership. Yet they nevertheless almost invariably take a much softer line on sanctions and other confrontational measures toward Iran than their Western—especially American and Israeli—counterparts.[69] This contrast has important geographic and geoeconomic origins that need to be understood, as they will likely color the evolution of Eurasian energy geopolitics going forward.

Iran, from an Asian standpoint, is arguably the most strategic nation in the Middle East, and one of the most strategic in the entire world. It stands at the entrance to the Persian Gulf, from which Asia gets well over half of its entire oil and liquified natural gas supply. The equivalent ratios for Europe and the United States are roughly one-third and less than a quarter. The Asian nations are also far more dependent on imported energy than the West—and growing more so, as their rapid growth increasingly outstrips domestic resources.

For India, Iran is a potential energy supplier not only by sea but potentially overland as well. The two countries are only barely separated from one another, by a sliver of Pakistani Balochistan. Indian Energy Minister Aiyar initialed a large-scale, if tentative, long-term contract for piped natural gas from Iran's South Pars field in 2006. That agreement has not been implemented, due to American pressure, but nevertheless represents Indian strategic interest in a traditionally friendly neighbor of over 2,000 years' standing. And the two countries began exploring further submarine pipeline options between them in 2010.

For China, Iran is also much closer geographically than often appreciated, due to the counterintuitive proximity of Xinjiang to the Persian Gulf, as noted above. Ongoing Pakistani infrastructure projects hasten the day on which large-scale overland commerce—both in energy and beyond—will be increasingly feasible across Western Asia. China is already, since 2009, Iran's largest foreign trading partner, with bilateral trade volumes exceeding $30 billion annually, and incentives for deepened interdependence in a diverse range of sectors are strong. Indeed, the Teheran-Beijing political-economic axis is a primary driver for deepened Eurasian continentalism.

For Japan, Iran is a traditional friend of more than a hundred years' standing, since at least the Russo-Japanese War of 1904–1905, when Iranians applauded Imperial Japan's unexpected victory over Czarist Russia. Throughout the ensuing century, Japanese and Iranians shared common geopolitical concerns about their looming Russian neighbor. And they share enduring common interests with respect to energy—contrasting relations with the United States notwithstanding.

Apart from Iran's role as an energy supplier and a natural geopolitical ally, that proud yet fragile country is also potentially important for Asia as a transit nation. The case of China excepted, the most feasible way for Asian nations to access the natural resources of Central Asia is via Iran. Even when those resources cannot be procured directly, it is easy for Asian firms to swap Central Asian resources provided to Iran in the north, where it is an importer from countries like Turkmenistan, for Iranian exports from the south, eastward across the sea lane, to India and beyond.

A final factor is the Israeli dimension. For the United States, in particular, Iran's potentially nuclear challenge to Israel is a matter of grave importance. Asian nations generally recognize Israel and support its peaceful integration into Middle Eastern affairs. Yet they are naturally much less sensitive to threats to its national security than Jerusalem or Washington, DC, given geographical distance and differing existential security conceptions. This difference in standpoint is another reason that Western and Asian stances toward Iran have subtly diverged in recent years, with even a fundamentalist Iran retaining geopolitical attractions for Asia that the West, especially the United States, has clearly foresworn.

THE INCREASED IMPORTANCE OF GEOGRAPHY
IN THE POST–COLD WAR WORLD

Geography and politics have always stood in complex interdependence with one another. Geographical realities provide a crucial basis for political calculations, and thus give birth to geopolitics, the study of the relationship between political power and geographical space.[70] Yet politics, through configuration of national boundaries, alliance relationships, transit rights, and conditions of access to and from neighboring countries, can also critically influence the extent to which natural geographic factors actually shape political-economic decisions.

Political constraints on the operation of natural geographical factors have waxed and waned in Eurasia across the centuries. In some cases, such as imperial prohibitions on oceangoing travel in feudal Japan and China,[71] political constraints were placed on maritime commerce and overseas travel by sea. More typically, however, such politically imposed travel constraints have applied to travel and commerce overland.

The Cold War was one such period, especially damaging to interchange across continental Asia's extensive land borders. Stalin, pursuing his autarkic concept of socialism in one state, sharply constrained travel between the Soviet Union and neighboring countries after 1926, disrupting international commerce in a wide arc stretching from Japanese-held Korea 5,000 miles westward to Turkey. Communist regimes in China, Vietnam, Korea, and Mongolia likewise restricted both international and domestic travel, while many Western nations, led by the United States, imposed inhibiting trade and travel embargoes also. Meanwhile, interchange in Southwest Asia was discouraged by Indo-Pakistani, Sino-Indian, and Israeli-Arab confrontations, as well as violent incidents and wars in the Middle East.

Following the Cold War, as we shall see in Chapter 3, political constraints on the operation of geography have been reduced, through discontinuous critical junctures such as collapse of the Soviet Union. Incremental normalizations, like the border agreements across Central Asia in the 1990s, have also helped. Clearly, as political constraints recede, geographical factors are growing more important in the post–Cold War Eurasian continental world.

CONCLUSION

In an increasingly global international community, the conventional wisdom is that the world is growing "flatter"—with geographical location rapidly declining in relative importance as globalization and the information revolution proceed, and as Cold War–induced political barriers subside. That may be true in finance, manufacturing, or service trade, but not, I argue, in energy. To the contrary, as worldwide energy demand steadily continues to rise, fueled by the gradual entry of 2 billion new Chinese and Indian consumers into the world economy, the restricted number of locations where hydrocarbons can be efficiently produced are growing more strategically important than ever before, not least for the peoples of Asia, who have far less energy than they need or expect to need in coming years. So are their principal transit routes, both maritime and overland. The age-old tyranny of location thus continues in the energy sphere, even in a global world—and nowhere more so than in energy-short Asia. It is a major factor driving the new Eurasian continentalism.

What specific impact does geography have on the political economy of supplying oil and gas to Asia? I have made nine distinct observations. First, I noted that the geographic concentration of resources—in the Persian Gulf and Russia—was functionally important, forcing Asian nations to pay particular attention to those potential suppliers and to their interrelationship with one another.

I pointed out that Asia had two distinct options for securing Middle Eastern energy resources—one by sea and the other by land. The land option, I argued, is more attractive to China and India, two of the largest consumers, who are increasing rapidly in importance, precisely due to their rapidly rising demand and its increasing concentration in areas close to the producing nations themselves. I noted the geographical importance of transit countries—particularly Pakistan and Turkey—and also, finally, the pivotal geopolitical roles of Russia and Iran. Based on this geographical evidence, including the underlying resource equation—West Asian abundance and East Asian scarcity—I must conclude that a new trans-continental energy geopolitics linking those two poles has a transcendent logic, of global importance. That Eurasian nexus of global geopolitics is only being enhanced by the dismantling of Cold War barriers over the past two decades. A Eurasian continental energy entente has a powerful logic, provided that politics does not stand in the way.

Chapter 3 Six Critical Junctures and Eurasia's Transformation

The nations of Eurasia in recent years have been backdoor neighbors to one another, at best. Centuries ago, in the pre-Columbian era, they had vigorous transcontinental commercial ties that lay at the core of the global political economy of the day. And many of these states, as some of the world's most consequential energy producers and consumers, share important complementarities today with respect to oil, natural gas, and uranium also.

Given these important potential synergies and their direct propinquity, why did the Silk Road states remain strangers to one another for so long? Why, suddenly, in the twilight years of the twentieth century, did their long-static ties begin to explosively and abruptly deepen? Why did their natural, symbiotic relationships not develop earlier and more gradually?

In this chapter, I consider the empirical paradox of emerging Eurasian continentalism—the changing reality of a continent for so many years static, segmented, and detached from the mainstream of world affairs that suddenly began transforming itself into something more. Quietly, with remarkably little fanfare, the nations of

East Asia, South Asia, the Middle East, and the former Soviet Union have, in the wake of the Cold War, become markedly more interactive with one another, across traditional geopolitical divides, in a discontinuous, unprecedented fashion. How and why has that unlikely change transpired? And what does it portend for international relations theory and for global affairs?

EXPLAINING EURASIA'S TRANSFORMATION

That Eurasia as a whole is changing profoundly and becoming an increasingly integrated and interactive unit, economically and diplomatically coherent, has been noted by a number of astute recent popular commentators.[1] What drives this deepening integration and determines the sort of political-economic profile that the increasingly integrated continent will exhibit, however, remains to be clearly explicated. And virtually no academic commentators have ventured to explain Eurasia's organization gap, or the continentalism that has begun to replace it, in more theoretical terms, despite the potentially important implications for how the global political economy functions.

Serious attempts to explain Eurasia's long-standing organization gap, and its recent erosion, have often been based on European experience, flowing from two streams of thought: the realist paradigm and institutionalist frameworks.[2] The realist tradition stresses the role of geostrategy in both creating and erasing the gap. The contrasting institutionalist tradition explains the organization gap and its erosion in terms of established norms and culture.[3]

There is definitely substantial variation in the salience of trans-national organization, and the degree of regional political-economic integration across the major global regions, and also in the profile of trans-national interaction within those regions. Abstract concepts like "hegemony" or "norms" fail to provide sufficient explanation for the variety that actually prevails in the real world. Neither "globalization" nor "market forces" adequately explain causality. Indeed, all of these notions are under-predictive, in explaining why regionalist configurations in the real world wax and wane.

As Mattli suggests, the critical equation definitely appears to be the demand for, and the supply of, regional institutions.[4] When economic interdependence is substantial, and technological change rapid, as has recently been the case within Eurasia, there tends to be demand from national leaders for new, stabilizing institutions, although that demand often remains unarticulated. Certainly energy interdependence, in the Eurasian case, is present as a driver. The supply of appropriate institutions, however, is by no means automatic.

In this chapter, I present the critical-juncture framework as a key explanatory variable in Eurasia's transition to more structured interdependence, and in trans-national institution-building more generally.[5] I suggest that developments at "critical junctures" open isolated states to new, more cosmopolitan options, and intensify demand for trans-national institutions, even very soft ones, while also helping to provide—as well as to configure—the supply of those institutions. I argue that individual decision-making at critical, historic turning points, both within nations and between them, thus profoundly shapes the ultimate institutional product, as well as the broader profile of socio-political interdependence.

Critical-juncture analysis stresses, in short, the dynamic interaction among individual decision-makers at critical decision points, against the backdrop of economic interdependence. In explaining outcomes, it combines insights from both historical-institutionalist and rational-choice models. Historical institutionalists have concerned themselves with persistent *legacies* from the past, which unavoidably configure the political-economic context within which individuals decide. New rules of the game, however, can and do emerge from *strategic bargains* among individuals, especially during periods of crisis and uncertainty. The eclectic critical-junctures framework incorporates central insights from both approaches.

The rational-choice approach, by contrast, too easily assumes that individual bargaining over new arrangements occurs on a blank slate, without regard to pre-existent understandings and institutional context, although it usefully captures the importance of individual decision-making.[6] In introducing the concept of critical juncture here, I outline a process by which rational actors modify their goals and perceptions in response to uncertainty, and by which they also bargain with one another in dynamic ways, often producing outputs that contrast to the embedded historical-institutional context in which they arose. Trans-Eurasian decision-making in the wake of the 1973 oil shock, the 1979 Iranian Revolution, or the 1991 Soviet collapse provide powerful illustrations of this tendency. Hopefully, testing will make it possible simultaneously to gain a deeper understanding of national transformation in key countries, the emergence of trans-continental interdependence across Eurasia, and also the political economy of regionalism, continentalism, and political development more generally.

CONCEPTUAL BACKGROUND OF THE
CRITICAL-JUNCTURE FRAMEWORK

The critical-juncture framework presented here is not commonly employed by specialists on regionalism and "proto-regionalism". A variant of this concept has been frequently and quite productively applied, however, to explain domestic institution-building. Indeed, a number of major works on nation-building find national policies and leaders' choices at critical decision points important in determining both the form and the function of political-economic institutions that later emerge.[7]

Sidney Verba recognized, in studying comparative national response to crises, that political development typically follows a branching-tree pattern. His approach conceptualizes such development as a sequence of points at which choices are made. From any given juncture, there are alternative next stages, depending on what choices are made. Yet choice necessarily forecloses some alternatives. On this issue Verba stresses the multiple options available at each decision point—and as a result, the non-determinist overall character of political evolution.[8]

Stephen Krasner suggests a similar "punctuated equilibrium" paradigm for understanding the state-building process.[9] Punctuated equilibrium, in his formulation, corresponds closely to Verba's notion of a branching tree. It suggests that institutional change is episodic and discontinuous, rather than incremental. Crises, in his formulation, are of central importance in determining long-term institutional outcomes. During a crisis, the choice made regarding which path to pursue forecloses other options, including potentially the paths that are most functionally appropriate to solving a problem. Employing the concept of punctuated equilibrium, Krasner suggests not only the constraints on institutional adjustments that pre-existing structures create, but also the converse opportunities for institutional innovation that crises provide. At each juncture, he contends, there is a chance for self-correction and choice of alternative political directions.

Stephen Skowronek similarly stresses the importance of political crisis, which he defines as "a sporadic, disruptive event that suddenly challenges a state's capacity to maintain control and alterns the boundaries defining the legitimate use of coercion."[10] Skowronek argues that "crisis situations tend to become the watersheds in a state's institutional development. Actions taken to meet the challenge often lead to the establishment of new institutional forms, powers, and precedents."[11] Skowronek's fundamental argument is that the

ultimate profile of institutions established during periods of crisis is a function of both environmental factors during such periods and pre-existing institutional structures. In short, the immediate interplay at a critical juncture
between events and the parameters that shape the meaning of those events to
decision-makers profoundly affects the institutional profile that ultimately
emerges from a crisis. Pre-existing institutions do not mechanically determine policy outcomes, he contends.

Crises reduce contradictions between state structures and the domestic
environment within which those structures exist, by provoking structural
change responsive to that environment. Yet following such crises, institutions
originally created to resolve the original incongruity take on a life of their own.
Bureaucracies and political parties, for example, configure themselves without necessarily responding to contemporary social changes, often leading to
increased tensions. These tensions in turn ultimately provoke further crises.
This dualism of changing circumstances and persisting institutions is central
to understanding the significance of crisis-generated critical junctures in political development.

Peter Gourevitch explicitly considered the relationship between crisis
and state, finding that crises both reflect developments within a given state,
and also in turn shape the configuration of states themselves. Gourevitch appreciated the importance of historical contingency, arguing that "in each crisis countries 'choose' a policy or a sequence of policies . . . but frequently in
decision-making we find neither consciousness nor coherence."[12]

In other work I have also personally applied the notion of crisis in explaining
public-policy profiles. In a formulation approaching that of the critical juncture, I describe the intervals surrounding a major political crisis as "climactic
periods, when long-established patterns are suddenly called into question,
and new, unusually enduring relationships are rapidly forged."[13] I note that
an explanation for policy change sufficiently predictive to suggest the direction of change needs to combine structural and historical approaches.

My 1988 study, considering Japan's post-World War II politicsl of public-
policy formation in comparative perspective, shows that in years of
turbulence—that is, periods when old relationships crumble and new ones
are rapidly forged—longstanding and often routinized circles of compensation are also reconfigured. The new institutions and policy patterns developed
during those short periods of flux often persist long after the original pressures
that forged them have disappeared. Detailed historical examination of both
pre-existing social structure and newly arising pressures for change during

periods of crisis, I thus argue, is critical. I see public-policy analysis, in other words, as a form of political archeology.

All of the preceding works highlight an important aspect of political development: crisis and individual response at a critical juncture. Every critical juncture, in the terminology of the branching-tree model, thus serves as a node from which different branches lead off in various directions. Decision-makers, given their own personal opportunities and constraints, unavoidably make choices regarding which branch to pursue at these individual decision nodes.

Going beyond this simplified paradigm, one can see variations on the branching-tree model theme. After a choice is made at a given decision mode and another decision point arises, distinct branches with divergent implications emerge down the road. Decision-makers who could potentially be different from those at the previous node, confront new opportunities and constraints, making choices as to which branch to approach. They may revise the thrust of the previous decision, even contradicting the former choice. Thus, over time, a more appropriate path—one that was foreclosed by the previous decision—may later reopen, as the actual process of making policy evolves.

The branching-tree model thus contrasts sharply with the realist paradigm, and also with historical institutionalism. This tree model, diverging from the realist paradigm, captures the actual dynamics of interactions at a critical juncture. In reality, power distribution and position in the international system, although important, do not determine the payoff structure and bargaining routes that are involved in an interactive decision-making process in any respect, and the branching-tree model is sensitive to this reality.

The branching-tree model also contrasts to the historical-institutionalist approach. The latter stresses determinacy in institution-building, while the former captures the deep contingency on events that is characteristic of critical junctures. Historical institutionalism focuses on the structural context of decision-making. The branching-tree model recognizes, however, the relative autonomy of individual choice, especially the inter-personal dynamics among individual policy-makers. Again, existing institutions provide important context for a critical juncture. Yet due to the distinctive, indeterminate nature of such potential turning points, as the following section makes clear, institutions by definition cannot conclusively shape the outcome of such a critical juncture. On the contrary, outcomes are typically dependent on individual decision-making, as well as the process through which individual preferences are determined and combined, even though that process tends to be spontaneously haphazard.[14]

SPECIFYING THE CRITICAL JUNCTURE MODEL

A critical juncture is defined here as a historical decision point at which there are distinct alternative paths to the future. For a decision point to qualify as a critical juncture, certain defining features are both necessary and sufficient:

1. A *crisis* typically exists, that calls the legitimacy of existing arrangements into serious question, regardless of whether those arrangements are formal or informal, institutional or hegemonic in character, and no matter whether the crisis involves a rapid change of power distribution within the system, or collapse of authority, or any form of violent conflict.[15] Crisis, in other words, meaningfully changes the pre-existing bargaining context, and opens periods of opportunity for change, thus generating new demand for institutions. Crisis also generates an initial stimulus for interaction, signaling the onset of a critical juncture. Crises can be strategic, economic, or a combination of the two: the 1962 Cuban missile crisis; the 1971 breakdown of the Bretton Woods system; the oil shocks of 1973 and 1979; the 1989 collapse of Soviet satellites in Eastern Europe; the 1991 collapse of the Soviet Union itself; and the 2008 global financial crisis are all illustrations.

2. Crisis breeds *stimulus for change*. It also generates, however, a parallel need for collective action to address a common challenge, thus catalyzing the process of institutional supply. The initial stimulus typically generates differing incentives for policy-makers, who themselves have diverse preferences and forms of leverage, which are defined by "states' international capabilities, and domestic coalitional stability, as well as elite beliefs and ideologies."[16] The actors, however, may—but do not necessarily—have the ability to resolve the problem at hand. If the nations involved lack the capacity to address the problem in question, and to undertake institutional innovations, then the crisis persists—with no decision made and no option chosen—until the crisis escalates to the point where actors emerge who are capable of innovating to solve the collective problem that they face.

3. The parties involved confront *intense time pressure*. Such pressure is a crucial element in a critical juncture, in that it constraints institutional supply, and the contours of the institutional proposals that emerge. Time pressure makes interactions hard to routinize, and limits the time available to search out options. As a result, decision-making takes place under severely bounded rationality. Decision-makers are forced into sudden, high-stakes decisions, with inadequate information, a combination which can fatefully affect policy outcomes.[17] The actors involved are forced to devise a solution within a

sharply limited period, after which opportunity for change which a critical juncture fortuitously presents may be lost. The pressure on individual policy-makers to negotiate a workable framework, intensified by their pressing need in a crisis to deliver results, distorts their pursuit of an optimal outcome. Consequently, the resulting institutions do not usually assume an optimal configuration; compromises and negotiations are therefore often central features of a critical juncture.

At a critical juncture, decision makers are clearly faced with enormous uncertainty and simultaneous time pressure to decide. The players are forced to take stands; failing to do so leads to lost opportunity to affect future changes. Crisis necessitates decisions and actions, and time pressure alters the contours of agenda setting, in turn decisively shaping the profile and resolution of issues. Interactions among individual leaders after a crisis tend to be conspicuously different from normal routinized interactions.

As a critical juncture contains a time pressure constraint, leaders of small countries that can afford to wait often enjoy considerable leverage in actual negotiations over traditionally dominant powers with responsibilities for system maintenance, who cannot wait. The dominant power is forced to accept a satisficing outcome in preference to a more ideal result, due to its own distinctive, asymmetrical need to conclude bargaining in a timely fashion to preserve system stability. Consequently, a dominant power, such as the United States in the post–Cold War world, cannot always get what it prefers at a critical juncture, even when it has global influence and a nominally full menu of options.

The Most Important Actors
in Critical Junctures

As Graham Allison suggested in *Essence of Decision*, players of governmental policy games tend to be defined by their positions. "The governmental actor is neither a unitary agent nor a conglomerate of organizations, but rather a number of individual players. . . . Players are individuals in jobs."[18]

Players at critical junctures are the individual leaders responsible for problem solving during, and in the immediate wake of, crises. They can be either the top political leaders, such as presidents, or otherwise designated negotiators interacting with other key decision-makers involved. In other words, the players at critical junctures are defined by the discretionary power that they can exercise in resolving issues at hand. Their source of influence includes either formal authority and responsibility or actual control over the resources necessary to carry out action.

Critical Junctures and Trans-National Institution Building

A critical-juncture framework clearly appears useful in intranational political development, as demonstrated in a wide range of previous studies. Yet there is an unwarranted lack of scholarly attention to the critical juncture mechanism in the study of trans-national institutional development and transformation. There is, as I have noted, a potentially catalytic link between the demand for such trans-national organization, flowing from either market pressures or security challenges, on the one hand, and the political supply. Coordination dilemmas make it easier for leaders to concur on new frameworks during critical junctures than at other times—and also more imperative. Such coordination dilemmas can also play a key role in dismantling pre-existing institutions, as happened in the last days of the Soviet Union.

Clear logical parallels can be drawn between national and regional institution building, especially when the units in a given region are highly interdependent, as in Europe, Latin America, North America, or East Asia. A continent could, for the purposes of this analysis, be considered a particular type of trans-national region. If the evolution of sociopolitical organization at the national level does not follow the path specified theoretically by historical institutionalism, there is no particular reason to believe that, at a regional or continental level, established precedents should necessarily determine future direction. If national institution building follows the crisis and sequence pattern, as the above scholarship suggests, then similar logic may be working at a regional level as well. This is especially likely when the constituent units of the region are highly interdependent, as the continent of Asia is becoming with respect to energy.

Indeed, the profile of regional institution building could be particularly responsive to crisis, given the fragility of institutions at the transnational level, the complex cross-pressures confronting regionalism, which only crisis can resolve, and the systemic imperative of coping with crisis when it actually emerges. This pattern could be particularly pronounced in areas of the world that are especially prone to political-economic crisis, such as the Middle East and Northeast Asia. These crises can in turn be a crucial catalyst for policy innovation, or for sociopolitical network building.

The Special Utility of Critical Juncture Analysis

Although alternative formulations have potential merits of their own, the critical juncture framework explains many dynamics and consequences of trans-national political evolution. Domestic institutions are the product of interactions among interest groups, organizations, administrative branches, and even individual leaders, in an effort to tackle common crises. Regional cooperation is therefore the product of dynamic interactions among countries with different interests and resources, seeking to solve emergent common problems or to fill a power vacuum, such as existed in Central Asia following the collapse of the Soviet Union.

Common goals, institutional environment, and case-specific factors—international power position, domestic coalition profile, and leadership beliefs, for example—offer broad parameters within which to modify context and seek better payoffs; their adaptation of bilateral or multilateral approaches, for example, is fatefully shaped by the process of interaction at a critical juncture. If policymakers aspire to create new institutions, they must first decide on the specific characteristics of those bodies or systems of rules, including the strength, nature, and scope of the arrangements in question.[19] The structural product of this critical juncture interaction is stabilized, codified, and in turn itself shapes the future contours of cooperation in a given region. The form and scope of regional cooperation are thus both perpetuated until another crisis occurs at a subsequent critical juncture.

Given the foregoing, the study of regionalism, including continentalism as a variant thereof, should thus find its roots in the understanding of critical junctures. Yet critical junctures do not, of course, fully explain regional development profiles. Historical and institutional factors naturally all contribute to the interactions among nations at critical junctures, by shaping the context of decision itself. To use another analogy, if preexisting institutions provide a menu of policy options for decision makers, crisis-induced critical junctures can (1) contract the repertoire, limiting available choices; (2) change the repertoire, ranking preferences differently; or (3) expand the repertoire, revealing fresh options that were imperceptible prior to the crisis. CJs can thus influence the decision-making processes of large, powerful nations just as profoundly as they do the policy profiles of smaller powers, if not more so, making critical junctures ultimately more fundamental to understanding policy outcomes, in many cases, than the power structures of domestic or international affairs.

At any given critical juncture, states may have multiple responses to trans-national crises. They choose one of them based on two-level game interac-tions with domestic interest groups and foreign counterparts.[20] Institutional development at critical junctures thus has inevitable discontinuity from a historical perspective—in both domestic and transnational decision making.

The impact of a critical juncture is not limited to the immediate handling of a crisis. Indeed, the policy networks established to deal with the crisis in question endure after the turbulence has subsided. Even when crisis-period actors fail to establish formal procedures or regulatory bodies to govern their own future relations, they build processes for interactions and coordination among the countries in question that continue to endure. Those processes can thereafter be reinforced by growing economic interaction in areas such as energy, or by deepening social interaction of various kinds.

Individual actors involved centrally in the policy networks created and strengthened through CJs tend to be prominent political leaders, specialists, and other influential figures in their own countries. In the process of dealing with crisis, they establish and solidify ties to actors from other countries. These trans-national relationships serve as communication channels for information and springboards for contemplating future collective action. After crises subside, actors participating in these transnational networks often continue making cooperative proposals for addressing subsequent issues that arise, using their new crisis-established transnational networks. After the 1997–1998 fi-nancial crisis in Asia, for example, such networks helped crucially in estab-lishing a multilayered institutional environment across that region, including that embodied in the May, 2000 Chiangmai agreement.[21]

CRITICAL JUNCTURES AND THE MAKING OF
EURASIAN ENERGY ENTENTE

Clearly there have long been profound and deepening complementarities of interest between the energy producers and the energy consumers of Eurasia, which could potentially lead to deeper and more intense regional ties, both formal and informal. The prospect of deeper relationships has persistently been intensified by the realities of geography, which naturally link Persian Gulf, Russian, and Central Asian producers intimately with Indian and

Northeast Asian consumers, both by land and by sea. These Eurasian energy complementarities and geographical proximity are much stronger than those with Europe and North America and should naturally lead to transcontinental energy entente. Yet such potential complementarities, as we have seen, were once long dormant, with little progress in realizing them outside the former Soviet Union, over the first eight decades of the twentieth century. Why then has continental interdependence begun to intensify so explosively in recent years?

Much of the answer seems to lie in a small number of intense political-economic crises in key Eurasian countries, unfolding sequentially across the last quarter of the twentieth century. These crises, in their totality, reoriented the continent's growth and energy profile, giving rise to deepened Eurasian political-economic interdependence, unprecedented since the demise of the Silk Road five centuries earlier. I point to six critical junctures in the recent history of Eurasia, during the fateful last three decades of the twentieth century, which together dynamically activated the powerful forces of integration and transformation now giving birth to new continentalist configurations of potentially historic significance.

Two of these junctures—Deng Xiaoping's Four Modernizations in the late 1970s and Manmohan Singh's Indian economic reforms of the early 1990s—activated the formidable growth engines of China and India, which in turn have been so fatefully important in stimulating energy demand in those two poor yet massive countries, with more than a third of the world's population between them.[22] The other four CJs—the 1973 Arab oil embargo and nationalizations, the 1979 Iranian Revolution, the 1991 collapse of the Soviet Union, and the 1999 advent of the Putin administration in Russia—transformed the political economy of key nations across Eurasia in fateful ways, both dismantling geopolitical barriers to the emergence of a more integrated continent and also encouraging deepening continental inclinations both to cohere regionally and to balance rather than simply bandwagon with the United States in international affairs. I begin my examination of these momentous transitions with the oil shock that reordered Eurasia's prospective role in global energy affairs, moving then to the liberalization steps in the continent's giant nations that unleashed their growth potential, and finally considering the key domestic political changes that magnified and channeled the consequences of that new Eurasian growth.

Oil Shock and the Changing Ownership of
Middle Eastern Energy (1973–1975)

> Oil . . . is the strongest of weapons the Arabs wield.
> —*Abdullah Tariki, Saudi petroleum minister and*
>   *cofounder of OPEC*[23]

One of the great political-economic bargains in world history, ranking with the legendary purchase of Manhattan for $24, was an obscure contract negotiated in 1933. For a loan of $170,327.50, Saudi Arabia's King Abdul Aziz ibn Saud granted the Standard Oil Company of California a sixty-year exclusive concession to 360,000 square miles of desert.[24] So huge were the oil reserves when finally discovered, and so massive the investment needs to develop them, that SoCal—Chevron to be—could not exploit these reserves alone. It took on partners, thus forming the Arabian American Oil Company (Aramco).

In the years to follow, Aramco indeed became a plum—the world's largest oil producer, sitting atop the world's largest oil reserves.[25] By the early 1970s, its average wells yielded 12,000 barrels per day, compared with the 18 barrels per day of the average U.S. counterpart.[26] Aramco's $20 billion refinery and petrochemical complex at Ras Tanura on the Persian Gulf, the largest in the world, could turn out more product (550,000 barrels per day), produce more petrochemicals (7 million tons per annum), store more oil, and load more supertankers than any other such facility on earth.[27]

Aramco's profits in the early 1970s were also immense. By early 1974 Saudi royalties and taxes had soared to $7 per barrel, while production costs remained only $1.20 per barrel. At that level, Aramco was netting more than $5 per barrel, pumping 7.3 million barrels per day. And it did not need to either ship or market the oil.

Handling the petroleum itself was the responsibility of Aramco's five owners. Four were American partners from among the so-called Seven Sisters—the world's most powerful oil companies, all from the Western world. SoCal (Chevron to be), Texaco, and Exxon each had a 22.5 percent interest, while Mobil held a 7.5 percent share. The fifth partner was the Saudi government, which bought a 25 percent share under a participation agreement in 1972.

Aramco, totally American run, did its best to stay out of Saudi politics and to help the country develop. Beginning in the early 1950s, it provided free health care, schooling, and no-interest home mortgage loans to its Saudi employees, while paying them well and training them carefully. It also guaranteed loans to Saudi entrepreneurs and introduced new agricultural techniques to local farmers.

Relations between Aramco and the Saudi government were for many years remarkably good. An American-run Aramco, after all, provided the Saudis not only with entrée for their oil to global markets and stable support from the oligopolistic Seven Sisters that controlled the oil industry, but also a powerful claim on political-military support from Washington. Even as Muslim nationalist pressures led to sweeping expropriations elsewhere—Mossadegh's move against British Petroleum in 1951, or Nasser's move against the Suez Canal in 1956, to cite just two conspicuous cases—neither the Saudis nor their conservative Arab neighbors in the Gulf touched the major Western oil companies. And even special deals offered by Italy's AGIP to Iran and by Japan's Arabian Oil Company to the Saudis and Kuwaitis did not lead to Middle Eastern action against the Western majors.[28]

Abdullah Tariki, the "Red Sheikh," who had been the first Saudi representative in Aramco's management and a founder of the Organization of Petroleum Exporting Countries (OPEC) in 1960, did broach the possibility of nationalization in 1961, shortly after being named Saudi petroleum minister.[29] Yet he was dismissed a year later. His successor, Ahmed Zaki Yamani, a confidante of Crown Prince Faisal, rejected Tariki's nationalization bias,[30] although by 1965 Yamani did open the door to more limited Saudi "participation" in Aramco.[31]

Over the ensuing years, pressures on the Saudi government to act against American dominance of Aramco steadily mounted. In addition to a drumbeat of criticism from the Arab street, and competitive enticements from less favored foreign nations, including Italy and Japan, there was Israel's preemptive attack on Egypt during the Six-Day War of 1967. On the eve of war, even Yamani threatened: "If the United States directly supports Israel, Aramco can anticipate being nationalized 'if not today, then tomorrow.'"[32] The Saudis did ultimately embargo shipments of oil to the United States and the United Kingdom, although their actions proved inadequate in constraining Washington, as the United States managed to raise its own oil production by 1 million barrels per day.[33]

By the early 1970s, the radical Arab regimes were growing more militant, putting further pressure on the Saudis. Following Qadaffi's 1969 coup, Libya established a national oil company and took over local BP and Conoco Philips operations during 1971. The Iraqi Baathist regime also began nationalizations in 1971 as well.[34] Yet the Gulf conservatives—with the bulk of regional and indeed global reserves, remained more hesitant. In October 1972, the Saudis and Aramco reached what for them was an unprecedented step—agreement for 25 percent Saudi equity participation, rising to 51 percent by 1983.[35] The United Arab Emirates (UAE) settled with its foreign partners along similar lines.

By the end of 1975—only three years later—matters were drastically different. Oil prices were more than four times what they had been in 1972. OPEC and the Organization of Arab Petroleum Exporting Countries (OAPEC) had been transformed into price-militant bodies, acting unilaterally rather than through negotiation with the Western majors. They had cut production and launched embargoes against powerful Western nations, including the United States. And virtually all the oil production in the Persian Gulf, as well as much international distribution, was in local hands. Saudi Arabia, the UAE, Qatar, and Oman—with 29.6 percent of world oil reserves between them—had claimed and already received 60 percent ownership of production facilities, while an even more militant Kuwait—pressed by an activist parliament and with a large local Palestinian population—had moved to 100 percent control, offering only $50 million compensation to previous foreign owners.[36]

These dramatic ownership changes in the Middle East were echoed by parallel developments elsewhere. In August 1974 a new Malaysian national oil company, Petronas, with exclusive ownership of domestic hydrocarbon resources, was born. In 1975, the Venezuelans took similar steps. In 1976 Bahrain and in 1977 Nigeria followed suit. By 1979, 42 percent of total world oil sales were in the hands of the exporters themselves—up from only 8 percent at the beginning of 1973.[37] And the overwhelming share of global reserves had passed into the hands of government-owned national oil companies in Eurasian nations, a pattern that persists to this day.[38]

CRITICAL JUNCTURE: UNSHEATHING THE OIL WEAPON

How did this historic change in the ownership and distribution structure of the world oil industry, from control by consortia of Western oil majors to dominance by producing nations themselves, actually occur? And what implications has this transformation had for intra-Eurasian political-economic relationships? As we shall see, a remarkably short, yet climactic, critical juncture centering on Saudi Arabia explains much of this change, which fatefully altered the character of transcontinental energy interdependence in future years.

The defining traits of critical juncture, as noted above, are crisis, stimulus to change, and time constraint. The 1973 events that catalyzed historic changes in the political-economic structure of the Middle Eastern oil industry fit this pattern well, because they were directly related to the Yom Kippur War between Israel and the Arabs in October 1973, when all three conditions were obviously present. On the holiest day of the Jewish calendar, 32,000 Egyptian troops, supported by 3,000 assault guns and sorties by over 220 MiG aircraft, stormed across the Suez Canal in broad daylight, even as Syrian tanks, backed by 700 artillery pieces, crossed into the Golan Heights.[39] Clearly this abrupt attack in a strategically vital part of the world provoked a crisis for all concerned, and a stimulus to change under severe time pressure, due to the impact on global energy prices, superpower relationships, and the security of Israel.

Although the military attack against Israel was launched by Egypt and Syria, the really potent oil weapon lay in the hands of King Faisal of Saudi Arabia. Although strongly anti-Zionist, he was also firmly anticommunist, and feared the spread of radicalism in the Middle East. He saw recent dangerous signs of Marxism in South Yemen, Sudan, and an abortive air force officers' plot in Saudi Arabia. He had always believed that oil and politics should not mix.

By early 1973, however, Faisal was beginning to change his mind.[40] He saw that global oil markets were tightening and that Saudi Arabia was displacing Texas as swing producer for the world. He was also impressed by the leadership change in Egypt—from Nasser, whom he distrusted, to Anwar Sadat, with whom he felt a closer bond. Sadat, Faisal sensed, was an Egyptian nationalist, trying to dismantle Nasser's legacy; a religious person; and an anticommunist, with the courage to expel Soviet advisors. Faisal himself, despite his long-standing pro-Americanism, was also frustrated with the unwillingness of the Nixon administration to move toward what he considered an even-handed stance on Israeli-Palestinian issues, despite the Saudi monarch's repeated and ultimately public entreaties.[41]

In late August 1973, Sadat visited King Faisal in Riyadh, intimating to the king that he was considering war with Israel. Sadat intimated that conflict would begin with a surprise attack and asked for Saudi cooperation. The king immediately pledged half a billion dollars to Sadat's war chest and promised to use the Saudi oil weapon. But he asked for a battle that would continue long enough for world opinion to be mobilized.[42]

Even after war began, and despite his private promises to Sadat, Faisal did not immediately respond. Along the Suez Canal and the Golan Heights, however, the fierce battle raged, running through huge military stockpiles on both the Arab and the Israeli sides. On October 10—only four days after the conflict began—the Soviet Union began a massive resupply, first to Syria and then also to Egypt, while putting airborne troops on alert and encouraging other Arab states to join the battle. In response, the United States quietly and reluctantly moved on October 14 to re-supply Israel, hoping to have its C-5As arrive discreetly from the Azores under cover of night. Due to adverse weather conditions over the Atlantic, however, many of the resupply planes were delayed and arrived conspicuously and dramatically after dawn, to the delight of the media and the Israeli public.[43]

American resupply of Israel—revealing clearly where the United States stood in an extremity—was the heart of the critical juncture. It triggered a fierce response from the Arabs, supported finally by an angry and anguished Faisal. On October 17, the Arab oil ministers agreed on monthly production cuts of 5 percent from the September 1973 production level, until their objectives were met, and also raised oil prices by a whopping 60 percent.[44] On October 20, after Nixon's announcement of a $2.2 billion military aid package to Israel the previous day, the Arabs went still further, announcing the suspension of all oil shipments to the United States. Aramco was ordered to implement the embargo against its own compatriots, "under threat of complete nationalization."[45]

Ceasefire in the Yom Kippur War itself came on October 24. A period of negotiation followed, culminating in significant Israeli withdrawals and an important Syria-Israel agreement that allowed Saudi Arabia, and the smaller OAPEC members with it, to suspend the embargo in March 1974. Yet the passions of the critical juncture, exacerbated by the unambiguous American re-supply of Israel at the height of the conflict in the face of Arab warnings, made nationalization at last politically imperative for Riyadh. In June 1974 Aramco reluctantly agreed to an adamant Saudi demand for 60 percent of Aramco's shares, and the era of majority American rule at the firm with the world's largest oil reserves was at an end. In 1980, following the Iranian Revolution—another critical juncture—the Saudi government acquired 100 percent of Aramco.

IMPLICATIONS FOR ASIAN INTEGRATION

Conflict in the Yom Kippur War only lasted eighteen days, and the Arab oil embargo for a scant five months. Yet the political-economic shock waves of this critical juncture triggered a major transformation in Asian and indeed in global affairs that has continued to this day. It proved to represent a critical deepening of Eurasian continental energy interdependence in three important ways.

First of all, and most important, the 1973 critical juncture provoked a historic ownership change in the world oil industry: the transition from Western multinationals to national oil companies as producers and, increasingly, as distributors as well. At the beginning of 1973, the Seven Sisters, led by Exxon, Mobil, Chevron, and Texaco, reigned supreme, based on their control of production at Aramco and of distribution in both the U.S. market and in Europe; two years later they had lost formal preeminence, due first and foremost to changes in Saudi Arabia—although not just there, but throughout the Gulf, and indeed throughout most of the producing world. By 2006, every firm in the top ten global reserve holders, with the ironic exception of Lukoil, was state owned, and eight of those firms were from within Eurasia.[46] Among the major international oil companies, Exxon Mobil was ranked fourteenth, BP seventeenth, Chevron nineteenth, Conoco-Phillips twenty-third, and Shell twenty-fifth.[47]

This new preeminence of national oil companies had concrete implications for Eurasia, particularly in distribution. It led ultimately to the emergence downstream of Eurasian producer multinationals, such as Saudi Aramco, in Asian consumer markets. Saudi petrochemical complexes and service stations began appearing in China's Fujian Province, as we shall see. The rise of the national oil companies also gave momentum to new Asian intermediaries, such as Japan and Korea's general trading companies, and China's national oil companies, which gained access to the newly dominant Eurasian national producers upstream. Dynamic new Asian national companies like Malaysia's Petronas, with multiple production and distribution functions, and special access to the newly dominant national oil companies of the Gulf, were also born. As Eurasian growth began to accelerate, these new Asian intermediaries would grow with the continent as well.

Second, the 1973 critical juncture inspired a new process of price setting and resource allocation, with major implications for Eurasia. OPEC, as it demonstrated dramatically with its unilateral production cuts and price increases amid the war, was the key decision maker on such vital questions. Vastly reduced in influence was the Western-dominated, oligopolistic producers' cartel, which had traditionally dominated supply and pricing worldwide through consortium ownership in Saudi Arabia and Iran, enforced by the long-standing swing producer role of the United States itself. OAPEC, which decreed the fateful production cutbacks of October 1973, had also temporarily gained prominence, although after 1980 it retired to organizing regional cooperation on more technical oil industry development matters.

The 1973 crisis, finally, led to deepening interpersonal contact between the Middle East and Asia farther east which created the personal basis for the vigorous dialogue to follow. In particular, the crisis invigorated ties between the Middle East and Japan, critically dependent on oil from the Gulf, which was initially declared an unfriendly nation, but made a rather dramatic pro-Arab shift in late 1973 that markedly changed its classification.[48]

The crisis enhanced the transregional standing of entrepôt centers like Singapore and Dubai, which began creating special expertise as catalytic intermediaries between parts of the world that had not previously known one another well. It also nurtured a group of resource-oriented leaders in Japan, such as Prime Minister Tanaka Kakuei and MITI Minister Nakasone Yasuhiro, who for years to come were to give special priority to Middle Eastern and Russian ties, in persistent efforts to procure adequate supplies of uranium, as well as oil, gas, and assorted minerals.[49]

China's Four Modernizations (1978):
Stimulating Growth and Energy Demand

"When China wakes," Napoleon once forecast, "it will shake the world." That massive nation, most populous on earth, has encountered many fateful transformations across its modern history, including the Republican revolution of 1911 and the Communist revolution of 1949. Yet no doubt the development most consequential for global political-economic affairs, and indeed ultimately for the deepening of China's ties westward with the energy producers of Eurasia, was the economic liberalization, beginning under Hua Guofeng, that was enunciated by Deng Xiaoping as the Four Modernizations at the Third Plenum of the Eleventh Central Committee of the Chinese Communist Party in December 1978.[50]

The concept of the Four Modernizations as Deng presented it—fundamental policy changes in the areas of agriculture, industry, and national defense, as well as science and technology—did not originate with Deng himself. The term was introduced by Prime Minister Zhou Enlai at the Conference on Scientific and Technological Work, held in Shanghai before the Cultural Revolution, during January 1963. Twelve years later, in one of his last public acts, Zhou made another pitch for the Four Modernizations at the Fourth National People's Congress. Yet in 1975 Zhou was suffering from terminal cancer and was too weak politically to confront Mao's wife Jiang Qing on this divisive issue, which related closely to the propriety of the Cultural Revolution that had ravaged China for the previous decade.

Deng Xiaoping was more combative. In the fall of 1975 he published three documents, which were ultimately to become the basis for the Four Modernizations in practice. The Gang of Four labeled these documents Three Poisonous Weeds and focused on Deng as target of the Anti-rightist Deviationist Wind Campaign. In his New Year's message of 1976, Chairman Mao warned against emphasizing material progress, and by April Deng had been dismissed from all his official government posts.[51]

Only ten months later, in October 1976, Mao was dead, and the Gang of Four had been arrested. By August 1977, Deng had been reinstated and soon thereafter delivered a speech to the Eleventh Party Congress stressing the Four Modernizations, which he interpreted as meaning "electricity in the rural areas, industrial automation, a new economic outlook, and greatly enhanced defense strength."[52] In February 1978, Chairman Hua Guofeng, who had been pressing individual liberalization steps for nearly a year, unveiled a ten-year plan for the period 1976–1985, embodying many of the same notions, although with a pronounced emphasis on heavy industry (steel, coal, electricity, and transportation infrastructure).[53] Deng, the more pragmatic, market oriented, and politically sensitive of the two, then made the definitive pronouncements that have endured across modern Chinese history, in December 1978.[54]

THE COMING OF CRITICAL JUNCTURE

Why should we consider the enunciation of the Four Modernizations to be a critical juncture? First of all, there was a pronounced crisis in the Chinese political economy following the ravages of the Cultural Revolution, centering on heavy industry, that urgently required resolution. Steel production in 1976 was only 21 million tons—down from 25.5 million in 1973, and a net gain of only 10 percent over the 1960 figure. In agriculture, the per capita output of grains was no higher in 1977 than it had been two decades earlier, in 1955. State enterprises, rather than being a source of profits, were absorbing large subsidies that necessitated the milking of agriculture. Oil fields like the famous Daqing fields in the northeast, whose workers once served as a paragon of the Cultural Revolution, were stagnating, while electric power infrastructure languished in disrepair. Meanwhile, and more urgently, on the military front, challenge from the Soviet Union was rising, giving Socialist China's economic weakness major national security implications as well. In February 1979, the Soviet Union had invaded Afghanistan and seemed to Chinese leaders bent on further expansion, generating in Beijing a profound sense of deepening international threat to China.

Second, there was major political stimulus for change in the PRC of the late 1970s. The country had experienced tremendous socioeconomic disloca-tion during the Cultural Revolution, and many, especially among more estab-lished groups, desperately desired a return to normalcy. Following the death of Chairman Mao, reversing the ravages of the Cultural Revolution at last became a possibility.

Finally, there was intense time pressure in implementing reforms during this period. Part of the perceived urgency was external, flowing from Soviet designs. Within China, Maoist forces remained strong, and the national po-litical situation was fluid. Foreign interests were as yet not well represented in China. There was a very real possibility that China could lurch backward to practices of Cultural Revolution days. In this environment, Deng Xiaoping and his allies felt that they had to move rapidly to consolidate a forward-looking set of economic policies.

The overall design was enunciated almost as soon as Deng took power, with initial implementation following soon thereafter. The early emphasis was heavy industry, with the $2 billion Baoshan steel mill near Shanghai being a first major step. As political conditions stabilized, Deng's approach progressively broadened beyond an initial emphasis on national self-reliance, to involve substantial foreign loans. In December 1978, for example, China arranged a $1.2 billion sovereign loan from a consortium of British banks, and by mid-April the PRC had received or arranged for a total of $10 billion in foreign loans. Five Special Economic Zones (Guangdong and Fujian in the south, Shanghai in central China, and Beijing/Tianjin in the north) were estab-lished, endowed with power to negotiate arrangements with foreign firms on the Yugoslav-Romanian model, thus melding socialist and capitalist systems. China also moved rapidly forward in technical education, expanding its sci-entific and technical workforce from 60,000 when the modernizations began to 400,000 by the early 1980s.

By then Chinese economic growth was surging into double digits—a pat-tern fated to persist for well over a quarter century. China's economy grew from eleventh largest in the world in 1980, according to World Bank calcula-tions, to second by 2010.[55] As indicated in Figure 3.1, China's gross domestic product (GDP) growth fell below 8 percent only seven times over the three decades from 1980 to 2010. During that period, China's overall economy expanded more than twenty-six-fold.

(Unit: $ billion)

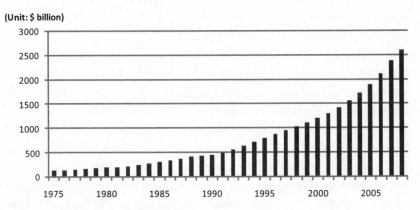

Figure 3.1A: China's high-speed growth following the Four Modernizations.
Source: World Bank, World Development Indicators Online, http://databank.worldbank
.org/.

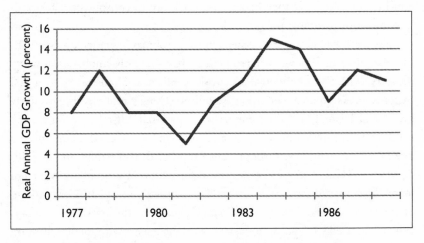

Figure 3.1B: China's economic acceleration under the Four Modernizations.
Source: World Bank, World Development Indicators Online, http://databank.worldbank
.org/.

For the first two decades, in particular, much of this growth was export-
led, with a heavy emphasis on exports to Japan and the United States. Foreign multinationals, which handled more than half of China's exports, also
played a major role. After 2000, however, this foreign dimension gradually
declined in relative importance, as the geographic sphere of China's growth
broadened westward, beyond eastern coastal areas into China's vast interior,
with domestic demand gaining substantially greater importance.

IMPLICATIONS FOR EURASIAN INTERDEPENDENCE

Before the Four Modernizations, China was an island unto itself—massive but economically static and self-absorbed. The modernizations and the ensuing growth surge that they inspired radically transformed this equation. With high-speed development, China—like Japan before it—began to rapidly outstrip its substantial domestic resource basis and grew increasingly import dependent, while also increasingly export oriented.

The initial impact was to deepen interdependence with Southeast Asia and the United States—primary Chinese export markets—more than with other parts of the world. Dependence on the U.S. market rose higher and higher—to its peak in 2002. A secondary effect, however, was energy-driven interdependence with Eurasia, which intensified greatly after 2000, and has become central to China's relations with the world since then, even as dependence on America has waned, as we shall see.

Since late 1993, China's previous long-standing oil export surplus has evolved into a massive deficit of over 6 million barrels of oil per day, with China's overall energy imports totaling over $124 billion by 2009.[56] Around 60 percent of all the oil that China consumes is now imported, and prospects are strong that China will import 80 percent of its oil needs—a significantly larger share than the United States—by 2020.[57] This historic transformation has propelled a spiraling and unprecedented hydrocarbon dependence on continental Eurasia—the Middle East, Russia, and the 'Stans—that is being complemented by broadening nonenergy relationships as well.

Another crucial implication of China's Four Modernizations for Eurasia's collective future concerns is the political context within which they were achieved. Unlike the Soviet Union, China pursued economic reform without engaging in political reform, through a process of gradualism, administrative decentralization, and particularistic contracting.[58] The PRC's special brand of communism—less institutionalized and more decentralized than that of the USSR—also facilitated this outcome. China thus emerged as a high-growth, yet soft-authoritarian power—only partially open and shallowly integrated with the world.[59] As a consequence of its distinctive critical juncture, dominated by the fear of resurgent anarchy through cultural revolution, the China that emerged casts an illiberal shadow over Asia that darkens broader prospects for a world of liberty and law.

India's 1991 Financial Crisis and Ensuing Reforms: Accelerating Growth and Burgeoning Energy Demand

Asia's other giant emerging economy, with a young and growing population of well over a billion people, is India. Like China, it was for many years a static, low-growth, and largely self-sufficient socialist economy, with a strongly protectionist, import-substituting orientation, epitomized by its expulsion of IBM in 1965.[60] Between 1970 and 1980, for example, Indian GDP growth averaged only around 3.2 percent annually.[61]

India's growth pattern, however, has sharply changed. As indicated in Figure 3.2, the discontinuity occurred in the early 1990s. The country experienced a severe foreign exchange crisis, during which India's foreign exchange reserves deteriorated calamitously: the country could barely finance three weeks of imports and was forced to pledge sixty-seven tons of national gold reserves as collateral for an emergency structural adjustment loan of $2.2 billion from the International Monetary Fund (IMF).[62] Meanwhile, the government was compelled to accept a sharp currency devaluation through which the Indian rupee fell from 17.50 to the dollar at the beginning of 1991 to 45 to the dollar by early 1992.

Following the crisis, and the ensuing set of economic reforms, India's economic pattern sharply changed, as we shall see. Growth began to accelerate, as noted in Figure 3.2, and averaged 6.7 percent real growth during the 1992–1997 period—more than double the average of the 1970s. After additional structural adjustment during the late 1990s, India's economy once again be-

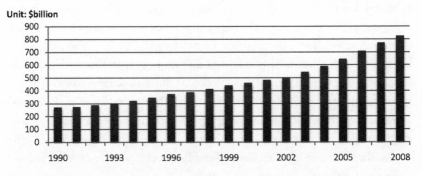

Figure 3.2A: India's recent high-speed growth.
Source: World Bank, World Development Indicators Online, http://databank.worldbank .org/.

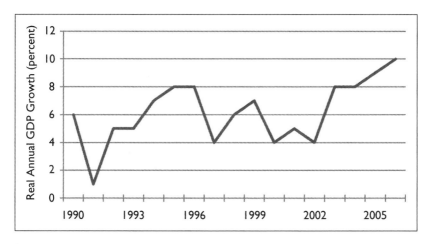

Fig. 3.2B: India's economic acceleration following the 1991 critical juncture.
Source: World Bank, World Development Indicators Online, http://databank
.worldbank.org/.

gan to expand, at a rate averaging 8 percent annually by the late 2000s. From
virtual insolvency in 1991, Indian foreign exchange reserves rose to nearly
$260 billion in 2009 and to even higher levels as the global financial crisis
abated late that year.[63]

PROFILE OF INDIA'S CRITICAL JUNCTURE

As in the case of China and its Four Modernizations, the stimulus for change
had been accumulating in India for many years. The deepening fiscal difficulties of the government (both national and provincial), intensified by the burden of subsidizing inefficient state enterprises and supporting a broad range of
commodity and fuel subsidies, were one key dimension: the gross fiscal deficit
rose from 9 percent of GDP in 1980–1981 to 12.7 percent of GDP in 1990–1991,
on the eve of the crisis. The government's internal debt also accumulated rapidly, rising from 35 percent of GDP in early 1981 to 53 percent of GDP a decade
later. Heavy government spending found its macroeconomic counterpart in
spiraling national current-account deficits.

The crisis that led India into its transformational critical juncture was
precipitated by the Gulf War. That conflict had an especially severe impact
on India's economy, due to the country's heavy energy-import dependence
and strong reliance on the Middle East for export markets and expatriate labor income. In the wake of Saddam Hussein's August 1990 invasion of Kuwait, India's oil import bill swelled, while export income and expatriate

remittances plummeted, and investors withdrew from India.[64] Large fiscal deficits, over time, had a spillover effect on the trade deficit, culminating in a serious external payments crisis.

By the end of 1990, India was in serious economic trouble. In addition to the burden imposed by rising oil prices, India incurred the substantial cost of repatriating from Kuwait 150,000 Indians endangered by violence there, while also losing the remittances of $4 billion annually that the migrant workers in the Persian Gulf collectively provided.[65] The country's fiscal deficit climbed to 8.4 percent of GDP and the external current account to 3.5 percent of GDP, while inflation nudged 13 percent (double India's historical rate), and foreign exchange reserves declined to just over $1 billion.[66]

The deepening structural crisis, as in China, generated stimulus for change, intensified by New Delhi's deteriorating reserve position. To an even greater extent than in China, this stimulus came from without, in what Gourevitch would call a case of "second-image reversed."[67] The IMF applied heavy pressure, in the form of a conditional loan. Diaspora Indians, wanting to see a more market-oriented Indian domestic economy in which they could hold a larger stake, also added their voices in support of reform.[68]

A key role, as a catalyst in concretely defining reform imperatives and configuring the reforms themselves, was played by Finance Minister Manmohan Singh. A confirmed liberal economist, later to serve successfully for many years as prime minister, Singh orchestrated reforms in five major areas: (1) fiscal deficit reduction, (2) industrial and trade policy, (3) agricultural policy, (4) infrastructure construction, and (5) social-sector development.[69] In the aggregate, these reforms represented a fundamental abandonment of the traditional control-oriented economic framework and a decisive shift away from socialism, toward market reliance.[70] The fiscal measures of course took precedence amid the crisis, which was primarily financial in nature, and thus an area where Singh could take direct action himself.

A third element of a classical critical juncture is typically intense time pressure on the parties involved, as previously noted. This pressure was quite severe in India's case during late 1991, due to the virulence of the foreign exchange crisis. India's pressing need for foreign exchange to finance vital imports, together with severe fiscal pressures, was used effectively during the crisis by reform-oriented officials like Manmohan Singh, in interaction with the IMF and the World Bank, to legitimize extensive privatization, an end to import licensing for capital goods, and expanded opportunities for foreign investment. In the wake of the crisis, 100 percent foreign ownership was authorized by the central government in a wide range of industries, and majority ownership in all except banking, insurance, telecommunications, and aviation.[71] This dramatic change in foreign investment policies, synergistic with the domestic reforms, played a key role in stimulating capital inflows, both direct and indirect, while also energizing India's highly creative business diaspora.

IMPLICATIONS FOR EURASIAN INTEGRATION

As in China, India's reforms fundamentally reoriented a static, inward-looking giant, and encouraged it to redeploy its resources, through market mechanisms, toward competition in the broader world. The reforms also encouraged a surge of investment into India from abroad, prompting Indian private firms and government enterprises to become more efficient at home. The net result was a sharp acceleration of economic growth, from around 3 percent before the reforms transpired to more than 6 percent in their immediate aftermath, and to around 8 percent today.

As in China, rapid growth acceleration and rising per-capita consumption in one of the most populous nations on earth led Indian demand to rapidly outstrip the country's modest natural resource base, putting rising price pressure on international commodity markets.

This pattern was especially pronounced in energy, leading to an intensification of continental interdependence, as in the case of China. India has traditionally maintained close economic and cultural ties with the Persian Gulf, predating even the days of British colonial rule, but these have further intensified in recent years. India has also deepened its energy ties with Russia and Central Asia, as its rising affluence over the past two decades has sharply stimulated demand for hydrocarbons. Greater stability in Afghanistan, coupled with improved Indo-Pakistani relations, would undoubtedly enhance these continentalist ties still further.

The Collapse of the Soviet Union (1991–1992): Catalyst to Revived Eurasian Interdependence

The history of the Silk Road over the centuries has been replete with openings and closings—the erection of mercantilist political barriers to commercial intercourse and their later demolition. The twentieth century was no exception. During Czarist days, up to 1917, transport across the great steppes and deserts in the heart of Eurasia was comparatively unencumbered. During

Stalinist days, however, most borders of the Soviet Union, including those in Central Asia, were hermetically sealed.

Following the Chinese Revolution of 1949, the two communist giants—the USSR and the PRC—contemplated symbolically consummating their alliance ties with a "Road of Friendship" between themselves, mobilizing youth of thirty-six nationalities to the "virgin lands" of Kazakhstan and Xinjiang, to build a historic railway line across the Eurasian steppes. An enormous white railway station, known as Druzhba, or "friendship" in Russian, was also erected at the Sino-Soviet frontier post. In 1961–1962, however, just as this ambitious cross-border railway line was moving to completion, Sino-Soviet relations suddenly cooled, Soviet assistance stopped, and Soviet technicians returned home. A direct railway link was no longer desirable for either side, and the Sino-Soviet border became once again a flashpoint of tension and conflict—an iron curtain within the communist world.[72] Such it was to remain for more than a generation.

The fateful change, transforming Central Asia from an isolated backwater within the communist bloc into a potentially dynamic, volatile zone of transnational economic intercourse and global geopolitical competition, was the collapse of the Soviet Union in late 1991. That momentous development emerged from forces that had been in motion for a decade and more. Yet it was utterly unanticipated until only a few months previously. The Soviet collapse demolished long-standing barriers to economic intercourse and political communication, many dating from Stalinist days, thus allowing Eurasia's remarkable growth and energy-demand equation of recent years to play itself out on a continental scale.

The sudden collapse of the Soviet Union was actually a decade and more in the making.[73] It had its roots in Soviet economic stagnation, failed attempts at reform, and the USSR's own overextension, relative to both its own capabilities and those of a rival United States, which proved much more adept at globalization.[74] A dramatic drop in the price of oil during the mid-1980s and a consequent lack of foreign exchange in succeeding years to purchase grain also severely complicated Soviet calculations, illustrating once again the decisive importance of energy in shaping global geopolitics, and generating stimulus for change, an important precondition for critical juncture.

The difficulties that ultimately brought down the Soviet Union arguably began with the Soviet invasion of Afghanistan in February 1979. Initially seen as an aggressive but shrewd effort to capitalize on the power vacuum in Southwest Asia created by the Iranian Revolution, the interminable conflict cost the Soviet military nearly 12,000 combat fatalities and provoked increasingly sharp political dissent within the Soviet Union itself by the mid-1980s.[75] The Red Army finally withdrew in February 1989—exactly a decade after the original intervention—further undermining Moscow's credibility in international affairs. The invasion, although futile, ironically served as a pretext for U.S. sanctions that deprived the Soviets of valuable foreign exchange, by preventing construction of major energy pipelines from the USSR to the European Union and Japan.

In 1985 Mikhail Gorbachev became general secretary of the Communist Party of the Soviet Union (CPSU), and in the same year the sharp decline in global energy prices began. In 1986, a serious nuclear accident occurred at Chernobyl, in the Soviet Ukraine, intensifying pressures for greater openness and social responsibility in Soviet society. Gorbachev responded with his glasnost (openness) and perestroika (restructuring) campaigns. Political turbulence intensified, ironically, after the Afghan withdrawal in early 1989, even though the withdrawal extinguished what had been a significant cause of previous dissatisfaction. In November 1989, the Berlin Wall went down, without a decisive Soviet response, deepening a sense—both in the Soviet satellites and within the USSR itself—that fundamental change was coming. In January 1990, however, countering rising discontent, the Red Army suppressed a major uprising in Baku, Azerbaijan, in which over 130 people were killed. Change was not coming easily.

Only a month later, continuing the liberalization trend even amid deepening discontent, the CPSU Central Committee decided to abandon its political power monopoly. This paved the way for competitive elections in all fifteen Soviet republics. A month later, Lithuania, one of the most restive republics of the USSR, declared independence, intensifying centrifugal pressures. Soon thereafter, the Red Army concluded a series of agreements to withdraw from former satellites in Eastern Europe, as Gorbachev moved to focus efforts on stabilizing the long-standing core of the Soviet Union itself.

In March 1991, a New Union Treaty, supported by Gorbachev and incorporating efforts to restructure the Soviet Union by decentralization so as to save it, was ratified in a national referendum by 76 percent of the vote. Only Georgia, Chechnya, and the Baltic states boycotted the event. In June, however, this new structure was gravely challenged by the election of Boris Yeltsin as president of the Russian Soviet Federative Socialist Republic, comfortably defeating Gorbachev's handpicked candidate Nikolai Ryzhkov.

Yeltsin, committed to radical decentralization, emerged as an outspoken and effective rival to CPSU General Party Secretary Mikhail Gorbachev himself.

THE COMING OF CRITICAL JUNCTURE

On August 19, 1991, Gorbachev's vice president, prime minister, defense minister, KGB chief, and other senior officials attempted a coup while he was vacationing in the Crimea. Yeltsin was quick to condemn the attempt and to amass popular support for himself. The organizers failed to arrest him, and after three days the coup collapsed. Gorbachev returned to power, but with his political position fatally compromised. Pressed by an ambitious Yeltsin, his legitimacy rapidly unraveled, generating both the crisis so often requisite for major policy change and the time pressure that typically configures resultant outcomes.

In September 1991, the USSR finally recognized the independence of the Baltic states, declared in Lithuania over twenty months previously. On December 1, Ukrainian independence was confirmed in a provincial referendum, attracting 90 percent support. The Alma-Ata Protocol, signed by all of the Soviet republics except Georgia, confirmed the dissolution of the union on December 21, followed by Gorbachev's resignation on December 25. At the end of 1991 all administrative organs of the USSR ceased functioning, opening a new post-Soviet era in Eurasian history.

IMPLICATIONS FOR EURASIAN CONTINENTALISM

With the collapse of the Soviet Union, many of the classic autarkic elements of Stalinist practice, descended from the days of "building Socialism in one state," abruptly disappeared. On January 2, 1992, acting as his own prime minister, Yeltsin ordered a sweeping liberalization of foreign trade, prices, and currency. Soon thereafter his market-oriented subordinates, headed by Yegor Gaidar, also took policy steps to encourage foreign investment. These focused on market-oriented measures such as price liberalization and financial stabilization, directed toward promoting a more favorable environment for capital inflows and deepened interdependence with the industrialized West.[76]

The most remarkable step was the liberal Foreign Investment Law of 1991, introduced just before the Soviet collapse, which promised "national treatment" of foreign capital inflows from abroad, allowing overseas capital into most sectors of the Russian economy. It also protected foreign investors against nationalization or expropriation and provided compensation when public necessity required it.[77] In many other parts of the former Soviet Union, outside the Russian Federation, officials also pursued policies supportive of foreign investment and expanded international trade. Most were not as fundamentalist as Gaidar and his neoliberal associates in Moscow at pursuing price reforms, but their general attitude toward expanded international transactions was positive.

In the more advanced western regions of the former USSR, the primary impact of the USSR's collapse and the sudden new market orientation was to deepen integration with Central and Western Europe, especially Germany. In Central Asia and the Russian Far East, however, market forces naturally exerted a stronger pull toward Asia than elsewhere in the former USSR, especially as Asian growth accelerated over the 1990s and beyond. China, India, Iran, Turkey, Japan, and Korea all deepened ties with the component parts of the former Soviet Union substantially as a result of the Soviet collapse, supporting a revival of classic Silk Road relationships. This time the new Eurasian continentalist interdependence was emphatically driven by energy demand (centering on China and India), and by energy supply from the former Soviet Union, although it had broader political-economic dimensions.

Most important, the collapse of the Soviet Union led to unprecedented new ties between the PRC and Central Asia. Between 1990 and 1992, just as the USSR was collapsing, trade between Kazakhstan and China rose tenfold.[78] As indicated in Table 3.1, and elaborated in Table 7.1, Central Asian trade with both China and Turkey also intensified for years following the collapse of the Soviet Union, sharply outpacing the still substantial trade with Russia and gradually reorienting the region in new directions. Indeed, by 2010, the volume of PRC trade with both Kazakhstan and Turkmenistan was signficiantly greater than the trade of those two former Soviet republics with Moscow itself, with the Central Asian states exchanging rapidly growing amounts of oil and gas for Chinese manufactures. Similarly, Turkey's trade with Azerbaijan also exceeded formerly Soviet Azerbaijan's trade with Russia.

Shortly after the Soviet collapse, an annual Urumqi Trade Fair was initiated in the PRC, with heavy Central Asian participation, while a Special Economic Zone was established in Xinjiang's Ili Valley, near the Kazakh frontier, to encourage cross-border exchange.[79] In October 1993, Kazakh President Nazerbayev went to Beijing, and just six months later, in April 1994, Chinese Premier Li Peng made a return visit to Almaty, Kazakhstan's capital. That visit came on the heels of a March 1994 boundary agreement between the two countries, to discuss concrete progress on cross-border infrastructure.[80]

Ultimately this high-level Eurasian diplomacy led to transcontinental railroads and pipelines that by 2010 conveyed 200,000 barrels of Kazakh oil

Table 3.1. Expanding Central Asian Trade with Russia, China, and Turkey (1990–2010)

Trade with Russia (millions of dollars)

	1990	2000	2010	2010/2000
Russia / Azerbaijan	288.5**	270.69	2,212.82	8.2
Russia / Kazakhstan	3,658**	4,443.45	16,138.43	3.6
Russia / Uzbekistan	1,685.3****	936.67	3,226.21	3.4

Trade with China (millions of dollars)

	1990	2000	2010	2010/2000
PRC / Azerbaijan	1.49**	6.168	930.58	150.9
PRC / Uzbekistan	52.165**	51.47	2,477.3	48.1
PRC / Kazakhstan	363.364**	1,556.91	20,313.6	13.0

Trade with Turkey (millions of dollars)

	1990	2000	2010	2010/2000
Turkey / Azerbaijan	123.213***	325.9	2,415.6	7.4
Turkey / Kazakhstan	130.85***	465.1	3,289.9	7.1
Turkey / Uzbekistan	245.531***	168.4	1,144.0	6.8

Source: International Monetary Fund. *Direction of Trade Statistics*, annual.
Notes: * Figure is for 1991, due to data availability. ** Figure is for 1992, due to data availability.
*** Figure is 1993, due to data availability. **** Figure is 1994, due to data availability.

exports daily, as well as 10 billion cubic meters annually of Turkmen gas, from deep in Central Asia 7,000 kilometers across China to Shanghai. In 2010 China also began sharply expanding both cargo and passenger facilities at Urumqi International Airport, as well as the nearby Special Economic Zone, in an effort to expand airborne trade with Russia and the neighboring Islamic world as well, in cooperation with both Turkish and Iranian interests, as will be recounted later in more detail.[81]

The Soviet collapse also led rapidly to new ties between Central Asia and large Islamic neighbors—especially Turkey and Iran—to the south and southwest. In February 1992, less than two months after the dissolution of the Soviet Union, the Economic Cooperation Organization, originally composed of Turkey, Iran, and Pakistan, convened at Tehran, with Iranian President Rafsanjani inviting all the newly independent Central Asian states to join. Two months later, Turkish Prime Minister Demirel undertook an extensive state visit across Central Asia, celebrating the solidarity of the 200 million Turkic people of the region, including Turkey's own 57 million.[82] Demirel also inaugurated a series of joint annual summits with Central Asia that continued for half a decade and established important new political and business networks transcending Cold War boundaries, which fostered the substantial trade depicted in Table 3.1. For its part, Iran, resisting pressure from the United States, concluded a $20 billion, twenty-five-year gas deal with Turkey in 1997, opening a major gas pipeline northward to Turkmenistan, in the same year.[83]

Japan and South Korea were likewise able to broaden and deepen their ties with the former Soviet Union—both Russia proper and the neighboring states known as the near abroad—due to the USSR's sudden collapse. Japan, in particular, invested heavily in Sakhalin energy, taking major positions in the Sakhalin I and Sakhalin II natural gas deals of the early 1990s. Both countries also invested in Central Asia, with the Korean commercial position strengthened by strong ethnic ties with both Kazakhstan and Uzbekistan, ironically due to Stalin's deportation of Korean *koryo saram*, originally living along the Pacific coast, to Central Asia during the 1930s. Japan and Korea both established deep energy ties with Central Asia in uranium, even though vast continental distances from their homelands inhibited the sort of explosive pipeline-based hydrocarbon trade that emerged between Central Asia and China after the 2008 global financial crisis.

India, curiously, was the one major Asian nation that did not initially benefit much from the breakup of the Soviet Union, despite its proximity to Central Asia and its established relationships with the region. As indicated in Table 7.1, its commercial ties with Central Asian states like Kazakhstan grew only modestly, compared to the explosive growth that the Chinese experienced. New Delhi had enjoyed an intense and profitable relationship with the Soviets since the mid-1960s, but that was disrupted by the collapse of the U.S.S.R. India is geographically close to Central Asia, but highly volatile Islamic nations of the region, including Pakistan and Afghanistan, stand in between. Furthermore, in the early 1990s, when the Soviet Union collapsed, India's remarkable subsequent growth track was not yet established.

The economic logic of consequential Indian relationships with energy-rich Central Asia is substantial, however, and will likely manifest itself in coming years, if political relationships in the turbulent region stabilize.[84] Indian energy ties with the Russian Far East have also deepened. India's Oil and Natural Gas Corporation has been involved in the Sakhalin I project and in 2008 acquired British interests in Russia's rich west Siberian oil fields.[85]

Central Asia also, of course, began to forge consequential new connections to the West, fueled by the collapse of the USSR. Most important, in the first instance, was foreign investment—especially that directed toward the Tengiz oil fields in Kazakhstan, which began production in 1993, and the Kashagan offshore fields at the northern end of the Caspian Sea, where production is expected later this decade.[86] American capital was central in both cases. There was also the Baku-Tbilisi-Ceyhan pipeline, from the Caspian to the Mediterranean, which opened in 2005.

Although Western firms are substantial investors in Central Asia, and to a lesser degree in the Russian Far East as well, the ultimate market for former Soviet energy, and the low-cost supplier of most manufactures required in the Asian regions of the former Soviet Union, is ultimately Asia itself. With East Asia growing, and needing more energy, extending economically westward across the continent, that relationship might naturally be expected to deepen on market grounds. The collapse of the Soviet Union, Central Asian openness to foreign investment, and subsequent Yeltsin laissez-faire policies within Russia itself in the early post-Soviet days, all galvanized the realization of underlying complementarities, bringing continental Eurasia together in unprecedented new ways transcending Soviet-era ties, and beginning to revive the classic Silk Road.

The Iranian Revolution (1979): An Islamist
State Estranged from Washington Emerges

Iran looms large, both over the past of Eurasian energy geopolitics and also prospectively over its future. With more than 77 million people, whose median age is twenty-seven, it is the most populous nation of the Persian Gulf area, and likely to continue in that role.[87] Also the second largest nation of the region geographically with an area of over 636,000 square miles, making it just slightly smaller than Mexico, Iran occupies the northern shores of the Persian Gulf, dominating the Strait of Hormuz, through which more than half of the oil flowing in international trade passes every day.[88] Iran also occupies the southern shores of the Caspian, thus dominating the geostrategically important Land of the Two Seas, discussed in Chapter 2.

Distinctively, among nations of the Islamic world, Iran is 89 percent Shiite Muslim and only 9 percent Sunni. Although Sunnis are generally in the majority across the Islamic world, Shiites are both numerous and dominant in Iran. The only major country where a comparable situation prevails is neighboring Iraq, which is 60 percent Shiite and around 32 percent Sunni. Shiites are, however, spread broadly throughout the Middle East, as well as South and Central Asia, as indicated in Figure 3.3—often in minority status.[89] Given their deep traditional sense of victimization, dating from a persecuted heritage during the early days of their religion,[90] the Shiites are a volatile element in the domestic politics of many Silk Road nations, especially following what they perceive as liberating political upheavals in their traditional homelands of Iran and Iraq.

In the world of energy, Iran is a potential superpower, distinguishing itself as the one nation that is already a major producer of both oil and gas yet also has the ability to readily expand production in the future. In oil Iran ranks as the number six producer and number eight exporter in the world, yet stands even higher—at number three—in reserves, after just Saudi Arabia and Venezuela. In natural gas, Iran ranks number five in production but number two in reserves, after only Russia.

Today, Iran finds itself entwined with Asia, especially China, in a steadily deepening embrace. Forty-five percent of its exports—of which 80 percent

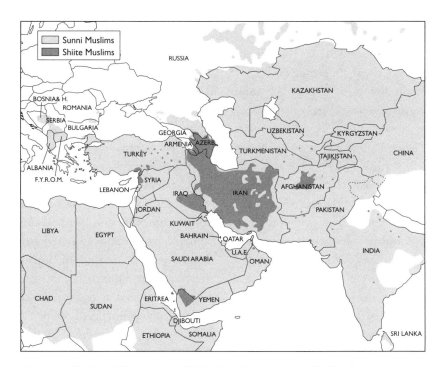

Figure 3.3: The broad distribution of Shiite Muslims across the Silk Road nations.

are hydrocarbons—flow to the four major economies of Asia: China (15.2 percent), Japan (14.2 percent), India (9.2 percent), and South Korea (6.4 percent). These are also, in that order, Iran's four largest global markets. On the import side the West looms somewhat larger, but four of Iran's five largest suppliers (UAE, China, South Korea, and Russia) are also Asian or Eurasian states.[91] Iran's trade with the PRC alone totals around $30 billion annually, and is recently growing nearly 40 percent a year.[92] A decade ago, that Iran-PRC trade was dwarfed by Iran's dealings with China's Japanese and South Korean neighbors, who imported substantial Iranian oil, and repaid in manufactures. Yet by 2010 Chinese trade with Iran was over double Japan's and nearly three times Korea's trade, as suggested in Table 7.1, illustrating the powerful momentum of China-centric, energy-driven Eurasian continentalism.

BEFORE CRITICAL JUNCTURE: IRAN AS PRO-AMERICAN STALWART

This intimate, and deepening, Iranian orientation toward Asia has a powerful rationality today, at once economic and geopolitical. Yet it was not always so. This Asianist orientation intensified sharply, as we shall see, in the wake of a critical juncture: the 1979 Iranian Revolution. That fateful development both estranged Iran from its previous deep moorings in the U.S.-dominated Western capitalist political economy and also opened it to the prospect of deeper ties to the East. Those ties, driven by both energy demand and geopolitics, began deepening over the 1980s, and have escalated remarkably since the mid-1990s, as China has become a major energy importer, and world energy prices have sharply risen.

To understand how the Iranian Revolution helped open a fateful new avenue for the global political economy—a new Eurasian continentalism, with China as the linchpin—it is important to grasp both how deeply Iran was moored in the U.S.-centric international system under Shah Reza Pahlavi's regime, and the complex resentments which that incorporation generated within Iran itself. During the early twentieth century, Britain had held the preeminent international role in Iran, bolstered by the economic strength and interests of the Anglo-Iranian Oil Company (AIOC), renamed British Petroleum (BP) in 1954.[93] After AIOC interests were nationalized in 1951, however, the United States, through CIA-inspired Operation Ajax, restored the shah to power in 1953 and became Iran's principal international partner.[94]

From the shah's return to power until the revolution of 1979, U.S. influence in Tehran was omnipresent. From 1954, American interests held 40 percent equity interest in the oil consortium that ran Iranian oil fields—

the same share as BP. In 1955, Iran joined the U.S.-sponsored Baghdad Pact regional defense organization. The CIA, together with Israel's Mossad, trained, equipped, and advised the shah's domestic security service, known from 1957 as SAVAK. Meanwhile, as the shah became the chief proxy defender of American interests in the Persian Gulf, the United States provided military advisors, who were granted controversial diplomatic immunity in 1964. Washington also supplied substantial military aid and support for expansion of the domestic defense industry, which by the 1970s employed more than 10,000 Americans around Isfahan alone.[95] By the time of the revolution, over 50,000 Americans in total were living in Iran—a fivefold increase within a decade.[96]

This broad and rapidly expanding American presence in Iran, much of it in explicit support of the shah, not surprisingly provoked a nationalist backlash within Iran itself, particularly as that presence coincided with major socioeconomic change and increasingly authoritarian policies on the part of the shah's government. Iran's population was growing rapidly—nearly doubling, from 19.3 million in 1950 to 33.7 million in 1975. By 1975, two-thirds of the population was under thirty.[97] Per capita income for the nation as a whole soared ten-fold in little more than a decade—from $200 per person in 1963 to $2,000 by the outbreak of revolution in 1979. Iran was taking in $20 billion a year in oil revenue after 1973. Yet youth unemployment stood stubbornly in double digits; the incongruity naturally stoked slowly smouldering dissent.

During the early post–World War II years, the United States had been relatively popular in Iran, having helped force Soviet withdrawal from the country's northwestern regions during the Azeri crisis of 1946. America's troubles with the Iranian public began with Washington's hand in deposing the popular nationalist Mossadegh government, which had nationalized AIOC in 1953.[98] The 1953 CIA-orchestrated coup against Mossadegh, which brought young Shah Reza Pahlavi back to power, alienated many Iranians from the young, inexperienced monarch. It also provoked a vicious cycle of repression, as well as perverse, deepening rentier dependence on foreigners and petrostate largesse that laid the basis for the revolution of 1979.

Resentment of the shah and the United States was focused and amplified by a variety of Islamist and Marxist intellectuals. Increasingly prominent among them, from the early 1960s, was the fiery cleric Ruhollah Khomeini of Qom. In January 1963, the still little-known Khomeini issued a strongly worded declaration denouncing the shah and his plans for a "white revolution," involving women's suffrage and other reforms. Khomeini also accused the shah variously of violating the constitution, abetting moral corruption, and being submissive to America and Israel. In late 1964, now more politically visible, Khomeini again denounced "capitulations" to the United States, in the form of diplomatic immunity to American military personnel. He was immediately arrested and deported—not to return to his country for fourteen long years, albeit ultimately in triumph.

THE COMING OF CRITICAL JUNCTURE

The critical juncture of the Iranian Revolution itself was not provoked by the classical factors that precipitated revolution in France, Russia, and China, such as defeat in war, financial crisis, peasant revolution, or military disaffection.[99] The stimulus for change came from a very different direction— the discontent of the mosques, the bazaars, and the lower middle class. They recoiled at the Westernization, inflation, inequality, and repression precipitated by the massive influx of petrodollars after the world price of oil was quadrupled—ironically, at the shah's own behest—in late 1973. "Steadily increasing prosperity," as de Tocqueville observed in another context, "far from tranquilizing the population, everywhere promoted a spirit of unrest."[100] No adequate conservative institutions existed in Iran to contain an explosion of rising expectations. And the deepening rentier petrostate character of the Iranian political economy allowed the shah's regime the short-term luxury of ignoring, repressing, or compensating the explosive new social forces that were steadily, if quietly, building within his empire.

The immediate catalyst for revolution was provided by character attacks by the shah's minister of information on Ayatollah Khomeini, who by the late 1970s had become a powerful expatriate moral force in the bazaars. These attacks provoked large demonstrations and a brutal police response at the holy city of Qom, early in 1978. A growing cascade of protests, many in the form of traditional Shiite fortieth-day memorials to the deaths of previous demonstrators, was accompanied in October 1978 by a crippling series of strikes in the bazaars, universities, newspapers, railways, government ministries, and ultimately the indispensable oil industry. In the face of spiraling economic and social chaos, longtime opposition politician Shapour Bakhtiar was named prime minister in late December as a last resort, with the shah and Empress Farah themselves leaving Iran within a month, ostensibly for medical treatment. Two weeks after their departure, Khomeini himself returned in triumph from Parisian exile, with 5 million people lining the streets of Tehran to witness his homecoming.

The ensuing three years (1979–1982) were a period of rapid and historic change in Iran, along both domestic and international dimensions—a true critical juncture. The crisis and time pressure for action were provoked by the exceedingly rapid collapse of the shah and the complex issues for immediate decision—economic, political, and diplomatic—that rapidly crowded in on the new and inexperienced revolutionary government. On February 11, 1979, the Pahlavi dynasty abruptly expired, with royalist Prime Minister Baktiar going first into hiding and then into exile. On April 1, an Islamic republic was established. The following October a new constitution was adopted, under which Ayatollah Khomeini held the position of *vali-ye faqih* (guardian jurist), with prerogatives including supreme command of the armed forces.

Meanwhile, on October 22 the former shah was admitted to the Mayo Clinic in the United States for medical treatment, with Ayatollah Khomeini angrily condemning this "evidence of American plotting." Revolutionary denunciation of the Great Satan (America) intensified. On November 4, Muslim Student Followers of the Imam's Line occupied the U.S. embassy in Tehran, precipitating a momentous hostage crisis with enduring consequences. The students successfully resisted discreet efforts by Prime Minister Mehdi Bazargan to get them to back down, due in part to Ayatollah Khomeini's support for their militancy. This deadlock led to Bazargan's resignation and a deepening of the international crisis. On April 7, 1980, after futile efforts to negotiate a release of the sixty-six American hostages, the United States broke diplomatic relations with Iran, and on April 25 made a futile attempt at a military rescue, Operation Eagle Claw, in the course of which eight U.S. soldiers died in a dust cloud accident at their initial staging area, near Tabas in southeastern Iran.[101]

GEOPOLITICAL IMPACT OF THE HOSTAGE CRISIS

The 444 turbulent days of the hostage crisis, which ended on the very day of Ronald Reagan's inauguration as president in January 1981, were a critical turning point, both in the history of the Iranian Revolution and in Tehran's relations with the United States. The crisis radicalized the revolution, rendering it explicitly anti-American, ruptured Iran's deep and long-standing political-military ties with Washington, and provoked an embargo on U.S.-Iranian trade. Because the crisis continued so long, with such salience in the politics of both countries, new, provincial domestic stakes in antagonism were created and institutionalized that later proved difficult to reverse.

The hostage crisis also inspired major geopolitical changes that intensified long-run continentalist tendencies in Eurasian geopolitics, even as they inspired deeper short-run American political-military involvement. The hostage crisis made it easier for the Soviet Union to move into Afghanistan (February 1979). That in turn encouraged the United States to enunciate the Carter Doctrine of national commitment to engagement with the Persian Gulf (January 1980), inaugurating three decades and more of deepened involvement.[102] The revolution also tempted Iraq's Saddam Hussein to capitalize on Tehran's estrangement from the United States to launch a massive invasion of Iran (September 1980).

IRAN'S DEEPENING CONTINENTALIST CAST

Saddam's invasion accelerated the reorientation of revolutionary Iran away from its traditional American moorings toward a Eurasian continentalist stance in international affairs, which had already begun. Much of Iran's weaponry remained American, as Khomeini had inherited the shah's vast armory, and Tehran went initially to countries with major American-made arsenals, such as Vietnam, for resupply. Yet Tehran also began urgently equipping its forces with non-U.S. weapons.[103] Access to Western European weapons was limited by Europe's distrust of Tehran's new revolutionary objectives. Access to Soviet munitions was also constrained by Moscow's alliance with Iraq, by the Soviet invasion of Afghanistan, and by Khomeini's own deep-seated distrust of communism. That situation left China, among major arms producers, as a key alternative.

China, itself just emerging as an active international economic power under Deng Xiaoping, and also intent on military modernization, saw the opportunity and took it, even though it had been a warm backer of the shah's regime up to its final days.[104] During the 1980–1988 Iran-Iraq war, the PRC became Iran's most important foreign supplier of munitions and munitions-producing capital goods, with North Korea often as a convenient intermediary, to allow Beijing to avoid unduly offending the United States. In 1982 China and North Korea together supplied 40 percent of Iran's entire imported arms arsenal. By 1987 this substantial share had grown even further, to 70 percent, helping to provide the basis for broader political-economic ties with Northeast Asia's communists that were to follow war's end.[105]

The Iran-Iraq War, itself precipitated by the Iranian Revolution, also intensified Tehran's estrangement from Washington, even as Tehran grew closer to China, and ultimately to Russia as well. Starting in 1982, reflecting Iranian successes on the battlefield and a desire to offset those military gains for the sake of Middle East equilibrium, the United States increased its backing for Sunni-led Iraq in its bitter struggle with Khomeini's Shiite Iran. Washington normalized relations with Saddam's regime, supplying it with economic aid, counterinsurgency training, operational battlefield intelligence, and ultimately weapons. In this connection Donald Rumsfeld visited Baghdad twice, in December 1983 and March 1984, as a special emissary of President Ronald Reagan. In all, the Reagan and Bush administrations approved at least eighty direct export shipments to the Iraqi military by 1990, including computers, communications equipment, aircraft navigation, and radar equipment.[106] Needless to say, this systematic American backing for the Iraqis incurred deep Iranian ire, even if it was offset, to some extent, by sub-rosa support from the Reagan administration under the Iran Contra program.

The estrangement between Washington and Tehran was further intensified, and institutionalized, by the protracted "Tanker War" during the later stages of the Iran-Iraq conflict. In 1984 Iraq began attacking Iranian tankers and the vast oil terminal at Kharg Island, while Iran struck back by attacking tankers carrying Iraqi oil from Kuwait, and then ultimately any tanker of the Persian Gulf nations supporting Iraq. In November 1986, Kuwait formally petitioned foreign powers to protect its shipping, with the USSR agreeing to charter tankers, and the U.S. Navy offering protection for tankers flying the U.S. flag in March 1987, thus defying the Iranian blockade. In April 1988, the frigate USS *Samuel B. Roberts* was badly damaged by an Iranian mine, in response to which the United States pursued naval operations in which two Iranian ships were destroyed and an American helicopter was shot down, killing the two pilots. In July 1988, on the other side, the cruiser USS *Vincennes* shot down an Iran Air civilian airliner, mistaking it for an Iranian F-14 Tomcat, with a loss of 290 civilian passengers and crew.

IMPLICATIONS FOR EURASIA'S FUTURE

The Iranian Revolution was an epic event, well described for scholars and journalists in its domestic context, whose broader implications for Eurasia's future and for that of the international system often go remarkably unexplored. This populist Islamic uprising unhinged the most populous nation of the Persian Gulf, with an unparalleled geopolitical location at the head of the Gulf and the base of the Caspian Sea, from a U.S.-centric regional security system in which it had previously been (1971–1979) the principal proxy for the United States itself. Khomeini's sudden triumph in Tehran provoked intense geopolitical jockeying by Moscow and Baghdad to capitalize on the new Southwest Asian power vacuum created by the unexpected demise of the shah. The revolution unleashed deep new Islamic fundamentalist aspirations, transnational in nature, that became an important feature of Eurasian politics in succeeding years.

The shock waves radiating out from Khomeini's triumph were felt with particular force across the Persian Gulf in Saudi Arabia, for both ideological and domestic political reasons. The Iranian Revolution—at once fundamentalist and Shiite—challenged Sunni Saudi Arabia's tacit claim to spiritual guardianship of the holy Islamic sites of Mecca and Medina, and of the Islamic world, with particular force, because it came from the right. This was especially disconcerting to the Saudis, because since the Wahhabi revival nearly 250 years previously Saudi Wahhabism had considered itself to be the ultimate in pristine Islamic puritanism.[107]

The intensity of Khomeini's direct attacks on the Saudis compounded Riyadh's anger and the impact within Saudi Arabia itself. Stressing Islam's general antipathy to monarchy, just as the shah's regime was collapsing in Iran, Khomeini harshly challenged the House of Saud, calling it an American satellite and condemning its conservative Wahhabi sect, improbably, as "American Islam."[108] Not surprisingly, this incendiary taunt encouraged the Saudis to demonstrate religious purity by supporting Islamic fundamentalist movements, including Sunni jihadists, in Afghanistan and elsewhere.

These impulses to seek legitimacy through more militant fundamentalism were intensified by the domestic unrest that Khomeini's vitriol provoked within Saudi Arabia itself, as well as elsewhere in the Gulf.[109] After the fundamentalist seizure of the Grand Mosque of Mecca on November 20, 1979, 12,000 Saudi National Guard troops were deployed to surround the oil fields in the country's Eastern Province, home to nearly 350,000 Shia. Defying government prohibitions, the Shia of Qatif, in the Eastern Province, decided to organize their religious ceremony of Ashura on November 27, many carrying portraits of Ayatollah Khomeini. Clashing with the Guard, demonstrators rioted, attacking army barracks, setting fire to industrial plants, and torching banks, in violence that boiled on for three full days.[110] The combination of the Grand Mosque occupation and the al-Qatif riots led both to major expansion of Saudi security forces and to Riyadh's increased backing for fundamentalist groups across the region.

Iran's revolution thus helped create new communal and religious uncertainties and tensions within continental Eurasia that continue to shape it today—all along the Silk Road, from the Persian Gulf, across Central Asia and Afghanistan, to Xinjiang and even eastward as well. In particular, Khomeini's revolution inspired the Islamic fundamentalist movement, soon fueled further by reactive Saudi and American backing in Afghanistan. Yet the revolution also opened the way to new patterns of trans-Eurasian interdependence, which tended to have an anti-American cast, due to Teheran's estrangement from Washington. The Iran-Iraq War, flowing directly from the revolution's naive early nativist fervor, which left the country so painfully exposed, forced Iran to seek out China and North Korea during the 1980s as major arms suppliers. The revolution also opened Iran to powerful complementarities of energy interests with nations to the east, born of high-speed East and South Asian growth, that are still deepening, and hold potential for transforming the world in coming years.

The Rise of Putin (1999–2008): Emergence of a Proactive Russian Petrostate

One key dimension of Eurasian energy geopolitics, as we have just seen, is the rising yet increasingly discordant role of Iran, radically transformed by the critical juncture of the Iranian Revolution. Another central element, profoundly shaped by recent political history, is the increasingly strategic role of Russia. This was configured fatefully by another critical juncture: the sudden rise of Vladimir Putin to the presidency of Russia in 1999, and his sure-footed conduct in the turbulent political-economic circumstances that followed, establishing energy as a central tool of Russian post–Cold War diplomacy. Putin, of course, continued as Prime Minister from 2008–2012, before running for President once again.

Although his family had some minor historic association with founding leaders of the Soviet Union, Putin himself rose from humble origins.[111] His mother was a factory worker, and his father a conscript in the Soviet Navy. After a career in the KGB, with extended service in Germany, he reconnected with Anatoly Sobchak, mayor of St. Petersburg and his former instructor at Leningrad State University, as the Soviet Union collapsed, and garnered a post as Mayor Sobchak's advisor on international affairs. In 1996 Putin moved to the Kremlin, and from then on his rise was rapid. In March 1997, President Boris Yeltsin named Putin deputy chief of the presidential staff. In 1998 he became head of the Federal Security Service and in August 1999, acting prime minister.

THE COMING OF CRITICAL JUNCTURE

Four months later, when Yeltsin abruptly resigned, Putin suddenly became acting president. In its suddenness, at a strategic political-economic turning point, Putin's emergence had the hallmarks of critical juncture. Russia was in crisis, there was powerful political-economic stimulus for change after the painful Yeltsin years, and time pressure to achieve that change, due to aftershocks from the 1998 financial crisis and the continuing Chechen insurgency.

Russia's economic circumstances at the time were dire. Russian GDP had dropped more than 40 percent between 1990 and 1995 and remained nearly 20 percent below 1990 levels close to a decade after the collapse of the Soviet Union. This decline in GDP was much more intense even than the 27 percent decline that the United States suffered in the wake of the Great Depression between 1930 and 1934.[112] Over 30 percent of the population was below the poverty line when Putin took office, the average salary only $80 per month, and mortality rates, not to mention unemployment, were soaring. Indeed, unemployment reached 41.6 percent among all adult Russian males in 1999.[113]

Due to a painful process of capitalist reform, the Russian economy had recorded an abysmal average annual growth rate of minus 5.4 percent across the eight years since the collapse of the Soviet Union at the end of 1991. Yet a legitimate market economy remained absurdly absent. In terms of economic freedom, Russia in 1999 ranked ninety-third among 123 countries surveyed, somewhere between Zambia and Bangladesh.

To make matters worse, credible legal parameters were almost totally lacking. Post-Soviet Russia offered no credible property rights to own land, only weak corporate governance standards, and an inconsistent tax system. It also suffered from high stock market volatility, rampant government favoritism and gross discrimination toward private firms, as well as a massive, inefficient bureaucratic complex even larger than that of the former Soviet Union.

All these serious structural problems rendered Russia's economy anemic and the Russian people cynical about the efficacy of any reforms. Amid reports that renewing Russia's defunct industrial base would require massive capital outlays of as much as $25 trillion over the ensuing quarter century, the much-hyped foreign commitments to invest in Russia remained painfully small. In comparison with China, Russia's small inbound foreign direct investment reflected the country's dismal economic performance, as well as substantial capital flight to other countries. In 1999, for example, China received $43 billion in direct foreign investment, and Poland $8 billion, while Russia—massively larger than Poland—received only $2–3 billion. Over the entire period of Yeltsin's presidency (1992–1999), China received $350 billion of inbound foreign investment, compared to a meager $11.7 billion for Russia.

This investment differential testified to Russia's uncompetitive international economic position. That in turn inhibited capital flows and made Russia a high-risk destination for future foreign investment. The near-absence of domestically funded projects further compounded the confusion, creating a situation where affluent Russians invested their funds abroad, largely in connivance with government officials at various levels. Meanwhile, poorer Russians were reduced to working in stagnant sectors where government control and subsidies remained high.[114]

Long before taking office, Putin had a clear recipe for Russian economic management and geopolitical success, in which both authoritarian capitalism and energy as a strategic policy tool loomed large. Many of the details were foreshadowed in his 1999 candidate of science dissertation at St. Petersburg's State Mining Institute.[115] Although quite possibly authored in substantial measure by others, Putin's thesis succinctly outlined key elements of what later emerged as his economic strategy in power, including the following major elements:

1. Russia's natural resource base would not only secure the country's economic development but also serve to guarantee the country's international position.
2. State planning needed to be at the heart of Russia's resource management.
3. Russia needed a number of state-dominated, vertically integrated financial and industrial corporations in the energy area (such as Gazprom ultimately became).
4. Russia should not cede full control of resource ventures to foreign investment, but should nevertheless harness foreign technology and other expertise, on terms favorable to Russia.
5. The state had the right and responsibility to regulate the process of acquisition and use of natural resources.
6. Foreign control of strategic resource projects, ceded in the years immediately following the collapse of the Soviet Union, was a costly mistake that needed to be corrected.

PUTIN INTENSIFIES THE GOVERNMENT ROLE AND FORGES STRATEGIC
ENERGY POLICIES (2000–2009)

Responding to the political-economic crisis created by the collapse of the Soviet Union and Boris Yeltsin's ineffective efforts to cope with it, Putin moved
to implement his strategy and to use Russia's underlying energy resources as
a tool for national political-economic revival. In doing so, he began transforming his country into perhaps the most self-consciously strategic petrostate on earth—one bent on using the country's immense energy resources as
a tool for recovering the international influence that Moscow had lost with
the collapse of the Soviet Union.[116] Given the rapidly rising energy demand
of Asia, fueled by Chinese and Indian growth, Putin's emergence, with such
an explicitly energy-oriented strategy, profoundly transformed Eurasian energy geopolitics.

Putin, amid the critical juncture provoked by Russian domestic political-
economic turbulence, took four major steps to build the strategic Russian
petrostate. First, he reined in the private-sector oligarchs who had so compromised presidential influence during the Yeltsin years. Most conspicuously,
Putin had Mikhail Khodorkovsky, president of the powerful Yukos oil company, arrested for tax evasion. At its peak Yukos was producing 2 percent of
the world's oil output and had dared to conclude independent pipeline deals
with China without consulting the Kremlin. Following Khodorkovsky's arrest, Yukos itself was systematically dismantled, ostensibly to pay tax obligations, with the component pieces acquired by rival, Kremlin-favored firms like
Rosneft and Gazprom. In May 2005, Khodorkovsky was sentenced to a nine-
year term for fraud and other offenses, which he served in a remote prison,
eight hours from the nearest airport, near the Chinese border in Siberia.[117]

Second, Putin consolidated government control over existing energy firms.
Apart from bankrupting Yukos, he reasserted Kremlin control over Gazprom,
the world's largest natural gas production and distribution firm, naming his
close confidante from Leningrad local government days, Dmitry Medvedev, as
its president. Putin also increased the government stake in Rosneft, Russia's
largest oil firm, and forced foreign investors to cede control of two major joint
ventures—TNK-BP (Siberian oil and gas development) and the huge Sakhalin
II gas development project. Putin likewise reasserted Kremlin authority in managing the national political economy as a whole, first by strengthening prosecu-
tors, intelligence agencies, tax police, and interior ministry paramilitary forces.

Then, in late 2004, he arranged that regional leaders no longer be elected directly but instead appointed by him, and then endorsed by local assemblies. Putin also moved to subdue the media irreverence of the Yeltsin years.[118]

RUSSIA'S PETROSTATE ON THE GLOBAL STAGE

With proactive national leadership, consolidated state control of the energy sector, and tightening global markets, Russia by 2005 began to loom larger and larger in global energy geopolitics, with innovative transnational networking devices like the exclusive Valdai International Discussion Club leveraging its role.[119] The first targets were the recalcitrant former Soviet nations of the near abroad—Ukraine and Georgia foremost among them—from whom Moscow summarily demanded sharp increases in natural gas prices, in the depth of winter in 2005–2006. Putin also moved to renegotiate joint venture agreements with foreign firms, as noted above, and to intensify pressure on recalcitrant Eastern Europe through the ambitious North Stream agreement, concluded in 2005. North Stream aimed to export Russian gas directly under the Baltic Sea to Germany, bypassing Eastern Europe, and thus destroying its transit leverage.

Putin also moved to strengthen the Gas Exporting Countries Forum (GECF), founded in 2001, whose regular active members account for over 70 percent of global gas reserves and over 40 percent of current production.[120] In April 2007, this group decided to set up a high-level committee, coordinated by Russia, to research markets and discuss how gas prices should be determined. The GECF is also becoming an umbrella organization for regional cartels and a major force inhibiting the emergence of a full-fledged international market for liquefied natural gas, thus supporting a key Kremlin objective.[121]

PUTIN'S PETROSTATE AND ASIA

The Russian petrostate of Vladimir Putin, consolidated and given clear definition domestically early in Putin's tenure, grew increasingly proactive in global energy affairs, especially in 2005 and thereafter. The initial focus of this activism, however, was Europe. Key domestic population and economic centers were in European Russia, after all, complementing Moscow's traditional Cold War geopolitical focus on NATO.

Intellectually, the cutting edge of a Russian reorientation away from the industrialized West toward new emerging powers in the East has been

Eurasianism—the argument that Russia is emphatically a nation of both Europe and Asia, destined to use its central location to enlarge influence with both.[122] This diffuse body of ideas has often been used to justify and reassert Russia's continuing significance in international affairs, especially in territories adjacent to Russia itself. A formalistic version of Eurasianism can be observed in the Russian diplomacy of Yeltsin's foreign minister, Andrei Kozyrev, as early as 1992, augmented by his successor, Evgeni Primakov.[123] The dominant variant since those days, pragmatic Eurasianism, perceives Russia's dual European and Asian identity as legitimizing Russia's interests in both the West and Asia, thereby necessitating a balanced foreign policy between the two vectors.[124]

Putin's pragmatic Eurasianism envisages Russia becoming a connecting link between Europe and Asia via physical steps, such as the construction of railway links between the two Koreas and the Trans-Siberian Railway, to transport goods to Europe cheaper and faster than the currently used sea route. It also envisions the construction of oil and gas pipelines from fields in Siberia and the Russian Far East to supply major energy consumers like China, Japan, and South Korea. Manifesting his interest in deeper engagement with Asia, Putin participated in the Organization of the Islamic Conference annual meeting (2003) and the first East Asia Summit (2005), both held in Malaysia, as an observer. Since then, Russian diplomats have repeatedly made persistent efforts to upgrade and deepen their nation's involvement in Asian organizations, especially those, like the Shanghai Cooperation Organization (SCO), that do not include the United States.

Economically as well, Moscow's ties to the East have been deepening, with Russia capitalizing on the waning of Cold War barriers to forge new energy ties across old ideological fault lines. A graphic case in point is Turkey, whose relations with the West have been complicated by both human rights differences and controversies over immigration and European Union entry. Russia now provides 40 percent of Turkey's oil, and also, through the ultra-deep, technologically advanced Blue Stream I pipeline across the Black Sea, nearly two-thirds of Turkey's gas.[125] Russia has also deepened energy relations with Iran, both through Gazprom's involvement in developing Iran's massive South Pars gas field and by agreeing to complete the controversial Bushire nuclear reactor, amid increasing international sanctions related to Tehran's controversial nuclear program.

The critical juncture of political-economic crisis in Russia at the dawn of the twenty-first century thus fueled the sudden rise to power of a distinctive type of leader: one who believed profoundly that energy held the key to Russia's economic recovery. The critical juncture also led, through its dynamic mode of resolution, to Russia's return to prominence in global affairs. Putin's instincts appeared to prove right and to reinforce his domestic leverage: energy prices rose sharply during his presidency, fueling an era of prosperity for Russia and immense domestic popularity for himself.[126]

In the initial stages of Putin's rule—amid the critical juncture of political-economic transition—he had focused primarily in his energy diplomacy on Europe and Central Asia as leverage. He had generated geoeconomic leverage for Moscow through pressure on energy-deficient Europe, using both Russia's own ample resources and also its transit position between Europe and gas-rich Central Asia. Going forward, however, the giants of Asia farther east—China and India, in particular—inevitably loom large as the major expanding markets of the entire world in their own right. The lingering uncertainty for the Russian petrostate is its political and psychological willingness to turn eastward—to muster sufficient resources and diplomatic effort to consummate the economic complementarities that earlier critical junctures across Eurasia, such as the collapse of the Soviet Union, made possible.

WHAT ABOUT THE ARAB SPRING?

In January, 2011, following protracted popular demonstrations, Tunisian strongman Zine el-Abidine Ben Ali fled into exile. Weeks later, mass demonstrations in Cairo's Tahrir Square, combined with Western pressure, toppled Egyptian President Hosni Mubarak. Less definitive political unrest convulsed Yemen, Libya, Jordan, Bahrain, and Syria.

Clearly the events of early 2011 were dramatic. Many analysts declared them a sea change in Middle Eastern politics.[127] In that there was a crisis, stimulus to change, and intense time pressure to effect that change, the Arab Spring can arguably qualify as a critical juncture, certainly for major national decision-makers in Arab nations. It clearly "puts democracy on the agenda" across the Islamic world in an unprecedented way.[128] It is, of course, difficult to foresee definitively how events will proceed in that volatile part of the world. Yet whether the Arab Spring will definitively re-shape the geopolitics of energy across Eurasia, from a long-term perspective, in the way that the six critical junctures outlined above have done, is, however, doubtful, for three reasons.

First of all, it is not yet clear how significant a long-term trend the Arab Spring represents. At the very least, its original achievements are fragile.[129] Even by late 2011 the movement appeared to have lost the powerful momentum it seemed to exhibit in the previous spring, due to opposition, both overt and sub rosa, from embedded interests. Democratic revolution rapidly triumphed in Tunisia, and forced the resignation of Egyptian strongman Hosni Mubarak, but met complex and often bloody roadblocks, as well as ambiguous outcomes, elsewhere, including in Yemen, Bahrain, Syria, Libya, and Jordan.[130] Even in Egypt populist forces were co-opted, attenuated, and redirected by the military and the oligarchy.[131]

Secondly, the Arab Spring has had surprisingly little impact on the production and export decisions of OPEC producer nations, partly because the unrest involved occurred almost uniformly in non-oil producing nations. Protracted conflict in Libya, the one major OPEC producer affected substantially by the chain of uprisings, reduced oil production volume there, until well after the death of Moammar Qaddaffi in October, 2011, while populist pressures and sabotage reduced natural-gas flows from Egypt to Israel. Yet otherwise the energy implications have been, and are likely to continue to be, distinctly limited. There were, to be sure, some minor echo effects in Saudi Arabia's oil-producing Eastern province. Yet unrest there was limited largely to the Shia population (a distinct minority in the Saudi kingdom), immediately repressed, and failed to have broader resonance among the majority Sunni.[132] Further, they stimulated large-scale Saudi stabilization policies, with both political-economic and military dimensions, that further blunted short-term prospects of instability in the Persian Gulf oil-producing nations.[133]

Thirdly, the Arab Spring does little to disrupt the geopolitical logic of deepening Eurasian continental energy interdependence, already established by the six critical junctures outlined above. China and India are continuing to grow rapidly, and need energy. Markets are encouraging producers in the near-by Persian Gulf, Russia, and Central Asia, to supply it. Since many producers are close geographically to suppliers, with political barriers between neighbors reduced through collapse of the Soviet Union, the logic of transcontinental energy ties is deepening, little influenced by the Arab Spring, whose concrete political-economic impact has been concentrated in North Africa. Those continentalist energy ties, mainly between China and various parts of the former USSR, continue to have a soft-authoritarian cast. If anything, the

Arab Spring, encourages that illiberal tendency, due to the political challenge it presents to the entrenched authoritarian powers of Eurasia, that continue to prevail far east and northeast of Tunis, Cairo, and even Damascus.

CONCLUSION: THE CONTINENTALIST WORLD
THAT CRITICAL JUNCTURES ARE BUILDING

Between western and eastern-southern Eurasia there is, as we have seen throughout this volume, a latent yet potentially fateful geoeconomic equation: the west of the continent has copious energy resources, while the east has a vast number of poor yet aspiring people. For many centuries, the relationship between those regions was a largely static one, like their respective economies and political systems, subsumed into broader currents of world affairs.

To be sure, some significant political-economic interchange did occur between eastern and western Eurasia across the 1950s, 1960s, and 1970s—notably expanding Japanese and then Korean imports of oil and gas from the Persian Gulf. The volume of trade was actually quite substantial. Yet it had remarkably little global geopolitical impact, being mediated largely through Western multinationals, between nations far removed geographically over the oceans, and within the context of a broader world political-economic order clearly dominated by the United States.

In this chapter, I have outlined six seemingly unrelated, discontinuous steps—critical junctures, I call them—which are the building blocks of a potentially different sort of world than we have known before. Together, these junctures have begun to unlock the static potential, and long-term geoeconomic logic, of a new continentalism—a deepening, territorially contiguous relationship among the Middle East, the former Soviet Union, China, and Northeast Asia that is not mediated by the United States. Although it is too early to judge conclusively, this emerging energy-driven interdependence could also well become a deeper relationship in which classical Western values and market principles prevail less clearly than in typical international relations of the past. Yet the new continentalism, unless countervailed, could nevertheless be a relationship of increasing consequence for global affairs as a whole.

Two of the critical junctures described here—China's Four Modernizations (1978) and India's economic reforms (1991)—opened the way to high-speed growth in the population giants of Asia, which between them are home to 37 percent of the entire world's people. Both China and India are poor countries, in which per capita energy demand is low. As their citizens grow more affluent and buy electric appliances, use air conditioning, and acquire an automobile, those per capita figures will soar. The critical juncture of transition to growth, therefore, has fateful implications for energy demand—not just at home, or across Eurasia, but around the world.

Then who will supply the burgeoning energy demand of Asia, led by its two new giants, and on what terms? With respect to that question, the other four critical junctures become distinctly relevant. The nationalization of Western energy multinationals in the Middle East, and the rise of OPEC during the early 1970s, accompanied by the rise of national oil companies, profoundly altered the energy distribution structure between eastern and western Eurasia, removing the Anglo-American middlemen. The collapse of the Soviet Union (1992) then opened important new prospects of supply from Russia and the near abroad—especially Central Asia. And it likewise opened important opportunities for overland supply—including direct pipelines from the Caspian to Shanghai, now operational, that would have been undreamed of three decades ago. As the "center of gravity" for China's growth and energy demand has moved westward and southward within China itself, driven by inland development stretching from Inner Mongolia and Xinjiang to Szechuan and Yunnan, the attractiveness within China of such continental pipelines has steadily risen.

The final two critical junctures—the Iranian Revolution (1979) and the sudden, unexpected emergence of Vladimir Putin (1999) as Russian president, have fatefully begun to shape the new energy and geopolitical relationships even now emerging across Eurasia, in the second, less unilateral phase of the post–Cold War world. Should the preeminence of the United States begin to decline, under the weight of a staggering national debt, coupled with enervating military conflicts in Islamic nations, the unipolar world of the early post–Cold War could morph into a less hegemonic and less rule-bound multipolar configuration. These last two critical junctures help us understand what that new post-post–Cold War world is coming to be.

The Iranian Revolution broke the traditional, Sunni-centric unity of the classic Islamic community, giving momentum to two alternative tendencies: Islamic fundamentalism and Shia nationalism.[134] Both have proven to be chronically destabilizing. Shia nationalism has unsettled the Persian Gulf, intensifying tensions with Sunni groups in Shiite majority states such as Iraq and Bahrain.[135] Iran's direct and indirect influence on Islamic fundamentalism has also been substantial, inspiring Hezbollah, Hamas, and other radical groups throughout the Islamic world. Iran has thus helped render Eurasian energy geopolitics significantly more volatile than they would otherwise be, in part by stimulating Saudi-based Sunni Wahhabism, which has also at times been highly inflammatory and destructive.

The critical juncture of Putin's emergence, finally, has also fatefully re-shaped Eurasian continentalist configurations. Since Putin became Russian president at the end of 1999, Moscow's energy policies have grown at once more coherent and more assertive. Russia is using energy ever more forcefully as a geostrategic tool, working, through the GECF and similar bodies, to unify producers in a common front, even as it refuses to formally join OPEC, the oil producers' cartel. Such machinations are of limited efficacy in relation to Europe and the United States, especially with the advent of shale-gas supply, supported by advanced fracking technology, in the West. Yet the Kremlin is more effective in fostering deepened ties with China, Central Asia, and the Middle East through such efforts, given their high rates of energy demand growth, more limited technological access and geographical proximity.

Thirty-five years ago, relations between the Middle East and the Soviet Union, on the one hand, and Northeast Asia on the other were quite distant. Today, that pattern has radically changed. The east and the west of Eurasia have grown more interdependent. And these six critical junctures, freeing the forces of energy economics, have played a central role in bringing that fateful continental confluence to pass.

Chapter 4 Comparative Energy Producer Profiles

The new energy Silk Road is not only a figurative highway, bounded by geography and animated by the still-living shadows of a venerable 2,000-year history. It is also a series of physical way stations, with definable boundaries and clear functional roles. Preeminent among these, of course, is the production of energy itself.

This chapter reviews, in comparative perspective, the oil and gas reserves, the production and export capabilities, and the production proclivities of the major exporting nations of Eurasia. It details the extraordinary concentration of reserves, and ultimately production also, within that sprawling continent. The impact of rising energy income on the domestic political economy of producer nations varies significantly from country to country, naturally provoking different utility trade-offs between short-run producer revenue and market stability, which are explored in Chapter 5.

THE MIDDLE EAST, RUSSIA, AND CENTRAL ASIA
AS PRODUCER AND STOREHOUSE

There are more than one hundred national producers of oil and gas in the world, with twelve of them being members of OPEC.[1] For most producing nations, energy production itself is a marginal enterprise for the overall national economy, and the output of these small-scale producers, conversely, has only limited consequences for world affairs. The output of small-scale hydrocarbon producers is, after all, utilized mainly for domestic consumption.

The United States occupies an unusual position in the world of energy. It is a major producer of oil and gas—second in the world for most of the past two decades, and first for most of the twentieth century. It once was a powerful exporter and fueled the arsenals of allies during two world wars from seemingly unlimited domestic oil reserves like the massive West Texas Field.[2] Yet America's own profligate domestic consumption, together with the massive requirements of aiding struggling allies in wartime, has gradually absorbed that slack. Since the early 1970s the United States has lost its long-standing role of producer for international as well as domestic markets and has loomed larger and larger as a consumer alone. In 2010, it imported 11.7 million barrels of oil per day—nearly twice as much as any other nation, and 61 percent of its total consumption.[3]

A handful of countries, however, remain major export producers for the world as a whole. As Figure 4.1 clearly shows, the vast majority of the largest current exporters lie within Eurasia, especially in the Persian Gulf. Their production capacities and incentive structures profoundly shape the terms under which oil and gas flow, over the short term at least, in international trade.

Over the long run, the prospects for Eurasian petroleum interdependence are even more compelling. The huge emerging consumers of the continent, China and India, have few places to turn aside from the Persian Gulf, because that is where the bulk of the reserves ultimately are. As Figure 4.2 suggests, over half of global proven reserves are in the Middle East.

As Table 4.1 also suggests, six of the ten top holders of petroleum reserves in the world are in Eurasia. Indeed, five of the top ten—and four of the top five—are in the Persian Gulf. Latin America and Africa can provide short-term alternatives, or low-probability long-term scenarios, but the options of Asia's consumers will likely narrow toward the Middle East, and particularly the Persian Gulf, in years to come.

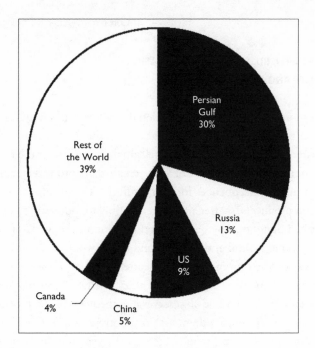

Figure 4.1: World oil production shares.
Source: BP, *Statistical Review of World Energy*, 2011 edition.
Note: Persian Gulf is defined as including Iran, Iraq, Kuwait, Oman, Qatar, Saudi Arabia, and the United Arab Emirates.

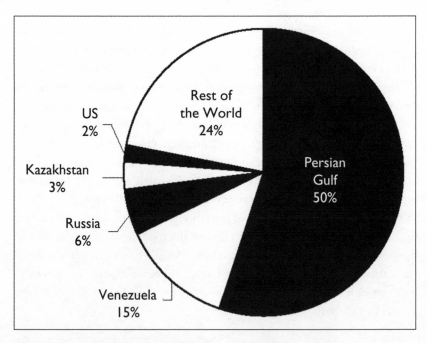

Figure 4.2: World proven oil reserves.
Source: BP, *Statistical Review of World Energy*, 2011 edition.

Table 4.1. Top Ten Oil Reserves

No.	Country	Oil Reserves (billions of barrels)	World Share (percent)
1	Saudi Arabia	264.5	19.1
2	Venezuela	211.2	15.3
3	Iran	137.0	9.9
4	Iraq	115.0	8.3
5	Kuwait	101.5	7.3
6	UAE	97.8	7.1
7	Russia	77.4	5.6
8	Libya	44.3	3.4
9	Kazakhstan	39.8	2.9
10	Nigeria	37.2	2.7

Source: BP, *Statistical Review of World Energy*, 2011 edition.
Notes: Figures are for proven oil reserves. In Venezuela's case, this includes large amounts of heavy oil, technically difficult to extract, included in self-declared reserve calculations for the first time in 2009, that were greatly expanded in 2010. Shaded countries are Eurasian continentalist states.

As global energy demand steadily rises, the Middle East will inevitably loom large as a global supplier, especially of oil. Indeed, International Energy Agency forecasts suggest that two-thirds of incremental oil exports globally between 2010 and 2035 will flow from that unstable region.[4] Three neighbors on the Persian Gulf—Saudi Arabia, Iran, and Iraq—together account for over 37 percent of the proven reserves on earth (Table 4.1).[5] Two additional states (Kuwait and the United Arab Emirates) account for another 14 percent, giving five Gulf nations over half of the proven oil reserves of the entire planet.

These countries float, in short, on an enormous ocean of oil, both figuratively and literally. And their substantial current exports are barely clearing their massive reserves. Ratios of reserves to production in Saudi Arabia and Iran are over seventy-two and eighty-eight years respectively (Figure 4.3). In the UAE the comparable figure is ninety-four years. These countries, in short, could continue producing for close to another century or more at current rates and not run out of oil—even if no new reserves were discovered.

Contrasts to the distribution of oil reserves elsewhere in the world reinforce conclusions reaffirming the long-term preeminence of the Gulf. The United States in 2010 reported only 2.2 percent of proven world reserves—including West Texas and the North Slope of Alaska. And America's proven

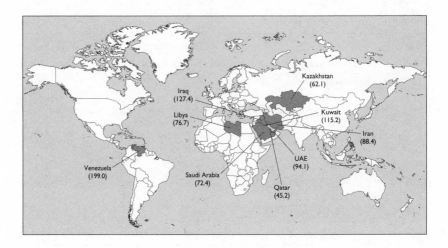

Figure 4.3: The concentration of high oil R/P ratios in the Gulf.
Source: BP, *Statistical Review of World Energy*, 2011 edition.
Notes: R/P ratio is the length of time required for proven reserves to be exhausted at current rates of production, in years. Figures for Venezuela include heavy oil.

reserves were expected to run dry, at current rates of production, in just 11.3 years, or more than half a century faster than in Saudi Arabia. Russia, with 6.4 percent of proven reserves and a reserve-production ratio of 20.6 years, as well as vast Siberian frontiers not explored, was clearly in a stronger position with respect to reserves than the United States.[6] Yet even Russia's oil riches pale in comparison with those of the Persian Gulf.

As a consequence of its massive reserve position and its minimal cost of production, the Gulf will inevitably loom increasingly large—the petroleum "supplier of last resort"—as resources everywhere else are progressively depleted. Former U.S. Secretary of Defense James Schlesinger estimated some years ago, for example, that Russia's share of global oil production and exports would peak around 2010.[7] The Middle East share, he suggested, would begin to rapidly expand thereafter, making the world as a whole more and more dependent on its oil. The International Energy Agency concurs.[8]

To say that the Middle East will inevitably loom large in coming years, especially for Asia, is not, however, to say categorically how its resources will be accessed. The traditional pattern of recent years has been the energy sea lanes from the Persian Gulf, through the Straits of Hormuz and Malacca, across the South China Sea, to Northeast Asia. Overland routes of various types are also possible, and growing steadily more prominent, as noted in Chapters 5, 7, and

8. Indeed, those overland routes are a fundamental aspect of the New Continentalism.

Many people speculate that Africa or Brazil could provide significant alternatives to the Middle East. This seems highly unlikely in the longer run, no matter how much media play China's energy ties with those two non–Silk Road regions may currently be getting.[9] The supply capacity of Africa south of the Sahara, in particular, seems grossly overrated. The fifty-three nations and eight dependencies within that huge region in 2010 held only 9.5 percent of global proven reserves, compared to 54.4 percent in the Middle East, 53.6 percent in the Persian Gulf as a whole, and 37.3 percent in the Big Three (Saudi Arabia, Iran, and Iraq) alone. Brazil, by comparison, held only 1.0 percent of proven global reserves.[10] Even the major offshore discoveries of late 2007 would only boost Brazil's total to around 1.4 percent of world reserves.[11] And global energy price volatility, such as was witnessed during 2008–2009, not to mention technical difficulties or major oil spills in the ultra-deep oilfields little more than one hundred miles south of Rio de Janeiro's pristine beaches, could critically slow their exploitation.[12]

Heavy Middle East Dependence on Asian Markets

The Middle East deals much less extensively with Europe and America, in its current oil trade, than it does with Asia, as has been noted. Its exports to Europe are less than 2.4 million barrels daily, and to the United States just over 1.7 million per day. The Western share of Middle East exports, relative to that flowing to Asia, has been steadily declining for a full generation, with the decline accelerating particularly since the Asian financial crisis, in the face of that dynamic continent's surging subsequent growth.

Even together, the substantial energy supplies moving from the Gulf westward are less than one third of the more than 14 million barrels daily that the Gulf sends east of the Straits of Malacca. That massive eastward flow represented over three-fourths of the region's total exports in 2010, and almost 27 percent of all the oil flowing in international trade.[13] It is thus one of the dominant realities of the global political economy. The UAE, Kuwait, and Qatar, in particular, have been viewing Asia as their major customer, with the Asian share of their oil exports ranging from 83 to 100 percent.[14]

Just as noteworthy as Asia's heavy current dependence on Middle Eastern energy, especially oil, are the trends over time. Northeast Asia, especially Japan and South Korea, have grown steadily more reliant on the Middle East

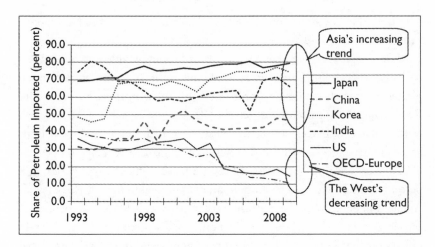

Figure 4.4: Major Asian consuming nations' petroleum import share from the Middle East.

Sources: Department of Energy, Energy Information Administration (Japan, U.S., and OECD-Europe figures); United Nations, Commodity Trade Statistics, http://comtrade.un.org (China and India figures); and Planning Commission of India, *Integrated Energy Policy: Report of the Expert Committee* (New Delhi: Planning Commission, Government of India, 2006).

Note: Indian data for 2000–2004 were not directly available, and are extrapolated from other verifiable statistics in the time series, including BP. *Statistical Review of World Energy.*

for their oil imports since the early 1990s, while Europe and the United States have become decidedly less so (Figure 4.4). While there was little difference between Asia and the West in their Middle East dependence during the early 1990s, the regional patterns have now sharply diverged.

The energy dependence of key Asian nations on the Middle East, although uniformly rising across all the key nations over the past two decades, does vary considerably from country to country, from the 80 to 90 percent level of Japanese dependence to China's much lower 40 percent reliance. India lies in between, at around 70 percent. Even so, all of these nations depend far more on the volatile Gulf region than does the United States, which receives only 18 percent of its oil from there. Indeed, America gets nearly 28 percent more oil from Latin America south of Mexico—mainly from Chavez's Venezuela—than it does from the entire Middle East. Indeed, 49 percent of America's entire imported oil supply comes from the Western Hemisphere, or around three times as much as from the entire Persian Gulf.[15]

Europe too has more important oil partners than the Middle East. It gets nearly six million barrels daily from the former Soviet Union, and slightly more than 2 million from the Middle East. Africa is an important alternative, providing Europe with significantly more than what it gets from the Middle East.[16] In total, the Middle East accounts for only around 16 percent of Europe's total oil imports—just slightly more than its very limited share of U.S. imports.[17]

More than 14 million barrels of oil flow east from the Persian Gulf to Asia every day. The largest national consumer is emphatically Japan, which takes over 3.6 million barrels daily—or nearly one-fifth of all Middle Eastern crude exports. In some Gulf countries, such as the UAE and Qatar, Japan's share often rises over half of local oil exports. Yet Japan faces rising long-term competition for Gulf supplies from China, which commands around 2.4 million barrels of Middle Eastern oil daily, as well as from Korea and the Association of Southeast Asian Nations, which take most of the rest of Asia's flow eastward from the Gulf. Asia's overall share of Persian Gulf exports, which is more than twice what any other part of the world

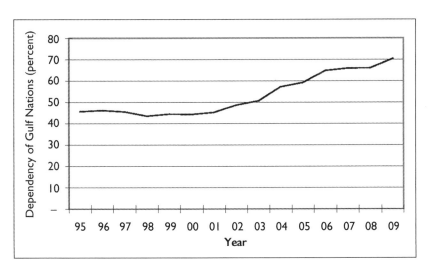

Figure 4.5: Rising dependency of Gulf nations on Asia-Pacific consumers.
Source: Organization of Petroleum Exporting Countries, *OPEC Annual Statistical Bulletin*, various editions.
Note: Gulf nations include Iran, Iraq, Kuwait, Oman, Qatar, Saudi Arabia, and the United Arab Emirates. Asia-Pacific nations include Australia, China, India, Indonesia, Japan, South Korea, Philippines, Singapore, Thailand, and Vietnam.

procures, has been steadily rising since the Asian financial crisis of 1997–1998 (Figure 4.5).

Asia's share of Middle Eastern energy exports fell, to be sure, during the crisis itself, dipping slightly from 56 percent of regional exports in 1996 to less than 52 percent by 1998–1999. Yet Asia's share rebounded thereafter, as local economies began to recover, to more than half of all the Persian Gulf's exports to the world by 2003 (Figure 4.5). That portion has since continued to rise sharply, to almost three-fourths in 2010, fueled by the rapidly rising demand of China and India.[18] Persian Gulf exports to Asia appear likely, as suggested in Figure 4.6, to rise even higher in the future, as demand in populous, high-growth developing Asia continues to increase, even in the face of periodic economic downturns in the West.

Apart from the Middle East, we cannot ignore the former Soviet Union. Russia itself, with the seventh largest oil reserves on earth (Table 4.1), has consistently ranked, together with Saudi Arabia, among the top two producers in the world since 2003,[19] and has naturally benefited from high world energy prices. After enormous adjustment problems following the collapse of the Soviet Union and during the financial crisis of 1998, Russia's economy has recovered smartly, especially since the advent of the Putin administration in 1999. During 2003–2008, its economic growth averaged 7.0 percent, compared to 2.4 percent in the United States and only 1.8 percent in the Euro area.[20]

Central Asia also has substantial reserves and will grow increasingly important in coming years, if energy prices remain buoyant.[21] As indicated in Figure 4.2, it has over 3 percent of proven world oil reserves, with substantial areas remaining unexplored. Kazakhstan, in particular, has the ninth largest reserves on earth (Table 4.1), with the huge Kashagan fields at the head of the Caspian still virtually unexploited.[22] Central Asia is also uniquely placed to supply demand from China and India via overland routes and has the capacity to steadily increase production for at least a decade. Accessing its substantial oil reserves, like those of Turkmenistan in natural gas, will likely be a major driver of the new Eurasian continentalism and will benefit from improved relations among the nations of the region—especially between China and the Central Asian states.

The Situation in Natural Gas

Like oil deposits, natural gas reserves are similarly concentrated in limited parts of the world, although the relative endowments of Russia and the Middle East are somewhat different. The Middle East as a whole holds just under 40 percent of global proven reserves (Figure 4.7), with Russia holding roughly a quarter and Central Asia another 6 percent. Thus it appears that around 70 percent of global conventional natural gas reserves lie on the Eurasian continent, with substantial areas, especially in northern Siberia, still remaining unexplored. East and South Asia will thus, over the long term, have great difficulty avoiding dependence on their Silk Road neighbors in natural gas, just as in oil, particularly given their high growth prospects, some local deposits of shale gas in China and India notwithstanding.

Within the Persian Gulf, Iran (15.8 percent) and Qatar (13.5 percent) hold the lion's share. The massive gas field beneath the Gulf, transcending the delicate national boundary between Iran and Qatar, known as the South Pars Field in Iran and the North Field in Qatar, is by far the world's largest single natural gas deposit, although Russia as a whole—the largest nation geographically on earth, after all—appears to hold more, in national-aggregate terms (Table 4.2).

Russia has formidable natural gas reserves that dominate the global standings, as suggested above. Its proven reserves comprise 23.9 percent of the global total, giving that sprawling country a reserves-to-production ratio of 76 years

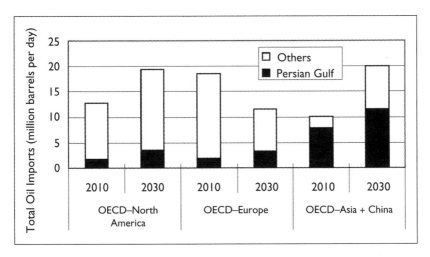

Figure 4.6: The deepening energy interdependence of Asia and the Persian Gulf.
Source: U.S. Department of Energy, *International Energy Outlook*, 2006 edition; U.S. Department of Energy, *International Petroleum Monthly*, June 2010 edition; United Nations, Commodity Trade Statistics, http://comtrade.un.org; and BP, *Statistical Review of World Energy*, 2011 edition.
Note: Northeast Asian members of the OECD include Japan and South Korea.

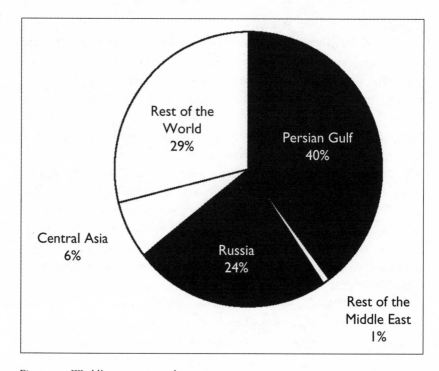

Figure 4.7: World's proven natural gas reserves.
Source: BP, *Statistical Review of World Energy*, 2011 edition.
Note: Figures as of December 31, 2010.

in one of the world's most crucial resources.[23] And much of Russia's vastness remains unexplored.

Central Asia also has significant endowments—more than double the share of world gas reserves that it holds in oil. Turkmenistan ranks fourth in natural gas, with 8.0 trillion cubic meters, followed by Kazakhstan, at eighteenth, with 1.9 trillion cubic meters.[24] Kazakhstan also ranks ninth in oil reserves, outranking the U.S., partly on the strength of its mammoth new Kashagan field, among the greatest global discoveries of the past two decades, followed by Azerbaijan (nineteenth, at 7 billion barrels).[25]

How will the substantial natural gas reserves of Central Asia and the Russian Far East be developed in future years? Asia will clearly have a major consumer role, at least for liquefied natural gas (LNG), and possibly for piped gas, due to its rapid economic growth and geographical proximity to the former U.S.S.R. Shale gas seems unlikely to undermine this prospect.[26] Both North America and Europe already have well-developed gas grids

Table 4.2. Top Ten Natural Gas Reserve Holders

No.	Country	Natural Gas Reserves (trillions of cubic meters)	World Share (percent)
1	Russia	44.8	23.9
2	Iran	29.6	15.8
3	Qatar	25.3	13.5
4	Turkmenistan	8.0	4.3
5	Saudi Arabia	8.0	4.3
6	United States	7.7	4.1
7	UAE	6.0	3.2
8	Venezuela	5.5	2.9
9	Nigeria	5.3	2.8
10	Algeria	4.5	2.4

Source: BP, *Statistical Review of World Energy*, 2011 edition.
Note: Countries shaded are within Eurasia. Reserve figures are for December 31, 2010.

that supply the bulk of their natural gas—Canadian gas for the United States, and Russian gas for Europe. Neither gets much piped gas directly from the Middle East, and shale gas may inhibit prospects for change in that situation, while also reducing Europe's vulnerability to pressure from Russia over gas. Given Central Asia's unique proximity to China and India and recent domestic infrastructure improvements in those giant nations, prospects for eastward gas flows appear brighter. Unprecedented overland pipelines and the emergence of a Eurasian gas grid inspired by Chinese demand are an emerging possibility, which will give momentum to the new continentalism.

With respect to LNG, a roughly similar pattern prevails: the Gulf is disproportionately dependent on Asia, and Asia, conversely, has more substantial dependence on the Persian Gulf than any other part of the industrialized world . This pattern is likely to intensify, as shale gas, in which Europe and the U.S. appear to be better endowed than most of Asia, and more capable of exploiting the resources they have, grows more important.[27] Europe, in particular, does have important alternative LNG suppliers in North Africa, deriving over 70 percent of its LNG from that source. Algeria is especially important to Europe, providing 9.8 percent of its total LNG supplies. Yet it is a partial exception, uniquely accessible for Europe, that demonstrates the broader rule: in LNG, as in oil, Asia—not America or Europe—is the major customer of the Middle East, and especially of the Persian Gulf. That deepening supply-demand relationship lies at the center of the deepening transcontinental Eurasian energy relationship.

CONCLUSION

Historically, the United States has loomed large as a global oil and gas producer—ever since the day in 1859 when the first modern oil well was drilled in northwestern Pennsylvania. For most of the ensuing century and more, in both war and peace, America dominated international production, while the Texas Railroad Commission played a key role in global pricing. Even as Middle East production began rising in the 1950s and 1960s, Anglo-American political-economic dominance in global markets continued, with the U.S.-led Aramco consortium controlling Saudi production, British interests dominant in Iran, and the Western Seven Sisters dominating distribution of petroleum products around the world.

Since the 1970s, the political economy of global energy production has radically changed. Market power has moved to the Middle East, and the Seven Sisters have largely given way, in global production and refining, to the national oil companies of the Gulf and Russia. Although Western multinationals retain formidable technical and capital resources, as well as market sophistication, control of reserves lies increasingly in other hands. The emergence of shale gas since 2008 as a plausible resource alternative, especially in the United States and Europe, modifies prospects for Western natural-gas import demand to some degree, but does not seem likely to affect supply patterns outside of the Atlantic Basin nearly as substantially—particularly trade between Northeast Asia and the Persian Gulf, where expensive infrastructure and long-term contracts inhibit rapid change in the status quo.

As the huge energy-hungry new consumers of Asia rise, they will no doubt seek to diversify sources of supply, for both economic and geopolitical reasons. In the end, however, they cannot easily avoid deepening reliance on their neighbors in Eurasia. In oil, this will preeminently mean reliance on the Persian Gulf, even though Russia and Central Asia also looms large in the short run, and are more intimately connected with East Asia overland than previously, due to new infrastructure like the East Siberia Pacific Ocean pipeline. In natural gas, Russia will likely be of rising importance, its role modified only marginally by shale-gas reserves in China and India, with the means of distribution—LNG or piped gas—fatefully shaping the geopolitical implications of interdependence. East Asia remains the only major industrialized global region without a continental natural-gas grid; incipient changes in this pattern over the past few years, as overland links among China, Central Asia, and Russia evolve, could ultimately have major implications for international affairs.

Powerful forces are thus in motion on both the demand and supply sides of the Old World energy equation. In the East and South, rapid growth in nations with limited domestic resources is compelling greater import dependence. And West Asia has the resources—more copiously than anywhere else on earth—to supply that steadily rising demand. Eurasia's extremities have enormous potential to grow more energy interdependent, with fateful future implications for the new continentalism.

Chapter 5 The Comparative Political Economy of Eurasian Petrostates

The major energy producers and energy consumers of Eurasia, as we have seen, are arrayed in remarkable geographical proximity to one another. Mere proximity, of course, does not necessarily imply economic interdependence, cooperation, or solidarity. Prospects for deeper cohesion and for reducing inevitable conflict are greatly enhanced, however, by domestic political-economic complementarity among the nations of the region.

This book seeks to understand the prospect for that deeper cohesion and the sort of world that deepening energy linkages across the Eurasian continent are creating. It argues that those transnational energy relationships, both maritime and overland, are more than mere arms-length, short-term economic transactions—they have prospect of transforming the nature of the world in which we live. They do so, in part, by deepening the role of energy in the domestic political economies of producer nations, a key topic that I examine in this chapter. Understanding the nature of any special domestic traits helps us grasp the broader political implications of the emerging transcontinental relationships themselves.

Over the past fifteen years, a substantial literature has developed in comparative politics about the "resource curse," suggesting that large natural resource endowments impair domestic prospects for economic development.[1] A narrower, but related petrostate argument contends that oil wealth undermines local prospects for democracy in developing nations.[2] As Tom Friedman put it succinctly, if grandiloquently, in enunciating his "first law of petro-politics": "The price of oil and the pace of freedom always move in opposite directions."[3]

While documenting concretely the impact of energy dependence on the broader political-economic functioning of producer states, this chapter strives to break fresh theoretical ground in two particular respects: (1) exploring comparatively the concept of petrostate, and (2) assessing the impact of different types of petrostates on international relations, particularly when they are interdependent with authoritarian capitalist consumer nations like China. The notion of a petrostate—a nation whose wealth stems primarily from the sale of oil—is a concise tool for understanding how nations are affected domestically by becoming major hydrocarbon exporters.[4] It also helps us understand the implications, in turn, of that historic transition to energy as a central political-economic concern for the Eurasian nations and for the global political economy as a whole.

Several arguments are made to explain the resource curse, which does appear to broadly prevail, in countries ranging from Africa to Southeast Asia and Latin America. One observation is that resource markets globally are prone to boom-and-bust cycles, which put extraordinary stress on the institutions and financial capabilities of developing states, impeding coherent development. Another is that abundant resources provoke high levels of domestic conflict, generating political-economic uncertainty that can be dysfunctional to development. Substantial resource revenue in the hands of the state can also put upward pressure on exchange rates, it is argued, leading to overvalued currencies that foster local imports and discourage exports.

OIL AND AUTHORITARIANISM?

Three causal mechanisms are typically suggested, linking oil and authoritarianism: (1) a *rentier* effect, through which governments employ a combination of low tax rates and high spending to inhibit pressures for democracy; (2) a *repression* effect, by which governments strengthen their internal security forces to ward off democratic pressures; and (3) a *modernization* effect, under which the failure of the population to assume industrial and service-sector jobs renders them less likely to press for democracy.[5]

In this chapter I consider in particular detail the recent political-economic evolution of three key Eurasian oil- and gas-exporting nations (Russia, Iran, and Kazakhstan), together with Saudi Arabia and the related Persian Gulf complex of related nations (the Gulf Cooperation Council, or GCC).[6] These cases were selected due to their scale of oil or gas production and to ensure geographical and political variety. They were chosen with a view to understanding the impact of energy wealth on political-economic development in the respective countries, and whether the countries in question will be "stabilizing" or "destabilizing" petrostates in their international behavior more generally.

There are two central dimensions of inquiry with respect to the domestic political economy of petrostates: (1) the impact of energy wealth on economic development (the resource curse); and (2) the impact of energy wealth on democratic evolution. The general hypothesis pursued here will be that oil and gas wealth gradually crowds out non-energy-related production, turning oil and gas producers with sufficient resources into undemocratic petrostates with erratic growth tracks and a bias toward corruption. Interdependence with authoritarian capitalist consumers deepens these perverse orientations, since such nations tend to reconfirm or reenforce them.

The argument here, tested in the cases of the GCC states of the Persian Gulf, Iran, Russia, and Kazakhstan (all among the nine largest oil exporters on earth) is that petrostates tend to be nondemocratic and prone to heavy military spending, as well as the proliferation of chemical, biological, and nuclear weapons, especially when they are clustered in close proximity to one another. Many, although not all, are "destabilizing petrostates," which routinely opt for high short-run producer prices, with only limited concern for long-run market stability. The rising dependence of Asian energy consumers—themselves only fragile adherents, if at all, to liberal norms—upon such illiberal producing countries, helps insulate petrostates from Western pressures for conformity with these international norms. The deepening of Eurasian energy interdependence thus could complicate prospects for democracy and the application of liberal values in significant parts of the world. Consumer political-economic interdependence with "stabilizing petrostates" may help moderate producer behavior in the short run, but the long-term stability of such ties, or of stabilizing petrostates themselves, is far from ensured.

These petrostates, it is argued, develop foreign policies of two varieties, depending on their populations and the related socio-military demands of those populations: (1) *stabilizing, swing-producer policies*, when the petrostates in question have small populations and large resources, such as in the nations of the GCC; and (2) *destabilizing, eccentric, rent-maximizing policies* when the petrostates have large populations and substantial budgetary requirements, as in the cases of Russia and Iran. In these latter countries, internationally disruptive behavior can actually work in the financial interest of the petrostate that foments it, by provoking fears of supply disruption that ratchet market energy prices upward.

A final concern of this chapter will be the orientation of key petrostates regarding the structure of the international political economy as a whole, given growing petrostate export dependence on Asia. It will be suggested that, as energy-export dependence grows in the petrostates, and energy dependence on Asia in particular rises, petrostate producers will find themselves increasingly independent of the cosmopolitan strictures of a "world of liberty and law" heretofore imposed from outside by Anglo-American hegemonic powers but lacking a strong, embedded domestic foundation in these energy-producing nations.[7] What new sort of norms and procedural rules may evolve out of their deepened petrostate interaction with increasingly Asian consumers, most importantly China, that are themselves at best fragile adherents to these liberal notions will be a key point of conjecture flowing from this chapter, to be further considered in the succeeding comparative chapter on major energy-consumer nations.

HEAVY ENERGY-EXPORT DEPENDENCE
OF THE EURASIAN PETROSTATES

To understand the central role that the major Eurasian energy producers play in their nations' broader political-economic relationship with the consumers of Asia, as well as the incentives that producers carry into that deepening transcontinental relationship, it is important to appreciate first the high, and generally rising, dependence of Eurasian petrostates on energy exports. As indicated in Table 5.1, each of the major Eurasian producers relies on oil and gas for at least two-thirds of its total national exports. Comparable ratios for the two major Organization for Economic Cooperation and Development (OECD) energy exporters, Britain and the Netherlands, are only around 14 and 17

Table 5.1. Heavy and Rising Reliance of Major Eurasian Producers on Oil and Gas Exports

	Fuel/Total Exports (percent)			
	1995	2000	2008	1995–2008
Eurasian Producer				
Kazakhstan	25	46	94	+69
Russia	57	52	67	+10
Saudi Arabia	85	95	93	+ 8
Iran	86[a]	95	80	−6
OECD Reference Cases				
Netherlands	8	9	17	+ 9
Britain	6	9	14	+ 8

Source: WTO website; and International Monetary Fund, Destination of Trade database.
Notes: (1) Oil and gas export dependence in the other largest GCC economies (UAE, Qatar, and Kuwait) is similar to that for Saudi Arabia. (2) Fuel export figures are from the WTO website, while total exports are derived from International Monetary Fund, *Direction of Trade Statistics* database.
[a]Initial figures for Iran are 1997 figures, due to statistical inadequacy.

percent respectively. They thus cannot qualify as petrostates, in the narrow sense of the term.

Trends over time in oil and gas export dependence are also important. Kazakhstan has clearly experienced an unusually rapid rise in energy export dependence, due to expanding production in the relatively new Tengiz and Kasharaganak fields. Yet reliance on energy exports has risen significantly since the mid-1990s in all the major Eurasian producing nations except Iran. Only international sanctions appear to have recently inhibited this general tendency toward increasing oil and gas export reliance, which also prevailed even in Iran until after 2000.[8] Dependence on oil and gas exports also increased in the major OECD exporting nations—Britain and the Netherlands—but from a much lower level of initial energy-export reliance than in the petrostates.

OIL AND GAS PRODUCERS: COMPARATIVE PERSPECTIVES ON EURASIAN ENERGY INTERDEPENDENCE

The major oil and gas producers of the world share a heavy common, and generally rising, dependence on energy exports—a pattern that is unusual for producers generally, when seen in comparative perspective. That common dependence qualifies them as petrostates. Social, economic, and political patterns in these major exporting nations do, however, covary with one another in other major respects, many of which are presented in Table 5.2. Broadly speaking, there are two varieties of petrostate: (1) large, populous nations with substantial financial requirements for economic development, as well as national defense, such as Russia; and (2) smaller countries, often very affluent, with less substantial domestic financial needs, such as the UAE.

The domestic political economies of the major Eurasian energy exporters have changed significantly over the past twenty years, in ways that help to promote long-term prospects for energy interdependence with East and South Asia. While becoming more dependent on Asian markets, the producers are also developing and consuming energy at home, thus acquiring stakes in the construction, hydrocarbon-processing, and energy-efficiency skills at which Asian consuming states are so proficient. To capture these important nuances and correctly portray the shifting configurations of producer national interest, I thus turn to country-specific analysis, starting with that most geopolitically important petrostate, the Russian Federation.

Russia: The Ultimate Destabilizing Petrostate?

The Russian Federation looms as a giant—not only among petrostates but among nations of the world more generally. It is, after all, geographically the largest nation on earth, stretching across nine time zones, and covering more than a ninth of the earth's entire land area.[9] Once heavily reliant on its military arsenal for global leverage, Russia has developed major influence in international energy geopolitics as well. It recently has been alternating with Saudi Arabia as the largest energy exporter in the world. With nearly $307 billion in oil and gas exports during 2008, a more than tenfold increase within a decade,[10] Russia is the only energy-surplus nation numbered among either the G8 or the five permanent members of the UN Security Council.

Russia also has a distinctive geographical centrality that is synergistic with its extraordinary size and makes it inevitably important in global geopolitics. The country lies precisely in the middle of the Eurasian land mass—literally astride Mackinder's heartland. The Russian Federation borders on fourteen countries by land (Norway, Finland, Estonia, Latvia, Lithuania, Poland, Belarus, Ukraine, Georgia, Azerbaijan, Kazakhstan, China, Mongolia, and North Korea) and shares maritime borders with Japan (by the Sea of

Table 5.2. Petrostate Profiles

A. Destabilizing?

	Population (millions)	Under 20/ Over 65 (percent)	Unemployment (percent)	GDP (Per Capita)	Military (active duty personnel)
Russia	140	21/13	7.6	10,602	1,046,000
Iran	75	34/5	14.6	4,739	523,000
Iraq	31.46	48/3	15.3***	2,629	245,782
Venezuela	29	40/5	12.1	13,113	115,000

B. Intermediate

	Population (millions)	Under 20/ Over 65 (percent)	Unemployment (percent)	GDP (per capita)	Military (active duty personnel)
Nigeria	158	52/3	4.9***	1,311	80,000
Saudi Arabia	26.2	40/3	10.8	16,531	233,500
Kazakhstan	15.7	30/7	5.5	8,081	49,000

C. Stabilizing?

	Population (millions)	Under 20/ Over 65 (percent)	Unemployment (percent)	GDP (per capita)	Military (active duty personnel)
UAE	4.7	26/1	4.0**	50,910	51,000
Kuwait	3	33/3	2.2*	38,359	15,500
Qatar	1.5	29/2	0.5	83,880	11,800

Reference

	Population (million)	Under 20/ Over 65 (percent)	Unemployment (percent)	GDP (per capita)	Military (active duty personnel)
Netherlands	16.6	23/16	5.5	46,882	37,368
Norway	4.8	25/16	3.6	86,082	26,450

Sources: International Institute for Strategic Studies. *The Military Balance,* 2011; World Bank. *World Development Indicator,* http://devdata.worldbank.org; and Central Intelligence Agency, *The World Factbook,* https://www.cia.gov.library/publications/the-world-factbook/, accessed August 2011. *Notes:* * Figure is for 2004 due to data availability. *** Figure is for 2008 due to data availability. **** Figure is for 2007 due to data availability. ***** Figure is for 2009 due to data availability.

Okhotsk) and the United States (by the Bering Strait) as well. Significantly, eight of Russia's neighbors were also former constituent parts of the former Soviet Union, and the additional three were nominally independent members of the Soviet bloc. Thus, embedded infrastructure and personal networks—the heritage of history—intensify Moscow's inclination and capability to assume dominion over surrounding nations, and indeed over the sprawling landmass at the center of which it lies.

Russia, as a nation in wrenching transition from socialism to capitalism, and to advanced industrial standing, has pressing social, economic, and (self-perceived) national security needs. Medical care has deteriorated precipitously since the collapse of the Soviet Union, with male mortality rates now among the highest in the industrialized world.[11] Infrastructure has also deteriorated, and state authorities consider that unmet national security needs are high.

Russia is, however, exceptionally well endowed with energy resources, as many of its neighbors also are. It has, as we have seen, the largest proven natural gas reserves in the world, with much of Siberia still promising in that respect, yet remarkably unexplored. Russia also has the second largest coal reserves on earth and the eighth largest global oil reserves. With four of the longest rivers in the world (the Ob, the Irtysh, the Yenisei, and the Volga) it has immense hydroelectric potential, concentrated in Siberia and the Far East. Given the crowded agenda of pressing perceived national needs and the scale of the tasks at hand, Russia has strong incentives to harness energy as a strategic tool for nation building and national aggrandizement, especially toward large-scale consumers lacking adequate domestic hydrocarbon reserves. It thus lies uniquely at the Asian nexus of energy and geopolitics.

RUSSIA'S RISING ENERGY DEPENDENCE

Given Russia's bountiful energy resource endowment, its portfolio of energy-intensive industries such as steel, petrochemicals, and aluminum production, as well as the general inefficiency of its economy just emerging from socialism, that sprawling nation, not surprisingly, both produces and consumes huge quantities of energy domestically. It has the world's eleventh largest economy, in terms of nominal GDP, and the eighth largest in terms of purchasing power parity. Yet it ranks fourth in electric power generation and stands third in overall energy consumption.[12]

Russia is, to be sure, the world's largest energy exporter. Yet domestic pressures to cross-subsidize domestic consumption from export revenue, to divert resources quantitatively from exports to domestic use, and to harness energy resources as a vehicle for generating state revenue for unrelated purposes continually bias Moscow's international energy policy calculus. They motivate Russian policymakers to demand the highest possible prices and the most expansive possible ownership rights from foreign partners, in the absence of countervailing diplomatic or geopolitical considerations favoring Moscow. These parochial domestic pressures, in short, provoke Russia to behave as a destabilizing petrostate.

Despite continual domestic pressures for consumption at home, Russia has, since the waning of the Cold War in the 1990s, become an ever more important energy exporter—supplying 40 percent of the global increase in oil consumption between 2000 and 2004, for example.[13] Energy has also assumed a more and more substantial position in the Russian national economy. Oil and gas exports rose, as a share of total Russian exports, from 57 to 67 percent between 1995 and 2008. Oil and gas production also now generate well over 20 percent of Russian GDP, and provided nearly half of national government revenue in 2010.[14] Russian energy is thus of increasing consequence, both for Russia itself and for the world as a whole.

Vladimir Putin systematically began to transform energy into a major tool of Russian foreign policy and domestic economic stabilization during his first presidential tenure (1999–2008), as noted in Chapter 3. Given Russia's resource endowments and geopolitical situation at the heart of the Eurasian world island, as described above, this geoeconomic approach appears to be a rational strategy, from the Russian standpoint. A lingering question, however, is what implications the distinctive domestic incentive structures of Russia in the energy sphere—rendered explicit and coherent under Putin—have for international affairs, for global energy markets, and especially for Asia, the dominant emerging energy market of the entire world.

The evidence presented here suggests, as indicated above, that Russia has strong incentives to behave as a destabilizing petrostate, since it is a producer heavily dependent on energy-export income. This dependence, we may hypothesize, makes Russia prone to press aggressively, and at times unrealistically, for energy price increases and to use strategic, often collusive means to achieve its energy-related objectives. Russia of course is a large nation, with major developmental needs, that likewise has national security incentives to press for increased revenue from energy. It also has the political-military resources to generate uncertainties in international affairs that can encourage higher prices in energy markets.

Russia's incentives to act as a destabilizing petrostate, often troublingly apparent in the Putin presidential years and subsequently, can potentially be mitigated by astute strategies pursued by its partners, sensitive to Moscow's enduring domestic weaknesses and inefficiencies. Russia has, for example, an acute need for foreign capital investment and technology to unlock its wealth of natural resources. It also has chronic energy efficiency problems. Asia, especially Japan and South Korea, has substantial ability to address these problems, especially capital supply and energy efficiency, and could thus potentially have a moderating impact on Moscow's global energy role in coming years.

The critical uncertainty for the Russian petrostate in the early 2010s was its willingness to turn eastward—to muster sufficient resources and diplomatic effort to consummate the deep prospective economic complementarity that energy potentially creates for it with Asia. Conflicts with Japan and China over Sakhalin II and the Eastern Siberia Pipeline suggested that a meeting of the minds between Moscow and some of the key Asian nations was yet to be achieved. Yet with energy demand rising across Asia, and turbulence in the Middle East continuing, Asian interest in Russia's petrostate and its capacity to supply oil and gas to the East is certainly persisting as well.

Kazakhstan: Rising Producer Literally in the Middle

Kazakhstan is one of the greatest energy storehouses on earth. It is home to the largest prospective oil field on earth outside the Middle East, and the largest oil discovery in the world since Alaska's Prudhoe Bay strike in 1979. It is also the largest uranium producer in the world, with 12–19 percent of global reserves.[15] The country also has substantial reserves of both natural gas and coal.

Despite its massive energy potential, Kazakhstan is also a highly constrained nation in physical terms. The ninth largest country in the world, it stretches over an area greater than all of Western Europe. Yet the country is totally landlocked—the largest landlocked nation on earth. And with only 15 million people, it has a low population density of about 2 people per square mile, compared to 12.8 and 134 respectively for the United States and Japan. Kazakhstan's combination of bountiful energy resources and limited population is similar to that of the stabilizing GCC producers of the Persian Gulf. This pattern contrasts markedly to the circumstances of populous producing nations like Iran, who tend to be the price hawks of OPEC.

Although the main trading routes of ancient days operated further to the south, Kazakhstan lies in the very heart of the Eurasian continent, close to the geographical midpoint, from east to west, of the classical Silk Road. It is neighbored clockwise from the north by Russia, China, Kyrgyzstan, Uzbekistan, and Turkmenistan, while also bordering on a substantial portion of the Caspian Sea. Across the Caspian, only Iran stands between Kazakhstan and the Persian Gulf. Its other prospective maritime outlet routes stretch across southern Russia to the Black Sea or alternatively down the Caspian and along the BTC pipeline through Azerbaijan and Georgia to Turkey's Mediterranean coast at Ceyhan.

Like many of the major energy-producing states, Kazakhstan is ethnically diverse and a newcomer to the international stage, with a relatively shallow sense of national identity. The country is home to 131 nationalities, including Kazakhs, Russians, Ukrainians, Uzbeks, Koreans, and Tatars, with much of the diversity stemming from Stalin's deportation policies of the 1930s. Across most of its early history, Kazakhstan was inhabited by nomadic tribes; by the mid-nineteenth century, however, it had been fully absorbed into the Russian Empire. During the twentieth century, it was the site of numerous major Soviet undertakings, including Khrushchev's Virgin Lands campaign, the Baikonur Cosmodrome, and the Semipalatinsk "Polygon," the Soviet Union's major nuclear weapons testing site. Many of Kazakhstan's sons also fought and died in World War II—playing a central role in the 1941–1942 defense of Moscow, for example—thus cementing Kazakhstan's Soviet identity in blood. And close to 40 percent of the Kazakh population in the early 1990s was ethnic Russian. Only on December 16, 1991, did conservative, cautious Kazakhstan declare its independence—the last Soviet republic to leave Moscow's formal embrace.

LEADERS AS CATALYSTS FOR CONTINENTALISM

Kazakhstan's one and only president since independence has been Nursultan Nazarbayev, born in 1940.[16] Before independence, Nazarbayev had served five years as chairman of the Council of Ministers of the Kazakh SSR (1984–1989), and then for two years as first secretary of the Kazakh Communist Party (1989–1991) in his own right. In a nation with multiple Kazakh tribes, myriad ethnic groups, a fractious bureaucracy, weak political parties, and shallow national traditions, Nazarbayev has been a singular unifying figure and a decisive, albeit authoritarian ruler. Kazakhstan under Nazarbayev has consistently ranked low on Freedom House and other human rights indices,[17] although it hosts well over $60 billion in foreign investment and is one of the few major energy-producing states that has allowed majority ownership rights to foreign investors. Multinationals active in Kazakhstan have included Chevron, Exxon Mobil, Agip, Inpex, Lukoil, and China National Petroleum Corporation.

Near-personal control of the massive income stream from his nation's rising energy production has greatly enhanced Nazarbayev's leverage over other social actors in Kazakhstan and his standing in international affairs.[18] And with proven reserves of almost 40 billion barrels, ninth in the world,[19] concentrated particularly in the gigantic yet still unexploited Kashagan offshore field, Nazarbayev's nation can greatly expand its current oil production.

Kazakhstan's natural resource wealth, of course, is of long-standing provenance—it has lain dormant within the earth since the late Devonian era, over 350 million years ago. Not even in Soviet days was that great wealth substantially exploited. Yet the Eurasian critical junctures of the 1970s, 1980s, and 1990s, as we have seen, created a vastly different and more dynamic world. Both China and India are nearby, and their economic reforms created a new continental dynamic, by the mid-1990s, of steadily rising energy demand from near neighbors.

Kazakhstan's central, albeit landlocked geopolitical position within Eurasia, nestled in the shadow of neighboring Russia, creates a national imperative for entrepreneurial, multidimensional foreign policy, using energy resources for leverage. That imperative Nazarbayev not only intuitively grasped but acted on with gusto, demonstrating the influential role that leadership can at times play in furthering continentalism. As first a provincial party boss in a remote corner of the then–Soviet Union, a decade before China and India emerged as major oil importers, and later as leader of a fledgling nation, he played a pivotal role in finalizing a historic 1993 agreement with the U.S. company Chevron to develop the huge Tengiz oil fields at the head of the Caspian Sea, now sixth largest in the world.[20] While maintaining cordial relations with Mikhail Gorbachev, and then Boris Yeltsin, Nazarbayev likewise negotiated Kazakhstan's peaceful exit from the Soviet Union, despite the USSR's substantial political-military interests there, including its major cosmodrome and nuclear testing site. Nazarbayev also shrewdly developed positive relations with China across the 1990s, following the collapse of the Soviet Union, using a central role in founding both the Shanghai Five (1996) and the Shanghai Cooperation Organization (SCO, 2001) to deflect Russian suspicion.[21] Moscow, after all, was included in those bodies, while Washington was not.

Nazarbayev also supervised the dismantling of Kazakhstan's nuclear arsenal, inherited from the Soviet Union, thereby neutralizing regional tensions.[22] Through this step he gained favor not only with the United States and its NATO allies, but also with Japan, the only direct victim of nuclear weapons. Tokyo built much of his new capital at Astana with its Official Development Assistance funds and added a major hospital at Semipalatinsk, near the former Soviet nuclear testing site. The United Nations, a variety of nongovernmental organizations, and even media moguls such as Ted Turner, founder of CNN, also warmed to Nazarbayev's nuclear disarmament initiative, rooted in his fateful and unique decision to forswear the substantial nuclear armaments left on Kazakh soil as a post-Soviet successor state. The Kazakh leader has likewise reached out to diverse religious groups around the world, drawing ecumenical conferences thousands of miles to Astana, which enthusiasts termed the "Singapore of the Steppes," a veritable crossroads, to press for global arms reduction.[23] Nazarbayev also used transnational ethnic ties and complementary energy interests to deepen relations with the two Koreas as well.

NEW ENERGY PROSPECTS IN A RECONFIGURED EURASIA

Due to the collapse of the Soviet Union—and Nazarbayev's appreciation of the new geoeconomic opportunities it opened—Kazakhstan thus gained scope for broad, multidirectional balance-of-power diplomacy, capitalizing on its central position between Russia, China, and India. This location, once remote to international transactions, suddenly attained crucial political-economic relevance as border tensions relaxed in the post–Cold War world and the populous Asian powers began to grow explosively. Kazakhstan's leverage was further enhanced by its substantial latent potential to expand oil production—possibly for more than a decade—particularly due to the as-yet undeveloped potential of the Kashagan field, expected to come online in the mid-2010s and to remain in production until 2042.[24]

The Kashagan field, discovered in 2000, holds prospective commercial reserves of 9–16 billion barrels of recoverable oil. That would give it between one-third and one-half of the proven oil reserves of Kazakhstan as a whole, or around half of the 28 billion barrels of proven reserves in the entire United States.[25] Kashagan will likely reach its peak production level of 1.5 million barrels per day around 2020.

The Kashagan project, although highly strategic for both Kazakhstan's future and that of continental Eurasia more generally, is still fraught with technical, financial, and political uncertainty. The field lies fifty miles offshore, in a demanding environment, where sea ice is omnipresent for a third of the year, and temperatures fluctuate from −35°C (−31°F) in winter to 40°C (104°F) in summer. Poisonous hydrogen-sulfide concentrations five times those considered dangerous in the Persian Gulf also complicate exploration and, potentially, production as well. Deposits are buried more than two miles beneath the seabed, under pressure 500 times that of the atmosphere at sea level.[26]

Not surprisingly, given the physical challenges, development costs at Kashagan are huge, with the whole project ultimately expected to cost more than $130 billion over its forty-year lifetime.[27] Those estimates more than tripled during the first decade of project development. A consortium of six firms, including Kazakhstan's own national energy company, KazMunaiGaz, is sharing the substantial risk, coupled with huge prospective reward, across five nations.[28] Yet looming political uncertainties, with President Nazarbayev in his seventies, and the shadow of possible nationalization on the horizon, still complicate a timely implementation of the mammoth project.[29]

Although long-run supply options still remain unclear, Kazakhstan's energy infrastructure links with the rest of Eurasia are deepening rapidly, giving critical momentum to continentalism. In the summer of 2009, the first major oil pipeline from the head of the Caspian Sea to China was completed—inaugurating a multi-trunked, 1.2 million bbl/day transcontinental energy network stretching all the way to Shanghai. Such a development appeared fantastical to seasoned area specialists little more than a decade previously.[30] Plans are underway to double that transcontinental capacity by 2014, supplied largely by Chinese equity oil from the fourteen PRC-affiliated production companies currently operating in Kazakhstan.[31] In December 2009, a 7,000-kilometer gas pipeline from Turkmenistan northeastward, across Uzbekistan and Kazakhstan to China's east coast, was also completed and launched personally by Hu Jintao, Nazarbayev, and the other related national leaders. In 2010 that pipeline transmitted 10 billion cubic meters (bcm) of natural gas to China, with volume rising threefold, to 30 bcm, by 2012. A second parallel pipeline is also being planned.[32]

Apart from its plentiful reserves of oil and gas, Kazakhstan also has massive uranium reserves, as noted above. These are attractive to all the major Asian nations, most of whom are continuing with ambitious nuclear expansion plans, despite the 2011 Fukushima tragedy. China is Kazakhstan's largest global customer, with contracts for over 55,000 tons of uranium across the next decade, while Russia, Japan, Korea, and India are also notable.[33]

As the new Eurasian energy geopolitics emerges, with China and India as rising consumers, Kazakhstan, at the heart of Central Asia, thus stands literally in a pivotal position, along a variety of resource dimensions. It could potentially align with neighboring Russia and Iran—both destabilizing producers—to force energy prices higher and gain more favorable conditions for the difficult and expensive Kashagan project now pending. Or Kazakhstan could evolve as a conciliatory, stabilizing producer like Saudi Arabia and the GCC states, trading concessions to consuming nations for support in its eternal geopolitical struggle for autonomy in the landlocked heart of Asia. As the wily Nursultan Nazarbayev would have it, Kazakhstan's ultimate choice remains unclear from the outside, yet of pivotal significance to the future of the New Silk Road.

Saudi Arabia: A Stabilizing Petrostate?

No nation looms larger in the geopolitics of international energy than Saudi Arabia. It is the largest oil producer in the world, pumping over 10 million barrels daily in 2010,[34] and still holding over 70 percent of OPEC's surplus capacity.[35] It is also the largest oil exporter on earth, supplying 8.7 million barrels of oil daily to the international market, and lies at the geographical heart of the compact Persian Gulf energy province, which provides 35 percent of all the oil moving in international trade.[36]

Looking to the future, Saudi Arabia holds by far the largest oil proven oil reserves in the world, with 265 billion barrels, or nearly 20 percent of total global reserves—over eight times the level of the United States, with much of the Empty Quarter (Rub al-Khali) remaining unexplored.[37] Its current production includes the largest oil field in the world and the largest offshore field on earth,[38] as well as the world's largest oil-loading terminal, at Ras Tanura. Saudi Arabia's gas reserves are also substantial (fifth largest in the world), but the Saudis are far more dominant in oil, with few incentives to prefer the substitution of gas for oil.

Oil also looms large for Saudi Arabia, relative to other sources of income and economic activity. The oil industry supplies around 90 percent of Saudi export earnings and roughly 80 percent of national budget revenues. It also generates a full 45 percent of national GDP, compared to 40 percent for the entire non-oil private sector. Saudi Arabia is thus in the truest sense a petrostate and has become emphatically more so over the past fifty years.

Saudi Arabia, of course, is only one of six GCC nations, which collectively hold well over 30 percent of the world's oil reserves and nearly the same proportion of its natural gas. Kuwait and the UAE, in particular, are important in oil, as well as Qatar and the UAE in gas. Yet Saudi Arabia has by far the largest oil reserves and is as a result the most involved in the global political economy, as the key stabilizing petrostate. Consequently, the political-economic analysis presented here focuses on the Saudis, with only occasional reference to the other important GCC energy producers.

The general consensus in the remarkably sparse academic literature on petrostates in comparative perspective, reviewed above, is that they tend to be undemocratic, with governments, generally unresponsive to their inhabitants, that play a destabilizing role in international affairs. Few would argue that either Saudi Arabia, a self-advertised theocratic state still governed by a hereditary absolute monarchy, or any of its GCC counterparts is domestically liberal.[39] Yet many knowledgeable observers do see the Saudis as a positive, stabilizing force in the global political economy.[40] Their strong vested interest in oil's continuing central role in global energy usage, due to their massive reserves and limited domestic financial requirements, has traditionally enabled their country to serve as a swing producer in international oil markets. The pages that follow first examine that classical Saudi role as swing producer and then move on to consider the domestic political-economic foundations of the Saudi petrostate, how they are changing, and how they relate to the prospective future Saudi international role, especially in relation to the rest of Eurasia.

THE HISTORIC SAUDI ROLE AS STABILIZING SWING PRODUCER

Saudi Arabia's first commercial oil field was discovered at Dhahran in 1938, with the first tanker load of petroleum being exported in 1939, both handled by the U.S.-dominated CASOC (later Aramco) consortium. By late 1947, as American civilian energy consumption began to surge in the aftermath of World War II, even as American domestic producers persisted with their traditional exports, shortages began to develop at home in the United States.[41] American leaders recognized that Europe's recovery, and U.S. military requirements overseas, would ultimately require expanded Middle East production, preeminently from Saudi Arabia, where American firms had a dominant stake.[42] The Saudis, especially after the discovery of the Ghawar elephant field, largest in the world, in 1948—the year of Israel's birth and the first Middle East war—recognized both their substantial supply capacity and the strategic need for American political-military support. Thus, the special U.S.-Saudi relationship, and ultimately the Saudi role as stabilizing swing producer for the broader world, were born.

The core of Saudi Arabia's supply policy over the past half century has been threefold: (1) to serve as oil supplier of last resort for the international economy in times of true extremity; (2) to encourage world oil prices to move within stable parameters; and (3) to quietly support important strategic interests of the United States, in return for credible American guarantees for Saudi security. Saudi Arabia has worked consistently to ensure that ample producer income be maintained but that prices not rise so precipitously that the world macroeconomy was damaged, or that consumers move decisively toward hydrocarbon alternatives.

This moderate, cooperative stance was evident during the Korean, Vietnam, Gulf, and Iraq wars, as well as World War II, when Saudi Arabia expanded production to accommodate U.S. military operations and directly supplied petroleum products to the U.S. military on a large scale in several cases.[43] The Saudis enlisted only reluctantly with the Arab oil embargo of Israel's supporters in 1973 and worked informally to limit its impact on the United States.[44] And they cooperated with the Reagan administration at crucial intervals during the 1980s in aligning world oil prices disadvantageously for the Soviet Union. This collaboration put excruciating financial pressure on the Soviets, just as the United States was intensifying its military buildup, thus facilitating the Soviet collapse that ended the Cold War.[45] During the 1990s Saudi Arabia was simultaneously also the largest single importer in the world of U.S. military equipment, America's largest market in the Middle East, and a strategic site from 1990 to 2003 for U.S. military bases. The air war over Afghanistan in 2001, for example, was coordinated by U.S. military air controllers from Prince Bandar Air Force Base in Saudi Arabia.[46]

Saudi Arabia's traditional tool for maintaining its flexible, geopolitically tinged swing producer role has long been to maintain around 1.5 to 2 million barrels per day of spare production capacity, often at short-term financial cost to itself. This slack has allowed Riyadh to satisfy suddenly emerging market demands that it considered legitimate and thus to put an upper lid on prices.[47] This spare capacity proved especially important after 1971, when pricing power in world oil markets began shifting from the Texas Railroad Commission to OPEC, since OPEC itself lacked an enforcement mechanism for its internal agreements and needed a large swing producer like the Saudis to play that coercive role.

Whether sufficient spare capacity can and will be maintained in Saudi Arabia is a key issue for global oil markets, and especially for Asia, which has accounted for the bulk of increases in world oil demand since the early 1990s, the period of the Asian financial crisis excepted.[48] Signs during the late 2000s were moderately encouraging, as the Saudis completed their five-year, $100 billion expansion of domestic oil production capacity to 12.5 million barrels per day.[49] King Abdullah has given the stabilizing producer role his explicit, personal support.[50] Yet the longer term remains more uncertain.[51]

Apart from maintaining excess production capacity to cope with contingencies, the obverse side of Saudi Arabia's stabilizing producer role is forcing other producers to collaborate. This is especially difficult, as suggested above, in the case of large, populous nations undergoing social transition, like Russia and Iran. The Saudis have, however, recently been quite successful in this task, inducing OPEC during 2009 to cut production by 4.2 million barrels per day amid the global financial crisis, for example, so as to boost oil prices from their low that year of around $32 to over $70 a barrel.[52]

Apart from its technical role in encouraging OPEC toward moderation in energy pricing, and its geostrategic role in expanding production to accommodate U.S. political-military concerns, Saudi Arabia has also served as a stabilizing petrostate by supporting a broad range of multilateral functions in world affairs. It helped organize the International Energy Forum (IEF), a diverse and important body involving industry leaders and policymakers of both producer and consumer nations, and has hosted the IEF Secretariat in Riyadh since that body's inception in 2003.[53] Saudi Arabia has also strongly endorsed and supported the IEF's Joint Oil Data Initiative database project, which disperses detailed oil and gas information from more than ninety nations and thus promotes transparency in hydrocarbon markets worldwide.[54] To further enhance its stabilizing global role, Saudi Arabia also serves as the one OPEC member of the G20 and has permanent representation on the executive boards of both the International Monetary Fund and the World Bank.

Despite OPEC protestations to the contrary, it does appear that the OPEC oil cartel, and no doubt Saudi Arabia specifically, were late to grasp the rising importance of Asian demand in world oil markets during the 1990s, or the converse deflationary impact of the Asian financial crisis of 1997–1998 when it first occurred. In December 1997, for example, OPEC increased its quota by 2.5 million barrels per day (10 percent), effective January 1, 1998, even though virtually all of Asia, OPEC's principal source of incremental demand for most of the previous decade, was in serious economic crisis. An important issue going forward is clearly how conscious OPEC—preeminently Saudi Arabia—will be of Asian consumer demand patterns, and what mechanism it will have for accommodating that increasingly important factor. The U.S.-centric mechanism of the past half century—involving Saudi surplus capacity, swing producer behavior, and sensitivity to American requirements in return for U.S. security guarantees—has been stabilizing, for Asia as well as the United States and the broader world. Yet whether it can and will persist, or what the alternative might be as Asian markets become increasingly central for Saudi Arabia and OPEC while dependence on the United States declines, is an important question just now emerging.

SAUDI ARABIA'S CHANGING DOMESTIC EQUATION

Saudi Arabia's long history as a stabilizing petrostate, predating even the Korean War, has rested on important political-economic foundations within Saudi Arabia itself. Most important, perhaps, has been the Saudi royal family, which established a fateful and positive relationship with the United States through the historic, catalytic meeting between King Ibn Saud, the founder of modern Saudi Arabia, and President Franklin D. Roosevelt on board the U.S. cruiser *Quincy*, in the Great Bitter Lake of the Suez Canal, during February 1945.[55] The hospitality that Roosevelt showed to King Saud, and the mutual rapport that they developed, set the tone for broadly positive top-level relations that continued between the two countries throughout most of the ensuing five decades. Dwight D. Eisenhower, and his firmness in sending U.S. Marines into Lebanon in 1958 to stabilize that nation, following a Nasserite coup in Iraq, also impressed Saudi leadership. In 1990 President George H. W. Bush's "line in the sand" decision to send 600,000 troops to Saudi Arabia to defend the kingdom and to evict Saddam Hussein from Kuwait, also had a powerfully positive impact on Saudi royal leadership, especially King Fahd. Saddam's brutal invasion, after all, gave Iraq control over 19 percent of the world's oil and threatened Saudi Arabia's major oil fields, concentrated in the Eastern Province, directly adjacent to occupied Kuwait.[56]

Complementing the royal family's role in creating and sustaining a stabilizing petrostate in Saudi Arabia has been the system of "segmented clientelism" prevailing domestically.[57] Powerful princes can assume direct and exclusive responsibility for priority sectors of the political economy, creating "islands of efficiency" insulated from pressure-group intervention.[58] The Saudi Arabian Monetary Agency (SAMA) and the Saudi Basic Industries Corporation (SABIC) are often considered such enclaves. Direct royal supervision, through the Supreme Council for Petroleum and Minerals Affairs (SCPMA), has also been crucial in preserving the autonomy and managerial efficiency of Saudi Aramco, fostered by American managers from the 1930s on.[59]

Two leaders of modern Saudi Arabia have been especially adamant in protecting the islands of efficiency: King Faisal (1964–1975), and the current

King Abdullah (2005–). Abdullah, as crown prince, was said to prioritize technical expertise above established personal ties in his choice of advisors,[60] and was less directly beholden than Fahd to traditional relationships with the United States. Significantly, Abdullah's first international state visits as king were to China and India, signifying a possible shift in Saudi priorities toward the East, or at least a clear appreciation of Asia's emerging global role.

A particularly important corporate actor in the Saudi petrostate is Saudi Aramco, the state-owned national oil company, which holds a monopoly on domestic oil production and sales. Founded in 1933, Aramco was under full American consortium ownership and management until the mid-1970s, when it was nationalized.[61] U.S. executives remained with the firm until 1988, however, when a fully indigenized Saudi Aramco was officially established, by royal decree. Current high-level Saudi Aramco leaders, just retiring, thus had strong exposure to the United States—most of them being educated there—and were highly conversant with American management and cultural mores.

Although Aramco still maintains important U.S. commercial ties, and sells roughly 1 million barrels of oil daily destined for the United States, its human and commercial networks have diversified greatly over the past three decades, especially in downstream operations. In 1992, for example, Saudi Aramco acquired a 35 percent interest in Korea's Ssangyong Oil Refining Company; in 1994 a 40 percent interest in the largest Philippine refiner, Petron; and in 1996 a 50 percent stake in Corinth Refineries of Greece. It was only in 1998, nearly a decade after its international downstream expansion began that Saudi Aramco established Motiva Enterprises, its first major U.S.-based refining and marketing joint venture. And the Saudi energy giant has been surprisingly inactive in the U.S. since then, given its long historical association with American corporations, government, and education. Aramco has been active in Asia, however. It invested substantially in a joint-venture oil refinery project in the northeast city of Qingdao during 2008, and then opened a major joint-venture oil refining and petrochemical complex in Fujian during November, 2009.[62]

Saudi Aramco is also diversifying into non-oil energy businesses with non-Western firms. In 2005, for example, Saudi Aramco and Sumitomo Chemical of Japan signed a joint-venture agreement for the development of a large integrated refining and petrochemical complex on the Saudi Red Sea coast that when fully operational will produce 1.3 million tons per year of ethylene and 900,000 million tons per year of propylene, with future ventures to come.[63] The Chinese have recently invested $3 billion in an aluminum smelter in the southern province of Jizan.[64] Japan's Arabian Oil Company has also been operating in Saudi Arabia and the Neutral Zone between Saudi Arabia and Kuwait since 1958.[65] The traditional U.S. monopoly has thus been broken, succeeded by a much more global pattern of relationships, with an increasing accent on Asia.

Within what might be termed the Saudi petroleum community,[66] the other two key bureaucratic entities, apart from Saudi Aramco, are the SCPMA and the Ministry of Petroleum and Mineral Resources itself. The former body, chaired by the crown prince and also involving the ministers of foreign affairs and petroleum, has the wide-ranging and strategic mission of determining oil and gas production levels, overseeing Saudi Aramco itself. It thus has the key role within the Saudi kingdom in setting oil prices and insulating petrostate institutions from domestic political pressures.[67] The Ministry of Petroleum, directed since 1995 by Ali al-Naimi, is responsible for originating and implementing virtually all petroleum policy initiatives, although it is not directly responsible for pricing.[68] Both the Supreme Council and the Ministry of Petroleum are heavily staffed and led by technocrats with advanced overseas education, particularly in the United States,[69] thus contributing further nuance and expertise to the Saudi petrostate's stabilizing international role.

Apart from running energy-producing bodies like Saudi Aramco, the government of Saudi Arabia has also initiated the ambitious National Industrial Clusters Development Program "to grow and diversify the Saudi Arabian economy by developing targeted industrial clusters that leverage the Kingdom's resources" with its abundant oil money.[70] This effort is administered by SABIC, founded in 1976, which like Saudi Aramco is a royally favored island of efficiency.[71] Projects have been initiated in sectors where the Saudis see long-term global competitive potential and that also provide diversification from a narrow hydrocarbon focus. Five specific clusters were being developed during 2006–2011, including automobiles, construction, metals processing, plastic packaging, and consumer appliances.[72]

Looking to the future, the dangers to Saudi Arabia's stabilizing petrostate appear not to center on a lack of technical expertise, at least among the elite bureaucratic corps, which is concentrated in the globalized islands of efficiency within the country. There are deepening problems, however, elsewhere in the configuration of Saudi elite society. The royal family itself remains important in balancing various factions, legitimating change, and mediating relations with the broader world.[73] Yet polygamy, high birth rates, and liberal membership rules are creating a proliferation of princes—all of whom receive handsome stipends and benefits—that could generate increasingly serious financial and political pressures for the country in the future.

Every male descendant of patriarch Abdul Aziz bin Abdul Rahman Al-Saud, who founded the modern Saudi kingdom in 1932, qualifies for annual stipends around $500,000 each; unlimited flights aboard Saudia, the national flag-carrier airline; and preferential access at low prices to land expropriated by the kingdom. There are currently over 5,000 such princes, with thirty to forty new princes born every month.[74] These princes, as direct descendants of their kingdom's founder, not surprisingly tend to have a strong sense of entitlement. The royal family, as Lacey points out, "built the kingdom. It carries their name. It would hardly be surprising if a large number of princes found it difficult to distinguish between what was theirs and what belonged to the still-growing state."[75]

These embedded commitments to princes, based on their powerful and legitimized sense of entitlement, threaten to become a deepening financial problem, despite Saudi Arabia's oil riches—especially as the Saudi state has run budget deficits for most of the past thirty years.[76] They could also well become a deepening sociopolitical problem, as the income of the average Saudi citizen has been volatile.[77] King Abdullah reportedly considered curtailing princely allowances early in his tenure, over a decade ago, but these measures have not as yet decisively materialized.[78]

A related danger, both domestically and internationally, is the institutionalized power of conservative organizations dominated by well-connected families, many of them with royal links. Many economic organizations qualify, as most are public corporations, or heavily regulated. So do the Majlis al-Shurai (what passes for a parliament) and the Council of Saudi Chambers of Commerce, both dominated by nonreformist stakeholders.[79] Clientelist pressures appear to have grown substantially, outside the islands of efficiency, since the major expansion of the Saudi state, fueled by oil money, during the 1970s and the 1980s.[80]

Saudi religious bodies, which have also been fueled increasingly by oil money since the oil shocks of the 1970s, also potentially jeopardize Saudi Arabia's international role as a stabilizing petrostate. There are, first of all, as a broad class, the ulama, or clerical legal scholars who are indispensable to the Saudi state due to its unique theocratic character as the defender of the holiest sites of Islam. Government authorities have expended considerable effort in bureaucratizing and incorporating this politically crucial group to help stabilize the regime.[81] The role of the ulama as legitimizers appears to have increased substantially since the 1979 Salafist occupation of the Grand Mosque of Mecca and the ensuing Qatif riots, which compelled the royal family to take forceful yet controversial stabilization measures.

The response of Saudi authorities to the occupation of the Grand Mosque, the holiest religious site in Islam, was especially problematic. On November 20, 1979, it was occupied by an isolated yet radicalized group of 200 to 500 Salafists, who denounced the royal family for welcoming Western values, allowing foreign exploitation, and thus helping to dilute Islamic preeminence in the birthplace of Islam.[82] The group also criticized the ulama for accepting bribes from the royal regime and condemned them for using Islam to prop up the "treacherous" rule of the Sauds.[83]

The government turned immediately to the ulama for a ruling on a permissible response. Five days after the seizure, the clergy lifted the traditional ban on use of weapons in the mosque. After a two-week struggle involving room-to-room fighting among the 270 vaults and chambers beneath the mosque, in which 255 pilgrims, troops, and fanatics were killed and 560 injured, the dissidents were finally dislodged by Saudi National Guard troops, who outnumbered the Salafists by as many as 100 to 1.[84] The political and psychological impact of the trauma, needless to say, was severe, both because the siege continued so long and because the government was forced to use violence to suppress it—a shocking and blasphemous act, in the eyes of many Muslims. The seizure's political impact was amplified further by the Qatif riots in the kingdom's oil-rich Eastern Province, including a major confrontation between the National Guard and Shiites on Ashura, one of the Shiite holy days, even as the Mecca siege was going on.[85]

The beleaguered Saudi King Fahd was thus suddenly confronted by dissidence from two contrasting and unexpected directions—fundamentalists who had traditionally supported his regime, and a marginalized group of Shia with limited sociopolitical influence, yet with the momentum of the ongoing Iranian Revolution only a few hundred miles across the Persian Gulf behind them.[86] Following the controversial military suppression by the Saudi National Guard, the king responded first with sharp retribution, and then with new prerogatives for the Shias, provoking Wahhabi fundamentalist backlash.[87] In response, a vacillating King Fahd revoked those new prerogatives, due to security concerns from the Right. This ambivalence, coupled with royal willingness to allow the presence of American troops on Saudi soil for more than a decade following Saddam Hussein's invasion of Kuwait in 1990, stimulated rising criticism from younger, nonestablishment ulama known as *sahwa* (awakening clerics).[88] It also provoked a round of Sunni terrorism, as expressed in the 1996 Khobar Towers bombing, the 1996 Riyadh bombing, the 2000 attack on the USS *Cole* in Aden Harbor, and ultimately 9/11, when fifteen of the nineteen suicide attackers on the World Trade Center, the Pentagon, and potentially other U.S. Government centers were Saudi.

The fateful events of late 1979 and beyond also gave momentum to the religious foundations, likewise supported by the state and wealthy individuals in an increasingly generous fashion. This support was, of course, nominally in accordance with basic dictates of the Koran, as it had always been.[89] Yet the petrodollars flowing into Saudi Arabia in such massive amounts following the oil shocks of 1973 and 1979, coupled with the political shocks of the Iranian Revolution and the domestic violence described above, led to even greater affluence and legitimacy for these groups than they had previously enjoyed.[90] Although the Saudi government clamped down sharply on local terrorists and their support base following suicide bombing attacks in Riyadh during May 2003, radical Islam is historically embedded in Saudi Arabia, so reducing its influence will take time.[91]

Beyond elite groups, dangers also appear to lie in changes within the broader society beyond the professional and technocratic institutions. Saudi Arabia, as a still-feudal society now modernizing, faces the classic problem of political development to which Samuel Huntington directed scholarly attention more than forty years ago: the difficulty of creating and sustaining institutions to accommodate the explosive desire for participation and service delivery in changing, developing societies.[92] This challenge is especially delicate in Saudi Arabia and its neighbors across the Muslim world, because population is so rapidly growing and urbanizing, with the many young people joining the workforce finding it difficult to find jobs, in an expertise- and expatriate-dominated society. The problem is also intensified, as we have seen, by the rigidity and conservatism of preexisting institutions.

PROSPECTS TO LOOK EAST: SAUDI ARABIA AND THE BROADER WORLD

The security and interpersonal ties between Saudi Arabia's current elites and the West—particularly the United States—are deep, as the foregoing examination of the Saudi petrostate has shown. Yet so were the ties between the United States and the shah's regime in Iran, just over thirty years ago. It would likely take an upheaval similar to Iran's 1979 revolution to produce a sea change in Saudi Arabia's international alignments over the short run, even if

potential partners in East and South Asia desired such a shift. Such a transformation is not impossible, as the previous analysis has suggested, although
probably unlikely. Under almost any scenario, however, Asia has substantial
political-economic utility for Saudi Arabia that can only continue to grow,
particularly if relations with the West grow more problematic.

"With China," as Prince Turki al-Faisal, former Saudi ambassador to the
United States and brother to Foreign Minister Prince Saud al-Faisal, points
out, "there is less baggage, and there are easier routes to mutual benefits."[93] The
same can be said of most Saudi relationships with Asia, as opposed to those
with the United States. In contrast to relations with the West, the heritage of
earlier colonial rule and differences regarding Israel do not lie persistently in
the background, to continually complicate mutual dealings. Besides, Asian
states tend not to be judgmental about the authoritarian-feudal cast of domestic Saudi politics, while both Asia and the Saudis are pragmatic about
taking advantage of economic globalization.[94]

Energy is clearly the major factor for Saudi Arabia that is driving deeper
relations with Asia, and especially with the continent's two emerging and
highly populous giants, as well as with Japan. Asia, led by Japan and China,
after all, is the largest customer for Saudi oil—indeed, over three times as
much Saudi oil flows to Asia as to the U.S.[95] Saudi Aramco now does almost
half of its business in Asia and since 2004 has had most of its offices there.[96]
Apart from exports, it is also expanding downstream investments in Asia and
has minority interests in major refining operations in South Korea, China,
and Japan.

For both Saudi Aramco and Saudi Arabia more generally, Asia is attractive
for the ways it can help the Saudis diversify beyond their basic role as an oil
exporter and also economize on the substantial quantities of energy that they
use domestically. The Saudis are spending $400 billion over the 2009–2014
period to upgrade national infrastructure, including construction of four new
"economic cities."[97] Japanese and Korean construction firms are world class,
while China and India can provide cost-effective skilled and unskilled labor.
The Asians, with their efficiency levels, can also help the Saudis save increasingly valuable energy.

Islam is also a significant consideration attracting deepening Saudi interest
in Asia. Asia, after all, has the largest Islamic population of any continent.
India alone has around 160 million Muslims—15 percent of its population,
and over six times the entire population of Saudi Arabia itself. China has

an additional 20 million. And Indonesia has the largest Muslim population in the world—two-thirds as large as all the Middle Eastern countries combined, including Iran.[98]

How Saudi support for Islamic movements in Asia is propagated could influence Saudi relationships further east, with the concern being that wealthy but unmonitored private Saudi religious foundations could have a destabilizing impact on local societies. There are between 8,000 and 40,000 madrassas in India, for example, but concerns are being raised in India that Saudi financing may also be introducing increasingly radical curricula.[99] Saudi links to jihadi groups such as Lashkar-e-Taiba, which has staged terrorist attacks in India, as well as links to Kashmiri separatist movements, are also a concern. Similarly, China is also apprehensive about possible Saudi support for dissidents among Xinjiang's 8 million ethnic Uyghur Sunni Muslims.

SUMMARY

Saudi Arabia is a crucial petrostate, from a global perspective, as the largest oil exporter on earth, with by far the largest reserves. By virtue of its huge reserves and its surplus production capacity, the country is also the actor most capable of serving as a stabilizing swing producer, accommodating sudden surges of demand due to military conflicts and other emergencies, and otherwise stabilizing global prices. This function is extremely important to the advanced economies of the world, and especially to the United States, given its security responsibilities, as well as Asia, due to its heavy reliance on imported energy.

The key question for the world, and the focus of analysis here, is whether Saudi Arabia will function in future as the sort of stabilizing petrostate that it has been since OPEC gained global price-setting capabilities in the early 1970s. As we have seen, the Saudi bureaucracy is developing increasingly impressive technocratic capabilities, and Saudi Aramco is gaining a global reach. The royal family plays an important and largely positive mediating role among diverse domestic groups and with the broader world. Yet the proliferation of princes and the deepening intrusion of well-connected families into economic life are both straining public finances and crippling prospects for reform in this distributive state, even as populist pressures from below are rising. Religious foundations and other ostensibly charitable groups, their coffers swelling with petrodollars, also hold potential for inflaming the situation, as do awakening clerics (*sahwa*). That Saudi Arabia is looking east appears certain, but whether it can continue to be a stabilizing petrostate in a broader global context is by no means ensured. Future prospects may well rest on interaction with the Islamic world's most consequential destabilizing petrostate—Iran—to which I now turn.

Iran: Destabilizing Petrostate and Beyond

Few nations loom as large in the world of global energy, both now and for the foreseeable future, as Iran. Even in the face of international sanctions, it remains the third largest crude oil exporter in the world. The country has the second -largest proven conventional oil reserves on earth, after only Saudi Arabia, with over 137 billion barrels, or nearly 10 percent of the world's total.[100] It also boasts the second-largest natural gas reserves, with 16 percent of the world's natural gas.[101] Its location, astride the Strait of Hormuz at the entrance to the Persian Gulf, through which close to half of the world's oil exports pass, only enhances the geopolitical importance that its massive energy resources provide.

As in the case of other major producer nations reviewed in this chapter, Iran's economy and public finance system are highly dependent on hydrocarbons, as they have been since the country first began oil production in 1913. In 2010 , Iran's net oil export revenues exceeded $67 billion. Oil exports generated roughly half of Iran's government revenues, while crude oil and its derivatives accounted for 80 percent of Iran's total exports.[102] Iran can thus for many reasons be considered both a quintessential petrostate and a key link in the global relationship between energy and geopolitics.

Iran today, however, is a most unusual petrostate. It is a relatively large country, with a substantial and rapidly growing population of over 77 million.[103] The median age is only twenty-seven years, and over 24 percent of the population is under fifteen. That population has nearly tripled since the revolution of 1979 and continues to grow rapidly, at over 1.2 percent annually.

Iran is also urbanizing rapidly. Today its population is over 71 percent urban, compared to 46 percent in 1976, shortly before the revolution.[104] The country as a whole is also much more affluent in per capita GDP terms than was true three decades ago, with GDP per capita having more than doubled during that period.[105]

To make matters even more difficult for economic planners, Iran is also a pluralistic and highly mobilized society, politically speaking, with a populist political-economic cast dating from the revolution itself. Although the country is 89 percent Shiite Muslim, it is only 51 percent Persian, with Azeri, Gilaki, Mazandarani, Kurd, Arab, Baloch, and Turkmen residents, among others, constituting significant elements of a voluble, interactive population that had 43 million cell phones in 2008. Civil society—especially the mosques and the bazaars—is well organized, a middle class is emerging, and democratic politics, while imperfect, are much more advanced than in most neighboring countries of the Persian Gulf, Saudi Arabia in particular. There are striking similarities between today's volatile Iran and the turbulent, imperfect emerging democracy of Taisho Japan (1912–1931), which was extinguished by depression, military intervention, and escalating tension with surrounding states prior to World War II.[106] Among Iran's many troubling socioeconomic maladies are high unemployment, which averaged 14.6 percent in Iran during 2010, and high inflation, of 10.1 percent in the same year. Both naturally intensify pressures on the state for welfare-oriented policies.

The postrevolutionary Iranian bureaucracy also finds coherent, programmatic policy response to emerging social pressures difficult. It is more poorly institutionalized and trained than Saudi Arabia's emerging technocracy, for example, as well as deeply stovepiped and factionalized. Major government institutions dealing with energy, such as the Oil Ministry, Energy Ministry, and Atomic Energy Agency, have their own functionally differentiated tasks, yet pursue divergent political objectives, with all the perverse consequences that such disjuncts can entail. In addition, there is reportedly inadequate coordination on energy policy between responsible energy sector officials and the ministries of trade, transportation, housing, and industry and mining, as well as programmatic duplication in areas like renewable energy.[107] Even the Energy Supreme Council, established in 2003, does not appear to have yet established adequate policy coordination.[108]

The consequence of these strong sociopolitical pressures, mediated through a fractious, inadequate bureaucracy, has been perverse, inefficient domestic oil and gas policies. They have encouraged, as we shall see, massive subsidies to nonindustrial uses of energy that have eaten badly into export revenues and intensified Iran's incentives to seek higher energy prices, if necessary through political belligerence and threats.[109] The same domestic fiscal pressures have encouraged Iran to covertly exceed established OPEC quotas to generate additional revenue and to pursue alternative energy programs, including nuclear power, to relieve domestic energy-supply dilemmas. Domestic sociopolitical pressures, in a word, have strongly intensified postrevolutionary Iran's underlying geopolitical incentives to act as a destabilizing petrostate in world affairs.

To understand the fateful international implications and possible strategies for transforming the status quo, it is important to review first the domestic biases that have helped make Iran a destabilizing petrostate in international affairs. These biases are rooted, most importantly, in the massive energy subsidies that the Iranian government has condoned.[110]

The domestic oil subsidies themselves are, ironically, a heritage of the shah's regime, rising from 12 percent in 1972, just before the first global oil shock, to 96 percent in 1979, when Pahlavi was overthrown. Subsidies have been maintained at roughly the percentage level that they attained in the shah's last days, although efforts have been made periodically to cut them, most recently in December 2010. The economic problem is that they have been used more and more extensively, primarily by the wealthy and the rising middle class, and have been set at absolute levels that do not anticipate increases in global energy prices.[111]

The energy subsidy consumed an estimated 11 percent of GDP in 1997–1998, 17 percent in 1999–2000 (because of sharp world price increases), and 34 percent in 2009.[112] The benefits of these large and unaffordable energy subsidies largely accrue to the rich, in some years by a 12:1 ratio. Explicit (budgeted) consumer subsidies have amounted to only 1.5–4 percent of GDP in recent years.[113] Through rationing, President Ahmadinejad has been fighting to cut the total subsidy (of about $90–100 billion) by $40 billion while the Majlis is pressing to limit cuts to $20 billion,[114] although whether rationing is effective is open to serious question.

Gasoline prices in Iran were maintained at a retail price of around 38 U.S. cents per gallon from 2007 to late 2010 by rationing, at the behest of President Ahmadinejad, who opposed the price increases that economists advised. In December 2010 he approved a substantial price increase, although the price remained below market levels. Due to the combined effect of rigid, unrealistically low, subsidized domestic prices and soaring global market demand, the cost to the national treasury of gasoline and related oil and natural gas subsidies by 2009 approached $30 billion annually, or roughly 30 percent of Iran's entire governmental revenue, forcing some belated efforts at rationalization.[115]

A variety of perverse international effects have flowed from these subsidy policies. Iran's retail prices for gasoline, at around 40 cents per gallon for several years, have been only one-third of those prevailing in neighboring countries, leading naturally to extensive smuggling.[116] Due to the diversion of supplies elsewhere and the disincentives created by low prices to refining capacity expansion within Iran itself, Iran was forced to become a major and growing gasoline importer—the second largest in the world by late 2010, despite its massive domestic energy resources. For example, gasoline imports in 2009 were about 40 percent of total consumption annually, creating a deepening geopolitical vulnerability for Iran itself and costing the Iranian treasury $4.6 billion in that year.[117]

The macroeffects of the subsidy policies and the populist economic approach of the postrevolutionary government more generally, within the context of the profound sociopolitical transition occurring in Iran, have been striking. Domestic energy consumption for individual and commercial use has soared, while other, more economically productive uses of energy have declined in relative terms. During 1976, for example, households and commercial enterprises consumed 20.7 percent of Iran's energy. By 2000, however, that ratio had soared to 40 percent.[118] Usage of energy for transportation also increased, from 18.6 to 23.6 percent of total consumption.[119] Underlying these sharp changes were a fourfold increase in the number of registered vehicles—passenger cars and motorbikes included—with half of the increase in Tehran alone. All of these vehicles, of course, had access to subsidized petroleum, the support of which was meanwhile putting considerable financial strain on the national budget.

Parallel, equally inefficient postrevolutionary shifts were occurring with respect to electric power usage as well. In 1976, industry used 58 percent of all national electricity consumed in Iran, while households and commerce accounted for only 40 percent. By 2000 these ratios had reversed, with industry accounting for only 35 percent, and households and commerce for a full 54 percent.[120] This development was, above all, due to the expanded use of household appliances and refrigeration, especially in the rapidly growing cities, and in higher-income brackets. Although inspired by populist sentiments, the benefits of subsidies, in many cases, were flowing primarily to the well-to-do, rather than toward the poor.

These misaligned populist policies, which postrevolutionary governments have either created or exacerbated, produced a remarkable transformation in the political-economic structure of the Iranian petrostate. From 1970 to 1978, just before the revolution, between 85 and 90 percent of Iranian oil production was exported annually. Between 1982 and 2005, however, the same ratio fluctuated between 59 and 76 percent, declining from 72 to 65 percent between 2000 and 2005.[121] By the latter year, petroleum exports had fallen to around 25 percent of national GDP and 50 percent of the government budget, despite the steady rise in global oil prices. Increasingly, national oil export revenue was being used to cross-subsidize wasteful domestic consumption, resulting in deepening fiscal pressures on the Iranian state.

The postrevolutionary Iranian government has oscillated between populist steps taken to placate the masses and contradictory, piecemeal steps intended to arrest the economic irrationalities inherent in its energy policies. The current president, Mahmoud Ahmadinejad, has persistently aggravated the populist bias, often with perverse economic effects. In 2005, for example, the Majlis introduced sweeping energy and food subsidies, ostensibly to aid the poor, freezing prices retroactive to 2003 levels.[122] The cost of these subsidies proved to be enormous, as oil prices internationally continued to rise. In 2007, to reduce the spiraling costs, Iran introduced gasoline rationing, at the behest of President Ahmadinejad, rather than implementing the price increases recommended by economists and actually voted by the Majlis itself.

The abrupt new rationing steps led irate citizens to set fire in protest to at least twelve gasoline stations in Tehran alone,[123] and rapidly inspired a flourishing black market for gasoline. In January 2010, the government announced a major new effort to replace energy and food subsidies with targeted social assistance to help cut fuel subsidies, whose cost had spiraled to $45 billion annually.[124] In December 2010, it quadrupled the price of subsidized gasoline, to the equivalent of 40 cents per liter, and reduced the subsidized quantity provided by 15 percent.[125] Yet how effectively these new measures, cutting against the political bias of postrevolutionary Iran, could actually be implemented, or whether they could be sustained in the face of renewed increases in commodity prices, remains to be seen.

The postrevolutionary Iranian petrostate, in short, has a strong populist bias. A large, populous country in the throes of social transition, with an explosively growing population, Iran is experiencing a sharp domestic surge in energy demand. The populist bias of the current government and the weakness of the national bureaucracy, in the face of a highly mobilized society, make it difficult for the state either to resist pressures for subsidies or to formulate coherent programmatic alternatives. The line of least resistance for Tehran is to press for higher oil and gas prices internationally, even through disruptive political-economic tactics, and then to relieve internal tensions by cross-subsidizing rising domestic commodity prices, as Ahmadinejad has recently done. Iran thus has strong proclivities, rooted deeply in its geopolitical positioning and domestic political economy, to be a destabilizing petrostate in international affairs.

IRAN AND THE LOOK EAST OPTION

Although the shah of Iran and his regime cultivated good relations with China, they were deeply entwined with the West, as noted in Chapter 3. Richard Nixon considered the shah as proxy defender of the Persian Gulf, on behalf of the United States. The revolution of 1979, followed by the Iranian hostage crisis and bilateral military confrontations—not to mention Iranian state support for terrorism, hostility to Israel, and covert efforts to develop nuclear weapons—have since deeply estranged Tehran and Washington, inspiring new directions in Iranian diplomacy and economic life that give vitality to the deepening Eurasian continentalist arrangements now emerging.

East and South Asia have deepening attraction, naturally, for a postrevolutionary Iran disillusioned with and embargoed by the United States, in cooperation with many of its Western allies. This attraction is clearly manifest in contemporary trade patterns. In 2010, Iran's five largest markets, based largely on energy sales, were China (16.2 percent of Iranian exports), India (12.6), Japan (9.9), Turkey (6.8), and South Korea (5.1). Iran's largest Western market was Italy. Iran's most substantial suppliers, conversely, were the UAE (16.7 percent), China (17.4), Germany (7.6), South Korea (6.3), and Turkey (4.8).[126] The overwhelming share of Iranian trade was thus conducted with Asian nations—a sharp departure from prerevolutionary patterns.

Investment ties between Iran and continental Eurasia are also deepening, even as Western embargoes discourage commercial relations with the United States, Europe, and to some extent Japan. Italy signed a major $1 billion buyback deal for Darkhovin oil field development in 2001, but most of the energy development deals since then have been concluded with Asia or Russia. The largest Iranian oil discovery of the past thirty years was made onshore in 1999 at Azadegan, with potential production of 300,000 to 400,000 barrels per day for twenty years. In 2004 Japan obtained exclusive rights to develop the field but refrained from pursuing the $2.5 billion project under pressure from the Bush and Obama administrations. After futile talks with France's Total and Norway's Statoil, Iran has more recently been negotiating with China and Russia on Azadegan oil development, as on South Pars gas development. Iran also concluded a twenty-five-year, $100 billion agreement with China in 2004 to develop the Yadavaran oil field, with options on 150,000 barrels of oil per day.

Iran and India also initialed a large-scale gas deal and pipeline project, on which New Delhi equivocated in the face of American pressure in 2008, amid price and security complications. After the Indian hesitation, Iran and

Pakistan continued to talk, finally reaching an agreement on a bilateral pipeline in 2009. By July, 2011 Iran had completed work on its portion of the bilateral pipeline, and Pakistan was preparing to commence work on its segment.[127] Following the Iran-Pakistan accord, India invited Iran to resume negotiations.[128]

Diplomatically and politically, Asia has special attraction for Iran, in that it is a growing region of the world, with rising economic potential, yet only limited previous association with the Western political-economic interests against which the 1979 revolution was waged. Iran's preeminent diplomat, recent Foreign Minister Manouchehr Mottaki (August 2005–December 2010), is a graduate of Bangalore University in India and a former ambassador to both Japan and Turkey. Even President Mahmoud Ahmadinejad, generally provincial as he has proven to be, has spoken approvingly of the importance of deepened relations with Asia.[129]

Soon after Ahmadinejad assumed the presidency in October 2005, his first vice president, Parviz Davudi, stressed a "look east (*negahe be shargh*) stance with a Eurasian tinge, emphasizing plans to bolster ties with East Asian countries, Central Asian republics, and Russia.[130] Ahmadinejad visited Tajikistan, India, Pakistan, Sri Lanka, China for the 2010 Shanghai Expo, and Turkmenistan to attend the inauguration ceremony for the second natural gas pipeline between Iran and Turkmenistan.[131] He also attended two SCO annual summit meetings as an observer and participated in the D8 summit of developing nations and in the 2010 Asian security summit.[132] He received Russia's Putin, Indonesian President Susilo Bambang Yudhoyono, Turkish Premier Erdogan, and Malaysian Prime Minister Datuk Seri Abdullah Ahmad Badawi, among a variety of world figures.[133]

In the wake of escalating Western sanctions, Iranian relations with China, in particular, are taking on more prominence, driven by a rapidly deepening, energy-based trade relationship. Chinese trade with Iran grew nearly 12-fold, from under $2.5 to nearly $30 billion, between 2000 and 2010, while Russia's trade with Iran grew only 1.9 times, Japan's 2.2 times, and Korea's 3.1 times. Meanwhile, American trade with Iran grew only four percent, over the course of an entire decade, showing the impact of recent sanctions.[134]

The PRC's permanent membership on the United Nations Security Council is one key factor in strengthening Beijing's relations with Teheran, as that standing allows China to inhibit seriously damaging sanctions through its veto power. The PRC's general willingness to supply technology and capital to Iran, in return for energy, is a second factor strengthening the bilateral relationship, as it shields Iran from international pressure, although determined

U.S. efforts intermittently inhibited traditional Chinese support for Iran from mid-2010.[135] Overall, China has emerged in recent years as Iran's most significant economic partner and diplomatic protector, with that relationship likely to deepen in coming years.

The central problem for Iranian relations with Asia, including China, is precisely Tehran's inclination to be a destabilizing petrostate, a stance seriously in tension with the predictability that Asia naturally desires as a high-volume, increasingly important consumer. Asia, however, does, on a more hopeful note, have the wherewithal to help alter the Iranian stance. A central reason for Iran's standing as a destabilizing petrostate is precisely that it is highly energy inefficient, for political reasons that are difficult for existing leadership to finesse. Energy consumption there is 6.5 times the global average, per unit of GDP.[136] And consumption has increased more than eightfold since the revolution, substantially outpacing growth of GDP itself. Expanding domestic energy usage, legitimated by the egalitarian, resource-nationalist policies of the 1979 revolution, is badly constraining the growth of oil and gas export income, the country's ticket to international autonomy, even as Western pressures on Iran intensify in the context of the dispute over its nuclear policies.

Asia, particularly Japan, has state-of-the-art technology for improving energy efficiency, in broad sectors ranging from industrial process controls to the design of home appliances. It also has pioneered energy-saving systemic innovations, such as expanded use of light rail in urban areas, as well as high-speed intercity rail transport. Railway systems are the great weakness of Iranian transportation—one that Northeast Asia is uniquely qualified to address. China has already built an extensive subway system for Tehran, Iran's capital and the city with the most pressing, energy-consuming urban transportation problems, just as Japan previously did for Dubai in the neighboring UAE.[137] Systematic Japanese, Chinese, and Korean assistance in improving Iranian energy efficiency and transportation systems, in return for enforceable restrictions on Iranian nuclear development with potential military applications, could constructively be on the global policy agenda and could serve as a means of productively deepening intra-Asian ties, while simultaneously also contributing to world peace.

CONCLUSION

Over the preceding pages I have reviewed the domestic political economies of four important petrostates—Russia, Kazakhstan, Saudi Arabia, and Iran.

These are all major energy-exporting nations, with critical prospective importance to the Eurasian future. We have considered their domestic resource endowments, their interest-group structure, and their administrative configurations, especially as those relate to energy policy, on the premise that subnational structure matters profoundly in orienting foreign policy, and ultimately in shaping the configuration of international relations itself. We have also catalogued the resulting dispositions of these producer nations to support or resist deepening ties with the Asian consumers that are growing so important for them.

The sort of comparative analysis of petrostates undertaken here is quite unusual in the scholarly literature. Others have surveyed individual petrostates like Russia in detail.[138] Still others have examined petrostates comparatively, with an eye to understanding their antidemocratic propensities and the structural determinants behind that tendency.[139] Yet few have considered the implications of domestic structure for foreign energy policy, especially for Middle Eastern, Central Asian, and Russian approaches to Asia, or the implications more generally of producer nation domestic structure for the stability of the international system as a whole.

In looking at major petrostates comparatively, our principal finding is that they can be broadly divided into stabilizing petrostates and destabilizing petrostates. The stabilizing variety are generally smaller nations, such as the members of the GCC in the Persian Gulf, which have small populations, large resource endowments, and stable political systems. Saudi Arabia at the moment qualifies—fatefully, for the international economy—although the future prognosis is uncertain.

Destabilizing petrostates are larger nations, with substantial populations, that face major developmental and national security demands, placing serious consequent strain on government finances. They are prone to promote sharp price increases or to engage in provocative political-military behavior that destabilizes energy pricing and supply parameters of the international political economy. Russia and Iran fall conspicuously into this category, as Saddam Hussein's Iraq once also did. Iraq today, as well as Kazakhstan, are in an intermediate classification, yet have socioeconomic profiles such that they could easily evolve in the destabilizing direction also.

We have found, of course, important nuances of difference among the nations in each category. Saudi Arabia, by virtue of its size, population, and domestic institutional complexity, has greater prospect of moving from the stabilizing to the destabilizing category than do neighboring GCC petrostates such as the UAE or Qatar—a Saudi Arabian transformation of that sort would clearly have catastrophic consequences for international affairs. Such a change is inhibited, however, by islands of efficiency in the Saudi system, like Saudi Aramco, SAMA, and SABIC, whose political viability is reinforced by both the royal family and transnational backing.

Among the current destabilizing petrostates, geopolitical considerations and domestic structure may well inspire Russia to a more proactive, disruptive role in international energy affairs than Iran, unless offset by a countervailing reset in international relations with Russia. These factors also conversely create counterintuitive possibilities for deepened international cooperation with Iran, based on energy efficiency, that have rarely been explored. Such inefficiencies are now deeply rooted in the Iranian political economy, exacerbated by Ahmadinejad's populism, and could be significantly ameliorated by Asian technical assistance, in both mass transit and energy efficiency, presumably after a nuclear settlement.

Internal differences among petrostates in incentive structure also seem consequential to their prospects for embracing the consuming nations of Asia, in a broader political-economic entente. Russia, for example, seems structurally oriented toward Europe, with vast pipeline networks to the west already embedded, and seeing leverage over Europe as central to enhancing its global role. Its trading patterns tend to follow this logic. Moscow also finds it institutionally and psychologically difficult to fully appreciate the immense emerging market and geopolitical potential that Asia presents, or to marshal the considerable resources needed to exploit it.

Iran, by contrast, cast off many of its European linkages in the 1979 Islamic revolution, and has stronger traditional ties with Asia. It also has, in its chronic energy inefficiencies, important functional reasons for rapprochement with Asia that could be deeper than those of Russia. Over the past three decades, it has grown strikingly more interdependent with Asia, especially China, its largest trading partner, due to energy complementarity.[140]

A final theme, comparing our four petrostates and relating to the conclusions of Chapter 3, is that most of these nations have been profoundly reshaped over the past generation by critical junctures that have reoriented them more intimately toward Asia than previously. For Kazakhstan, the shift—the collapse of the Soviet Union—was particularly dramatic and substantive. Before 1992 it had little relation to China, yet now over 200,000 barrels of oil daily are pumped from the perimeter of the Caspian to the vicinity of Shanghai, and other political-economic ties with the PRC are steadily deepening as well, encouraged by national leadership. For Iran, the critical juncture of the 1979 revolution was fateful in political-military as well as economic terms— the country shifted dramatically, from being a proxy state for the United States under the shah to being a close associate of Russia, China, North Korea, and other destabilizing powers today. Even for Russia, a critical juncture introduced fateful new dimensions—Moscow under Putin has proved to be far more strategic in dealing with Asia than it had previously been, as demonstrated both by nationalization of the Sakhalin II project in which Mitsubishi and Mitsui held a central share, and by simultaneous pragmatic discussions between METI and Gazprom regarding technical cooperation.

The one major petrostate we have surveyed that has not as yet undergone a truly wrenching critical juncture is Saudi Arabia. Its nationalization of Aramco in the mid-1970s ultimately produced fundamental change in the global political economy of energy distribution, but did not substantially offset domestic Saudi politics. Riyadh's relations with the broader world are remarkably similar to those of a generation ago. The Seven Sisters no longer dominate Aramco, but prominent Saudi engineers still attend Texas A&M or Colorado State. The foreign minister is a Princeton alum. At the level of human networks, at least, Saudi Arabia appears to have changed less than elsewhere, and technocrats, rather than politicians, hold sway, at last in their isolated islands of efficiency. Yet demographic and political pressures are rising, and whether the conservative ulama and an efficient security police force are enough to inhibit their advance into economically critical globalized sectors like energy remains unclear.

In all the petrostates, the one clear constant is the energy logic born of Asia's remarkable and continuing growth. Asia, with every passing day, is becoming a more and more important market for these producers, even as the producers themselves grow affluent, consumption oriented, and desirous of the energy efficiency technologies, not to mention the cost-effective manufactures, that Asian energy-consuming nations have at their command. Asia's need for producer hydrocarbons still has a long way to go, given the still-low rates of per capita demand in the emerging Asian giants, while the absorptive capacity of the petrostates for Asian manufactures is likewise substantial. Still, in a globalized world, these consumers too have multiple options. It is to their domestic structures, and to what these crucial, if subnational, configurations mandate for energy geopolitics, that we now turn.

Chapter 6 Energy-Insecure Asian Capitalist Consumers

The major producing nations of the Middle East and the former Soviet Union, as we have seen, are a distinctive set of petrostates—heavily dependent on hydrocarbon exports, energy inefficient, intent on diversifying, authoritarian, and increasingly oriented to the East. The world may be globalizing and flat, in its financial and industrial dimensions, but in energy geographic logic still matters. Dealing in oil and gas with neighbors is often easier than working with those who are continents removed, if the underlying producer/consumer relationships are complementary. And for Eurasia's producers—concentrated in the Land of the Two Seas (the Persian Gulf and the Caspian)—the most attractive emerging markets are remarkably close by.

In this chapter, I review the major national markets across Asia with which the petrostates of the Middle East and the former Soviet Union must deal: China, Japan, India, and South Korea. All share a crucial common feature: chronic energy insecurity. Two of them—the more mature economies, Japan and Korea—have virtually no domestic oil and gas. The other two—China and India—struggle

with huge populations, explosive growth, and limited domestic energy reserves apart from heavily polluting coal. Together, these four nations rank
among the five largest oil importers in the world, following only the United
States.[1] Yet none of the four are home to preeminent multinational energy
firms. And all lack the political-military leverage, particularly on the high
seas, to ensure unimpeded transport for their imported energy supplies. The
consumers of Asia, in short, confront a radically more demanding supply
environment for the imported oil and gas that they need so badly, than the
United States, Europe, or the producing nations themselves.

CENTRAL IMPORTANCE OF THE PERSIAN GULF

The four major Asian consuming nations also share, as we shall see, a geographically conditioned preference for Persian Gulf energy supplies. That
preference appears to be intensifying, even as the reliance of the West on the
Gulf declines, as Figure 6.1 suggests. The Gulf lies less than 1,000 miles directly across the Arabian Sea from one of the major Asian energy consumers

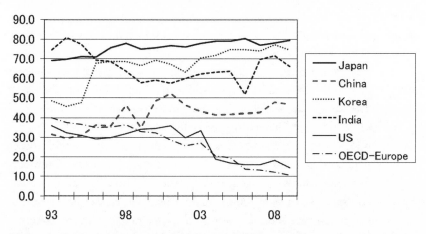

Figure 6.1: Rising Asian reliance on the Persian Gulf (1993–2010).
Source: Department of Energy, Energy Information Administration (Japan, U.S., and
OECD-Europe figures); United Nations, Commodity Trade Statistics, http://comtrade
.un.org (China and India figures); and Planning Commission of India, *Integrated Energy
Policy: Report of the Expert Committee* (New Delhi: Government of India Planning
Commission, 2006).
Notes: Percentage of energy supplied by Persian Gulf states. India figures for 2000–2004
were not available. Asia includes Japan, China, South Korea, and India.

(India) and closer than most other potential suppliers to the other three. For Europe and the United States, the Gulf is much farther away, and the incentives of Western firms to distribute Gulf oil are much weaker than they traditionally were, since the nationalization of their Gulf production facilities in the 1970s.

The PRC has somewhat lower reliance on the Persian Gulf than Japan and Korea, which are U.S. allies (Figure 6.1). Africa in particular does have some appeal for China on geopolitical grounds, as it affords diversification of supply away from a volatile Middle East, toward areas where Chinese political influence is greater. Yet Africa's reserves cannot compare with the Gulf's, and that continent is considerably more distant. In the long run, the interdependence of all of Asia's consumers with the Land of the Two Seas—the Persian Gulf and the Caspian—must inevitably deepen.

THE DEEPENING CONTINENTAL DIMENSION

There are also increasing prospects that the overland dimension of Asia's energy relationship with the Gulf—and also the Soviet successor states—will deepen, drawing those areas into a more intimate mutual embrace. Indeed, following Asia's rapid recovery from the 2008 global financial crisis during 2009–2010, land-based interdependence rapidly intensified, driven by a completion of new pipelines from Turkmenistan, Kazakhstan, and Russia, among others, to China. Pipelines provide diversification, and greater security of supply—especially for nations like China that are nervous about American dominance in the energy sea lanes.

As the geographical locus of energy demand within China itself shifts westward, as Indian growth accelerates, and as energy prices rise, the economic logic of transcontinental pipelines also intensifies. In contrast to other major industrialized regions of the world—Europe and North America—pipelines have never been a major feature of the Asian regional energy equation. The emergence of a full-fledged Asian energy grid, most probably focusing on natural gas, would thus be a major new political-economic development, likely to intensify and solidify the new continentalism.

A final broad commonality among the four major Asian consumer nations lies in the corporate area and in linkages to government-business relations. All four have institutions for trading and developing oil and gas that systematically reduce market risk.[2] Japan, Korea, and India have powerful industrial groups that can comprehensively handle complex export, import, and resource-development deals. Japan and Korea, in particular, have large, efficient general trading companies that can handle barter as well as market transactions. China and India also have resource corporations with substantial public-equity participation, while the governments of all four proactively intervene to help defray the risk their firms typically incur in large-scale energy-related transactions.

While the four major Asian energy-consuming nations have important commonalities in the way that they approach energy questions, they also have important differences that nuance their response to the challenge of hydrocarbon supply. After outlining the distinctive features of each consuming nation's energy challenges, the following pages detail their country-specific national responses. A detailed look at each consumer nation makes ever clearer the broad range of considerations, both domestic and international, that dispose them collectively toward deeper ties with the Eurasian oil and gas producers, by sea and, increasingly, overland as well.

China: Consumer Catalyst for Eurasian Geopolitical Change

China's energy and resource circumstances are at once simple and fateful, with three major aspects. First, China is the most populous nation in the world, with well over 1.3 billion people. Second, its per capita consumption of energy, and most other resources as well, remains extremely low—less than one-third of Russian and less than one-fifth of comparable American levels.[3] Third, China's per capita energy consumption, amplified massively at the national level by its huge population, is rising sharply as its people grow more affluent. And that per capita usage, fueled by rising automobile and consumer appliance ownership, as well as China's growing, energy-intensive industrial base, will likely continue to rise. China's energy consumption from 2007 to 2035 is expected by the U.S. Department of Energy to rise at an average rate of 3.1 percent annually.[4]

China's geopolitical circumstances are equally simple and fateful. First, the country is centrally located in Asia, the most populous continent in the world, bordering on fourteen other nations. Second, China has hegemonic potential within its region, due to its enormous scale, both geographically and demographically. Only India comes close to China's huge population, and it is considerably smaller and less central geographically within the Asian continent. Third and finally, due to the PRC's commanding geopolitical position within Asia, it has both land and sea options for dealing economically and politically with the broader world.[5] In this respect, China is far more fortunate than Russia, for example, which although a heartland power is largely landlocked, or Japan, whose peripheral island location consigns it to inevitably being a sea-based power, with limited potential for influence on land.

Taken together, China's underlying demographic and geopolitical circumstances naturally suggest a profound future impact on the global political economy. Certainly this is predictable with respect to energy, a field where income growth, rising per capita consumption, and population scale all leverage one another, and where Chinese circumstances are unusual in all three respects. Yet the truism can easily be distorted or misunderstood.

To say that current Chinese circumstances, or emerging trends, will have broad, momentous future impact is not to say either that Beijing will directly dominate beyond its borders or even that it will necessarily attempt to do so. The PRC's soft power may also be limited.[6] Many of the key implications of Chinese growth and rising affluence will, in short, be indirect and often unintended within China. It is what the Chinese do for domestic reasons, as their global shadow lengthens, that could exert the most fateful international impact. Certainly unintended consequences of this sort may substantially contribute to the building of a transcontinental Eurasian energy relationship, since well over half of the distance from the Caspian Sea and the Persian Gulf to Beijing and Shanghai lies within Chinese borders.

Across China's remarkable 6,000-year history, national unity and stability, together with economic survival, have been the three impulses classically galvanizing Chinese leadership.[7] When Chinese leaders have commanded the resources needed to act, they have typically done everything possible to ensure these elemental ends, which traditionally determine their ultimate standing in the scales of Chinese history. And the meteoric growth of the past three decades, since Deng Xiaoping unveiled the Four Modernizations of 1978, have assuredly given both China's government and its citizens the resources to pursue their classical national goals—not to dominate the world, or even to enhance China's power abroad, but first and foremost to ensure harmony and prosperity at home.

A PRIMARY IMPULSE: ENSURING DOMESTIC HARMONY AND PROSPERITY

What then do ensuring unity, stability, and prosperity mean concretely for China itself, at the dawn of the twenty-first century? Most important, they mandate sustaining economic growth sufficient to keep unemployment down and government revenue up. Infrastructural spending is a priority tool for achieving both, as manifest in the 2008–2009 global financial recession, at the onset of which China promptly announced one of the largest Keynesian stimulus packages in history, totaling nearly $600 billion.[8] Ensuring adequate export opportunities is obviously another national imperative, albeit one of slowly declining importance, as the Chinese domestic economy itself grows in relative size. Even reliance on the U.S. market, traditionally crucial, is of declining relevance, with the share of Chinese exports going to the United States peaking in 2002, as opportunities elsewhere in the world continued to rise.

In ensuring stability, unity, and even prosperity, the unsettled circumstances of China's periphery—precisely the areas that connect the PRC overland to other sections of the Silk Road—loom large. Neither Xinjiang nor Tibet, adjoining Central Asia and India respectively, have clear Han majority populations, nor long histories of settled Beijing dominance. Both have proud local populations with rich histories of their own and a fear of seeing their longstanding identities submerged in a unitary, monocultural China, however dynamic and prosperous that sprawling unit might be. These fears collide head on with a resurgent China's renewed aspirations for unity and stability; sentiments on both sides are growing ever stronger as China's rapid growth continues.

Thus, for primarily domestic reasons—to safeguard stability and to deepen national unity—China has embarked on an ambitious program of deepening domestic linkages to its restive western and southern peripheries. The core has been the Open the West Program (*xibu da kaifa*), directed at deepening central access to and control over Xinjiang and Tibet. The following pages describe these primarily domestic efforts and then outline the fateful international contribution to the building of a more integrated Eurasia, which they entail.

DOMESTIC CAUSE AND GLOBAL CONSEQUENCE: CHINA'S WESTERN POLICIES
AND THE EMERGENCE OF THE NEW SILK ROAD

> The frontiers of China are moving, even if its boundaries are not.
> —*Indian Defense analyst, IDSA, New Delhi*[9]

Kashgar, in the far southwestern reaches of Xinjiang, was once a key way station on the classic Silk Road. For centuries it was impossibly distant from China's eastern centers of power, and the pathways for reaching them were rudimentary, to say the least. Eastern coastal Chinese did trade in Kashgar's markets for highly valued jade, however, where they also sold silk, chinaware, and tea. These wares were then distributed widely—north to Mongolia, south to India, southwest to Persia, and west to Europe. Kashgar was thus decidedly a key crossroads of the ancient Silk Road, although far-distant from its terminus on China's eastern shores.

Today an integral part of the People's Republic of China, Kashgar operates, like the rest of the PRC, literally on Beijing Standard Time. Twice as close to the Strait of Hormuz or the Caspian Sea as to Beijing and Shanghai (Figure 6.2), Kashgar residents thus rise to prepare for work and government engagement at 5:00 A.M. local time, with the sun, so as to reconcile political imperatives and geographical location.

The task of reconciliation is by no means merely a mechanical matter of coordinating schedules across multiple time zones. Culturally, economically, and politically, Kashgar is light-years from China's heartland, over two thousand miles to the east. The per capita income of Kashgar inhabitants, 82 percent of them Uyghur, and most of them Muslim, is half that of Hupeh or Zhejiang, whose populations remain almost entirely Han.[10] And the people

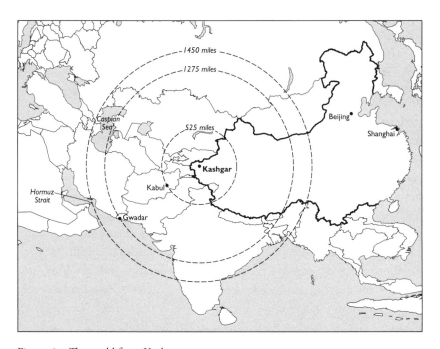

Figure 6.2: The world from Kashgar.

of Kashgar, with little relation to Chinese authority until barely a century ago, concede only ambivalent allegiance to Beijing even now.[11]

In June 1999, during a major policy speech at Xian, the ancient Tang dynasty capital, a thousand miles to the west of Beijing, President Jiang Zemin announced a campaign called Open Up the West. Its central purpose was emphatically to improve infrastructure between eastern China and the western borderlands, especially Xinjiang, whose name, attached by the Ching in the late eighteenth century, literally means New Frontier.[12] Four years later, Jiang's successor, Hu Jintao, reaffirmed the western development policy. And he threw sharply expanded resources behind it, drawn from the fruits of China's explosive growth, to redress internal income inequality, while also securing the borderlands.

During late 2008, in an aggressive effort to mute the domestic effects of the global financial crisis, Hu's administration expanded spending on infrastructure still further, concentrating new countercyclical funds, once again, in road, rail, air, and pipeline links to the West. High-speed rail connections, provincial airports, and long-distance pipelines—all domestic, but with broader continental implications—were among the special priorities.[13] During 2009–2010, following ethnic riots in Xinjiang that left over 200 people dead, China's central government announced an additional plan to spend over $100 billion in the West on railroads, airports, power grids, and other infrastructure. It also designated the West as the bedrock of China's energy programs.[14]

Chinese Domestic Drivers of Continentalism

Thus, as we shall see, China is aggressively building infrastructure westward from its east coast for a variety of domestic reasons, aided by technical developments such as high-speed rail and ultra-high voltage (UHV) power transmission.[15] These efforts are indirectly yet fatefully promoting continentalism: transforming the political economy of Eurasian regional development far beyond China itself. Hormuz and the Caspian are coming closer to Shanghai, because China's domestic imperatives are driving the Beijing authorities to cover the two-thirds of that distance lying within their borders, so as to connect Shanghai and Kashgar—however culturally, economically, and indeed geographically removed those two spots, at opposite ends of China, may be from one another. Chinese leaders, in short, are even now inadvertently forging the sinews of a more integrated Eurasia in the course of dealing with their own challenges of domestic cohesion and development.

Asia's Energy Platform

This inadvertent Chinese domestic catalyst for Eurasian continental integration has a long pedigree—a set of aspirations for Chinese internal modernization reminiscent of late-nineteenth-century America that date back at least to Sun Yat-sen. Sun, in 1922, published *The International Development of China*, in which he argued that the post–World War I foreign powers should invest in his country's western regions for economic reasons, to create the huge Chinese market that they desired ultimately to service.[16] In the 1960s, Mao Zedong made a different yet parallel plea, contending, in his Three Front Strategy, that China's interior provinces should be developed as a strategy for national defense.[17] Deng Xiaoping also supported Western development, but in the context of a broader "two overall situations" approach. This placed priority first on support to the coastal areas of China, due to their stronger prospective export competitiveness in the early stages of the Four Modernizations, before then turning westward.

The intellectual basis for the Open Up the West campaign of recent years was laid by Hu Angang, director of the Research Institute on National Conditions and a distinguished academic at Tsinghua University in Beijing.[18] Hu authored or coauthored a series of studies on China's regional disparities, which he contended were seriously deepening during the 1990s, after a respite during the 1978–1990 period. Hu stressed an economic gap between eastern and western China, in particular, that he argued was so excessively large that it should not be allowed to grow further.[19] Indeed, Hu found that gap to be even larger than those prevailing in the disintegrating polity of Yugoslavia, whose economic model Chinese scholars and policymakers had traditionally followed with great interest. Hu stressed that while the market's role was to safeguard efficiency, that of government was to realize equality and justice, particularly in the western regions, where aggrieved and restive ethnic minorities were concentrated. Preferential support of the West needed to be carried out, Hu argued, through financial transfers and extensive construction, supporting the weaker and more remote provincial units.

Jiang Zemin reportedly bought Hu's big-picture intellectual argument and linked it to his own legacy: the notion of a historic, far-sighted national policy shift appropriate to the coming of the millennium, the transition to new leadership, and also China's expected World Trade Organization (WTO) accession.[20] Long Yongtu, chief WTO negotiator, echoed the latter theme: Only if western China were allowed to march toward the world would it be able to establish an adequate development mentality, to absorb the inflow of international factors of production, and to raise its overall quality through the global exchange of information.[21]

These broad, abstract, and idealistic international themes were translated into actions that, for a mixture of domestic and broad global purposes, ultimately ended up indirectly privileging the New Silk Road. Numerous new infrastructure projects were authorized: the West-East Pipeline, from Xinjiang to Shanghai, long considered economically infeasible, which was nevertheless completed in 2004; the Langhai-Lanzhou-Xinjiang railway; and the proactive development of the Tarim Basin in Xinjiang, including the Desert Petroleum Highway, running across the Taklamakan Desert.[22] These projects bridged with Chinese government concessional funding the vast distances between China's economic centers on the east coast and distant outposts in Xinjiang adjoining Central Asia and the Middle East. The projects also encouraged commercial and industrial development in Xinjiang itself, proving to be an indispensable catalyst for China's practical relations with the traditional Silk Road nations.

The mutually reinforcing synergies between Chinese politics under Hu Jintao and the evolution of the New Silk Road should also be noted. Hu had extensive experience with western regions before his ascension to overall leadership in China, as had prime minister-to-be Wen Jiabao. Hu had served previously in Gansu and in Tibet; Wen in Gansu as well. As deputy prime minister, Wen had also directed, under both Jiang Zemin and Zhu Rongji, the Western Region Development Leading Group, which coordinated national policy formation on such issues within the State Council.[23]

Upon Hu Jintao's ascension to overall leadership, he had selected income differentials, and advocacy of the poor, as transcendent concerns. These were salient problems in the west, where income levels were generally lower than in most regions,[24] and fit his personal agenda perfectly. In addition, the political balance of power in the Politburo that accompanied Hu into office strongly supported western development. Fully one-third of the twenty-four full members had a personal background in the west, including President Hu and Prime Minister Wen. In addition, fortuitously, Wang Lequan, the Chinese Communist Party (CCP) boss of Xinjiang, was promoted to the Politburo in 2002, just before Hu's ascension to leadership.[25]

Collectively, China's new leadership after 2003 strongly supported Western development for its congruence with five discrete domestic policy agendas: (1) quest for equality, (2) foreign investment, (3) infrastructure investment, (4) nationalities issue, and (5) sustainable development.[26] Western development was also politically attractive in Beijing, for the renewed raison d'être that it gave conservative forces. The CCP and state investment, in particular, played much greater roles in lagging areas like Xinjiang than in more attractive areas on the east coast, where market forces and overseas Chinese investment held sway.[27]

Xinjiang as a Continentalist Growth Pole?
In March, 2010, the State Council announced strategic plans for Xinjiang to achieve "leapfrog development and lasting stability," announcing a package of measure to both boost the local economy directly, and to encourage greater investment in both public services and peoples' livelihood programs.[28] A central element was a "pairing assistance" program, that mobilized 19 affluent provinces and municipalities on China's east coast to invest more than 3 billion yuan (over $466 million), and to carry out 150 pilot projects in the region.

The 19 local-government aid providers, including prominently Shanghai and Guangzhou, have made a ten-year commitment, and agreed to invest 66 billion yuan ($10.15 billion) between 2011 and 2015.[29]

Supported also by accelerated central-government infrastructure spending, which will bring high-speed rail and expanded international airports to China's western borderlands by 2014, Xinjiang's GDP in 2011 was outpacing the national average by nearly 2 percent annualized, and foreign trade between Xinjiang and the world was growing explosively as well.[30] China Southern Airlines has made Urumqi International Airport a passenger and cargo hub for trans-continental flights from Guangzhou to Istanbul, Teheran, Novosibirsk, Dubai, and Islamabad, with a dedicated terminal freshly built, while Urumqi in September, 2011 also inaugurated an annual China-Eurasia Expo.[31] The city is also expanding its export-processing zone, in cooperation with Turkish, Iranian, and Chinese partners, to provide halal-observant processed food products and other specialities for export to the broader Islamic world. Kashgar, nestled near the Kyrgyz, Tajik, and Pakistani borders along the historic Silk Road, is taking similar steps to strengthen its continentalist ties, as are the 29 border crossings connecting Xinjiang with six surrounding Eurasian nations.[32]

Tibetan Development and New Southward Continental Linkages
Like Xinjiang, Tibet is literally one of the last frontiers for Beijing dominance in the entire PRC. Located at China's extreme southwestern periphery, Tibet occupies fully one-sixth of the PRC's entire land area, with a population that

remains less than 10 percent Han Chinese.[33] Beyond the Himalayas, of course, lies teeming India, growing at over 8 percent annually, and soon to surpass China as the most populous nation on earth. Tibet's own total population, however, remains less than 3 million—or less than one-four hundredth that of China as a whole. Tibet's current indigenous majority could thus easily be overwhelmed by Han in-migration from China proper.

Infrastructure clearly plays a key role, as in Xinjiang, in uniting Tibet more closely with the rest of the PRC, and thus indirectly in connecting China itself to regions beyond. The first step in recent years came with the building of the Qingzang railway, connecting Xining, in Qinghai Province, to Lhasa, the capital of Tibet.[34] A remarkable feat from an engineering standpoint, the Qingzang is the world's highest railway track, running as high as 16,600 feet above sea level, much of the way over permafrost, and providing both oxygen and ultraviolet radiation protection to each passenger. Construction involved more than 20,000 workers and over 6,000 pieces of industrial equipment, with the finished railway line being inaugurated by President Hu Jintao himself on July 1, 2006.[35]

Although intended initially to draw Tibet closer to China proper, the Qingzang railway and related infrastructure across Tibet will also ultimately deepen China's links with South Asia as well, potentially increasing still further an explosively growing transnational economic relationship that already involves well over $60 billion in annual trade, up more than twentyone fold since 2000.[36] In April 2008, the Chinese announced, with Nepalese concurrence, an intention to extend the railway from Lhasa to Khasa, on the Nepalese border, by 2013.[37] Another line will extend from Xigaze, Tibet's second city, to Yadong, also on the Indian border.[38] From those border posts, railway lines would presumably connect to parallel infrastructure extending northward from India, augmenting other direct linkages between China and India across the Himalayas. Economic exchanges have thus far been limited by the absence of easy land transport links, even though Nepal shares an 875-mile border with China. That infrastructural constraint on interdependence, however, is steadily eroding.[39]

Deepening Continentalist Ties with Southeast Asia

China's continentalist relationships are also deepening rapidly with Southeast Asia. PRC trade with the ten nations of ASEAN quadrupled between 2003 and 2008, from $59.6 billion to $192.5 billion, following the November, 2002 agreement among the eleven countries to establish a free-trade area by

2010. The FTA was formally established, on schedule, on January 1, 2010, together with a parallel arrangement between ASEAN and India. Trading relations among all parties have continued to grow rapidly, with those along China's land borders, particularly Laos, Vietnam, and Myanmar, being especially dynamic. Chinese trade with these three continental neighbors grew over the first decade of the twenty-first century (2000–2010) by 26, 12, and 7 times respectively, while it grew by only 5.7 and 5.3 times respectively with more distant and maritime Indonesia and Singapore.[40]

As in Chinese relations with Central Asia and Pakistan, infrastructure is a key aspect of deepening economic ties. Major oil and gas pipelines are in progress across Myanmar, connecting the Bay of Bengal with China's Yunnan province.[41] China is investing heavily in Burmese electric-power infrastructure. In the context of its domestic regional development schemes, the PRC has designated Guangxi, bordering on Vietnam, as a free cross-border renminbi settlement trial location, to expand trade cooperation, strengthen investment, and promote the development of coastal high-tech and modern service industries.[42] And high-speed rail lines are under construction across Vietnam, Cambodia, Laos, and Thailand from Nanning to Singapore,[43] and also across Laos and Thailand from Kunming to Singapore, to be completed by 2015.[44] China's continental ties are thus expanding steadily across its land borders to the south, as well as to the north, the west, and to the southwest.

ENHANCING ENERGY SECURITY ABROAD

Chinese domestic stability imperatives are thus a significant contributor, however little noticed, to the rapid emergence over the past two decades of Eurasian energy interdependence. There are, however, natural national security concerns, including energy security, that are more directly international. After all, since 1993 China has rapidly emerged as a large-scale oil importer— bringing in nearly six million barrels per day by the end of 2010.[45] And since 2007 the PRC has become a significant importer of both piped and liquefied natural gas (LNG) as well.[46]

China's energy-security problem is subtly different from that of Japan and South Korea. The United States, after all, dominates the sea lanes to the Persian Gulf and points beyond, from whence most of China's oil and gas derive. And China, unlike its two Northeast Asian neighbors, is in no sense a clear-cut U.S. ally. China's energy import demand is also growing much more rapidly than theirs, making the securing of supplies much more urgent than for its neighbors.

China is taking five major domestic steps to enhance its energy security, which in turn deepen its political-economic ties with Eurasian continental producer nations. First, the PRC is working actively to enhance the equity oil share of its imports, by aiding national champions like China National Petroleum Corporation (CNPC) and Sinopec in their global acquisitions.[47] In doing so, it is also enhancing national control of the value chain, including refining, along which oil and gas proceeds from oil field to consumer.[48]

CNPC and Sinopec, for example, have signed contracts with Iran to develop that country's North Azadegan and Yadavaran oil fields. Meanwhile, in July 2009, CNPC also won a bid to develop the Rumalia oil field in southern Iraq, one of the country's largest.[49] Overall, China's overseas equity oil production grew almost 8 percent in 2008, representing 29 percent of China's total oil production at the end of that year.[50] CNPC alone was active in twenty-nine countries.

A second Chinese initiative to enhance energy security has been to intensify downstream investment ties with foreign energy firms, thus giving these companies a more direct corporate stake in supplying China with both crude oil and refined products. ExxonMobil, for example, recently partnered with Sinopec, Saudi Aramco, and Fujian Province to build China's first integrated oil-refining and petrochemical facility involving foreign participation.[51] More than $4.5 billion was invested in the complex, built to produce 240,000 barrels per day of transportation fuels, ethylene, and other refined products.[52] Completed in late 2009, the project supplies over 750 service stations and other terminals in Fujian province.[53] In 2006, Sinopec and Kuwait Petroleum Corporation have also built another $5 billion oil refinery and ethylene plant near Guangzhou.[54]

China has likewise encouraged its own national champions to acquire refinery stakes in other countries. Petrochina (CNPC), for example, purchased a $1 billion stake in Singapore Petroleum. In June 2009 it also received approval to acquire 49 percent of Nippon Oil's Osaka refinery in Japan.[55]

A third Chinese energy security initiative has been to expand the national strategic petroleum reserve, originally created in 2001. Under phase 1 of this program, completed in 2009, China stockpiled 103 million barrels of oil, or twenty-five days' supply at current consumption levels. Under phase 2, completed in 2011, capacity was raised to a total of 270 million barrels. This complemented the 300 million barrels of currently existing commercial crude oil storage capacity in the PRC, with much of the stockpiled oil naturally flowing from the Middle East.

A fourth Chinese energy security initiative is to reduce import dependence on the Strait of Malacca—a potential choke point for China's maritime oil supplies, which could easily be blocked by the U.S. Navy or even by terrorist action. Pipeline projects through Myanmar to the Bay of Bengal, and from Pakistan to the Arabian Sea have the dual benefit of both finessing the Strait of Malacca and funneling seaborne hydrocarbons from the Middle East and Africa into parts of China's western and southern periphery, from Xinjiang to Yunnan, that could not efficiently be supplied with hydrocarbons transported by sea to China's east coast.[56] More directly, ambitious pipelines from Kazakhstan and Turkmenistan are bringing oil and gas in increasing quantities overland, direct from Central Asia into the western PRC. Beginning in late 2009, oil has begun flowing southward into China from Russia as well.

CHINESE DOMESTIC IMPERATIVES, PIPELINE ECONOMICS,
AND CONTINENTALISM

These transcontinental pipelines are a perfect illustration of the changing political economics of energy—driven by Chinese domestic imperatives—that are so dynamically and rapidly deepening Eurasian continental energy interdependence. Explosively growing demand within China's interior, of course, is the prime mover. Yet this could not express itself in the form of transnational pipelines, as from Kazakhstan into the PRC, had not the political barriers of the Cold War era not been removed, amid the critical junctures of the 1990s described in Chapter 3. Also important was the active Chinese domestic infrastructural spending of the Open Up the West Campaign, heavily subsidized to promote national unity, employment, and Han settlement in Xinjiang. It was under this program that the first west-east gas pipeline, 2,500 miles from the Tarim, Qaidam, and Ordos Basins of Xinjiang directly to Shanghai, was completed in 2004. Once this line reached Xinjiang, opening access from the west to the large markets of eastern China, pipelines still further westward—to Turkmenistan and even to the Caspian and the Persian Gulf—naturally became more feasible. Recent transnational pipeline initiatives into China are depicted in Figure 6.3.

Since 2004, pipeline connections across China, and linking China overland with Central Asia and Russia, have proliferated to a remarkable and once unimagined degree. In this transformation, domestic energy shortages and the imperatives of domestic economic stimulus are playing a key role. In 2006, the 1,050-mile Western China Refined Oil Pipeline, linking Urumqi in Xinjiang with Lanzhou in Gansu Province, began operations, followed by a

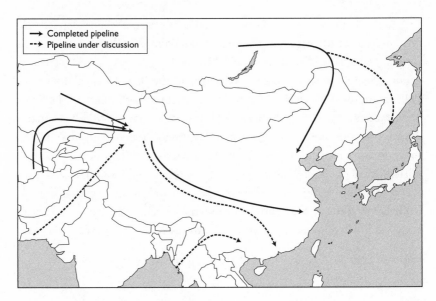

Figure 6.3: International pipelines to China.

parallel crude oil pipeline during 2007. Also in 2006, China inaugurated its first transnational oil pipeline, a 200,000 barrels per day energy link extending 620 miles across the border, between Atasu in Kazakhstan and Alashankou on the Chinese side. In December 2009, the first phase of the East Siberia-Pacific Ocean pipeline was finished, delivering 300,000 barrels per day of crude oil to the Chinese border and ultimately, through Chinese domestic pipelines, to refineries in Daqing.

Gas pipelines have also proliferated, building on rising energy demand within the PRC, and the new transportation economics created by the original West-East Pipeline of 2004. Using government economic stimulus funds, generated to fight the global financial crisis of 2008, CNPC has built a second west-to-east trunk gas pipeline, at a cost of over $10 billion, with more than twice the capacity of the 2004 version.[57] The Chinese portion of the new line spans spans more than 4,000 miles from the Sino-Kazakh border to Guangzhou, and became fully operational in June, 2011, several months ahead of schedule.[58] This domestic line links up with the massive Central Asian Gas Pipeline, running from Turkmenistan's immense South Yolotan gas fields 1,440 miles across Uzbekistan and Kazakhstan into China, which was inaugurated by Hu Jintao and Turkmen President Berdimuhamedov in December 2009.[59]

Within China itself, a third west-east line equal to the first two in scale is being built at a cost of nearly $15 billion to convey even more Turkmen gas to China's east coast. Fourth and fifth domestic lines are in the prefeasibility study stages, facilitating still larger imports from the west. CNPC has also signed memoranda of understanding with Russia's Gazprom for two pipelines from the Russian Far East into China over the next decade.[60]

CHINESE RAILWAYS, SUPERHIGHWAYS, AND CONTINENTALISM

Oil and gas pipelines are being rapidly supplemented by other infrastructure, as noted above. In 2006, for example, China proposed a Pan-Asian Railway Network to connect twenty-eight countries with 81,000 kilometers of railways.[61] A principal route is to originate in Urumqi and connect Central Asian countries with Germany via high-speed rail by 2025.[62]

En route to these longer-term goals, the PRC has sharply accelerated railway construction, in the context of its massive antirecessionary stimulus package. Operating mileage in the west jumped to 38 percent of China's total at the end of 2008 and is scheduled to rise 70 percent further by 2020.[63] To facilitate high-speed travel over vast continental distances, China's WuGuang rail system will involve dedicated lines, similar to Japan's Shinkansen or Germany's InterCity Express, built in cooperation with major multinationals, including IBM, General Electric, and Germany's Siemens and Max Bogl.[64] The emerging high-speed rail network, expected to have over 800 high-speed trains in service by late 2012 and reaching deep into the interior of China, is depicted in Figure 6.4. By the end of 2013, construction is expected to reach Urumqi, capital of Xinjiang, in its steady Silk Road progression to the West.

Apart from its ambitious program of domestic railway expansion, which by definition covers two-thirds of the distance from Shanghai to the Strait of Hormuz and the Caspian, China is also promoting the international linkages that would transform its new domestic routes into a truly transcontinental system. The PRC has, for example, helped fund a railway line from Gwadar to Dalband in central Pakistan, which will then be integrated with existing lines linking Pakistan to Iran.[65] It is likewise funding lines from Xinjiang to Pakistan, rail links through Kyrgyzstan and Uzbekistan, and other routes to Mongolia that directly deepen transnational interdependence across the broad continental expanses of Eurasia.[66] It is also greatly expanding and upgrading airports in western and southern cities such as Urumqi, Chengdu, and Kunming, just as Korea is doing in Uzbekistan, in an effort to establish strategic Eurasian continental transportation hubs.

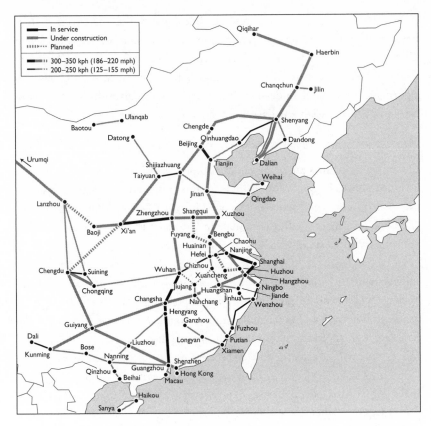

Figure 6.4: China's ambitious high-speed rail network.

Ambitious expansion of superhighways helping to integrate the continent is also underway, with Chinese domestic expansion once again serving as catalyst. In 2005, the PRC's National Expressway Network Plan was authorized, providing superhighways connecting all large and medium-size cities in China by 2020, to create a nationwide superhighway network totaling 53,000 miles in length.[67] Already China's Highway 310 connects Lianyungang Port on the east coast with Khorgos, nearly 3,000 miles away on the border of Kazakhstan. Highway 312 similarly connects Shanghai to Urumqi, the largest city in Xinjiang, at the edge of Central Asia, via the Gobi Desert.[68] This Chinese domestic highway network is, like high-speed railway expansion, giving a powerful infrastructural jump start to Eurasia's deepening continental interdependence, while also providing it with a massive potential feeder network from the populous East (Figure 6.5).

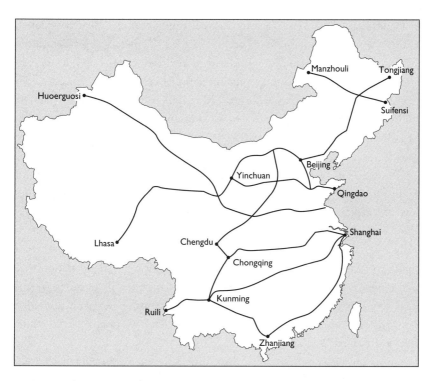

Figure 6.5: China's sprawling superhighway network.

SUMMARY

Trans-Eurasian continental infrastructure involving China has expanded greatly following the Cold War, and especially since the global financial crisis of 2008. In 1992, immediately following the Soviet collapse, Mitsubishi Corporation and CNPC, soon joined by Exxon, began exploring the feasibility of a 6,000-kilometer trans-Asia pipeline bringing Turkmen gas to Shandong, and thence via another 2,000-kilometer undersea pipeline to South Korea, and ultimately to Japan.[69] Despite the revolutionary political changes underway at the time, many considered the study economically fantastical—as they did the entire notion of Silk Road revival. Around the same time, Japanese Official Development Assistance (ODA) officials considered supporting the construction of a west-east gas pipeline across China, but likewise considered it impractical and impossibly expensive. So did several Western oil companies, including Shell, ExxonMobil, and Gazprom.[70]

Little more than a decade after these feasibility studies were completed, China's West-East Pipeline was a reality, in 2004. It emerged, however, under PRC governmental auspices, subsidized by the state to provide both energy and employment, while also enhancing national cohesiveness. For parochial reasons of domestic energy security, China thus became a powerful catalyst for larger transnational schemes that are bringing Eurasia together, through a process driven powerfully, if indirectly, by the PRC's remarkable economic growth.

China is a player sui generis in the political economy and geopolitics of Eurasian energy, with four defining characteristics—huge population, low per capita energy consumption, rapid economic growth, and central geographical location within the continent as a whole. The PRC is emphatically a heartland state—one with even more favorable geopolitical prospects for the twenty-first century than Russia, the classic heartland nation, has ever enjoyed. China may not have strongly expansionist pretensions. Yet its explosive economic growth is nevertheless generating new continentalist political-economic realities across Eurasia, which have fateful implications for international affairs.

For its own domestic reasons, the Chinese national government is, amid the rapid growth of the past generation, becoming strongly assertive about national unity, stability, and welfare. And it has the resources to vigorously pursue these goals. Concretely, pursuit of national unity and stability has come to mean asserting stronger dominion over what have traditionally been borderlands with tenuous ties to Beijing—Xinjiang and Tibet. Both are home to proud and venerable civilizations, and peopled primarily by non-Han ethnic groups, so the process of asserting Beijing's dominance and enhancing the role of local Han residents has been a delicate proposition for all concerned.

A major part of Beijing's domestic strategy for integrating Xinjiang and Tibet—invested with macroeconomic attraction as well in periods of economic crisis—has been large-scale infrastructural spending. The central government has spent massive amounts on highways, railways, telecommunications networks, power grids, and pipelines—all intended to make China a more coherent union. Since 2000 there has been a particularly strong infrastructural emphasis on Xinjiang and Tibet, which has accelerated still further since 2008.[71] Yet this process of national infrastructure building has generated fateful, unanticipated international consequences as well—deepened political-economic ties with Central Asia, the Middle East, and Russia that lay the basis for a stronger Eurasian continentalist cast in world affairs.

India: Rising Energy Player of the Coming Decade

Current political-economic analysis in the West of global energy issues focuses heavily on China's powerful impact on world supply, demand, and prices. While this is by no means to be depreciated, it is incomplete and in some ways myopic. Asian energy demand has two powerful national engines, with India rising steadily in importance. In the geopolitical calculus also, India's shadow is lengthening and will likely continue to do so for decades to come.

The underlying demographic equation of India, making its energy and environmental future so fateful for the world, is fundamentally similar to that of China. India has a huge population, second only to that of the PRC and totaling well over 1.2 billion in early 2012.[72] By 2025, that population is expected to be the largest in the world.[73] India's people, however, remain generally poor, with a per capita income, in purchasing power parity terms, of only $3,500 per year. Per capita energy consumption, accordingly, remains low, at less than one-third the global average, or only one-fourteenth that of the United States.[74] Many Indians do not yet have the income to consume large amounts of energy, or to buy the goods that might indirectly inflate such consumption.

Those demand-inhibiting circumstances, however, are beginning to change. India's population, first of all, is growing rapidly—much more rapidly than China's. India's birth rate in 2011 was nearly 21 per 1,000—almost double that of the PRC.[75] India's population is also substantially younger (Table 6.1), with a median age nine years less than in China. Given these contrasting demographic trends, India is likely to become the most populous nation in the world within a generation, decisively eclipsing the PRC.

While growing more populous in coming years, India is also likely to become more affluent. As the foregoing figures suggest, it starts from a significantly lower base than China, in terms of per capita GDP and energy consumption, and also from a lower rate of national economic growth. Yet there are strong reasons to believe that India's per capita income will rise substantially and its population as well. The country's GDP growth in 2010 reached 10.4 percent, and has averaged 7.8 percent since 2008, based on strong competitiveness in

Table 6.1. Latent Future Energy Demand Prospects?

	Median Age	Age Span, 0–14 (percent)	Population Growth (percent)	Birth Rate (per 1000 people)	Urban Population (percent)	GDP per Capita: PPP	Energy Demand per Capita (Kg)
India	26	29.7	1.3	20.9	30	$3,500	545
China	35.5	17.6	0.5	12.3	47	$7,600	1,598

Sources: Central Intelligence Agency, *The World Factbook*; and World Bank, *World Development Indicators.* http://devdata.worldbank.org.
Notes: (1) Birth rates are live births/1000 population; (2) 0–14 indicates an age span, in years; (3) Energy demand figures are per capita annual consumption, expressed in kilograms of oil equivalent, for 2008.

services, including health care. These sectors are expanding on a global basis and are likely to sustain rapid growth, rising affluence, and greater energy consumption within India also.

Social transformation inside India itself, notably the rapid expansion of the middle class, will reinforce these other trends. Currently the middle class—households with disposable incomes ranging from 200,000 to 1,000,000 rupees per year—comprises at least 50 million people, or around 5 percent of the population, although there are a variety of estimates.[76] By 2025, according to Deutsche Bank, a continuing rise in personal incomes will spur a tenfold expansion in this pivotal group of consumers, enlarging the middle class to about 583 million people, or 41 percent of the overall Indian population.[77] Discretionary spending as a share of total income will also rise, by McKinsey's projections, from 52 to 70 percent of total private spending. This combined dynamic will open the way for sharply accelerated purchases of automobiles and consumer durables, naturally leading to major subsequent increases in energy consumption.

Infrastructural improvements—new roads, airports, and railways—will also stimulate Indian energy consumption, as well as closer ties between India and its continental neighbors. The country already has a vast network of national highways, covering more than 40,000 miles, but most are poorly paved and crumbling. The government recently launched a nationwide initiative to upgrade those highways, centering on the Golden Quadrilateral project, now virtually complete. The new network will connect India's four largest cities—New Delhi, Kolkata, Chennai, and Mumbai—with four- to six-lane expressways, forming a semi-quadrilateral configuration.[78] India already maintains a Golden Quadrilateral railway system similar to its emerging highway complex, which carries 65 percent of India's freight traffic and 55 percent of its passengers.[79]

Energy consumption is thus likely to expand sharply across India over the coming years, as that in China has already done. China's final energy consumption during the two high-growth decades following the Tiananmen crisis (1990–2007) rose 88 percent.[80] The International Energy Agency's (IEA) forward projections for Indian energy consumption over an equivalent time period (2009–2030) are for a comparable increase of 88 percent.[81]

INDIA'S DEEPENING TIES WITH THE ASIAN AND EURASIAN PETROSTATES

Relative to the other three major energy consumers of Asia, India's existing ties with the petrostates—particularly Iran, Saudi Arabia, and Russia—are particularly strong and venerable. Historical, political, and economic factors are all at work. Here I review reasons for these enduring Indian petrostate ties and consider how they contribute to the emergence of the New Silk Road itself.

History looms especially large between India and the rest of Asia, with underlying religious affinities being a key connector. Buddhism, of course, was born on the Indian subcontinent and made its way eastward to China via Central Asia, and ultimately to Japan and Korea.[82] Islam also has a venerable relationship with India, predating even the Muslim conquests of the seventh and eighth centuries. Today nearly 15 percent of the Indian population, or over 160 million people, are Muslim—the largest minority Islamic population in the world, and the third largest national community of Muslims anywhere, after those of Indonesia and Pakistan.[83] Three former presidents of India, numerous former ministers, and CEOs of such prominent firms as the informatics leader Wipro are Muslim.

It took 700 years for Islam to penetrate India—more by suasion than by force. Islamic rulers were common in India, beginning with the Delhi Sultanate of the twelfth century and continuing with the Mughal Empire (1526–1858). There were, accordingly, definite secular benefits to be had traditionally by being Muslim. Yet many Islamic rulers of India, including Akbar the Great, were tolerant of Hinduism and not insistent on conversion. Under this liberal yet alluring incentive structure, Islam gradually spread across the subcontinent and retains a substantial, moderate, and often firmly rooted presence in India today, especially in Assam, Uttar Pradesh, Kerala, and Bihar, where Muslims constitute well over 15 percent of the local population.

Long-standing Islamic ties retain practical relevance for India internationally—reinforcing relations with fundamentalist Middle Eastern oil producers, in particular. They appear, for example, to have recently eased New Delhi's relations with Saudi Arabia, otherwise complicated by India's close ties to Israel, and by the bitter Kashmir standoff between India and Pakistan. In January 2006, Saudi Arabia's King Abdullah was guest of honor at India's Republic Day celebrations, bringing with him a 200-member delegation and a personal desire to consolidate a special relationship with India. Among other conciliatory gestures, including preparations for major bilateral agreements on counterterrorism and cross-investment, King Abdullah proposed that India, with its substantial Muslim population, be accorded observer status in the global Organization of the Islamic Conference.

Commercial ties between India and neighbors to the north and west are also long-standing and synergistic with cultural connections. A southern branch of the Silk Road, after all, once passed through northern India, crossing always-turbulent Afghanistan en route from Central Asia. Kashmiri shawls, as well as Indian ivory, sugar, dies, and carpets were traditionally in great demand in Bukhara, Samarkand, and beyond.[84] Indians were also major traders and moneylenders along these routes, together with Parthians and Sogdians, with more than 8,000 Indians reportedly living in Central Asia by the middle of the nineteenth century.[85]

Another element of embedded history, crucially relevant to future Eurasian energy geopolitics, is India's long-standing and intimate relationship with the Persian Gulf. Dating from pearl trading in ancient times, this relationship intensified under the British Raj, when the empire exercised hegemonic sway over much of the Middle East, including the Gulf, from Calcutta and New Delhi, rather than from London.[86] The vision of Britain's Victorian-era viceroy, Lord George Curzon, was emphatically Indocentric, but expansive, and included the India-Persian Gulf dimension as a central element.[87] Many of the civil servants who administered British policy in the Gulf were Indians, and the majority of the soldiers enforcing it were Indian volunteers, serving in Britain's Indian Army. More than 1 million of these *sepoys* served in World War I; India also provided substantial manpower and logistical support for British World War II campaigns in the western desert of Egypt and in ousting hostile local regimes, ranging from the Vichy French in Syria to the pro-Nazi government of Iraq.[88]

The human connections forged between India and the Gulf during those imperial years continued and intensified following the formal British withdrawal in the 1960s and 1970s, as the Gulf's civilian manpower needs grew, together with its newfound energy-driven prosperity. By the time Saddam Hussein invaded Kuwait in 1990, remittances back to India from workers in the Gulf had reached 7 percent of India's GDP.[89] Today, there are over 4.5 million Indian migrant workers in the Gulf, making up close to half of the local population in some countries.[90]

Historically embedded yet ongoing Indian ties with Russia, dating from Soviet days, remain important in pulling India away from abject globalism and back to more parochial Eurasian continental associations. From the mid-1960s until the end of the Cold War, nominally neutralist Indian governments cultivated increasingly intimate relations with the Soviet Union, driven by the Sino-Indian border war, the Sino-Soviet split, and America's geopolitical tilt toward Pakistan, as well, ultimately, as China also. The Indo-Soviet partnership was highly complementary: it involved energy and arms supplies for India, as well as technical exchanges in the medical, pharmaceutical, and information technology areas that covered Soviet weaknesses and laid the groundwork for post–Cold War developmental cooperation as well.

Russia remains by far India's largest arms supplier, as it has been since the 1960s, currently providing around 70 percent of India's military hardware.[91] In March 2010, India signed five deals to purchase more than $7 billion in hardware and expertise from Russia, procuring an aircraft carrier and a fleet of MiG-29 fighters, as well as defense and space technology.[92] The MiG's first delivery will be made in 2012.[93] In December 2010, during Russian President Dmitry Medvedev's state visit to New Delhi, Russia and India also agreed to codevelop a fifth-generation fighter aircraft with stealth capabilities and to pursue plans to build two new Russian nuclear reactors in India.[94]

In contrast to China, which lies geographically at the center of the Asian continent, India is a great peninsula, extending deep into the Indian Ocean, somewhat detached from its terrestrial neighbors. As a consequence, India only borders on five countries, compared to fourteen in the case of China. And some of those nominal neighbors are separated from India proper by formidable physical barriers, such as the Himalayas. India is thus less automatically immersed in broader Asian continental geopolitics than China; domestic political-economic decisions, including local infrastructural policies, likewise have less bearing on broader international relationships than they do in the PRC.

Yet India is an explosively growing economy, whose already substantial national energy requirements will inevitably rise. Indeed, they may well grow even more rapidly than those of China. India's income level, after all, is much lower than that of the PRC, and its population is expanding more rapidly. India will also inevitably need to forge deeper energy ties with the petrostates of the Persian Gulf and the former Soviet Union. To secure adequate energy supplies, New Delhi will, however, also need to build the requisite infrastructure and cater to the developmental needs of these major energy exporters, across Afghanistan, Pakistan, and other currently turbulent areas, giving it strong energy-related incentives for regional political stabilization.[95] India will likewise have to confront the deepening geostrategic reality that the other large consumers of Asia—China, Japan, and Korea—will similarly require access to the resources of the petrostates, whether via sea lanes passing close by India's own shores or by continental pipelines.

FUTURE PROSPECTS

Three major issues arise for India, flowing from its own expanding energy needs, in the context of Asia's broader energy geopolitics: infrastructure, support for the developmental needs of the petrostates, and national defense. These questions are recent in origin, beginning to deepen less than a decade ago, as India emerged from the pariah status that followed its nuclear tests, and as the substantial resource requirements flowing from its rapid economic growth became increasingly manifest. These concerns will inevitably energize India's Look West policies toward the West Asian petrostates and its Look East policies toward the similarly energy insecure East and Southeast Asian consuming nations as well.

India confronts major infrastructure challenges in three dimensions. First, there is the challenge of providing electricity generating and transmission infrastructure, in a country where 40 percent of residences remain without power, and where one-third of local businesses see unreliable electricity as a primary obstacle to doing business.[96] Seventy percent of India's electricity is currently generated in polluting coal-fired plants, so there is also an environmental dimension. Major efforts are being made to shift from coal to gas-fired and nuclear power plants; India currently has fourteen nuclear reactors in commercial operation and recently bought ten more from France and Russia.[97] Efficiency and safety in the electric power sector, including the nuclear dimension, is an area where India's fellow Asian consuming nations, as well as the West, can also be supportive. Indeed, they need to be, given India's vast emerging energy requirements.

Other aspects of the infrastructure issue are the construction of pipelines and ports to accommodate India's rising demand for imported oil and gas. Currently India imports roughly 2 million barrels of oil per day, or more than 72 percent of its domestic requirements, and around 20 percent of its natural gas, mainly in the form of LNG.[98] These import requirements will rise sharply in coming years, with IEA projections suggesting a tripling of oil imports and a quintupling of natural gas imports by 2030.[99] Overland options are considered in Chapter 7.

Amid the continuing complexities of regional pipeline politics, prospects are rising that primary Indian reliance on LNG will continue for the foreseeable future. Currently India imports nearly 90 percent of its LNG from Qatar, in the Persian Gulf. It is also considering the Russian Far East as a major LNG option, where the Indian major Oil and Natural Gas Corporation holds a 20 percent equity stake in the Sakhalin I oil project and shows a keen interest in Sakhalin III, scheduled to be both an oil and an LNG operation.

EMERGING SYNERGIES WITH THE PETROSTATES

A major recent concern in all the major petrostates, as we have seen, is finding long-term options for economic development that promote diversification away from those nations' own finite hydrocarbon reserves. Even the largest exporters increasingly recognize the enormous losses, both physical and financial, that they incur through wasteful domestic consumption. India's capabilities uniquely complement petrostate aspirations in some important areas, building on the long-standing human ties with both the Persian Gulf and Russia that are outlined above. India and Saudi Arabia, for example, have signed agreements to cooperate in the fields of hospital consultancy and management, to import Indian pharmaceuticals into the Saudi Kingdom, and to train Saudi nurses in India.[100] India's world-class information technology firms, such as Wipro, have also invested or established subsidiaries in Saudi Arabia's new Knowledge Economic City at Medina.[101]

INDIAN SECURITY CONCERNS

India's rising energy requirements, and the increasingly competitive geopolitics of Eurasian energy, also raise new hard-core national-security issues. These inevitably deepen Indian interactions with other neighboring states, despite New Delhi's traditional geopolitical detachment. Most important, rising seaborne import requirements, for both oil and LNG, increase the strategic importance of sea lanes to the Persian Gulf, as well as India's underlying interest in the stability of the Gulf itself. India, after all, obtains over 70 percent of its oil and 90 percent of its LNG from the Gulf, while more than 4 million Indians earn their livelihood there. The intensity of this interaction is hardly surprising, since the Gulf lies only a thousand miles from India's own western shores.

The strategic importance for India of the Gulf and the energy sea lanes is further heightened by the deepening reliance on the same sea lanes of other major Asian consumers farther east. Extending deeply into the Indian Ocean, directly across the most direct route from the Strait of Malacca to the Gulf, India has natural political-military leverage on Japan, Korea, and China, provided that it maintains either an adequate level of domestic military capability, credible alliances with other maritime powers, or both. The Indian government, and particularly the Indian Navy, thus watches Chinese steps toward development of a blue-water fleet of its own with particular trepidation.

Although India remains more detached geopolitically from the Asian continent than does China, New Delhi must nevertheless also be concerned about its northwest frontier. Throughout history, it has been out of this volatile, mountainous, poorly governed region that violent intrusions into the fertile, populous South Asian flatlands—including recently those of al-Qaeda and Lashkar-e-Taiba—have come. The stable futures of Pakistan, Afghanistan, and Central Asia, as well as the relations of these buffers to potential rival powers, are thus all high priority to New Delhi. Endemic concerns will be intensified in future years by the potential of those areas for energy supply and transit.

India's most immediate preoccupations with its northwest frontier are twofold: terrorism and China. The terrorism issue has exploded dramatically in India of late, through such brutal events as the November 2008 slayings in Mumbai, which killed 173 people and wounded over 300.[102] Terrorism is deeply related in Indian eyes to the struggle with Pakistan over Kashmir and the depredations of Islamic fundamentalist groups such as Lashkar-e-Taiba—based in Pakistan, but with broader connections and aspirations.[103] A principal rationale for India's Central Asian initiatives since the mid-1990s has been a fear that instability in places like the Ferghana Valley of Uzbekistan could create a breeding ground for Islamic terrorist movements endangering India itself.[104] This persistent apprehension has also been a principal motive behind India's interest in observer status at the Shanghai Cooperation Organization, whose principal successes thus far have been in coordinating national counter-terrorism efforts.

India's second concern in the northwest is increasingly China, especially in conjunction with the traditional Pakistani threat. The PRC, ironically, is drawn toward involvement in Central Asia by some of the same forces that attract India—energy and terrorism. In China's case the short-run economics are particularly compelling, due to the PRC's rapid current growth, its proximity to Central Asian energy reserves, and the stability of prospective transit routes. The Chinese presence is expanding rapidly and giving India, as a potential rival, rising incentives to countervail it. India is much more comfortable with the long-standing presence of Russia, a tacit geopolitical ally in the region.

SUMMARY

India will inevitably loom larger in the geopolitics of Asian energy in coming years, just as China will, for similar reasons. Both are populous yet poor, with prospects of rapid future macroeconomic growth in a globalizing world, coupled with increasing affluence, that will encourage rising energy demand. With a substantially younger population and a much higher birth rate than China, however, India will soon have more people than the PRC and could well outpace China's rate of increase in energy demand as well. India, in short, is a prospective future energy consumption superpower, whose broader political-economic prospects and requirements cannot be ignored.

Although the drivers of India's expanding role as a major energy consumer are generally similar to those of China, the prospective geopolitical expression within Eurasia is likely to be different. India is a maritime power, with deeply embedded historical ties to the Persian Gulf, and secondarily to Russia. Its rising domestic energy requirements make pipelines into Central Asia a plausible option, if political stability can be ensured. Yet pipelines cannot emerge so directly from domestic imperatives, as in the case of China, due to the constraint of Pakistan. This also complicates Indian access to Iran. The prospects for an Indian priority on seaborne energy supply—imported oil and LNG—are conversely stronger than in the Chinese case, again due to regional politics. India is also likely to play a more direct geopolitical role in the Middle East than is China, given long-standing human ties, more positive security relations with the United States, and deeper, albeit discreet, relationships with Israel.

Japan: Mature Yet Underestimated
Energy Superpower

Japan attracts remarkably little attention in world affairs, considering its massive economic scale. With a GDP of over $5 trillion, the country has the third largest economy in the world after the United States and China.[105] It also has the second largest foreign exchange reserves on earth, at well over $1 trillion, following only China.[106]

Unlike China and India, Japan is clearly a maturing nation, with all the strengths and weaknesses which that situation implies. The median age in Japan is almost forty-five, as opposed to twenty-six in India and thirty-five in China.[107] Japanese gross savings and capital outflows, including ODA, are among the highest in the world, as are educational levels. Japan may not itself be a catalytic agent of transformation, but it has enormous development experience and much to contribute in terms of technology, capital, and organization.

The huge Japanese macroeconomy rests on a remarkably small geographical base—at 378,000 square kilometers, the entire country is slightly less than the size of California. Like Britain, but unlike any of the other major Asian energy producers or consumers, Japan is an island nation—isolated to a meaningful degree both geographically and historically from the teeming continent next door. It is a stable country, one of only two among the eight I am examining that has not experienced a sharply reorienting critical juncture over the past four decades. Japan is also more ethnically homogeneous and distinct than most of the other energy players considered here, being, together with Korea, one of only two major producers or consumers that lacks a substantial Islamic population. For a variety of reasons, Japan is thus more detached than its neighbors from the emerging geopolitics of Eurasian continentalism, and a potentially important interlocutor between the continental and Pacific powers like the United States.

UNDERLYING ENERGY INSECURITIES

Japan does, however, suffer from some radical energy insecurities, which can best be seen in comparative context. Among the most pronounced and unsettling is the almost total absence of oil and gas reserves—Japan's entire proven domestic reserves of around 44 million barrels would supply the country for less than nine days at current rates of consumption.[108] Total domestic proven natural gas reserves would last a bit more than two months.[109]

Table 6.2. Japan's Low Energy Self-Sufficiency in Comparative
Perspective (2010)

	Japan	France	Italy	Germany	U.S.	U.K.
Domestic Energy/ Total Energy Supply	19.2	51.4	16.9	39.0	77.9	73.3
Oil Dependency/ Total Energy Supply	40.9	29.5	39.0	31.8	36.1	31.9
Net Imports/ Total Oil Supply	101.6	97.2	93.7	96.3	57.9	16.0
Imports from Middle East/ Total Oil Supply	86.9	15.5	36.6	4.7	10.7	5.4

Sources: International Energy Agency (IEA). *Energy Balances of OECD Countries,* 2010 edition.
Paris: International Energy Agency, 2011; and IEA. *Oil Information—Crude and Product Imports,*
2010 edition. Paris: International Energy Agency, 2011.
Notes: (1) Japanese oil imports exceed total supply/demand due both to stockpiling and Japanese
re-export of refined oil products. (2) These factors aside, Japan's imported 97.7 percent of the oil it
consumed in 2008, as noted above.

Only Korea and Taiwan, among major Asian economies, are so conspicuously devoid of hydrocarbons.

Four key statistical indicators, presented in Table 6.2, clarify Japan's extraordinarily low level of energy self-sufficiency. Japan has by far the lowest
ratio of domestic energy production to total consumption (19 percent) among
the major industrialized nations. It is more dependent on oil as a share of total energy consumption (41 percent) than any other G8 nation. Furthermore,
it imports a higher share of the oil it consumes than any other G8 member.
And a higher share of Japan's precious oil comes from the volatile Middle
East than any other industrialized country.

Market economists, of course, would not necessarily consider the foregoing as either a weakness or a deficiency. If international markets are prop-
erly functioning, they would argue, Japan could benefit, especially during
periods of major energy price decline, from its lack of embedded commitment to a domestic resource base. During the 1950s and 1960s, for example,
Japan did in fact profit economically from a long-term secular decline in oil
prices and the improved terms of trade that it enjoyed thereby as a major
importer. Some casual observers of the Asian scene have actually criticized
sustained Japanese policy efforts over the past three decades to reduce imported energy dependence on such grounds.[110]

Whatever the abstract economic merits, there is little question that Japanese
policymakers and corporate leaders themselves have regarded low energy

self-sufficiency over more than a century as a major national vulnerability, for a combination of sociocultural and institutional reasons.[111] On the cultural side, traditional Japanese distaste for the unknown, and uncertainty avoidance, probably come into play. Yet fundamental structural factors are also at work, both in the global political economy and within Japan itself, that help generate a profoundly different notion of energy security than that prevailing in the West.

JAPAN'S ENERGY ANGST

To differentiate it from more market-oriented Western conceptions, traditionally insensitive to the marked political-economic advantages that dominance in the global political economy gives to the United States and Britain, in particular, Japan's conception might be termed energy angst.[112] In its essence, this energy angst is an aversion to low domestic energy self-sufficiency, in part environmentally and institutionally determined, without regard to short-term market fluctuations. It has consistently influenced Japanese geopolitical calculations and energy policies for most of the past century.

Energy angst is rooted, of course, in Japan's radical lack of energy resources, as outlined above. Yet the problem, as Japanese policymakers and industrial leaders see it, is much deeper. Another key dimension is Japan's enduring sense of inadequate geoeconomic leverage in the global political economy. It has rarely perceived itself as a core member of the Western industrial world. Since World War II it has lacked the major political-military capability to exert international influence that the major Western nations, preeminently the United States, have possessed. And its multinationals have not exercised the direct corporate control over energy resources that many of their counterparts in the West have done, or that Japanese policymakers desire for their country in the future. Indeed, even today only around 15 percent of Japan's oil supply is equity oil, compared to the target of 40 percent for the year 2030 set by the powerful Ministry of Economics, Trade, and Industry (METI).[113]

Japan's energy angst is intensified by the domestic configuration of public and private institutions. Japan's Energy and Natural Resources Agency, for example, is a central component of METI, which rose sharply in stature through the 2001 reorganization of the Japanese government. This agency is also probably the part of METI that has retained the greatest regulatory discretion, amid the sweeping globalization and deregulation of Japanese industry that has transformed Tokyo's policymaking over the past three decades. The two oil shocks of the 1970s, the perceived national security imperatives that they generated, and the support of the politically influential electric power industry shielded the energy agency from the sweeping erosion of regulatory authority that plagued much of the Japanese bureaucracy. And the energy bureaucracy—as a heritage of Japan's turbulent history of depression and war—has long been uncommonly cohesive and well-developed institutionally.[114]

The institutional configuration of Japan's energy-related private sector also intensifies energy angst. The electric power industry, for example, has traditionally been among Japan's most profitable and influential, reflecting the pronounced community spirit of the leading firms in the industry and their traditionally close relationship to the powerful industrial bureaucracy. Virtually all of Japan's regional business federations have power company CEOs at their heads, who contribute liberally to both civic projects and influential local politicians, although the Fukushima accident has complicated their civic and political role since March, 2011.

Within the domestic political economy, general trading companies, steel, and banking also have strong interests in energy sector development. The general-trading companies—internationally distinctive in their ability to profit from diverse export, import, and investment transactions—are especially important as energy development project catalysts. Their powerful incentives to generate trade flows out of developing regions, such as India, China, and Central Asia, influence banks, manufacturers, and ultimately government in the same direction.

Japanese patterns of corporate governance also contribute to the resource development bias of Japanese energy policy, highly synergistic with that of the petrostates. Stakeholders are dominant in most energy firms, with shareholders largely drawn from friendly, affiliated financial institutions. Combined with a stable, hospitable regulatory environment, this institutional pattern gives the Japanese energy sector a long time horizon and high risk tolerance—much more pronounced than in the Anglo-American tradition. Even the sweeping political shift of September 2009 from one-party conservative dominance to somewhat more liberal administrations has not fundamentally changed this dynamic, since prevailing systems of corporate governance, privileging both executive and labor stakeholders, have not changed.

The energy angst of Japan's elite institutions, both public and private, has generated a distinct, embedded heritage that should continue to powerfully shape Japan's energy policies in the future as it has in the past, shifting

Table 6.3. Japanese Energy Policy Achievements (1973–2010)

	1973	2010
Oil Stockpiling (Days)	56	199*
Diversification (percent)		
(1) Oil	77.4	42.7**
(2) Nuclear	0.6	15.4**
(3) Natural Gas	1.5	17.0**
Energy Consumption Index (Manufacturing)	100.0	55.6

Sources: METI. *Enerugī Hakusho* [*Energy White Paper*], 2011 edition, http://www.enecho.meti.go
.jp/info/statistics/sekiyubi/pdf/h23/1110719oil.pdf ; METI. *Enerugī Hakusho* [*Energy White Paper*],
2010 edition, http://www.enecho.meti.go.jp/info/statistics/sekiyubi/pdf/h22/100215oil.pdf.
International Energy Agency. *World Energy Outlook, Natural Gas Information*,2011, p.IV238.
Notes: * Figure is for 2009. **Figures are the International Energy Agency's estimates for 2010.

political party configurations notwithstanding. Despite the rigidities and
resource misallocations that it undoubtedly bequeaths to the uncertain
political-economic future, that embedded angst has generated dramatic improvements in Japanese energy security since the oil shocks of the 1970s. Japan has more than tripled its oil stockpile since 1973 (Table 6.3). Meanwhile,
it has sharply diversified away from oil. And Japanese policy has greatly reduced the energy intensiveness of the national economy as a whole.

JAPAN'S IMPRESSIVE ENERGY POLICY COUNTERMEASURES

Japan has made remarkable strides over the past four decades in energy efficiency, cutting energy consumption per unit of GDP by well over 30 percent
since 1973. Today, it consumes only one-half of the energy per unit of GDP
that the United States and the European Union do, and only one-eighth as
much, by the same measure, as China and India.[115] Japan's sectoral approach
has led to such savings as a 35 percent reduction in steel industry energy consumption per unit of production since the 1970s and a heavy concentration of
energy-efficient, low-emission vehicles on Japanese highways.[116]

How Japan allayed its energy insecurities by diversifying away from oil and
achieving impressive energy efficiencies illustrates that country's most important synergy with other Eurasian nations—the efficacy of its energy policy
model, the 2011 Fukushima nuclear tragedy notwithstanding. There are three
dimensions of special relevance: (1) restrictions on oil use; (2) positive supports
for alternative fuels, including nuclear and solar power, as well as LNG; and (3)
energy efficiency policies. Japan's experience is relevant not only to consuming

nations such as China, India, and Korea, but also to the petrostates, which are striving to diversify away from hydrocarbon usage to conserve that increasingly valuable resource.

Japan's aggressive energy program has been powerfully driven of late by the extreme insecurity that the country felt following the oil shock of 1973, when the international price of oil abruptly quadrupled, compounding the inflationary pressures generated by the Nixon Shock counterstimulus package of 1971–1972. Japan experienced simultaneous demand-pull and cost-push inflation, with the consumer price index shooting up by nearly a quarter in a single year (1974), and widespread consumer shortages suddenly emerging. Tokyo's stock market also declined sharply, with the most severe recession in over two decades ensuing.

Amid the oil crisis, Japan took three important policy steps.[117] First, it passed the Petroleum Supply and Demand Optimization Law (late 1973), which set oil-supply targets and restricted oil use. Reinforced later by supplemental tax measures, this legislation encouraged industrial consumers in energy-intensive sectors such as steel, paper, and petrochemicals to economize on oil consumption, through such techniques as cogeneration. Second, it passed three laws in support of the nuclear industry (June, 1974). These encouraged the rapid expansion of reactor use from three in 1970 (two experimental) to forty-six in 1993, accounting in the latter year for 30 percent of total national electrical generation. Third, it passed the Petroleum Stockpiling Law (1975), which provided financial assistance to private firms in maintaining a seventy-day supply of petroleum products. Together, these three crisis-driven measures were the crucial policy steps generating the impressive diversification outcomes just described (Table 6.3), although the nuclear emphasis obviously had drawbacks that emerged in later years.

Japan's most notable energy policy success may well be in the area of energy efficiency. As noted in Figure 6.6, Japan has the lowest ratios of primary energy consumption to GDP of any major nation. While embedded decisions of the past, such as heavy reliance on commuter rail service rather than automobiles, are partly responsible for these formidable results, recent policy has powerfully shaped this outcome, especially in the industrial sector.

Japanese industrial energy efficiency, as discussed above, was powerfully stimulated by both restricted oil use and higher taxes, as well as a sectoral approach that concentrated conservation efforts on industries like steel and petrochemicals, where prospective gains were expected to be high.[118] These measures encouraged a remarkable round of corporate innovation in industrial processes

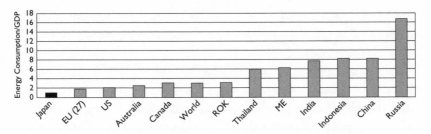

Figure 6.6: Japan's remarkable energy efficiency levels in comparative perspective.
Source: METI, *Enerugī Hakusho* [Energy White Paper], 2010 edition, http://www
.enecho.meti.go.jp/topics/hakusho/2010energyhtml/2–1-1.html.
Notes: (1) Primary energy consumption/GDP indicates energy efficiency. (2) ME
indicates Middle East. (3) Statistics are for 2007.

at the plant level, particularly in the recycling of waste energy, accompanied by substantial capital investment in energy-efficient facilities.[119] This combination cut Japanese industrial usage of energy up to 40 percent in high-consumption sectors such as steel, paper, and petrochemicals, producing the same product with a fraction of the energy.[120] Indeed, at the macro level, Japan today produces close to twice the level of industrial output as in the early 1970s, while its overall annual energy consumption has remained almost unchanged.[121]

In the 1980s, Japanese policymaking moved beyond heavy industry, to stress energy efficiency and alternate energy potential in the residential and commercial sectors. One early step was to enforce consumer appliance product standards that both increased energy efficiency and also enhanced functionality in other respects. A major beneficiary was the Japanese refrigerator, which has doubled in size since 1981, even as its energy usage per liter has fallen by 80 percent.[122]

In 1993, Japan's New Energy Development Organization implemented the New Sunshine Project, to consolidate domestic renewable research and development programs and to innovate in crucial areas.[123] The Top Runner Program, for example, was inaugurated to identify the most energy-efficient model in a variety of product lines, insisting that new products meet that high standard of efficiency. The program broadened in 2008 to encompass new vehicle efficiency standards, to be introduced in 2015. Energy efficiency standards were thus extended to progressively broader areas, supported by tax incentives to encourage introduction of standards-conforming equipment. Alternate energy was also encouraged by similar carrot-and-stick mechanisms, supporting the emergence of new industries like photovoltaics.[124]

Japanese energy policies have typically been distinctive not only in their details but also in their holistic character. They promote, in short, not only specific new technology or manufacturing processes, but also new paradigms for system design, that save more energy than alternative methods of organizing production or even of organizing daily life. Japan's current pioneering efforts to introduce smart electrical power grids are a case in point.[125] These encourage use of information technology to balance power supply and demand, filling two objectives: (1) increasing efficiencies in the utilization of existing equipment and appliances; and (2) making it technically feasible to harness electricity produced through solar and wind power to support broader electric power grids.[126] Being holistic, these innovative, highly efficient new power transmission systems are easily introduced even in rapidly growing economies, providing special complementarity to China, India, and the Eurasian petrostates.

IMPLICATIONS FOR FUTURE EURASIAN INTEGRATION

Japan is an island nation and a mature but highly affluent political economy. As such, Tokyo is unlikely to be a catalytic change agent, dramatically transforming broader Eurasian geopolitical equations or being decisively shaped by them. Neither is it likely to be a disruptive, destabilizing force. Yet Japan's technology, capital, and policy expertise could be very useful at times in cooperation with Western powers like the United States, in addressing the epic developmental problems that the large emerging consumers—China and India—as well as the petrostates are likely to confront. Japan has a geopolitical autonomy from continental Eurasia, coupled with strong technical capacity to assist its development, that makes it a potentially pivotal figure in global efforts to direct continentalism toward broader, less parochial goals.

Among the major energy producers and consumers of Eurasia, none exhibits higher levels of industrial and process technology than does Japan. Indeed, in many areas of consumer electronics, precision machinery, transportation, new materials development, and construction technology, Japan leads the world. As the first non-Western industrial power and as a country that has continued to assimilate Western technology and also to innovate in its own distinctive fashion, Japan has the expertise to help make Eurasia relatively self-sufficient in a broader global context.

In earlier sections of this and the previous chapter, I identified three major developmental imperatives common to both petrostates and large consumers: infrastructure building, energy efficiency, and structural transformation away from energy, toward high-growth and high value-added, yet less energy-intensive sectors of the future. Japan's own evolution, as the second largest economy in the world, can support progress toward the latter two goals. It can also aid technically in achieving the first, although Japan's own infrastructure building, within its confined island archipelago, does not have the broader, Eurasia-wide geopolitical consequences of China's Open Up the West program, for example.

Japan's synergies could be particularly strong with the petrostates, especially with respect to energy efficiency and energy demand management. As was noted earlier, Eurasian petrostates like Russia, Iran, Saudi Arabia, and its GCC neighbors have some of the most energy-intensive economies and the highest rates of energy demand expansion on earth. Indeed, especially in larger petrostates in the throes of political-economic transition, where populist pressures are strong, as in modern-day Iran, Japan's technical expertise in energy efficiency, mass transit, and alternate energy development is particularly needed. Such countries otherwise have a structural tendency to become destabilizing petrostates. Through its capital and technical expertise Japan could, *in the wake of a nuclear settlement*, potentially play a significant future role in helping stabilize the standing of petrostates like Iran in the broader international energy system.

As mentioned in Chapter 5, petrostates, especially those with a long history of reliance on hydrocarbon exports, are intent on preparing themselves for the day when their reserves are gone. Many understand that they have to develop themselves while they still have the financial wherewithal to do so, and that Japan can be helpful in that endeavor. For example, Sumitomo Corporation recently won a bid to build a futuristic power station and desalination complex with a power output of 1 million kilowatts in Saudi Arabia. The Saudis are also highly interested in Japan's advanced medical and optical-fiber communications equipment.[127]

SUMMARY

Japan, as a high-growth economy without appreciable domestic oil or gas reserves, has for more than a century been a major factor in the energy equations of both Asia and the broader world. Japan's involvement in World War II, including its fateful December 1941 attacks on Pearl Harbor and the Dutch East Indies, had an important energy-geopolitics dimension.[128] Yet Tokyo has not figured prominently and directly in the geopolitical calculus of energy for half a century and more. Its domestic politics, like its diplomacy, have been relatively stable and uneventful.

Japan's massive and continuing hydrocarbon import demand thus helps sustain the Middle East's deepening orientation toward Asia—Japan is, for example, the largest energy customer of both Saudi Arabia and the United Arab Emirates (UAE). Yet that has been true for many years. Japan has not provided the critical junctures—the radical political-economic departures—to give geopolitical momentum to that historic development.

Japan's contribution to the building of Eurasian energy relationships, as we have seen, is a subtler one than that of China, India, Russia, or Iran—less directly immersed in geopolitical ententes and rivalries, as it is a noncontinental power. It stands somewhat aloof from the integrationist pressures of pipeline politics and conversely suffers when continentalist alignments, as well as complexities in U.S.-Japan relations, encourage nations like Russia and China to pressure it for diplomatic concessions. Yet Japan nonetheless figures significantly in the geoeconomic calculus of Eurasia. Tokyo provides a massive market, as well as moderating technical and economic support. Japan's energy efficiency best practice is globally preeminent and addresses one of the greatest needs of the petrostates. Japanese ODA and technical support for infrastructure in countries ranging from India, China, and Central Asia potentially to a nonnuclear Iran, can have substantial future economic and geopolitical significance, both for Eurasia and for partners outside the region.

South Korea: Coping with the Ultimate in Energy Insecurity

Korea, unlike nearby Japan, is geographically a piece of the Asian continent, sandwiched between Russia and China, and divided into North and South only by an armistice line. The peninsula is thus inevitably more enmeshed in continentalist Eurasian geopolitics than the isolated Japanese archipelago. The South is also significantly smaller than Japan—the size of Indiana rather than California—with a population only 40 percent of Japan's and an economy just one-third as large.[129]

A SEVERE ENERGY CHALLENGE

The Korean peninsula confronts some of the most severe and intensely geopolitical energy security challenges in the world—a heavy burden for a relatively small nation. Those dilemmas form an unusual triad combination, intensifying the complications that they present to the country's economic future and magnifying the importance of both energy diplomacy with the major petrostates and potential alternatives to hydrocarbon dependence.[130] Most fundamentally, Korea lacks domestic sources of energy to fuel its own rapidly growing and energy-intensive economy. To make matters worse, it is unusually dependent on oil as a fuel source. In addition, most of the oil that Korea consumes, together with much of its natural gas, comes from the Middle East, and this Middle East reliance is rising.

This acute shortage of natural resources leaves Korea no choice but to rely heavily on imports. Of its total energy supply, 88.7 percent comes from abroad—one of the highest levels in the world. By comparison, Japan imports 88.8 percent of its energy, Germany 61.0 percent, and the United States only 22.1 percent.[131]

The problem of extraordinarily high energy import dependence is compounded for Korea by the fact that its economy as a whole is relatively small but very open and trade dependent. It suffers badly from oil shocks and financial crises, as in 1973, 1979, 1997, 2008, and 2011, because fluctuations in the exchange value of the Korean won typically magnify the domestic impact of these painful oscillations. Both energy and financial crises often sharply increase the price of scarce and vital energy in local currency terms. Nearby Japan is not affected nearly so severely, despite its similar resource deficiencies, due to the much greater scale of the Japanese economy (nearly three times Korea's size) and Japan's more limited trade dependence.

South Korea (Republic of Korea, ROK), which obtains around 50 percent of its primary energy from oil, compared with a global average of 38 percent, is thus also unusually dependent on oil as a fuel source. Apart from oil's heavy use in transportation, as Korea becomes increasingly an automobile society, the country also uses oil extensively to fuel power plants and provide home heating, with gasification still underdeveloped in comparative terms. To compound the country's problems, Korea has one of the highest levels of oil dependence on the volatile Middle East of any nation in the world—a dependence that has risen steadily over the past decade. By early 2010 the Middle East dependence exceeded 84 percent of Korea's entire oil imports.[132] Japan, at around 87 percent, was the only major consuming nation that was more Middle East dependent.[133] Continental pipelines from Russia would thus have some attraction for Seoul, if North Korea's belligerence and unpredictability did not so severely complicate the transit equation.

THE ROK'S DYNAMIC RESPONSE

With energy challenges so severe, and memories of traumas inflicted capriciously and unpredictably from abroad so vivid, perhaps it is not surprising that Korea's policy responses to its energy and financial dilemmas have generally been quite decisive and far sighted. Cold reality has required realistic action. Effective response has also been aided by political stability. Korea has fortunately been one of the few major Eurasian unaffected over the past two generations by a critical juncture reconfiguring its energy needs and orientations, allowing it to concentrate single mindedly on technical and diplomatic resolutions.

The quality of Korea's response to its daunting energy challenges has been enhanced by certain institutional features of the ROK's domestic political economy, many more conducive to efficient response even than those of Japan. First of all, the country's political structures are relatively well suited to crisis management. The ROK has a strong presidency, with the president elected for a single five-year term—a pattern contrasting with Japan's factionalized parliamentary system and frequently weak national leadership. Korea also has a unicameral National Assembly, contrasting to Japan's complex bicameral version. Furthermore, the ROK has a strong, strategic bureaucracy, including a Ministry of Foreign Affairs and Trade (MOFAT), which merges functions divided in Japan between the Ministry of Foreign Affairs and METI—and consequently the subject of sharp bureaucratic conflict. Largely for structural reasons, Korean policy responses are thus often more rapid and proactive than Japanese, an advantage that has often benefited Korea competitively in recent years.

Structurally, the Korean and Japanese private sectors are similarly organized in many ways. Both countries feature institutions—notably industrial groups (*chaebol* in Korea, paralleling *keiretsu* in Japan) and general trading companies—that prove highly functional in dealing with developing economies like those of China, India, and the Eurasian petrostates described above. Private sector competitive behavior has also often been more vigorous in Korea, however—partly due to larger numbers of competitive firms, but also partly due to more decisive governmental support, and also to more shareholder-oriented patterns of corporate governance. These became much more pronounced in the ROK during and just after the traumatic 1997–1998 Asian financial crisis, in contrast to a much slower and more limited pattern of transformation in Japan. Korea's smaller scale and greater dependence on the global economy, including multilateral institutions like the IMF, made this move toward shareholder dominance as a matter of necessity.

Policy-wise, one of Korea's most distinctive recent departures—a trait that symbolizes the country's deepening creative entrepreneurial spirit—is the proactive way that it has embraced the information revolution. In the mid-1990s, the Ministry of Information and Communication and the Informatization Promotion Committee were created to promote national informatization, and the government enacted a Framework Act on Informatization Promotion. Since then, the government has effectively pushed ahead with informatization, guided by a continually updated informatics vision, from Cyber Korea 21, to e-Korea 2006, to Broadband IT Korea Vision 2007, to the u-Korea Master Plan. As a result, Korea was ranked sixth in the 2008 UN e-Government Readiness Index and second in the 2008 e-Participation Index.[134] Korea garnered second place, after only Sweden, in the ICC Development Index 2007, and placed first in the percentage of fixed broadband Internet subscribers in the entire Asia-Pacific region. Korea's e-commerce volume rose over ten-fold between 2000 and 2008. Meanwhile, information and communication industry sales growth has averaged more than 10 percent annually since 1999.[135]

With respect to energy specifically, several Korean domestic policies at home have been particularly innovative, and have provided an enhanced basis for deepened Eurasian continental relationships in future. Korea has, for example, actively built its substantial and growing petroleum stockpile by encouraging foreign firms to stock oil in Korea under their ownership, on consignment, as an informal part of Korea's own national stockpiles, at special storage rates. The government has thus both expanded the national stockpile and provided foreign firms a potentially attractive business opportunity. Korea has also begun building a national gas grid, thus enhancing opportunities for LNG providers such as Qatar, and opening the way for deeper future relations with Russia, the world's largest piped-gas supplier, as well.[136]

The Korean energy policy most pregnant with international implications has been the ROK's dynamic civilian nuclear program. Korea built its first nuclear reactor in 1978 with U.S. technology, and the sector has grown rapidly in sophistication, landing a $40 billion export deal in the Middle East only thirty-one years later.[137] Over 36 percent of Korea's electricity is now derived from nuclear power, and that ratio has been rising steadily for the past two decades, little influenced by the Fukushima tragedy in neighboring Japan.[138] Korea currently has twenty reactors in operation, configured in four large nuclear complexes. Twelve additional domestic plants, presumably to be supervised by Korea Hydro Nuclear Power, are currently in the construction or planning phases.[139] When completed, these will further increase the nuclear share in Korea's domestic electricity consumption to a projected 59 percent of electricity supply by 2030.[140] Since 1995, all nuclear plants in South Korea have been built almost exclusively with local technology, and this pattern will likely prevail in the future as well.

EMERGING SYNERGIES WITH EURASIAN PETROSTATES
AND EMERGING CONSUMERS

Korea, although continental, is relatively detached geographically from the major petrostates and developing economies of Asia, other than China, as Japan also is. Korea is likewise small enough that its own economic evolution has only very limited international implications. Yet the ROK can nevertheless contribute significantly to the development of nations elsewhere across Asia, by helping provide infrastructure, as well as capital and consumer goods, and technology. In many cases the ROK can supply other nations more cheaply and rapidly than Japan, with the additional supportive factor of close, interactive government-business relationships.

For its part, South Korea clearly needs the other six developing nations considered here, due to their expanding markets and, in the case of petrostates, their energy as well. As noted above, Korea's energy needs are substantial: although only the thirteenth largest nation in the world, in terms of economic scale, it is the fifth largest oil importer on earth.[141] And these needs will rise steadily with Korea's economic growth, as the ROK has few domestic energy resources.

The one plausible escape for South Korea from its domestic energy dilemmas—nuclear power—is also felicitously a major potential source of export revenue as well.[142] Half of the world's current inventory of 436 nuclear reactors is scheduled for retirement by 2030, and with long-term energy prices rising, there is clearly replacement demand, the Fukushima incident not withstanding. In addition, economic growth in Asia and the Middle East generates important new commercial opportunities there, despite post-Fukushima controversies about nuclear power in the G-7 nations. India and China, for example, are planning to build roughly 150 new nuclear plants between them.

The Persian Gulf also has ambitious plans, not least because it commands 75 percent of the desalinization capacity in the world and can only desalinate large quantities of seawater efficiently using nuclear power.[143] According to the World Nuclear Association, ten of the eleven reactor projects on which construction started in 2009 were in Asia—West, East, or South. And thirty-six of the fifty-four reactors currently being built worldwide, at any stage of construction, are located on the continent as well.[144]

Under President Lee Myung-bak, himself a former president of Hyundai Engineering and Construction,[145] the ROK has targeted the civilian nuclear sector as a high export priority for the foreseeable future. By the year 2030,

Korea's Ministry of Knowledge and Economy has set a national goal of exporting eighty reactors, which it estimates would be worth around $400 billion. This target, if realized, would prospectively make South Korea the third largest nuclear exporter in the world, with a 20 percent share of the global market.[146] Presumably sales along the rapidly growing New Energy Silk Road across Eurasia, as the Koreans call it, would constitute a major share of the ROK's total.

Seoul suddenly established itself as a credible international competitor in the nuclear marketplace early in December 2009, when it won a spectacular contract to build and service four 1,400 megawatt nuclear reactors, priced at $5 billion each, in the UAE. The total contract price tag, including $20 billion for servicing, maintaining, and supplying fuel for the reactors over their sixty-year life span, came to $40 billion—the biggest single contract that South Korean firms had ever secured overseas.[147] And this was Korea's very first nuclear export contract bid—landed just twenty-two years after the country built its own first nuclear plant at home, relying entirely on imported technology.

The huge UAE export contract is unlikely to be Korea's last, particularly since Japanese competition has been blunted by the Fukushima accident. The ROK has set an ambitious goal of garnering six additional multibillion-dollar reactor orders by 2012, beyond the four just contracted in the UAE.[148] Prospects appear to be especially good elsewhere in the Middle East. Korea and Turkey have been negotiating a protocol to cooperate on the construction of Turkey's second planned nuclear plant, at Mersin, on the Mediterranean coast.[149] Jordan, which has to import nearly 95 percent of its energy requirements, at a cost of a fifth of its GDP, and which also has severe water shortages that make nuclear-powered desalinization attractive, has also concluded contracts with the Koreans.[150]

Nuclear power is far from the only area where Korea's technical skills match developmental needs elsewhere along the New Silk Road, in a cost-effective manner. Civil construction is another important sector. In early 2010, Korea reached an important milestone in that regard, with the dedication in Dubai of the $1.5 billion Burj Khalifa. With that ceremonial conclusion, the new skyscraper became the tallest building in the world, built by Samsung over six years of construction. Hundreds of miles away, Korean Airlines is also transforming the Navoi International Airport of Uzbekistan, turning it into a major Eurasian cargo transshipment center.[151]

In a variety of service sectors apart from construction, Korea is deepening its relations with other continental Eurasian states also. In 2009, it welcomed more than 60,000 medical tourists from around the world, with a special focus on Middle Easterners, providing food and religious facilities to meet their special needs.[152] It is also deepening bilateral service ties with Russia. In 2009 South Korea sent its first astronaut, Yi So Yeon, into space aboard a Russian Soyuz rocket, after completing training in Russia.[153] Korean firms also outsource considerable research and development in Russia, capitalizing on that country's excellent work in the basic sciences and software, combining it with Korean strengths in digital electronics, to improve their air conditioners, digital TVs, and cell phones.

SUMMARY

Korea, with an exposed high-growth economy but virtually no domestic oil or gas reserves, has some of the most difficult energy challenges in the world. Its vulnerabilities are similar to those of Japan, but in an economy only one-third of Japan's size, which is much more trade dependent and more reliant on foreign capital flows than is Japan. A divided nation located physically on the Eurasian continent, Korea is inevitably more geopolitically engaged than insular Japan, although its peripheral position on the continent makes it of consequence to energy geopolitics first and foremost on matters relating to North Korea and Northeast Asian energy pipelines. As its politics have been stable, however, South Korea has not contributed critical junctures that have so critically intensified Eurasian geopolitical relationships.

Korea is, however, a significant catalyst for more technical energy relationships among East Asia, Eurasia, and the Middle East, that can also substantially aid the development of Asia's emerging giants, China and India. The ROK's institutions and its transnational networks—including a strong presidency, proactive ministries, general trading companies, and diaspora networks of ethnic Koreans in Russia and Central Asia—all play a role. Korea's particular competitive strengths lie in infrastructure and, recently, nuclear plant construction, enhanced significantly by close business-government coordination, and aggressive support from top levels of the Korean government.

CONCLUSION: BROADENING EURASIAN POLITICAL-ECONOMIC COMPLEMENTARITY

Across the preceding pages, surveying the major energy consumers of Asia, we have found enormous complementarities among them, many of which they share more profoundly with one another than they do with the broader world. We first considered the two great developing economies, China and India—the most populous nations on earth, with 40 percent of the human race dwelling within their collective borders. And we noted the enormity of the challenge posed to future global energy supply and environmental quality by their still humble economic circumstances—some of the lowest per capita rates of energy consumption in the world.

Those individual consumption rates will inevitably rise, with growing income, propelled by broad global demand for the cost-effective products and services of these nations. And as they consume more, China and India both will need more energy, particularly of the less polluting varieties—gas and nuclear power. The emerging Asian giants will also need more energy infrastructure and more support for their other, varied developmental requirements.

The two great consumers of industrial Northeast Asia—Japan and Korea—are more advanced economically. Although Japan is significantly larger, more affluent, and in many ways more advanced technologically, Korea is more dynamic politically, with a more cost-competitive panoply of products and services in most areas. Both are natural suppliers for the continent, both to the petrostates and to the two large Asian consuming economies as well.

The world economy, of course, is increasingly globalized, with most products and services traveling transcontinentally with ease. Yet the world is by no means totally "flat," as Tom Friedman would have it, especially with respect to energy supply and demand.[154] Geography still matters. The West of Eurasia, on the one hand, and its populous East and South on the other, arguably have a natural complementarity and synergy with one another, geographically as well as culturally, that they do not share with the broader world. Through the country-specific analysis of the foregoing pages, we have gained important insights into just what those intracontinental synergies might be, and it makes sense to summarize them here.

First of all, the petrostates and consumers of Eurasia are drawn together economically by energy itself—the consumers need it, and the producers need to sell it. World markets, to be sure, are global. Yet the most rapidly growing continental market is in Asia, and well over half of the Persian Gulf petrostates' production flows there. Within a decade, due mainly to Asian growth, that share will rise to 75 percent. The Asian consumers, as we have seen, are conversely also in great need—either due to their rapid growth, as in China and India, or due to their radical insufficiency, as in Japan and Korea. Fortunately, they are also competitive manufacturers, capable of supplying a broad range of products that the petrostates do not readily produce themselves.

Second, the Eurasian petrostates and consumers also have a geographically ordained complementarity that cannot be ignored. All of the consumers, as well as the Persian Gulf petrostates, such as Saudi Arabia and Iran, are connected by highly direct, if lengthy, maritime routes. And many of the parties, including China, Russia, and Kazakhstan, have direct overland connections on the Eurasian continent as well, that are rendered ever more attractive by accelerating growth and energy demand in the interior of Asia. With time, the pipeline linkages, like other infrastructure, will likely grow increasingly intimate, their long-distance economics transformed by China's explosive growth, and the thirst for energy, as well as westward and southwestward bias, which such growth inspires.

The two most economically advanced Asian consuming states, Japan and South Korea, also have industrial, financial, and technical capabilities that are unusually complementary to those of the other six developing economies we have examined—the four petrostates, together with China and India. Those complementarities lie in two areas: infrastructure and economic transformation.

Japan and Korea both have sophisticated industrial groups, and within them general trading companies, that are well versed in turnkey projects. These in turn comprehensively involve resource extraction, processing, transportation, and even financing. Northeast Asian industrial groups have no precise analogues in the West and are uniquely suited to projects in developing nations that require barter or compensation transactions and that generate multiple trade flows. Both Korea and particularly Japan also pursue extensive government aid and technical assistance programs that can augment the capabilities of the private sector. And both countries have strong incentives, rooted in energy insecurity, for doing so.

In a world of rising energy prices—stimulated in a basic, enduring way by the rise of the rest[155]—the petrostates enjoy increasing affluence, of course, but also important new developmental challenges. One, ironically, is energy efficiency. Hydrocarbons are not only depleting resources but also growing extremely precious. Particularly in the larger petrostates now undergoing social transformation, notably Russia and Iran, pressures to subsidize and squander them are strong. These countries badly need technical and policy advice on both how to economize and also how to reorder their societies to cut energy usage. Even where hydrocarbons are not depleting to the point of scarcity, as in the Persian Gulf, it is very costly to squander them. Japan and Korea are uniquely capable of aiding both stabilizing and destabilizing producers in their economizing task, helping to moderate the behavior of all parties along the way.

Japan and Korea today—as well as China and India in the future—can also aid the petrostates in developing new energy alternatives to hydrocarbons, including nuclear power. The Asian consumers are particularly well equipped in this regard due to both their broader industrial efficiency and also their own energy insecurities, which they have tried to reduce by moving beyond oil and gas. Japan is particularly competitive in photovoltaics and has dominated the solar power market for most of the past decade. Traditionally Japan has been stronger in the nuclear sector, but Korea dramatically showed its rising capabilities in December 2009 in landing the $40 billion UAE nuclear contract, against stiff Japanese, American, and European competition. In the wake of Fukushima, that Korean competitive advantage may have lengthened in the short-run, although Japanese technical strengths and ability to learn from the past remain formidable.

Over the past two chapters, I have focused on eight trees in the forest of Eurasian energy geopolitics—four producers and four consumers. In doing so, I have tried to peer inside the black box of individual nation-states and to identify the subnational challenges, actors, incentives, and policies driving the key Eurasian political economies. We have found remarkable complementarities and synergies, unlocked by the critical junctures of the past four decades. I explore these transcontinental synergies further in the pages to come, profiling the Eurasian nexus of deepening energy interdependence that is steadily bringing both a new energy geopolitics and a new continental interdependence of global importance fitfully into being.

Chapter 7 Emerging Ententes Amid Complex Continentalism

Clearly there are important complementarities between the petro-states and the energy-insecure consumers of Eurasia, as we have seen in the past two chapters. The petrostates need markets for their hydrocarbons—readily available and geographically accessible to the East, in Asia. The petrostates need technical assistance and manpower to assist their development—also accessible in Asia. And many of the most chronic inefficiencies of the petrostates, as we have seen, are in energy usage, construction, and mass transport—all areas of Japanese, Korean, Chinese, and Indian technical as well as industrial strength.

For many years, despite the latent complementarities that so clearly prevail, the Eurasian nations failed to cohere, or even to deal pro-actively with one another, especially across their land frontiers. Their static economies generated few incentives for interchange, and the rigid political barriers of the Cold War inhibited what limited efforts were made. Many of these nations were bystanders to history, failing to play out their parochial aspirations substantially on the broader world stage.

Six critical junctures, as we saw in Chapter 3, began to transform this continental picture of rigidity, hesitance, and inaction. Sweeping Chinese and Indian reforms fatefully set new growth engines in motion that became ravenous for energy; the transformation of the Soviet Union, Saudi Arabia, and Iran, as well as the role of multinational energy firms, engendered new political-economic means of supplying it. Through these historic junctures, new prospects were created for transforming the latent underlying complementarities of the petro-states and consuming nations of Eurasia into concrete new relationships, more direct and seriously interactive than ever before.

Not all the new relationships, of course, were cooperative. Deepening continental interdependence bred new rivalries and distrust as well, notably among China, India, and Japan. Yet economic forces have mitigated these tensions and at times generated collective interests also.

This chapter examines the collaborative new transregional relationships that have begun fitfully to emerge, linking East, South, and West Asians and Eurasians once again with partners across their heretofore disjointed continent. These emerging relationships are subregional in character. They by no means create, in the aggregate, a cohesive Eurasian economic, political, or geostrategic entity, however much they foster long-term interdependence. These new collaborations, or ententes, as I call them, take many forms—diplomatic, commercial, political-military, corporate, and even cultural.[1] They are conducted at many levels—subnational, national, and, at the multinational level, in many forms—bilateral, minilateral, and multilateral.

These entente relationships are by no means all mutually collegial—rivalries, to repeat, have not disappeared from Asia. Yet a palpable new connectivity and interdependence that has been insufficiently remarked, which I call "complex continentalism," is nevertheless slowly emerging.[2] Asia, at last, is "a continent created."[3]

A COLD WAR HERITAGE OF DIVISION

To understand what is new and distinctive about now-emerging Eurasian ententes, it is especially useful to contrast them with the rigid and ideologically bounded configurations that increasingly constrained the continent for nearly seven decades from the late 1920s, in the wake of the Russian and then the Chinese revolutions. First Stalin erected an autarkic "socialism in one state" (1924–1926),[4] cutting the Soviet Union off from long-standing Central

Asian and East Asian ties that even Czarist Russians and early Bolsheviks had nurtured.[5] Then Mao and his American adversaries, working at cross-purposes yet ironically, in tandem, cut mainland China off from traditional ties with the rest of the continent, following the Chinese Revolution of 1949.[6] The Korean War intensified U.S. determination to isolate the fledgling PRC, leading to both diplomatic ostracism and an economic embargo with which Washington induced nearby allies such as Japan, South Korea, and Southeast Asian states, not to mention Taiwan, to cooperate.[7] Yet bitter, lingering wartime memories made it virtually impossible for these American allies—especially Japan and South Korea—to cooperate with one another.

To complete the fragmentation of the continent, China and the Soviet Union split, in acrimony, during the late 1950s, with Soviet advisors being expelled from China and the Sino-Soviet borders closed to most commerce and human traffic for over a generation, from 1959 until the mid-1980s.[8] China and India, collaborators in the nonaligned movement of the 1950s, were also subsequently estranged by their border war of 1962, and their mutual frontiers closed. Relations between China and the Soviet Union continued to spiral downward amid the ensuing Cultural Revolution, and the two communist giants actually came to blows on Damanskii Island (Zhenbao to the Chinese), atop the frozen Ussuri River, in early March 1969.[9]

The Cold War pattern, in short, was one of isolation and fragmentation among the nations of Eurasia, from the 1920s well into the 1960s. The only formal entente to speak of, on the communist side, was the Sino-Soviet Pact of February 1950, which effectively became a dead letter within a decade of its signing. On the capitalist side of the Cold War, key nations were incorporated, either multilaterally, as in the case of the Southeast Asia Treaty Organization, or bilaterally, through a hub-and-spokes network of individual treaties, in a Washington-centric web of security arrangements, supplemented by preferential economic access to the massive American market.[10]

The Cold War international order, starkly bipolar at the global level, divided Eurasia quite definitively into three categories: (1) allies of the United States (Japan, South Korea, Taiwan, Iraq until 1958, South Vietnam until 1975, Iran until 1979, and Thailand); (2) allies of the Soviet Union (China until around 1960, North Vietnam and then unified Vietnam after 1975, North Korea); and (3) a group of intermediate powers, including most conspicuously India and most of the Middle East and Southeast Asia, as well as China, following the Nixon Presidential visit of February 1972. Over the course of the

1970s several countries within this intermediate group began nurturing ties at various levels with the two principal international blocs; Indian technological exchanges and arms deals with the Soviet Union, together with countervailing economic and financial ties to the United States, were cases in point. Yet even though the rigidly bipolar Cold War system was beginning to blur at the edges in this fashion, it was not until the six critical junctures enumerated in Chapter 3, stretching from the early 1970s through the late 1990s, that new, decisively post–Cold War configurations began clearly to emerge.

IMPULSES FOR RISING CONTINENTAL COHESION

Energy, as we have seen, provides a powerful background rationale for the new and much more dynamic transcontinental relations across Eurasia that have begun to emerge in the wake of recent critical junctures. The advent of rapid growth in India, combined with continuing expansion in China, have proved synergistic to regional economic ties with Middle East and Central Asian energy producers. This "Chindian" growth has made Central Asia—a relatively high-cost supplier with infrastructural problems, located fortuitously close to the two Asian giants—a much more consequential factor in global energy equations than heretofore. Important new energy projects, such as the Tengiz and Kashagan fields in Kazakhstan, supported by multinational capital and technology, are aiding this integration process.

There are, however, other powerful indigenous forces at work also. As we have seen, East Asia, India, and the Middle East have a long-shared history of pan-Asianism. Pax Americana has been powerful in recent years, but it has stirred backlash as well.

Resentment of American global dominance has intensified since 2000, because of both Washington's persistent unilateralist tendencies early in the decade and its intrusiveness. Nowhere have these dual trends manifested themselves more clearly than across Eurasia. Never the home of stable democracy, and never previously the location of American military bases, Central Asia and Afghanistan have been pressed to host a U.S. presence since the September 2001 terrorist attacks on the World Trade Center and the Pentagon. Under the Obama administration, U.S. involvement in the area has continued to be intense, even as Washington has endeavored to strike a more multilateralist pose.

Border Agreements

Shifting regional politics over the past few years have fueled resentment against the West and animated intraregional diplomacy. The early origins of deepened Eurasian ties lie back in the late 1980s, as China and the former Soviet Union slowly repaired their ruptured bilateral relations. In 1987 those congenitally closed and suspicious communist giants began historic negotiations to delimit their 4,600-mile land border, which significantly helped to improve their ties. These border talks, concluding successfully with a 1997 treaty on military frontier force reduction, were paralleled by bilateral border discussions by both the Chinese and the Russians with Kazakhstan, Kyrgyzstan, and Tajikistan, which have all proved generally successful.

China's surprisingly flexible attitude proved to be a key catalyst for broader territorial accommodation in the heart of the continent. The collapse of the Soviet Union presented China with an ideal opportunity to regain the more than 34,000 square kilometers of territory it claimed in Central Asia. In the context of ethnic unrest, however, the PRC chose to improve ties with the newly independent states, so as to deny external support to separatist groups in Xinjiang.

China first pursued compromise in its dispute with Kazakhstan, Xinjiang's largest neighbor, starting talks less than a year after the collapse of the Soviet Union. In 1994, 1996, and 1997 bilateral agreements concluded with Kazakhstan, China made significant concessions, retaining only 22 percent of disputed areas. In 1996 and 1999, the PRC made similar concessions in agreements with Kyrgyzstan, where it received about 32 percent of the bilaterally disputed land. A civil war that erupted after the collapse of the Soviet Union, however, stalled negotiations with Tajikistan. Talks resumed in 1997, leading to a preliminary agreement in 1999, dividing one disputed sector evenly, and to a supplemental agreement in 2002. Beijing made a major concession in this latter agreement, dropping most of its traditional 28,000-square-kilometer claim in the Pamir Mountains, which it had pressed since the late nineteenth century.[11]

The Challenge of Ethnic Diversity
and the Specter of Irredentism

Eurasia, except for homogeneous Japan and Korea in the Northeast, has long been an ethnically, linguistically, and religiously diverse continent—the product of vigorous migrations and intermingling, driven variously over the centuries by conquest and by trade. That pervasive diversity has often complicated governance and not surprisingly rendered the region's elites congenitally apprehensive. Over the past two decades the endemic challenge of managing the diversity that governments in the region face has been complicated by social mobilization (education, urbanization, and so on). It has been intensified by major changes in political boundaries and leaders—many related to the 1991 collapse of the Soviet Union and the sudden creation of new successor states with limited legitimacy of their own.

Almost all of the Eurasian continental states have substantial, restive minorities, on which local elites unavoidably cast a nervous collective eye. The three large non-Muslim countries (China, Russia, and India), for example, all have significant Muslim populations—20 million in China, over 15 million in Russia, and 160 million in India. Indeed, India's Islamic community is the second largest in the entire world, even though the huge figure comprises less than 15 percent of India's overall population.[12] And Uzbeks, Uyghurs, Tatars, Azeris, and Russians, to name just a few, are all scattered across several frontiers, with associations and claims transcending national boundaries. Their claims enhance prospects for both commerce and the sort of explosive ethnic conflict that erupted in Xinjiang in June 2009, in Kyrgyzstan a year later, and to a lesser degree in Xinjiang once again during the summer of 2011.[13]

Common Fears of a Rising Fundamentalist Threat

The original contacts and confidence building that set continentalist ties among China, Russia, and the other post-Soviet states in motion at the personal level were initiated through the border talks of the mid-1990s. The determination to proceed to deeper cooperation beyond border negotiations alone was intensified further by a common perception of rising Islamic fundamentalist threat, shared from the late 1990s on by elite groups throughout the region. The core nations all have substantial—and restive—minority Islamic populations, as I have noted, while Islam is the dominant religion throughout Central Asia also. Although Russia had been conscious of this issue from Soviet days, in part due to its own protracted struggles in Chechnya and Afghanistan, Islamic fundamentalism was a newer concern for the Chinese and the fledgling nations of Central Asia.

Xinjiang, in the heart of the continent—a major energy producer, and growing rapidly—has been one conspicuous flashpoint for nearly two decades. Four major developments contributed to rising turbulence there, in China's most heavily Muslim province, where the Turkic-speaking Uyghur people make up roughly 45 percent of the population, compared to slightly over 40 percent for the Han Chinese.[14] First, the initiation of Deng Xiaoping's economic reforms in the late 1970s released Xinjiang from the quasi-military rule that had prevailed since the communist takeover in 1949 and, to a substantial extent, for more than a century before that. Second, the opening after 1987 of China's western border with Central Asia ended Xinjiang's forty-year isolation from its neighbors, allowing the renewal of trade and contact with the rest of Central Asia. Third, the collapse of the Soviet Union at the end of 1991, and the establishment of independent states by Islamic (Turkic and Iranian/Tajik) neighbors created a model of political sovereignty and cultural autonomy that inspired many Turkic Uyghurs in Xinjiang. And finally, the defeat of the Soviet Union's Red Army by Islamic fundamentalists in Afghanistan, the revival of Islam itself in post-Soviet Central Asia, and the emergence of well-funded radical Islamic movements in both of those regions inspired many of Xinjiang's Muslims to redefine their aspirations in religious terms.

By the mid-1990s, Xinjiang, after generations of isolation, was thus suddenly China's only province bordered by eight countries—with all of which it had economic and cultural contact.[15] And five of those eight new neighboring nations were predominantly Muslim, with several having substantial Uyghur populations, dating from classic Silk Road days.[16] Given Xinjiang's own Turkic and Islamic heritage, that China would fear unrest and desire for cooperation from its neighbors in mitigating that danger is not surprising.[17]

Rising Elite Support for Defensive Multilateralism

Apart from broad collective-defense organizations, such as NATO and the Warsaw Pact, multilateralism did not flourish in the bipolar Cold War era, outside of Western Europe. Even ostentatious gatherings like the Bandung Non-Aligned Conference of 1955 generated few enduring institutional consequences. Postrevolutionary China also was broadly reluctant about multilateralism.[18] Yet in June 1996, PRC leaders nevertheless took the initiative in establishing the so-called Shanghai Five grouping, a distinct innovation for continental Eurasia, explicitly directed against "the three hostile forces: terrorism, separatism, and extremism,"[19] with its defensive concerns about stability in Xinjiang clearly important in the background. During the same year, the PRC also launched its Strike Hard campaign against separatists in Xinjiang, following this with a New Criminal Law in the spring of 1998. This statute redefined "counter-revolutionary crimes" as "crimes against the state," and included within this definition actions "stirring up anti-ethnic sentiment."[20] China's initiative in cofounding the Shanghai Five—with Russia and three neighboring Central Asian Islamic states—thus appears clearly related to deepening fears among the Chinese elite, following the breakup of the Soviet Union, concerning the prospect of ethnic unrest in Xinjiang. Zhongnanhai realized that it needed to coordinate with neighboring governments to contain any possible unrest and to avoid provocations encouraging neighbors to play the ethnic card.

Creation of the new security framework could not alone, of course, immediately stem the tide of violence. In February 1997, there was a large riot in the Xinjiang town of Yining, and a Xinjiang train was derailed by a bomb. Later the same year bus stations in both Beijing and Urumqi were bombed. Two years further on, in July 1999, a power station at Hejing (in Xinjiang) was similarly attacked.[21]

Whatever general biases against multilateralism China may previously have entertained, trans-Eurasian cooperation in the late 1990s did promise to inhibit subversive transnational activity involving Xinjiang's neighbors and expatriate Uyghurs living outside China. This incentive has been intensified over the years by continuing turbulence, particularly since 2008.[22] As long as the danger of significant fundamentalist violence in Xinjiang persists, that prospect will provide at least one continuing motivation, quintessentially defensive, for Chinese activism in promoting multilateral cooperation across Central Asia.

Trade as a Background Determinant

To get a more concrete sense of just how continental Eurasia is gaining increasing coherence and along what axes, it is useful to consider recent regional trade patterns. Trade, after all, is one of the most easily quantifiable and acceptable indicators of interdependence. Bilateral trade among the eight major energy producers and consumers of Asia that we have been following has been growing explosively, the concrete details of which are presented in Table 7.1.

Several conclusions can be drawn from reviewing this Eurasian trade data. First of all, the rate of increase in virtually all major bilateral intra-Asian trade relationships has been more rapid over the past decade than that of world trade in general. World trade has grown over 94 percent since 2000; only bilateral trade between Japan and Korea (+31 percent); Japan and Iran (+87 percent); and Russia and India (+67 percent) has grown more slowly.[23] In each of those cases, there is a plausible explanation—political tensions in

Table 7.1. Eurasia's Dynamic Regional Trade Relationships

A. Traditional Relationships (millions of dollars)

	1990	2000	2010	2010/2000
Russia/Kazakhstan	3,658**	4,443.45	16,138.43	3.6
Russia/Uzbekistan	1,685.3**	936.67	3,226.21	3.4
Russia/India	1,391*	1,637.3	4,621.11	2.8
Japan/Saudi Arabia	13,844.91	17,276.76	42,360.65	2.5
Japan/Iran	5,086.30	5,928.72	13,239.74	2.2
Russia/Turkmenistan	172**	602.88	1,287.25	2.1
Japan/ROK	29,242.10	51,156.49	90,919.05	1.8

B. Renewed Relationships (millions of dollars)

	1990	2000	2010	2010/2000
Russia/PRC	4,406.5*	6,180.62	56,015.40	9.1
Japan/Russia	3,481.06*	5,124.23	24,230.50	4.7
Japan/PRC	18,201.43	85,512.02	302,995.03	3.5

C. Emerging Relationships (millions of dollars)

	1990	2000	2010	2010/2000
PRC/Turkmenistan	4.463*	16.16	1,566.55	96.9
PRC/Uzbekistan	52.165*	51.47	2,477.30	48.1
PRC/India	270.14	2,911.16	61,735.72	21.2
India/Iran	557.64	679.5	13,429.01	19.8
PRC/Saudi Arabia	417.10	3,098.23	43,230.42	14.0
PRC/Kazakhstan	363.36*	1,556.91	20,313.60	13.0
India/Saudi Arabia	1,724.16	2,022.75	24,562.14	12.1
PRC/Iran	335.10	2,486.47	29,332.66	11.8
ROK/India	718.80	2,310.87	17,109.05	7.4
ROK/Kazakhstan	10.8*	131.77	938.32	7.1
ROK/Russia	192*	2,846.39	17,659.29	6.2
PRC/ROK	669.11	34,500.45	206,834.39	6.0
Japan/Kazakhstan	96.16***	160.17	828.66	5.2
India/Kazakhstan	1.016***	58.25	294.66	5.1
ROK/Iran	1,580.4****	3,768.12	11,536.96	3.1
Russia/Iran	306.4*	683.28	1,322.99	1.9

Source: International Monetary Fund. *Directions of Trade Statistics.* http://www.imf.org/external
/data.htm, accessed 2011.

Notes: * Figure is for 1991, due to data availability. ** Figure is for 1992, due to data availability.
*** Figure is for 1993, due to data availability. **** Figure is for 1994, due to data availability.

the former two cases, and the unwinding of strong Cold War economic ties between Moscow and New Delhi in the latter.

A second broad pattern evident in Table 7.1 is that nontraditional, emerging trade relations—mostly transcontinental in nature—are growing very rapidly, albeit often from a relatively small base. India-Iran, China-India, China-Kazakhstan, and China-Iran trade ties, in particular, are deepening very rapidly. Many of these emerging relationships involve China, and only one (with Kazakhstan) involves Japan, suggesting that China may benefit disproportionately from the new continentalism. "Renewed" relationships, those plagued by intermittent historical or territorial difficulties subsequently overcome, such as Japan-China after Koizumi's Yasukuni Shrine visits, or Russia-China after their 1959 split and later reconciliation, are in an intermediate category.

A third broad pattern is the rapid pace of expansion in Chinese and Indian trade relationships with other major Eurasian nations, such as Kazakhstan and Uzbekistan. This pattern, of course, is inspired by the rapid economic growth of those giants, and is not in itself surprising. It does suggest, however, that they are playing, and can continue to play, a key role in determining future regional political-economic configurations. In contrast to Russia, however, China and India do not have many arms, or much oil and gas, to supply other nations of the region.[24] Their attraction is mainly in their manufactures, and in processed agricultural goods.

A fourth pattern is the striking pace of trade across old Cold War boundaries, especially over the past decade, and especially when the nations in question had been the object of a critical juncture. Trade among China, India, Kazakhstan, and Iran demonstrates this point. Border trade between China and Turkmenistan has also been booming, driven by natural gas flows; in 2010, it actually surpassed Turkmenistan's trade with Russia itself, although Moscow has other sources of leverage, as we shall see.

Russia as a Catalytic Force

Of all the six critical junctures that have so fatefully configured the Eurasian political economy over the past few decades, none have been more important than the two that fatefully transformed the Soviet Union during the 1990s. The collapse of the USSR at the end of 1991, first of all, allowed the Central Asian republics to reach out to the east and the south for the first time in three-quarters of a century, forging new relationships with China, India, Iran, and Turkey, as well as Japan and Korea. As we have seen, some of these associations, especially with China, have become most dynamic. Second, the advent of the Putin administration in December 1999 began the revival of Russia as a proactive force in continental integration—using energy and arms shipments, rather than military force or trade, as principal tools of reassertion—both with Central Asia and with East and South Asia as well.

Russia, especially under Putin and Medvedev, has had uniquely powerful incentives to form and to lead a balancing coalition, beginning in the near abroad and its immediate environs, to offset American global power and to preempt its further expansion. Balancing, after all, had been the quintessential Soviet role during the Cold War, and that was the great-power role that many domestic interests in Russia, as well as Kremlin leadership itself, wanted the country to reassume. American assertiveness during the 1990s, epitomized in the expansion of NATO and the Kosovo War, intensified Moscow's long-standing great-power sentiments. Russia also felt a strong defensive need to stabilize its periphery, seemingly threatened by terrorism, Islamic fundamentalism, and—to the Kremlin—perverse variants of democratic pluralism. Moscow's interests have been intensified by the presence of 6.5 million Russian citizens in the Central Asian successor states of the former USSR.[25]

Moscow has not had the industrial prowess nor the affluent market that the West, Japan, or even China possess as levers for asserting regional dominance. That weakness is evident in the anemic Russian trade figures in Table 7.1. Yet the Russians have had some potent tools for creating a new geopolitical order along the old Silk Road. Russia is by a considerable margin the largest arms exporter to most of continental Asia, although less prominent than the United States in global arms export standings.[26]

The bulk of Moscow's arms exports go to the largest, most rapidly growing nonaligned powers, China and India, for both of which it is also by far the largest supplier. In 2010, for example, Russia supplied nearly $2.9 billion in weaponry to India and over $400 million to China, representing 86 percent and 73 percent respectively of their foreign weapons procurements.[27] Although Russian arms sales to China declined for some years early in the 2000s, due to Russian fears of reverse engineering, they surged again in 2010 at the high end of the market, with Moscow's sale of forty-eight Sukhoi-35s, Russia's most advanced jet fighter, to the Chinese air force.[28] Chinese cash will apparently go far toward financing Russia's new fifth-generation fighter program, competing with the U.S. F-22, and could be a sign of a new, cooperative continentalist relationship between the two neighboring giants. Development of a fifth-generation fighter with stealth capabilities also was agreed at the December 2010 Indo-Russian summit meeting.[29]

Barack Obama's November 2010 visit to India did result in some American inroads there, but future prospects remain unclear,[30] and Russia maintains a clear quantitative lead in arms sales to New Delhi. Since the collapse of the Soviet Union in 1992, Russia has supplied over $28 billion in arms to China and over $18 billion to India (Figure 7.1), even before the December 2010 fifth-generation fighter agreement between Moscow and New Delhi. Russia also supplies virtually all of Central Asia's weapons and significant amounts of Iran's armaments as well.[31]

Russia's trade relations with the rest of Asia remain surprisingly weak in general, although they are growing rapidly with some key nations—notably China. In 2010 , Russian trade with the PRC totaled over $56 billion, compared to only $4.97 billion in 1999, the year that Vladimir Putin came to power.[32] Russia's other major regional trading partners include Japan ($24.3 billion in 2010), South Korea ($17.7 billion),and India ($8.5 billion).[33] In each case, the bulk of Russia's exports are energy related, and its overall trade with

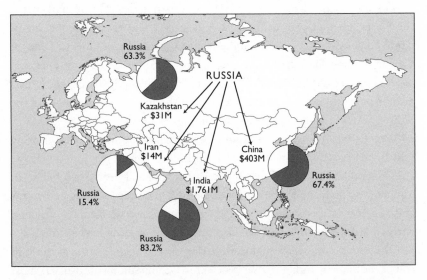

Figure 7.1: Russia's key arms-supply role.
Source: Stockholm International Peace Research Institute, Arms Transfers Database, http://www.sipri.org/databases/armstransfers/armstransfers.
Note: Figures are for Russian 2009 foreign arms sales, and percentage of shares of counterpart nation's arms imports. The bulk of Iran's weapons not supplied by Russia come nominally from China (84.6% of Iran's arms import total for 2009), although a significant quantity of the Chinese share is reported to actually originate in North Korea.

the countries in question is much smaller than that of Japan, China, or in many cases South Korea. Only energy and arms make Russia a trading partner to be reckoned with.

Russia has played a leadership role in initiating and strengthening some regional organizations such as the Collective Security Treaty Association (CSTO), as we shall see, especially where these bodies afford it hegemonic leverage. And with the largest natural gas reserves on earth, as well as a strategic transit position astride the export routes of others, not to mention large oil reserves, nuclear technology, and geopolitical power, Moscow is in a position to use energy to leverage its broader interests in ways that few other nations are equipped to do. Not surprisingly, Russia is the most proactive proponent of narrowly regionalist arrangements, excluding the major Western powers, in Eurasian energy geopolitics today. It has the political, military, and economic resources to exert leverage close to home, and it is conversely weak on the broader global stage.

ANATOMY OF THE EMERGING ENTENTES

How then should we characterize these new relationships emerging across Eurasia, many cutting across fault lines of the past, that are now bringing the continent's constituent parts into deeper interdependence than they ever attained during the Cold War? These emerging ententes have three special characteristics as a group, which distinguish them collectively from counterparts of past eras. Most important, they are transcontinental in scope, transcending parochial configurations like the neo-Confucian culture area, which itself has deepened its own internal cohesion in recent years.[34] Because these Eurasian ententes link partners over great distances and across cultures—Beijing to Teheran, Seoul to Tashkent, or Tokyo to Abu Dhabi, for example—they help catalyze the genuine continent-wide integration, provoked by deepening energy ties, that has begun to characterize Eurasia so clearly over the past decade. This economic integration does not extinguish national rivalries, of course, but it does inhibit their degeneration into armed conflict.

Second, the recent ententes are multilevel—that is, transnational relationships not only among nation states, but also linking a complex mixture of subnational and supranational actors. Groups ranging from the Collective Security Treaty Organization (CSTO) to the Central Asian Cooperation Organization, the Commonwealth of Independent States, the Central Asia South Asia conference, the Eurasian Economic Community, the Transport

Corridor Europe-Caucasus-Asia, and the Asia-Europe Meeting (ASEM) are involved. Third, these emerging relationships are by and large driven by energy or geopolitics—inspired by the deepening political-economic ties that energy interdependence creates, even when those ties do not provide direct vehicles for procuring hydrocarbons per se.

DIVERSE VARIETY OF EURASIAN ENTENTES

As political-economic interactions across Eurasia intensify, driven by energy transactions, arms exports, improved transcontinental infrastructure, and the force of critical junctures, connectivity emerges in various forms. As outlined in the following pages, one can distinguish a variety of ententes—hegemonic, multilateral, corporate, and even pariah ententes. Relationships are not uniformly collaborative, but they create a much more interactive continentalism than ever before, and a bias toward rising interdependence. There are also fluid and still nascent international configurations—notably the "strategic triangle" among Russia, China, and India—that have potential to become more systematically cooperative relationships, with prospectively fateful geopolitical consequences. This section profiles these emerging ententes and strategic configurations, as well as the larger continental connectedness— pluralistic and fraught with occasional tension, but more fundamentally unifying—that they call into being.

Hegemonic Entente: Resecuring
the Near Abroad

For over 120 years, before the collapse of the Soviet Union in 1991, Central Asia had been part and parcel of the Czarist, and then the Soviet, empires. For over 150 years, the same had been true of the Caucasus as well. Kazakhstan, at independence, had a population that was nearly 40 percent Russian, with ethnic Russians demographically dominant in the north of the country, bordering Russia itself. Across the Central Asian near abroad lived well over 10 million Russians—the majority having been born there.[35]

Not surprisingly, as Moscow has recovered its confidence and assertiveness since the advent of Putin, among its first aspirations has been recovering influence and, to the extent feasible, even dominion within the former boundaries of the USSR where assertion is cost effective. To that end, since Moscow lacks general trade competitiveness, it has devised three major nonmarket tools to employ: economic assistance, military collaboration, and geoeconomic leverage on energy-related matters. All have proved efficacious in Central Asia. Moscow has also formed a customs union with Kazakhstan and created a $10 billion regional development fund to aid economically distressed backwaters of the near abroad, including Kyrgyzstan and Tajikistan.[36]

In the military realm, Russia performs a comprehensive range of services, ranging from manning border posts on the Tajik frontier with Afghanistan to stemming the flow of drugs northward; serving as both exclusive supplier of military equipment in the region and as principal supplier of military intelligence;[37] assisting with internal security and counterinsurgency training; and even informally staffing certain local military forces, such as Turkmenistan's navy. In the energy field, Russia buys natural gas from Turkmenistan and Uzbekistan, albeit often on rather coercive terms. Moscow, after all, enjoys substantial leverage, especially in relation to Central Asian exports to Europe, due to the paucity of alternatives to shipping gas westward through the Russian domestic gas grid system. Moscow also continues to assist in Central Asian resource development, especially in the less sophisticated areas that do not readily attract multinationals on acceptable terms. Gazprom, is, for example, currently exploring for energy in Tajikistan.[38]

Moscow under Putin and Medvedev, in short, has gradually, yet persistently, worked to reverse the collapse of the Soviet Union, which Putin in 2005 called "the century's greatest geopolitical catastrophe."[39] Apart from various collaborative bilateral activities with individual former Soviet republics, Russia has also worked to strengthen its influence within the former Soviet space through multilateral bodies. To best understand these bodies and their potential for promoting broader regional cohesion, it is important first to consider the geopolitical dynamics that shape international relations across the Eurasian heartland today.

The Core Strategic Triangle: Russia, China, and India

Dominating the heartland of Eurasia, considered by geopoliticians since Mackinder to lie at the core of global power politics, stand three large nations: Russia, China, and India. Together they are home to nearly 3 billion people, or almost 40 percent of the world's entire population (Table 7.2). Their combined land area stretches across one-fifth of the terrestrial surface area of the globe and occupies the bulk of Mackinder's strategic "world island" at the epicenter of human civilization. With over 4.6 million men under arms, these nations collectively have the largest militaries in the world, outside the United

Table 7.2. Eurasia's Strategic Triangle in Comparative Perspective

	Russia	China	India	Combined	Combined/ Global	U.S.A./ Global
Population (Million)	140	1,354	1,214	2,708	39.0%	4.6%
Defense Budget ($ Billion)	41.4	76.4	38.4	156.2	10.8%	47.7%
Military (Thousand)	1,046	2,285	1,325	4,656	22.9%	7.7%
GDP ($ Trillion)	1.49	5.73	1.55	8.77	13.9%	23.1%
Area (Million KM²)	17.098	9.597	3.287	29.982	20.1%	6.6%

Source: International Institute for Strategic Studies. *The Military Balance,* 2011; and Central Intelligence Agency. *World Factbook,* 2011.

States, and all possess nuclear weapons. Their combined defense budgets, totaling close to $150 billion, dwarf any in the world, save that of America.[40] And their combined GDP of more than $7.5 trillion is growing, however erratically, at well over double the pace of the United States.

It is fatuous to assume, of course, that Russia, China, and India together form any sort of coherent entente today, or even that they will necessarily do so in the future. Many thoughtful observers have stressed the inherent bilateral tensions within each of the dyads—especially between China and India.[41] Yet Russia at least clearly has strong incentives, building on its energy endowments, military prowess, and consolidation of the former Soviet heartland, discussed above, to encourage such a configuration. Rapidly deepening energy ties within the triangle are presented in Figure 7.2. And there is a logic for all three parties in the broader trilateral dynamic, such as local regional stability in the face of ethnic tensions, or the ability to balance against forces outside the region, which national-level analysis can easily neglect. To understand the emerging political economy of Eurasia, and how energy is driving new patterns in post–Cold War international affairs more generally, it is important to see how the mutual relations among these three giants are deepening at the supra and subnational levels, driven by energy, geopolitics, trade in manufactures, and shared domestic stability concerns. And it is instructive to explore what changes within the strategic triangle might portend for the broader region, and ultimately for the wider world.

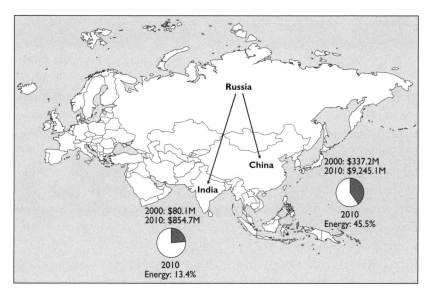

Figure 7.2: Energy linkages within the strategic triangle (2000 vs. 2010)
Source: United Nations Commodity Trade Statistics database, http://comtrade.un
.org/db/.
Note: Energy trade here includes coal, crude oil, natural gas, uranium, and nuclear
reactors and parts. Numbers on the figure are total energy imports from Russia. In
2010, China imported oil ($7,303.0 million, 79.0 percent), nuclear reactors and parts
($850.0 million, 9.2 percent), coal ($930.4 million, 10.1 percent), uranium ($97.1 million,
1.1 percent), and natural gas ($64.6 million, 0.1 percent). In the same year, India
imported nuclear reactors and parts ($586.2 million, 68.6 percent), oil ($123.1 million,
14.4 percent), natural gas ($61.7 million, 7.2 percent), uranium ($56.1 million, 6.6
percent), and coal ($27.6 million, 3.2 percent).

Well over a decade ago, in the early post–Cold War days, Russian Foreign
Minister Yevgeny Primakov during a late 1998 visit to New Delhi urged
creation of a strategic triangle among Russia, China, and India, to "ensure
regional peace and stability."[42] Primakov, longtime director of Moscow's Oriental Institute and simultaneously former director of the Russian FSB intelligence services, was also one of his country's premier Arabists and well-known
in Moscow for farsighted geopolitical thinking. He had been strongly opposed for years to U.S. unilateralism in the Middle East, having worked fe-
verishly on the diplomatic front at the end of the 1991 Gulf War to forestall
Saddam Hussein's total defeat. Primakov was clearly motivated in his Delhi
remarks by opposition to the American Desert Fox campaign of air raids on

Iraq, as well as the U.S. air war in Kosovo, which were current Russian concerns at the time.

When Primakov's remarks were originally made, they evoked a mixed response. His Indian hosts listened politely, but Chinese diplomats demurred from afar, stressing blandly and vaguely that they believed in maintaining positive ties with all nations.[43] Many dismissed the proposal as tactical—a mere attempt to enhance leverage in the UN Security Council. Yet seven years later, in June 2005, the foreign ministers of the same three nations assembled for their first, historic trilateral meeting at Vladivostok, in the wake of "color revolutions" against traditional Soviet-era leaders in Ukraine, Georgia, and Kyrgyzstan.[44] By 2011, trilateral foreign ministers' meetings had been held eleven times, on an increasingly routine, annual basis.[45] Late in the decade the trilateral concept was broadened and globalized to include Brazil, with BRIC (Brazil, Russia, India, China) summits being held at Ekaterinburg, Russia, in 2009, Brasilia in 2010, and Sanya, Hainan, in 2011.[46] Yet the core interactions continued to be among the original three Eurasian continental powers.

The original impulse for the Russia-China-India entente was clearly defensive. All of the three powers, beginning with Russia, were uneasy about the steady post–Cold War expansion of American influence in the world generally, and within continental Eurasia in particular. The initial impulse behind Primakov's 1998 initiative, as noted earlier, was opposition to the U.S. Desert Fox air campaign against Saddam Hussein and the Kosovo War campaign against Serbia, in which the Chinese embassy in Belgrade was also hit. U.S. inroads into Central Asia after 9/11, the Bush West Point "preemption" speech of 2002,[47] the invasion of Iraq in April 2003, and the color revolutions of 2005 all later gave momentum for the balancing impulses implicit in the entente, especially for Russia and China.[48]

Domestic political stability at home and in neighboring countries, particularly defense against terrorism, has been another shared concern of the triangle. As noted above, all three nations have substantial and restive minority Muslim populations of their own. They are also concerned at the rise of radical movements, such as Uzbekistan's Islamic Movement of Uzbekistan (IMU), in Central Asia, as well as ongoing instability in Afghanistan.[49] In 1999–2000 both Kyrgyzstan and Uzbekistan suffered attacks from IMU fighters trying to break into the Fergana Valley through the Batken Mountains.[50] The IMU is reportedly also engaging in terror-related activities in the lawless tribal areas of northwest Pakistan, next to the Afghan border, and disturbingly close to Central Asia's major population centers as well.[51]

With the Obama administration's pledge to start withdrawing its forces in Afghanistan, Kabul and its neighbors have begun quietly shifting their orientations, in anticipation of future power vacuums that might emerge in the region. In his June 2010 address to a national loya jirga, Afghan President Hamid Karzai admonished Western troops for causing civilian casualties and conducting night raids, then reached out explicitly to the Taliban in conciliatory terms.[52] Karzai has also been active as an informal observer at recent summits of the Shanghai Cooperation Organization (SCO), initiated by China and Russia, in which the United States is pointedly not welcome.

Although India is a democratic state, and the other members of the triangle are soft authoritarian, India lies in close proximity to both Afghanistan and Central Asia, from which it has endured incursions from time immemorial. India also has had vivid recent experiences with domestic terrorism, such as the bloody 2008 and 2011 Mumbai attacks, that strengthen incentives to support stability-preserving regimes of whatever persuasion. There is also substantial support inside India both for positive relations with Russia—the key instigator of this triangle—and for balancing policies that dilute the hegemonic influence of the United States in international relations.[53] China, for its part, shares all these objectives,[54] and in 2009 became India's largest trading partner, surpassing the United States and the UAE.[55] In 2010, Sino-Indian trade exceeded $60 billion, with agreements at the December 2010 Wen-Singh summit to increase bilateral trade volume to $150 billion by 2015.[56] High-level communication mechanisms were also put in place to assist in resolving border disputes, expanding trade, and enhancing bilateral consultations under multilateral frameworks, such as the BRIC and G20 summits.[57] In the face of enduring geopolitical tensions, Sino-Indian interdependence is clearly deepening, and networks for conflict management between these continental giants are deepening as well.

The Iran Factor

The core actors of the strategic triangle—Russia, India, and China—share strong regional stability concerns in the face of dual domestic and extraregional challenges. They are in no sense strongly revisionist regarding the structure of the international system more generally. Yet all three do harbor great-power aspirations and resentment about unipolarity, that tempt them toward balancing American power.

How does this Silk Road triad relate to postrevolutionary Iran? Obviously, its strategic transit location and massive hydrocarbon reserves are attractive,

especially to China and India. Tehran's revisionist stance in international affairs also has attractions, especially for Russia, which as a fellow petrostate
with "de-stabilizing" incentives particularly appreciates Tehran's hawkish stance
on oil and gas pricing, not to mention its persistent criticism of the United
States. Yet the intensity of Iran's nuclear confrontation with the West, the
stridency of its confrontation with Israel, and Tehran's transnational ties with
groups like Hezbollah and Hamas give all three members of the strategic
triangle pause. At present they are pursuing a hedging strategy toward Iran,
of expanding trade; according it observer status in their multilaterals; providing limited arms supplies, often using surrogates like North Korea; and cau-
tiously pressuring its nuclear program. Given Iran's social, economic, and
political-military scale, as well as its location, not to mention its massive hydrocarbon reserves, the country's future role in Eurasian energy geopolitics is
among the continent's most critical uncertainties.

Pariah Ententes: WMD Trade along
the New Silk Road

Several Eurasian nations have a disturbing propensity to treat their potent
weaponry as a commercial proposition, for potential diffusion to others at an
attractive price. This propensity seems related particularly to their domestic
politics: internationalist groups with a stake in stable interdependence with the
broader world are relatively weak in such nations as Pakistan, Iran, Syria, and
Libya, for example, even if they cannot unambiguously be considered "shuttered states."[58] Chauvinist, parochial groups intent on chemical, biological,
and nuclear (CBN) armament, even at the cost of international ostracism,
tend to be conversely powerful in such troubled nations. And when they trade
at long distances across Asia, with nations to whom they have no geographical
propinquity—as North Korea does with Syria and Iran, for example—the
more shuttered countries, such as Iran and North Korea, appear to be especially uninhibited in their behavior. Both their mercurial tendencies and
their sense of mutual solidarity are exacerbated at the regional and global
levels by their isolation from international society—which is why I call these
configurations "pariah ententes."

The clearest and most egregious example of CBN commercialization, of
course, was the nuclear black-market network of A. Q. Khan, the founder of
Pakistan's nuclear weapons program. Former International Atomic Energy
Agency director general Mohamed El Baradei was quite correct in dubbing it
"the Walmart of private-sector proliferation."[59] Khan's network helped supply

critical bomb-making expertise and components to North Korea, Libya, and Iran.

For at least twelve years, Khan is believed to have led this lucrative multi-national black-market export operation, which netted more than $100 million from Libya alone.[60] It provided blueprints, technical design data, specifications, components, machinery, enrichment equipment, models, and notes on first-generation P-1 and next-generation P-2 centrifuges. To market his dubious wares, Khan used transit points and intermediaries in Dubai, Germany, Malaysia, South Africa, Turkey, Switzerland, and Britain, among a group of around thirty countries.[61] In February 2004, Khan confessed (reportedly in English on Pakistani television) for abetting nuclear proliferation and took sole responsibility, in return for a pardon from President Musharraf.[62]

The original heart of the continentalist arms connections, which provided the technological base for Khan's own Pakistani nuclear program, and ultimately for his black-market network as well, appears to have been the relationships between China and to some extent North Korea, on the one hand, and Pakistan and Iran on the other.[63] Those trans-Asian ties date back at least to the 1980s, when China and North Korea were Iran's major weapons suppliers during the Iran-Iraq War.[64] During the mid-1990s, under heavy American pressure, and as a result of improving relations between the United States and China, the PRC moderated its arms exports to North Korea, together with its supply of weapons technology.[65] Pyongyang, however, has apparently continued its transactions with Iran and Syria, in particular, to the extent that it has been able, as discussed later.

Beginning in the 1970s, following Pakistan's disastrous 1971 war with India, in which Bangladesh won its independence, China began forging an intimate military relationship with Pakistan, its strategically situated, continentalist Islamic neighbor across the Karakorum mountains. In 1989, the two countries signed a ten-year memorandum of understanding providing for military cooperation in the fields of purchase, joint research and development, joint production, transfer of technology, and export to third countries.[66] In 1993 China also agreed to provide credits for Pakistani arms purchases. Over time, China thus became Pakistan's principal military patron, providing both defense-related exports of all kinds and production facilities for jet aircraft, tanks, artillery, and missiles.

Of even greater importance, China also provided critical assistance to Pakistan in the development of its nuclear weapons capabilities, furnishing it with uranium for enrichment, advice on bomb design, and possibly the use of its own nuclear testing site at Lop Nor to explode a nuclear device.[67] China likewise provided Pakistan with 300-kilometer-range M-11 nuclear-capable ballistic missiles, contrary to an agreement with the United States, in return receiving midair refueling technology and Stinger missiles (intended for Afghan insurgents) from Pakistan.

During the Iran-Iraq War, China also became Iran's most important supplier of munitions and munitions-producing capital goods, providing everything from antitank missiles to F-6 fighter aircraft. The PRC ultimately supplied Iran with 22 percent of its weapons, worth $2.1 billion, by far the largest share, followed by North Korea ($913 million) and Iraq's longtime ally, Russia ($302 million).[68] Following the 1980–1988 war, Beijing remained important in the supply of delivery systems, especially missiles. In the mid-1990s, China provided Iran with a new generation of substantially more capable antiship missiles, the C-801 and C-802, and in 1999 also assisted in developing a portable surface-to-air missile, Misagh 1. In 2000, Beijing sold Tehran another class of missile-armed fast-attack craft, the Chinese Cat.[69]

During the late 1980s, Iran also became firmly resolved to move toward weapons of mass destruction (WMD), as a result of its traumatic experiences in the Iran-Iraq War of 1982–1988, together with the continuing threat of Saddam Hussein.[70] As with delivery systems, the PRC initially aided this WMD effort. In the mid-1990s, China, for example, began assisting Iran to develop dual-use chemical facilities. The PRC was suspected to have supplied several virtually complete factories capable of producing chemical weapon agents, including nerve, riot-control, and tear gas precursor chemicals, and 40,000 barrels of chemicals used for chemical weapon decontamination. Early in 1998, a Chinese chemical company was reported to have completed construction of a new large production facility on the outskirts of Tehran, that was capable of producing nerve gas.[71]

Support for Iranian nuclear programs was also a key element of Beijing's effort to forge a partnership with Iran in the 1980s and 1990s. In 1985, during Rafsanjani's visit to Beijing, China and Iran secretly concluded a protocol for cooperation on the peaceful use of nuclear energy that provided Iran with four small teaching and research reactors. In 1990, China announced its deal with Iran on a ten-year agreement for further nuclear cooperation, sending a 27-megawatt reactor and 1,600 kilograms of refined uranium products. In September 1992, President Rafsanjani visited Pakistan together with Iranian nuclear experts, and then continued on to the PRC, where he concluded another agreement on nuclear cooperation. In February 1993, China then agreed to build two 300-megawatt nuclear reactors in Iran. Thereafter, the PRC transferred significant nuclear technology to Iran, while training Iranian nuclear scientists and engineers, as well as providing Iran with a calutron enriching device and other cutting-edge nuclear technologies. In 1995, however, the PRC, under American pressure, agreed to cancel the sale of the two reactors, formally suspending the 1985 agreement in 1996.[72]

Significantly, China's agreement to end its nuclear relations with Iran occurred in advance of the October 1997 U.S.-China summit. The Clinton administration indicated that it had received a firm written assurance that China would end nuclear dealings with Iran, although two small ongoing projects—a zero-power nuclear reactor and a factory to produce tubing for nuclear fuel rods—would continue.[73] U.S. diplomacy with China thus appears to have disrupted a perverse Silk Road linkage—a significant success case with tangible relevance for the Sino-American policy future.

Apart from Russia, China, and in some respects Syria, North Korea is Iran's most important ally. This relationship was forged amid the long, bitter Iran-Iraq War (1982–1988), as noted earlier, during which the DPRK served as Iran's largest arms supplier. After the war's inconclusive finale, bereft of allies, and faced with a continuing threat from Saddam Hussein, Iran began to feel the need to develop WMD. It did so just as North Korea, faced with the collapse of the Soviet Union and the uncertain sympathies of China, began to sense the same geopolitical imperatives. Not surprisingly, the two continentalist pariahs, at opposite ends of Eurasia, became strategic partners.

North Korea supplemented Chinese military assistance to Iran by shipping the ayatollahs modified Scud missiles, training Iran's air defense teams in the use of Chinese mobile surface to air missiles (SAMS), and instructing the Revolutionary Guards in unconventional warfare techniques.[74] It also aided Tehran in developing its own production facilities for these missiles. After a successful test firing in the Sea of Japan, the DPRK further agreed in 1993 to supply Iran with its 600-mile-range Nodong I mobile missiles. It is also believed to have subsequently cooperated with Iran in the development of the longer-range and multistage Taepodong missile technology.

North Korea's relationship with Iran appears to be substantially broader and more multifaceted than mere arms supply. Iran is, for example, reportedly a major financial source of the DPRK's weapons development programs, helping to bankroll research on the Scud Model B (with a 320–340-kilometer range and a 1,000-kilogram payload), the Scud Model C (with a 500-kilometer range and 700-kilogram payload), and the Nodong 1 (1,000-kilometer range and a 700–1,000-kilogram payload).[75]

North Korea has also helped Iran produce, test, and develop arms. In 1987, for example, North Korean engineers flew to Iran to "help convert and construct production and maintenance facilities," as well as to help Iran produce the Shahab-1 and then the Shahab-2, which has a 500-kilometer range.[76] The arms production of North Korea and Iran is closely interrelated, since Shahab-3's critical components are North Korean.[77] Iran also appears to have shipped at least nineteen missiles directly from North Korea around 2005.[78] In 2010, earlier news reports of these shipments were corroborated by secret State Department cables made public by Wikileaks.[79]

There is a significant possibility that these two pariah nations may strike a deal over energy and arms exchanges. Iran seeks North Korean assistance to increase its missile capabilities. In exchange, North Korea needs a new energy source, other than China, which in 2005 cut off its oil export to North Korea for a considerable interval. With more hard currency, North Korea may continue to improve its military program, with Iranian cooperation.[80]

Iran also has long been reported to be one of North Korea's two major oil suppliers, the other being China. During the 1980s and 1990s, Iran supplied as much as two-thirds of the DPRK's oil, a highly strategic role. Israeli sources have claimed that a follow-on missiles-for-centrifuges technical exchange barter deal was struck between Pyongyang and Tehran. Under this putative arrangement, in exchange for Iranian assistance with uranium enrichment, the DPRK provided Iran with engines for the Nodong missiles (the precursors of the Iranian Shahab-3 missile) and worked out Shahab-3 manufacturing problems in Iran. The Shahab-3, which successfully completed its test program in July 2003, is thought to be able to carry a 1,000-kilogram payload for 1,500 kilometers.[81] Further, Iranian scientists were reported to have observed the DPRK's missile and nuclear tests.[82]

North Korea's trans-Asian ties are by no means limited to Iran. Indeed, the DPRK is the leading exporter of ballistic missiles to the entire developing world, and its exports have continued despite its various flight-test moratoria. Yet all of North Korea's major missile technology partners are continental powers in Eurasia. This is not surprising, because all six of the non-UN P-5 nations possessing intermediate-range ballistic missiles, with a range of 1,000 to 3,000 kilometers, are Silk Road nations. Apart from Iran, Libya, Pakistan, Syria, and possibly Egypt have also received some missile systems from Pyongyang.[83] There have also been persistent allegations of Syria–North Korea nuclear cooperation, which appear to have prompted an Israeli air strike on an alleged nuclear reactor under construction in northern Syria, during early September 2007.[84]

Apart from North Korea's suspect transactions with national governments in the Middle East, another concern of Western diplomats, defense officials, and intelligence specialists has long been possible dealings with terrorists.[85] The North, of course, during the 1980s itself used terrorism as a weapon of policy, assassinating South Korean Director of Economic Planning Kim Jae Ik, three other Cabinet ministers, and thirteen other senior, non-Cabinet officials in Rangoon, Burma, on October 9, 1983. Pyongyang's agents also blew up a Korean Airlines civilian airliner en route to the Middle East in November 1987, high over the Andaman Sea.[86] Although there is no evidence of DPRK plotting with Islamic terrorists, the prospect is not fanciful, given North Korea's past history and its willingness to undertake a wide variety of adventurous military and illicit commercial pursuits if well compensated.

Multilateral Ententes

Key parts of Eurasia are slowly gaining enhanced political-economic connectivity in varied ways. We have considered hegemonic ententes, strategic triangular coalitions, and pariah ententes, all of which link important parts of the continent in novel ways. To meet the dual challenges of stability and economic development across this vast region, while providing some geopolitical insulation from American pressure, multilateral institutions have begun evolving as well.

STABILIZING THE NEAR ABROAD: RISING RESPONSIBILITIES FOR THE CSTO?

The CSTO is a joint national-security body, dominated by Russia, and arising out of the Confederation of Independent States (CIS). This CIS was created in 1991 as the Soviet Union was collapsing, in an attempt to maintain coherent political, military, and economic relations among the Soviet successor states. Founded in October 2002, CSTO itself today has seven members—all formerly republics of the USSR, and arguably the seven still closest to Moscow. All of the Central Asian states except traditionally reclusive Turkmenistan participate.

Until the ascent of Vladimir Putin, the CIS had little cohesion, although matters changed soon thereafter, with CSTO becoming a major vehicle for reasserting Russian influence on political-military matters in the near abroad. The CSTO holds periodic military command exercises, such as Rubezh 2008, carried out in Armenia, where a combined total of 4,000 troops from all seven members conducted operational, strategic, and tactical training. In September, 2011 it convened Center-2011 in Central Asia involving over 10,000 troops and 70 combat aircraft.

In February 2009, a CSTO Collective Rapid Reaction Force was created, ostensibly to repulse military aggression, conduct antiterrorist operations, fight transnational crime and drug trafficking, and mitigate the effects of natural disasters.[87] Although CSTO did not intervene directly in the June 2010 Kyrgyz crisis, it provided supplies and equipment to Kyrgyz authorities and could well intervene to restore public order in similar future domestic crises in Central Asia. Iran has explored membership, and CSTO appears open to the prospect of expansion beyond the borders of the former USSR, as well as cooperation with other continentalist counterparts.[88]

In January, 2010 a sub-group of CSTO nations—initially Russia, Kazakhstan, and Belarus, created a customs union to help deepen their economic relationships. In October, 2011 Kyrgyzstan also elected to join the union. In early 2012, further-progress toward a common economic space was made.

THE COMING OF THE SCO

Early in 2001, Russia and China concluded their first major treaty in fifty years, formally the Treaty on Good-Neighborly Relations, Friendship, and Cooperation. This provided for increased Russian arms sales to China, and the training of Chinese officers at Russian military schools. In June 2001, the two countries followed up this agreement by initiating the six-nation Shanghai Cooperation Organization, also including Kazakhstan, Tajikistan, Kyrgyzstan, and Uzbekistan. The SCO was a more institutionalized version of the Shanghai Five of 1996 with the addition of Uzbekistan, a body established five years earlier to build mutual trust in border regions following the Cold War. The new organization, given strong momentum by the positive personal relations between Chinese and Russian leaders at the time, established an autonomous secretariat in Shanghai, with the former Chinese ambassador to Russia, Zhang Deguang, as its first secretary-general.[89]

The addition of Uzbekistan was significant, as it was the one member not directly bordering Russia. Its entry clearly suggested that the SCO had transcended its border-negotiation origins and was intending to focus attention, only three months before 9/11, on the deepening, nearby terrorist threat in Afghanistan. Indeed, Kazakh President Nursultan Nazarbayev remarked at the founding session: "The cradle of terrorism, separatism, and extremism is the instability in Afghanistan."[90]

Significantly, Iran, India, Pakistan, and Mongolia are SCO observers, and the first three have applied for full membership.[91] Afghanistan itself is affiliated through the SCO-Afghanistan Contact Group. With these additional nations, more than half the population of Eurasia, from the Baltic to the Pacific, are arrayed in this loose political, economic, and military agglomeration.

All of the member states had two important bottom-up incentives for meaningful cooperation: border disputes and the threat of terrorism. These motives drove the early activities of the SCO. Apart from creating a regional antiterrorism structure in Tashkent (2004), the SCO set up a cross-border drug crimes program (2006) and held a series of large-scale joint military exercises, beginning in 2005 and continuing annually or biannually since then.

The SCO also established a clear-cut legal framework for operationalizing practical interaction among the member nations in combating terrorism. This effort seems to have paid off. Kazakhstan and Uzbekistan collaborated, through the SCO, to discover and localize underground cells of the Islamic Jihad. Russian and Tajik law-enforcement agencies worked together to apprehend members of the Islamic Movement of Turkestan around Moscow in 2009. A secure database and unified search registry have been created, which includes over 1,100 people put on an international wanted list for terrorist and separatist offenses, as well as information about forty-two organizations banned in the member states.[92]

The American presence in Central Asia since 9/11 has been a continuing implicit concern for several members of the SCO, especially Russia and China. It provides a continuing incentive, from their perspective, to enhance solidarity and exclusivity among the SCO members themselves. The Russian military has been especially concerned about NATO overtures to Central Asia under the Partners for Peace program and increasingly determined to counteract those inroads. The Russians have also been wary of overtures from Japan. In the early days of the organization, Kazakh President Nazarbayev reportedly raised the prospect of Japanese membership, due especially to Tokyo's potential financial contribution, although that was apparently rejected by Russia and China.[93]

While the initial conflict in Afghanistan raged with full force, before the fall of the Taliban regime in late 2001, none of the SCO members criticized the concept of Western involvement in Central Asia. Yet voices of opposition began to arise with the outbreak of the Iraq War and intensified following the so-called color revolutions in Georgia, Ukraine, and Kyrgyzstan. As the United States, beginning in early 2005, became correspondingly proactive in supporting democratization around the region, the Russians, in particular, became conversely critical within the SCO of the United States and its Central Asian base activities. The U.S. application for observer status in the SCO was formally rejected that year. During 2005–2006, the SCO also became a forum for exerting major pressure on Kyrgyzstan, in particular—the one nation that continued to accept the presence of American bases, following U.S. withdrawal from Manas, Uzbekistan, at the end of 2005.

The primary emphasis, and achievements, of the SCO have been in the security area, especially in confronting terrorism. No doubt that institutional concern will continue to be strong, as the U.S. presence in Iraq and Afghanistan continues to recede. The SCO has, however, begun trying to broaden its economic activities also, building on the deepening energy ties among its members, including Russia and China. In October 2005 the Moscow Summit of the SCO agreed to prioritize joint energy projects and the joint use of water resources, while establishing an SCO Interbank Council to fund such projects.[94] Soon thereafter, Russia announced plans for an SCO Energy Club. Although that was slow to materialize, the 2008 summit again affirmed the importance of energy security. At the 2009 Yekaterinburg SCO Summit, China announced plans to provide member nations with a $10 billion loan to aid them amid the ongoing financial crisis, in energy and other areas.[95] In 2010 Chinese Premier Wen Jiabao personally proposed enhanced cooperation on energy efficiency, new transnational pipelines, the development of solar and wind resources, reconstruction of electric power grids, and measures to ensure the uninterrupted and efficient use of energy facilities.[96] In 2011 the summit reaffirmed the importance of cooperation on terrorism and drugs, while expanding the common agenda to water resources and the creation of a new global currency. Conference chair Nursultan Nazerbayev also speculated openly that the SCO could well assume responsibility for many issues in Afghanistan after the withdrawal of NATO coalition forces in 2014.[97]

Even more important than specific cooperative steps in the economic area has been the SCO's role in legitimating bilateral cooperation, especially between China and the Central Asian nations. These countries, after all, were under Moscow's direct control during Soviet days, so China's deepening economic ties with them naturally provoke some resentment in Russia. It is thus easier for China to build pipelines and engage in other forms of active bilateral energy cooperation with Central Asia within the context of a multilateral framework like the SCO, which also includes Russia as a key member.

TRACK TWO MULTILATERAL ENTENTES: AMED AND BEYOND

At a less institutionalized level, dynamic new transregional networks are beginning to evolve across Asia at an explosive pace. Within East Asia itself, China's Boao Forum, South Korea's Jeju Forum, and Japan's Nikkei Dialogue have grown rapidly in both scale and regional influence over the past decade.[98] An even broader leadership network, with substantial recent promise, is the Conference on Interaction and Confidence Building Measures in Asia (CICA).[99]

Political dialogues between the Middle East and East Asia have likewise deepened since the late 1990s. During consultations in Egypt, Singapore Senior Minister Goh Chok Tong proposed a biannual Asia-Middle East Dialogue (AMED), along the lines of ASEM, which he also initiated in 1996. AMED convened for the first time at the Shangri La Hotel in Singapore during June 2005, with a follow-up working session in Cairo two years later, and a second full-scale, high-level conference at Sharm El-Sheikh in February 2008. AMED III convened in Bangkok, Thailand during mid-December, 2010, with 300 participants from 31 countries.

Increasingly frequent state visits have also helped to deepen elite networks, build multinational institutions, and stimulate policy innovation. In a sign of the times, Saudi King Abdullah made China, India, and Malaysia his first foreign ports of call in January 2006, immediately following his coronation, with Pakistan his next destination, in the following month. Chinese President Hu Jintao conversely headed directly for Riyadh, Saudi Arabia, following his visit to Washington in April 2006, while Japanese Prime Minister Abe Shinzo made a similar combined Washington–Middle East junket the following spring. These sorts of high-level initiatives provoked intensified Track Two (policy-oriented private-sector) brainstorming and networking in their wake, just as Goh Chok Tong's AMED initiative had done.

Hydrocarbon Ententes and Continentalism in a Risky yet Collaborative World

Among the most distinctive and important realities in the traditional political economy of Asian energy is the lack of a continental natural gas grid. In contrast to patterns in Europe and North America, Asia lacks a continental system of piped natural gas supply. This embedded reality not only deprives Asians of an energy-efficient, environmentally attractive fuel source but has also impeded the emergence of broader continentalist political-economic ties.

Oil and gas projects, especially pipelines and green field hydrocarbon development, are, by their nature, capital intensive and fraught with risk—both project-specific and more generally political-economic in nature. Neither commodity prices nor the stability of host regimes—nor even their investment policies or export terms—are anything close to certain, especially for foreign investors, in an era of rapidly shifting exchange rates. These problems are compounded in the heart of Eurasia by insufficient transparency, poor legal regimes, and lack of infrastructure or even basic information. Energy infrastructure is potentially a key facilitator for continentalism, as it links geographically contiguous producers and consumers overland, but for many years such infrastructure did not emerge easily in the Eurasian context.

Developments in the wake of the 2008 Great Recession suggested that the pace of Eurasian continental infrastructure building could at last be quickening. In early 2009 the first Kazakh-PRC pipeline was completed. In December of the same year, Turkmen gas began flowing to China. And in January 2011, 300,000 barrels per day of Russian oil began flowing overland to China for the first time, through the East Siberia Pacific Ocean (ESPO) pipeline.[100]

The previous pages suggest a powerful logic, over the coming two decades, to transcontinental Eurasian oil and gas development projects in general, for three key reasons. First of all, demand and supply are strongly aligned. Asian energy demand, driven by inevitably significant per capita increases in the teeming markets of China and India, will sharply rise. And the only parts of the world, in the long run, with the reserves to reliably accommodate massive potential demand increases are the Middle East and the former Soviet Union.

The second factor at work is geographic. The areas of greatest demand and inevitable supply lie in remarkably close proximity to one another, especially as the economic center of gravity in China shifts westward, to Szechuan and beyond in the context of Beijing's domestic demand stimulus and regional equalization programs. The westernmost reaches of China and India, after all, are both little more than a thousand miles each from the Persian Gulf, making overland access attractive, since pipelines are highly cost effective at distances under 2,000 miles. Sea routes from the Strait of Hormuz across the Arabian Sea to India, and then eastward to China and Northeast Asia, are also relatively direct and cost effective, compared to longer and more complex transport westward to Europe and America.

The final factor is political. Certainly there are domestic political uncertainties along the Silk Road, together with terrorist dangers and political-military wariness as well. Yet the thrust of our analysis here is that prospects for inter-state warfare within continental Eurasia itself are waning, the endemic Indo-Pakistani conflict notwithstanding, while institutions for regional conflict management are conversely emerging, in response to both terrorist challenges and economic interdependence. Despite episodic, and sometimes dramatic, expressions of geopolitical rivalry, ranging from textbook controversies to fishing boat confrontations in disputed waters, there has not been a single major intra-Asian interstate war, apart from Saddam Hussein's depredations, since the Sino-Vietnamese border conflict of 1978. This remarkably pacific pattern stands in stark contrast to the turbulence that prevailed across Eurasia during the first half of the twentieth century, which persisted in certain quarters into the 1960s and 1970s. Growing economic interdependence clearly seems to inhibit the conversion of inevitable animosities into open conflict, especially when it is accompanied, in contrast to the early twentieth century pattern, by advanced communications and sophisticated transnational political, military, and economic networks, which are beginning to emerge in continental Asia, as they did earlier along its maritime periphery.[101]

The remarkable growth and transformation across Eurasia that has since occurred—described in our chronicle of critical junctures in Chapter 3—has sharply expanded both energy demand and continentalist economic interdependence. Yet it has been accompanied by a remarkable degree of stability in state-to-state relations among Eurasian nations themselves. The major national-level conflicts that have since occurred—Afghanistan and Iraq—have been driven primarily by foreign interventions from outside the region, rather than by local determinants.

Potential for transcontinental cooperation within Eurasia is thus growing, even where rivalry remains a subtheme, at both the national and the corporate levels. Herewith we consider a variety of ententes specially related to energy, animated by the remarkable growth of the region. After surveying sector-specific cooperation, we move on to particular geographic permutations and to the role of political-economic catalysts capable of pulling these configurations together over time, into more broadly cohesive groupings.

Natural Gas and Nuclear Power Development Ententes

Given Asia's distinctive energy insecurities and environmental challenges, especially the continent's heavy reliance on coal,[102] there is a powerful rationale for expanding usage of natural gas and nuclear power. Yet usage in both categories remains remarkably low, especially compared with other regions of

Table 7.3. Developing Asia's Limited Reliance on Natural Gas and Nuclear Power

Primary Energy Demand Share	U.S.* (percent)	EU** (percent)	OECD Pacific*** (percent)	Non-OECD Asia** (percent)
Natural Gas	25.2	25.1	16.8	7.8
Nuclear	9.8	13.9	13.1	0.9
Oil	36.1	34.5	39.9	21.4
Coal	23.0	18.8	26.2	51.3

Source: International Energy Agency. *International Agency Statistics, Natural Gas Information.*
2011 edition, Part IV, 24 and 396; OECD, *World Energy Outlook,* 2010, 638 and 666.
Notes: (1) OECD Pacific includes Japan, South Korea, Australia, and New Zealand.
(2) Non-OECD Asia does not include Asiatic Russia.
*Figure for 2010 estimate by OECD. **Figure for 2008. *** Figure for 2009 estimate by OECD.

the world (Table 7.3). The developing nations of the region (including both China and India) get less than 1 percent of their primary energy from either of those potentially important sources, with more than half of their primary energy coming from highly polluting coal.

Southeast Asia has the rudiments of a natural gas grid, while South Korea and Japan have domestic liquid natural gas (LNG) distribution pipeline systems. Yet there is no region-wide transnational grid, despite the close proximity of large reserves in both the Middle East and the former Soviet Union to potential Asian markets.

For Northeast Asia, especially Japan and Korea, there is a strong logic for LNG, given that region's distance from continental sources of gas, the infrastructural costs of pipeline construction, and the geopolitical uncertainties of the region. Together, Japan and Korea are, not surprisingly, markets for nearly half of all the LNG moving in international trade worldwide.[103] Yet for China and India, with their greater proximity to Russia and the Middle East, their rapidly rising energy demand, and their heavy reliance on coal with its severe environmental consequences, pipelines are more economically attractive. Deepening continental interdependence and the gradual waning of political conflict enhance that attractiveness still further.

For China and India, there are fundamentally three near- to medium-term natural gas access options: (1) Russia, especially Sakhalin and the large Kovykta gas fields north of Lake Baikal; (2) Central Asia, particularly Turkmenistan; and (3) the Persian Gulf, notably the integrated South Pars and North Field, which Iran and Qatar share. Due to maritime access, Sakhalin and the Persian Gulf are both potential LNG options, while the others presuppose piped gas. Long-distance pipelines from the Persian Gulf to India, or even potentially to China also, are not technically unfeasible, if political uncertainties can be overcome or neutralized.

The Geopolitical Challenge of Supplying
Central Asian Energy to the World

Central Asian gas access issues are currently the most dynamic and contentious of the three categories, from a political-economic point of view. Central Asia, after all, is geographically situated close to the two energy-hungry giants, China and India, and has large, undeveloped gas fields, especially in Turkmenistan and Uzbekistan. It is also relatively stable politically and more hospitable to foreign investment than Russia, in particular, appears to be.

Central Asian energy issues are inevitably politicized, as the region is landlocked, and access to global markets must consequently be negotiated. As indicated in Figure 7.3, there are four basic access options: (a) north across Russia; (b) eastward to China; (c) southward across Iran; and (d) westward to

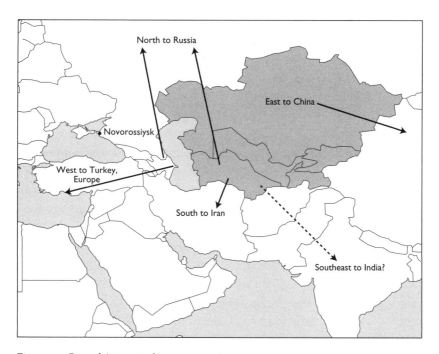

Figure 7.3: Central Asian pipeline access options.

Turkey and thence onward to Europe. Historically, virtually all of Central Asia's gas has flowed northward into Russia, through the former Soviet Union's extensive trunk pipeline network, with Russia extracting substantial price concessions and transit fees in return. Both multinational producers in Central Asia and the host nations themselves consequently seek alternatives.

Southward access through Iran is complicated by conflicts of interest between Iran and the Central Asian states, as well as lack of infrastructure, not to mention international sanctions against Iran. Yet eastward access to China is a viable proposition, which is developing rapidly. A major pipeline from Turkmenistan through Uzbekistan and Kazakhstan to Xinjiang, connecting into China's domestic network to Shanghai, was completed in December 2009, with additional lines to follow. By mid-2010, Turkmenistan was supplying China at the rate of 13 billion cubic meters of gas annually—already larger than supplies to Russia—with the likelihood that such supplies would triple to 40 billion cubic meters by 2012.[104] This rapidly expanding pipeline network is being reinforced by positive political relations among Kazakhstan, Uzbekistan, Turkmenistan, and China, as well as multilateral interactions through the SCO and other bodies, discussed above.

Chinese success in energy deals with Central Asian countries is by no means due to market factors alone. Generous economic aid is also at work. Since 1998, when China seriously began to think about energy security, as its imports rose amid the uncertainties of the Asian financial crisis, China has provided total aid of $3.9 billion to Kazakhstan, $783 million to Turkmenistan, and $652 million to Uzbekistan.[105] China has also cultivated Central Asian elites and promoted cultural diplomacy, in an effort to develop the human ties needed to make much-needed energy projects like transnational pipelines politically viable. The PRC has at times pursued multilateral approaches, such as Hu Jintao's offer of energy loans to member nations at the 2006 SCO summit, but bilateral tactics have been more common, with multilateralism often a cloak to legitimize increasingly substantial Chinese inroads into Russia's near abroad.[106]

The final, and in some ways the most geopolitically important, access route for Central Asian hydrocarbons—an implicit geopolitical entente—is to the west, via Georgia, to Turkey and the Mediterranean, through the so-called BTC (Baku-Tbilisi-Ceyhan) pipeline. Turkey is thus a crucial transit country. The BTC runs from the Caspian to the Mediterranean, without crossing Russian territory, thus providing leverage for Central Asian producers with the Russians (Figure 7.4). Together with the companion Baku-Supsa

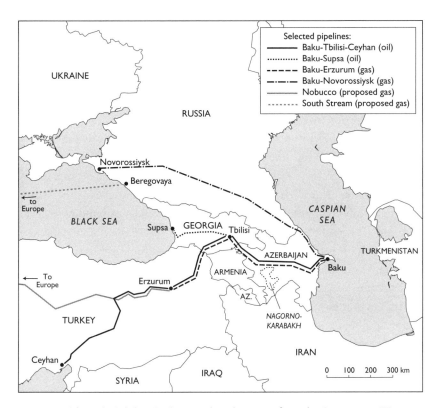

Figure 7.4: The Baku-Tbilisi-Ceyhan pipeline: key route from the Caucasus to Western markets.

natural gas pipeline across Georgia, BTC provides the only independent access for energy from former Soviet Central Asia to Western markets that is not controlled by the Russians. Yet Turkey also has important energy-related incentives to desire regional cooperation and stability, not least because it relies on Russia for nearly two thirds of its own natural-gas imports, supplied across the Black Sea via Moscow's Blue Stream I pipeline.[107] "New Silk Road" energy access options to India, recently supported by the United States, will be discussed later in the chapter.

Ententes with the Persian Gulf

With more than half of the world's proven oil reserves, and over a third of its natural gas, the Persian Gulf is clearly an inevitable long-term option for rising consumers such as China and India. Maritime access out of the Strait of Hormuz is naturally one possible route, both for oil and for LNG. That option implies the importance, which I explore further in discussions of strategic issues in Chapter 8, of supportive ties with major naval powers, including preeminently the United States. Pipelines, however, are also a possibility, and substantial consideration of plausible pipeline alternatives is actively in progress. The expansion of continental pipeline networks inevitably draws nations of the region into deeper political-economic relations with one another.

One concrete pipeline option eastward from the Gulf is the so-called Iran-Pakistan-India (IPI) pipeline (Figure 7.5). In 1993, Iran and Pakistan agreed to build a gas pipeline between their countries, which Iran later proposed to extend to India. This alternative, still to be realized, is known as the "peace pipeline," embodying the hope that it will be a confidence-building mechanism for the volatile Southwest Asian region, by fostering economic interdependence. IPI is prospectively a 1,724-mile overland project, carrying natural gas from Assaluyeh, Iran (near the huge South Pars gas field), through northern Pakistan, and on to Rajastan in India. There it would interconnect with the Indian domestic gas network. The entire IPI pipeline is expected to cost over $7.4 billion and to take three to five years to build.[108] When completed, it could carry 55 billion cubic meters of gas annually.

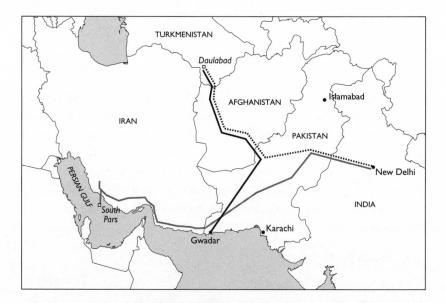

Figure 7.5: The Iran-Pakistan-India pipeline.
Notes: Gray line represents projected IPI pipeline. Dotted line represents TAPI pipeline. Black line represents TAP LNG export variant.

Agreement on the full IPI pipeline is still not finalized, due to India's wariness in undertaking such a delicate project with its long-time rival Pakistan. In June 2010, however, Iran and Pakistan did exchange final papers on their portion of the project, providing for Iranian supply of up to 21 million cubic meters annually of natural gas to Pakistan, beginning in 2013.[109] Construction on the pipeline has begun inside Iran, managed by the engineering arm of the Islamic Revolutionary Guards, although domestic security challenges remain. Pakistan may have difficulty ensuring security for the pipeline, if and when it is completed as 475 miles of it would pass through Balochistan, a turbulent region whose separatist tribes have often targeted energy facilities in the past.

Faced with India's ambivalence regarding IPI, Pakistan, in 2008, invited China to become an additional partner.[110] Meanwhile, political-economic ties between Iran and China were also deepening, raising the serious prospect that IPI gas could be diverted from India to China. Piping gas from Iran through Pakistan and across the Karakoram to Xinjiang would be technically feasible, and the PRC has been acquiring Iranian concessions that would provide a source of supply. In 2004 Iran rewarded China for broader economic and political support, including its work in providing Iran with infrastructure to serve as a transit gateway for Caspian oil, by giving it rights to develop the massive Yadarvan oil field, with the formal contract being signed in December, 2007.[111]

China has already built a major transshipment port at Gwadar in western Pakistan, with capacity for docking major naval vessels that could prove useful in transshipping Iranian gas. In mid-2011, following the death of Osama bin-Laden in a unilateral U.S. military strike inside Pakistan, the Pakistanis reportedly gave the PRC formal rights to deploy there, while the PRC reciprocally promised Pakistan 50 new JF-17 fighters.[112] In August, 2011 it launched Pakistan's first communications satellite,[113] and agreed to engineer and finance the Iran-Pakistan gas pipeline.[114] China is also supporting construction of pipelines and highways northeast from Gwadar through Pakistan, skirting India, that could connect across the Karakoram Mountains into Xinjiang, to interlink with China's own domestic gas grid and highway system. Like India and Western nations also, in pipeline politics the PRC strives to minimize the number of transit countries through which its pipelines pass, and then to develop strong geopolitical leverage, through economic assistance, military deployments, and elite network contacts, to ensure the stability needed for pipeline systems to operate smoothly. It clearly appears to be doing that in transforming the IPI pipeline project to its own advantage.

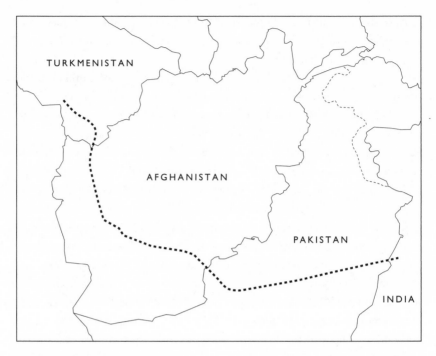

Figure 7.6: The TAPI pipeline option.

One other pipeline option from Central Asia has powerful economic and geopolitical logic, even though it remains to be operationalized: the Turkmenistan-Afghanistan-Pakistan-India (TAPI) pipeline. This line, as shown in Figure 7.6, would originate in the gas fields of southern Turkmenistan, a nation with the fourth-largest reserves on earth, and run 1,000 miles southeast across Afghanistan to the Indian subcontinent. First conceptualized in the 1990s by Unocal and Bridas, an Argentinean firm, the TAPI option has been intensely studied by the Asian Development Bank, which did feasibility studies in 2005 and 2008, estimating capital costs of $7.6 billion.[115] A revised gas pipeline framework agreement, signed by representatives of the four participating nations in September, 2010, envisaged construction to begin in 2012, and gas to begin flowing by 2015.[116]

Armed conflict in Afghanistan obviously makes the TAPI pipeline infeasible for that conflict's duration, although the Afghan government has committed up to 7,000 troops to enhance security. Yet the project has major intrinsic merits for a wide variety of related parties that could create powerful incentives for peace, for multilateral cooperation, and for peacekeeping capabilities in the area sufficient to ensure stable development.[117]

For India and Pakistan, TAPI would of course address energy deficits, which are growing steadily more severe. For Turkmenistan, it would generate revenue and diversification of export routes. And for Afghanistan it would provide revenue for development—an estimated $300 million annually—and gas for industrial enterprises along the pipeline.

Geopolitically, TAPI would also be highly attractive for Central Asia, India, and potentially the United States, in particular, as it would diversify Central Asia's energy options, provide new material incentives for stability in Afghanistan, and weaken the leverage of Russia and China in Central Asia. Russia also, however, during 2010–2011 apparently began to see merit in the proposal, as the prospect of Gazprom commercial involvement emerged.[118] That support from Moscow, plus enthusiastic backing from Washington, and India's energy needs make prospects for concrete progress in project preparations brighter, as the Afghan conflict begins to wane.

Energy Ententes with Russia?

Russia has by a substantial margin the largest natural gas reserves in the world. Yet exploiting them has proven to be a surprisingly complex political-economic proposition, despite Russia's clear intent, especially under Putin, to do so. Numerous plans have been advanced for developing Siberian hydro-carbon reserves and exporting production across the Eurasian continent to the East. Yet of all the three pipeline options available to the consumers of Asia, those emanating from Russia have been the slowest to develop and have caused the most frustration to foreign partners.

To be sure, a few energy partnerships with Russia have operated smoothly. Conspicuously, the Sakhalin I gas and oil project, involving the Japanese government-affiliated Sakhalin Oil Development Corporation (SODECO), in partnership with India's public Oil and Natural Gas Corporation (ONGC), and Exxon Neftegaz, in a joint venture in which Russian partners (Rosneft affiliates) have only a 20 percent interest, appears to have proceeded smoothly—after fifteen years of preparation, it has been in production and operating relatively uneventfully, albeit imperfectly, from an Exxon and SODECO perspective, since 2006.[119]

Also, after more than a decade of planning, the ESPO pipeline was completed physically in August 2010, from Russia's east Siberian oil and gas fields via Tayshet to Skovorodino, on the Chinese border (Figure 7.7).[120] In November 2010, northeastern China's major oil-refining center at Daqing actually started to receive Russian oil on a test basis, with full-scale exports beginning

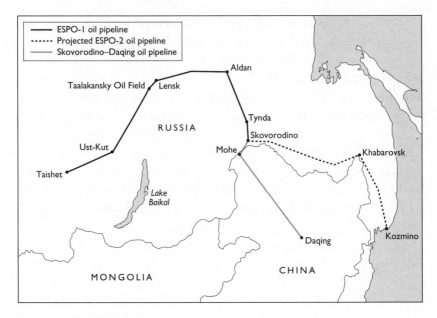

Figure 7.7: The ESPO pipeline.

two months later.[121] ESPO is scheduled to continue eastward by 2014 to Kozmino port, close to Nakhodka on the Pacific coast, where a modern new oil transport terminal was opened in January 2010,[122] and thereby onward to the international market, including Japan.[123] Indeed, GS Caltex, SK Energy, ExxonMobil, and Mitsui are already on the client list, with signed contracts.[124] Significantly, however, the project has been completed first to China, despite long-standing tensions between Moscow and Beijing.[125] As the first major transnational pipeline project to be completed between those two neighboring giants, in the face of numerous political, logistical, and economic obstacles, ESPO's extension to Daqing represents another major step in the emergence of Eurasian continentalism.

Considering why the ESPO pipeline has been completed at last, after more than a decade of negotiation, provides insights into accelerating pressures for continental political-economic interdependence more generally. Rapidly rising Chinese energy demand, fueled by the PRC's remarkable economic growth, is making an increasing number of China-related projects feasible, especially those for overland oil and gas supply, which the PRC prioritizes for security reasons.[126] China is also incresingly able to unilaterally provide strong financial incentives for their completion. Turkmenistan and Kazakhstan have agreed to supply China on favorable terms and have substantial added capacity to do so, thus increasing pressure on Russia to supply China as well, whatever Moscow's lingering misgivings might be.

FUTURE CATALYSTS FOR INTEGRATION

Trans-Eurasian political-economic relations are intensifying in the energy sector, due to the accelerating pace of pipeline construction, giving increased political-economic support to continentalism. Parallel but less geographically ambitious previous regional experience in Northeast Asia, where sectoral trade and financial ties have led, over time and through critical junctures, to more formalized regional institutions,[127] suggests that this Eurasian "protocontinentalism" could well evolve into something more substantial, and of major global importance, although the prospect is by no means certain. The New Silk Road is another laboratory for exploring whether integrative patterns that have emerged in Northeast Asia—from informal networks to soft institutionalism, via critical juncture, and onward to more formal institutions, as economic interdependence rises—may be replicated elsewhere as well.

Looking to the future, it is useful to consider what forces might catalyze the enhanced Eurasian connectivity that critical junctures have facilitated, and that transcontinental economic interdependence—especially energy complementarity—continues to stimulate. This section of the research identifies two: (1) the entrepôt ministates, such as Singapore and the UAE, which stand outside the large, overregulated petrostates and authoritarian capitalist consumers, providing services to the others; and (2) individual leaders, ranging from Goh Keng Swee to Vladimir Putin. Together, these two groups further accelerate emergence of a more highly interactive continentalism within Eurasia.

The Entrepôt Ministates

Eurasian continentalism is a product not only of political-economic forces, geopolitical logic, and business organization, but also of distinctive social interactions, which need a supportive physical arena. Key people, capable of integrating diverse nations, often far across the world from one another, and of diverse cultural backgrounds, need to come into contact, in the sort of stable, user-friendly environment where they can make business deals and conclude congenial political arrangements. In this respect, as in energy demand and supply, geographical location definitely continues to matter, even in the globalized world of the twenty-first century.

In that new, brave, globalizing world, the ability to foster and energize so-cioeconomic networks is a fundamental source of national strength and helps to fuse broader transregional relationships as well.[128] The Eurasian nations are fortunate to have within their midst a small yet substantial number of entrepôt ministates that are particularly well adapted to fill these catalytic functions. City-states such as Singapore, the UAE, and increasingly other Persian Gulf locales such as Bahrain and Qatar have a combination of qualities that help them accelerate a process of long-term continental inter-dependence that energy-sector complementarities make attractive in any case. Within larger nations, some multi-cultural cities like Urumqi in Xinjiang are coming to play such catalytic trans-national roles as well.[129]

The ministate catalysts of the New Silk Road—descendants of medieval entrepôt like Venice and Genoa—have six concrete traits that make them important as arenas for regional commerce, networking, and other forms of soft integration. Most important, they have open economies with low tax rates. Indeed, many of them, such as the UAE and Singapore, are duty-free ports. This openness promotes entrepôt commerce and provides the entrepôt states with commercial advantages vis-à-vis their more shuttered neighbors, such as Iran in the Gulf and Indonesia in Southeast Asia, that in turn helps integrate those neighbors more smoothly into international economic affairs.

These catalytic ministates also typically enjoy solid infrastructure, both physical and intellectual, further facilitating transregional transactions. Both Singapore and the UAE, for example, have global-standard accounting sys-tems, the rule of law, and a broad range of multinational financial institutions. English is widely spoken, expatriate staffs frequently have Anglo-American edu-cations, and many global firms locate regional headquarters in such locales.[130] Telecommunications infrastructure and pricing are also global standard.

Democracy is not necessarily typical in these strategic entrepôt centers—indeed, the reverse is generally the case. Political systems are typically feudal or soft authoritarian, allowing technocratic dominance. The most dynamic Gulf arenas for integration, for example, are typically run by Arab hereditary princes with a sense of long-run economic imperatives, while in Singapore a close-knit meritocratic group also prevails.[131]

Although leadership slots may be closely held among a united elite, the en-trepôt centers now knitting the nations of Eurasia more closely together are typically cosmopolitan and transregional, at many levels, in their ethnic and cultural composition. Both Singapore and Dubai, for example, have large numbers of expatriate executives and technical specialists; both also hire large numbers of guest workers in more menial positions. Both have particularly large concentrations of Chinese and Indians, supporting their transregional linkage role.

The key entrepôt centers naturally have substantial energy-sector expertise—a key qualification for further transcontinental relationships that, in the final analysis, are heavily driven by energy. Few of the entrepôt centers themselves are major energy producers—neither Singapore nor Dubai, for example, generate any local energy production at all. Yet they do enjoy associated expertise and connections. Singapore is, after Rotterdam, the second largest oil-refining center in the world, with an active energy-trading market. Dubai, although it has no oil, is a part of the UAE, a loose confederation with the fifth-largest oil reserves on earth, two major airlines, and a broad representation of multinational banks and trading firms, although it has a population of only 6 million inhabitants, including those of Dubai, of whom only 15 percent are Emirati citizens.[132]

The entrepôt city-states, finally, all have proactive transregional diplomacies, rooted in endemic regional vulnerabilities, which force them to consult beyond their shores and to strengthen the multilateral environment within which their own local economies operate.[133] As longtime Singapore Prime Minister Lee Kuan Yew observed, "Your best friends are never your immediate neighbors."[134] Singapore, with its ethnic Chinese majority, its tiny area of 624 square kilometers, and its miniscule 2.7 million population, for example, lies both wealthy and surrounded by often hostile and resentful Islamic Malay nations. Vulnerability thus forces it to forge strong transregional ties.[135] In the security area this has meant close cooperation with both the United States and Israel.[136] To countervail resentment of this stance, however, Singapore has also forged elaborate ties with a variety of Islamic states and played a leading role in fostering the AMED dialogue with the Middle East, as noted above.[137]

The major entrepôt ministates of the Persian Gulf are in a situation strikingly analogous to Singapore's, which also encourages them to forge transregional ties. The UAE, Bahrain, and Qatar all have Sunni Muslim leadership elites, yet live in the shadow of a potentially nuclear Shiite Iran, and a Shiite Iraq in the midst of uncertain transition. All have huge expatriate populations that outnumber local citizens, with Bahrain even having a Shiite majority. All are wealthy, yet only lightly armed.

For such Persian Gulf entrepôt states, as for Singapore 3,600 miles to the east, transregional ties are indispensable. The United States is clearly a key factor in that mix, but hardly the only one, even in security matters, particularly in the uncertain post–Iraq War era that is now emerging. In economic, financial, and even security affairs, Eurasia's role is substantial and rising, driven by burgeoning energy transactions, even as Europe and to a degree America also grow more distant.[138] And with the Western financial world in debt and in confusion, the interests of Asia and the Gulf—the major surplus regions in global finance—are growing even more closely aligned. The entrepôts—both east in Asia and west in the Gulf—have the resources, incentives, and increasingly the networks to link East Asia, South Asia, the Middle East, and potentially Russia as well. And they are rapidly becoming arenas for fostering such trans-continental integration.

Leaders as Catalysts

Economic complementarity, as we have seen, does not translate neatly and smoothly into interdependence. Policy change, in particular, is often a painfully discontinuous process. Vision and entrepreneurship, not to mention compatible institutions and policies, are clearly necessary to transform economic logic into new realities on the ground. At the transnational level, a clear perception of common destiny on the part of key leaders is crucial to successful regional integration, as the evolution of Europe since the 1950s shows.[139] And such shared perceptions frequently fail to evolve in the absence of powerfully shared experience.

Vision has been crucial in the growing impulse of first the East Asian region and more recently the nations of Eurasia, spanning the entire Asian continent, to seriously interact. Early in the twentieth century such vision was mainly the province of intellectuals divorced from policy, although a few national policymakers, such as Sun Yat-sen, did articulate pan-Asianist sentiments also. Following World War II, there were intermittent Asianist leaders, including Zhou Enlai, Nehru, Sukarno, and Nasser, many of whom assembled at the landmark Bandung Afro-Asian Summit of 1955.[140]

Leaders are especially important as prospective catalysts for Eurasian continentalist integration for five reasons. First, and perhaps most important, they help their countries change direction, especially at the critical junctures, which history shows have brought Eurasian continentalism into being. However rational the Silk Road orientation may be in economic and domestic security terms, especially with usable energy in short supply, and civil strive endemic, it is an unconventional one in operational terms for most of the countries involved. Top-level initiatives have thus been critically important in orienting nations toward dealing with other Eurasians at substantial cultural and geographic distance from themselves.

Malaysian Prime Minister Mahathir Mohammed's "Look East" initiatives of the 1980s and 1990s, redirecting Malaysian policies away from an Anglo-Saxon focus toward Japan and Korea, as well as Saudi King Abdullah's 2006 Look East overtures toward China and India, have been clear cases in point.[141] Turkey, Iran, South Korea, China, and Singapore have all taken similar transregional steps.[142] And Iran for several years (August 2005–December 2010) did so under a foreign minister, Manouchehr Mottaki, with a BA from the University of Bangalore, who also served for several years as ambassador to Japan (1994–1999).[143] Vladimir Putin, has also played an influential role, variously as Russian President and Prime Minister since 1999, in deepening cooperation among energy producers for well over a decade, especially with regard to natural gas.[144] Indeed, his sudden advent in 1999 was itself a critical juncture that greatly intensified the geopolitical cast of Eurasian energy relations, as noted in Chapter 3.

A second catalytic function of leaders in the building of trans-Asian continentalism is to help compatriots create international networks. Such networks are especially important in Eurasian relationships, because many of those ties cut across traditional Cold War political lines and are also transcultural. Working-level bureaucrats, politicians, and businesspeople among the SCO or AMED nations, for example, simply do not know each other. Top leaders, by heading delegations and making legitimating introductions, can put such middle-level functionaries in contact with one another across political and cultural boundaries, so that serious working-level interchange can begin.

Singapore, as we have seen, is a key catalytic arena for deepening New Silk Road ties. Senior Minister Goh Chok Tong, who has long promoted interregionalism, has played an especially proactive personal role.[145] His extensive travels across the Middle East in 2005–2006 together with Singapore businesspeople, and his initiative in convening AMED in June 2005, are clear cases in point.[146] Russian President Putin similarly promoted the interests of Gazprom and other Russian energy firms by frequently taking their leaders along or introducing their issues during his state visits abroad.[147] Kazakh President Nazarbayev and Turkish Prime Minister Erdogan have also been influential in this way.

A third, related leadership function is to help build trust and leverage overseas. Leaders, by virtue of their position, carry the prestige of their office and help confer it on delegation members by association. When leaders travel widely across Eurasia to confer, as has become increasingly common since energy prices began spiraling upward in 2004–2005 in particular, they increase regional trust and confidence. Periodic high-level conferences such as AMED, SCO, and CICA, together with bilateral state visits like those of Saudi King Abdullah to China and India, and those of Japanese leaders (Koizumi, Abe, and Fukuda), Chinese leaders (Hu and Wen), and Korean leaders (Roh, Lee, and Han) to the Middle East and Central Asia, appear to be building some trust and rapport. Meanwhile, Russian energy sector consolidation, coupled with high energy prices and aggressive diplomacy, are steadily reinforcing a Russian leverage which has long-term implications for Eurasian interdependence more generally, despite frequent short-term resistance to Russian geopolitical maneuvering.

Leaders are important, fourth, for their agenda-setting role, as distinct from their administrative functions. Former Indian Petroleum and Natural Gas Minister Mani Shankar Aiyar, for example, developed a comprehensive Asian regional energy strategy for India that was substantively important, by promoting such ideas as the Asian Gas Grid, connecting Asian countries with 55 percent of world natural gas reserves.[148] He also established the logic of energy relations as a tool for transcending and reducing geopolitical tensions, by personally building energy bridges to China, Myanmar, and Iran.[149] Even after Aiyar left ministerial office in January 2006, after a short tenure of only twenty months, his emphasis on regional projects to ensure energy security continued to animate Indian foreign economic policy.

Korean President Kim Dae Jung promoted important ideas personally, such as the concept of the Iron Silk Road railway across Eurasia and the "Sunshine Policy" for dealing with North Korea.[150] He also inspired important new organizations to promote concepts of Asian regional integration, such as the Asia Vision Group, proposed at the December 1998 Hanoi ASEAN Plus Three summit, and chaired by former Korean Foreign Minister Han Sung-joo.[151] President Lee Myung-bak and Prime Minister Han Seung-soo strongly emphasized Eurasian energy diplomacy and the concept of an Energy Silk Road, beginning in early 2008.[152]

Leaders are also crucial, finally, for the resources they mobilize on behalf of their priority strategies. Japanese Foreign Minister Obuchi Keizō, for example, was instrumental during the late 1990s in orienting Japanese foreign policy more strongly toward Central Asia, due to the strong intraparty political influence that this prime minister-to-be possessed with the Japanese foreign aid program. That leverage allowed Obuchi to commit new resources to Central Asian policy objectives that gave real credibility to his Silk Road policy goals.[153] The crucial role of Putin and his successor Medvedev in mobilizing Russian political and economic resources in support of New Silk Road diplomacy at a critical time, with broader geopolitical consequences, goes without saying. Indeed, the suddenly proactive role of Russian leaders after 2003 in energy diplomacy, as global prices began to rise, driven by Asian economic growth, has been one of the central factors giving increasing reality and concreteness to the notion of an incipient Eurasian balancing coalition in world affairs.

CONCLUSION

Powerful economic complementarities have long existed between the vast hydrocarbon resources of the Middle East and the former Soviet Union, on the one hand, and the vast consuming populations of East and South Asia on the other. Yet for many years, despite the coming of industrial and automotive revolutions that hurled the world abruptly into the petroleum age, the two geographical antipodes of Eurasia remained economically and politically remote from one another, save only for the unobtrusive, apolitical trading state activities of Japan. Indeed, it took six critical junctures to spur the growth and dismantle the barriers requisite to bringing the Islamic and Confucian corners of that vast continent into broad-based interdependence once again.

This chapter has presented the story of how and why Eurasia has become a more interactive and in many ways more cohesive continent, following the Balkanization of the Cold War years. It also considers what sort of continent Eurasia is becoming. Three powerful forces have been at work: elite fears of the instabilities created by ethnic diversity; fears of a rising fundamentalist threat; and the role of Russia as catalyst. Russia itself has been driven by two basic impulses: (1) acting to stabilize its regional environment by repelling disruptive forces, including those from the West; and (2) enhancing national influence by using energy as a geopolitical tool. Interestingly, the former impulse has been more productive for Russia in eliciting regional cooperation, although Moscow's latent leverage on energy matters remains one of the most effective elements in its diplomacy.

In sharp contrast to Western patterns, trade and finance have not been principal drivers of political integration between the east and the west of Asia, however important they have been in subregions such as the Northeast, and

increasingly between India and China.[154] Key nations of the Eurasian continent are linked more by geopolitical calculations, including arms contracts,
development assistance, and, increasingly, energy pipelines and other infrastructure, than they are by nonenergy trade and investment. This distinctive
reality naturally shapes the sort of transcontinental ententes that are emerging,
as well as the prognosis for those bodies, many of them potential forerunners
for more formal integration, and in that sense protocontinentalist.

I have identified several types of emerging ententes in continental Asia:
hegemonic, multilateral, pariah, and corporate, as well as a strategic triangle
of great powers. None are as cohesive or transparent as Western alliances, but
they (particularly hegemonic ententes like CSTO) could potentially provide
the basis for incipient balancing behavior versus the West at the international
level, catalyzed by Russia. At a minimum, the constituent nations are trying
to create an autonomous space in the heart of Eurasia where American superpower is not determining. They are achieving a degree of success, which could
be enhanced by the decline in U.S. Afghan involvement. Moscow's dominance
through hegemonic ententes in the near abroad, coupled with leverage through
arms supply and energy in the strategic triangle, give it local influence, despite its relatively weak regional trade ties. Eurasian continental energy and
arms ententes thus have potentially significant strategic implications, likely
to grow more important in future, which are explored in greater detail in the
next chapter.

Chapter 8 Strategic Implications

The economies of East Asia, South Asia, the Middle East, and the former Soviet Union have changed sharply of late and have grown markedly more interactive, as we have seen, under the impact of historic critical junctures. Virtually every nation along the vast continental expanse from Beijing to Tehran and beyond is much wealthier now—both absolutely and relative to virtually every other global region—than a decade ago, the recent succession of financial crises notwithstanding. The growth explosion that began with critical junctures in China (1978) and India (1991) broadened further to Central Asia in the late 1990s, following the Soviet collapse of late 1991, with that critical juncture opening former Soviet realms to deepening interdependence with the rising Asian giants.

Growth then accelerated in the Middle East, reflecting long-term global energy price increases that have begun to transform the very structure of world affairs. The Iranian Revolution, followed by shock waves in Saudi Arabia and Afghanistan, as well as the rise of Putin, injected the uncertainty of Islamic jihad, and more extensive Russian use of energy as a policy tool. The global financial crises that followed, during 2008–2009 and 2011, enhanced the relative international importance of intra-Eurasian energy geopolitics still further, through their disproportionate impact on the industrialized West.[1]

Despite continuing rivalries and tensions, the nations of the New Silk Road are thus becoming a critical mass in the international system, with their energy ties growing at once deeper and more geopolitical. Expanding, energy-driven interdependence among the Middle East, East Asia, and elements of the former Soviet Union has major strategic consequences, born of earlier critical junctures, that are just becoming manifest. To reiterate, divisive rivalries across this complex emerging region continue to exist. Yet continental Eurasia is nevertheless growing both more coherent and more consequential, with rising potential to undermine the preeminent global geopolitical position of the United States, should Eurasia's political-economic integrity continue to deepen. This chapter explicates those emerging prospects, stressing their still-inchoate nature. It lays groundwork for the conclusion to follow, which presents a program of needed proactive response, on the part of both Americans and the broader global community.

THE IRONY OF AMERICA'S CHANGING ROLE

Although continental Eurasia's profound political-economic transformations of the past generation were fatefully shaped by critical junctures within, they took place in response to a broader pattern of historic and far-reaching globalization during the 1970s and the 1980s—the most sweeping in nearly a century.[2] The United States, it should be remembered, played a central role in catalyzing those revolutionary global forces. The breakup of AT&T, together with large-scale defense research and procurements under Ronald Reagan, helped to provoke the communications revolution. Similarly, the global growth and entrepreneurial vigor of American multinationals, coupled with their adamant trade liberalization strategies, also helped to accelerate market expansion around the world.[3] Unfortunately, however, the very same forces that have spawned such international dynamism, nurtured and supported politically in the United States, have also, with time, begun to undermine the preeminent global geopolitical position of the United States itself and the strategic assets at its disposal for coping with the Eurasian continental nations. Although that position remains strong, adverse trends will make proactive, corrective steps increasingly urgent in future years.

For the past half century and more, the core of the global political economy has been the United States—a massive continental power, blissfully separated by vast oceans from all potential rivals, in sharp contrast to other potential superpowers. China, for example, has Japan, Russia, and India directly on its frontiers. Russia, meanwhile, must contend geographically with not just China but also Iran and Germany, while lying in close proximity to the powerful, industrialized West. Western Europe is also preoccupied with regional concerns close at hand, including the intermittent threat of financial crisis.

Apart from America's favorable, detached location, it also has a near monopoly of first-rank military capabilities. It is one of less than ten nuclear powers—the one with preeminent delivery systems—and accounts for nearly half of global defense spending.[4] Although U.S. land forces are far from the largest in the world, American air and naval power are second to none—in scale, in technical sophistication, in combat experience, and in geopolitical leverage flowing from their far-flung deployment patterns.

America also retains formidable geopolitical influence through the strategic presence of its forward-deployed military forces in several of the largest and potentially most powerful nations of Eurasia (Figure 8.1). Throughout the first post–Cold War decade and beyond, the United States maintained roughly 100,000 troops in Europe, centering on Germany, Italy, and Great

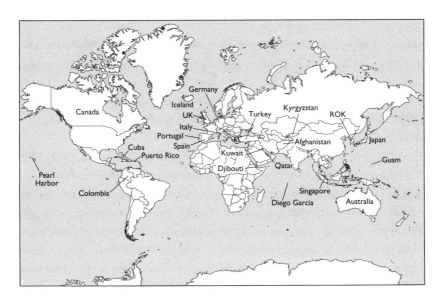

Figure 8.1: American military deployment network.

Britain. Simultaneously, it based close to 100,000 American troops in Northeast Asia, mainly in Japan, South Korea, and afloat with the Seventh Fleet. Even two decades after the collapse of the Soviet Union, the largest contingents of American troops in the world, outside Afghanistan, were still forward-deployed in Germany, Japan, and South Korea. In all these cases, their presence was reinforced by strong host-nation financial support.[5]

Just as important as the global sweep of American military deployments is their strategic configuration. U.S. forces are substantially deployed in the power centers of the OECD world—Western Europe and Northeast Asia—simultaneously reinforcing America's network of rimland alliances and inhibiting the emergence of balance-of-power tensions among these major nations. U.S. and NATO troops are also deployed strategically along the energy sea lanes from the Persian Gulf to East Asia, in locations ranging from Bahrain, headquarters of the Fifth Fleet, and al-Udeid Airbase in Qatar, to Diego Garcia, Singapore, and beyond to Japan and Korea, with powerful air and naval capabilities all along those strategic thoroughfares. America's political-military position is also reinforced by prepositioning, access agreements, training programs, and military sales.[6]

Apart from its military strength, and the broad, strategic deployment thereof, the United States has a broad range of other power resources with which to potentially confront or co-opt any competitive Eurasian configurations in the emerging global political-economic system of the twenty-first century. Deeply related to military strength, first of all, are American intelligence collection and assessment capabilities. Apart from the world's preeminent network of reconnaissance satellites and a formidable human intelligence configuration, the United States also has the world's best analysts and research institutions, both within and outside government, working in intimate interaction with the broader global community.

Aside from military capabilities, the United States also has formidable embedded political-economic strength.[7] This entrenched influence flows from its role in helping create virtually all the major institutions of the postwar world, including the Bretton Woods system of international trade and finance, now defunct; the United Nations; the World Bank; the International Monetary Fund; and the World Trade Organization, just to name a few. Emblematic of America's massive embedded advantages is the dominant global role of the U.S. dollar, recently providing 33 percent of global reserve-currency financial assets, compared to 14 percent for the Euro, a distant runner-up.[8] The dollar's persistent preeminence has been nothing short of amazing, given the nearly $650 billion in trade deficits[9] which the United States recorded in 2010, together with the massive net-debtor circumstances in which it currently finds itself—not to mention the serious 2008 crisis of its major financial institutions, the rancorous budget debate of 2011, and the credit-rating downgrades that followed.

Even more important to U.S. global preeminence than the scale of America's financial resources, or even their complex linkages to the very fabric of international life, is their geographical distribution. Virtually every national government—not excepting even pariahs like Iran and North Korea—holds U.S. dollars as the core of their foreign-exchange reserves. Indeed, Pyongyang has paid Washington's financial hegemony the ultimate compliment of producing "superdollars," counterfeits of the U.S. currency itself.

The United States also has substantial embedded "soft power" capabilities to engage, and thereby to influence, the wider world.[10] Apart from preeminent universities, with their global alumni networks, there are also powerful mass media, such as CNN, the *New York Times*, the *Washington Post*, and the *Wall Street Journal*, which play a key transnational role in agenda setting. These media networks enjoy broad, influential audiences worldwide, magnified by the global role of the English language, forcing not only the American but also foreign governments to respond to what they broadcast.

Given its diverse range of power resources—in finance, mass media, and intelligence gathering, as well as military affairs—the United States has, for half a century and more, been more than able to provide sufficient blandishments to rimland powers like its G7 allies, to balance Russia and other Eurasian nations. The dramatic collapse of the Soviet Union at the end of 1991 was only the most dramatic expression of that potency. Globalization, to be sure, benefited the United States greatly in its early stages, as both Jimmy Carter and Ronald Reagan well understood; embedded American strengths clearly persist in the global world now emerging. Yet the rise of new energy-driven ententes, as well as rising trade imbalances and volatility in global finance, are threatening U.S. dominance, even as shale gas allows the United States itself to become somewhat more self-sufficient in energy. The world must be conscious of all those portents in future years.

Deepening Challenges

Amid the steady drumbeat of American triumphalism, which intensified for a decade and more following the Soviet Union's collapse, many core supports for U.S. preeminence have been slowly wasting, in part due to the rise of the

New Silk Road itself. This erosion of the long-standing geoeconomic Pax Americana has occurred most obviously in three key areas: finance, conventional energy, and military basing, as discussed above. More subtly, years of persistent overseas military interventions, however unavoidable, have exacerbated a mountain of U.S. national debt, both by increasing current expenditures and by magnifying future obligations for veterans' pensions and medical expenses.[11] They have also provoked a surge of anti-Americanism and resentment of U.S. hegemony, especially in the Middle East, Latin America, and Europe.[12] The net consequence of all these developments, as we will see, is gradually becoming clear: a new, more volatile era of multipolarity, beyond American Afghan involvement, in which Eurasian interrelationships can at last emerge, however inchoate, as one increasingly significant tier among many new, often interrelated political-economic configurations.

In finance, the primary engine of change has been America's prodigious government debt, swollen by a decade of war in Iraq and Afghanistan, and recently aggravated by domestic stimulus. That debt has been rising steadily since the early 1990s, accelerating markedly since 9/11, and totaling around $14.8 trillion in September 2011.[13] U.S. government debt outstanding in 2010 was roughly four times as large as in 1990 (Figure 8.2).[14]

To be sure, recent levels of American public debt have been exceeded in the past—notably at the height of World War II. Indeed, in 2008 the country's debt was only half of what it was in 1945, when the cost of waging World War II propelled it to 122 percent of GDP.[15] Yet the fiscal constraints on American foreign policy seem fated to grow even more constraining in future years,

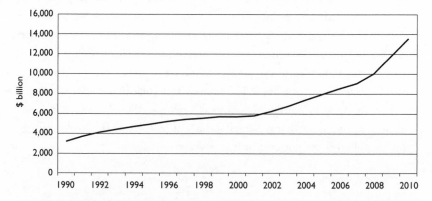

Figure 8.2: Expansion of outstanding U.S. public debt.
Source: U.S. Department of the Treasury, http://www.treasurydirect.gov/govt/reports/pd/histdebt/histdebt.htm.

driven by debt service and spiraling entitlement obligations, even if programs like the massive $780 billion stimulus package of 2009 are not repeated.[16]

America's 2011 fiscal deficit was around $1.3 trillion, and the Congressional Budget Office projects that annual deficits will average $1 trillion annually for the next decade.[17] For fiscal 2011, debt service already consumes 10 percent of federal government revenues. And that share is expected to rise to 17 percent by 2019 and to exceed national defense spending by 2030.[18]

On the entitlements front (primarily Social Security and Medicare), U.S. government unfunded obligations (traditionally covered on an intergenerational basis) are over $61 trillion, or over four times current U.S. GDP.[19] Funding current obligations occupied fully 40 percent of the federal budget in 2008. And with the aging of the 77-million-strong baby boomer generation, the first members of which turned sixty-five in 2011, entitlement expenditures will spiral still further. Pension and health care (public and private) consumed 4 percent of U.S. GDP in 2008, but this ratio is expected to rise—for demographically predictable reasons—to 18 percent by 2050.[20]

Rising International IOUs

The IOUs flowing out of the United States are rapidly accumulating in the hands of Europeans, Japanese, Chinese, and recently Indians and Russians as well.[21] China and Japan are now by far the most important creditors of the U.S. Treasury (Figure 8.3). Together they hold 65 percent of world foreign exchange reserves,[22] most of which are held in dollars, and are said to routinely

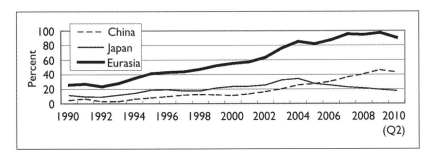

Figure 8.3: China, Japan, and Eurasia: combined shares of global foreign exchange reserves.
Source: International Monetary Fund, International Financial Statistics, http://www.imfstatistics.org.
Note: Eurasia includes China, Japan, India, Hong Kong, Russia, Republic of Korea, Bahrain, Kuwait, Qatar, Oman, Saudi Arabia, and the United Arab Emirates.

purchase more than 20 percent of the outstanding securities that the U.S. Treasury itself issues. Eurasians as a group held fully 90 percent of the foreign exchange reserves on earth in mid-2010.[23]

Significantly, since 2004 the relative shares held by Japan and China have reversed, to the disadvantage of America's longtime ally Japan, with potential longterm political-economic implications for America and the stability of the dollar's global role that remain to be explored (Figure 8.3). There are also strategic issues on the horizon: How actively and at what cost will the United States be able to pursue or even credibly commit to undertake military deployments that its major bondholders do not like? The shadows of the world that will follow America's costly Iraqi and Afghan interventions are looming.

Related to America's rising liabilities, the changing profile of asset holders, and the expanding role of sovereign wealth funds (SWFs), discussed earlier, is the crucially important question of the dollar's future role in global finance. This appears secure in the short run, despite the S and P downgrade of July, 2011, especially given the ongoing Euro crisis and persisting financial disarray among Eurasian creditors. Yet the long-term picture is less sanguine, given the vast scale of American debt.

Within the developing world this shift away from the dollar has been especially pronounced, with East Asian and Middle Eastern nations leading the way. The share of dollar reserves in total reserve assets of those countries fell from 46.1 percent to 34.2 percent between 2000 and 2010,[24] with some major actors, such as Iran, rejecting the dollar as a reserve currency entirely.[25] Recently the Asian surplus nations have invested more heavily in gold.[26] Developing nations have also placed a rapidly rising share of their assets in SWFs, as indicated earlier, which have clear long-run potential for subverting the global role of the U.S. dollar, as attractive nongovernmental investments increasingly emerge outside the United States. Capital-intensive Eurasian infrastructure projects could have a catalytic role in this regard.

Sovereign Welfare Funds: Catalyst for an Expanded Eurasian Global Role?

On the financial side of the energy-geopolitics nexus, a strategic arena where the impact of America's high propensity to consume crucially intensifies the challenge of dollar decline, globalization is inspiring a parallel development that seems destined to leverage Eurasian influence in global political-economic affairs, most probably at the expense of the United States. SWFs are "pools of money derived from a country's reserves, set aside for investment purposes that will benefit the country's economy and citizens."[27] Many such funds hold the bulk of their nation's foreign exchange reserves. Since the first SWF was established by the Kuwait Investment Authority in 1953, SWF assets have expanded to over $3 trillion, with a study conducted under the auspices of the Council on Foreign Relations forecasting that these assets will nearly quadruple, to $12 trillion by late 2012.[28] By comparison, hedge funds worldwide held assets of a "mere" $1.67 trillion as of March 2010.[29]

SWFs relate profoundly to the rising role of Eurasia in the global political economy, because the large SWFs are almost exclusively located in New Silk Road nations. Nine of the ten largest SWFs in the world are based in Eurasia— five in East Asia and three in the Middle East, plus Russia (Figure 8.4). None are in Africa or Latin America. The only exception to the Silk Road monopoly is Norway, which helped popularize and legitimate the SWF concept globally in 1990 and actively uses an SWF to invest the bulk of its proceeds from oil exports.[30] The largest American SWF, that of the state of Alaska, is the seventeenth largest in the world, with assets of just over $40 billion.[31]

As Figure 8.4 makes clear, the large SWFs are of two varieties. Most important are the SWFs of major oil and gas exporters, particularly from the Persian Gulf, which collectively hold roughly two-thirds of SWF assets worldwide.[32] The UAE's fund, the world's largest at over $600 billion, is in a sense typical. The UAE is a huge oil exporter, at over $70 billion annually (or 2.5 million barrels per day), with two-thirds of its production going to Japan.[33] Despite its huge exports and the considerable revenue therefrom, swollen by high energy prices, however, the UAE has very limited local absorptive

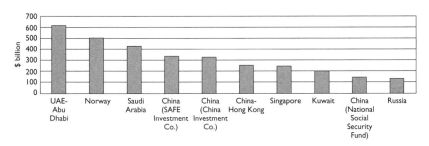

Figure 8.4: Large sovereign wealth funds of the world.
Source: Sovereign Wealth Fund Institute, http://www.swfinstitute.org/fund-rankings/.
Note: Figure for China (SAFE Investment Co.) is a best-guess estimation. Russia figure (National Wealth Fund) includes the Russian oil stabilization fund. Figures are the latest available as of November 2010, according to the website.

capacity. Its local population, after all, is only 4.5 million people, of whom less than 20 percent are citizens.[34]

The second group of substantial SWFs belongs to East Asian manufacturing-exporting nations. The largest Asian SWFs, those of the PRC, hold total assets of roughly $350 billion each, or about a quarter of China's overall foreign exchange reserves in total.[35] Such SWFs are essentially recycling the product of trade surpluses between East Asia and Western industrial nations, although Japan, as of early 2012, did not yet have one.

SWFs thus recycle a high and rising fraction of the huge surpluses from energy and manufactured trade that the Eurasian nations have been running with the rest of the world, particularly with the United States and Europe. Those funds have expanded rapidly since 2000, as both energy and nonenergy trade surpluses between Eurasia and the rest of the world have soared. Between 2000 and 2006, as energy prices rose, for example, the trade surplus of the Middle Eastern countries minus war-torn Iraq with the broader world tripled, from $88 billion to $252 billion. Meanwhile, the trade surpluses of Russia and the Central Asian countries, minus Kyrgyzstan and Tajikistan, more than doubled, from $58 billion to $139 billion. That of China, trading heavily with the United States and Europe, rose more than ninefold, from $18 billion to $169 billion.[36]

UNIQUE POLITICAL-ECONOMIC LEVERAGE

The SWFs have unique potential for revising the course of world political-economic affairs, due to their organizational structure and decision-making criteria. Their managements are typically businesspeople rather than bureaucrats, and their investment criteria are performance oriented. SWFs have no direct regard for macroissues in political economy, like the seigniorage role of the U.S. dollar, and most countries have no systematic way of incentivizing them to do so.

Unlike conventional sovereign asset pools, which have typically been conservatively invested in gold and the sovereign debt instruments of key currency nations, such as U.S. Treasury bills, SWFs invest much more broadly, often at the subnational level. The Abu Dhabi Investment Authority, for example, bought 4.9 percent of Citigroup for $7.5 billion, while China Investment Corporation, one of the PRC's largest SWFs, took a 10 percent share in the Blackstone Group, a highly influential boutique American investment firm, for $3 billion.[37] Dubai International Capital has likewise bought heavily into several Asian industrial enterprises, including Sony and HSBC.[38] A growing number of Japanese companies, including Nippon Telephone and

Telegraph, Sony, and Mitsubishi Heavy Industry, have courted potential investors in the Middle East, the global financial downturn notwithstanding.[39] They find that the financial crisis, having crippled so many Western institutions, made Middle Eastern alternatives relatively more attractive.

This unprecedented new diversification of reserves on the part of surplus nations, primarily those of Asia and the Middle East, has two potentially historic long-term implications for the global political economy. Both of them are subversive of the American financial hegemony that has been so central to global political-economic affairs since the Bretton Woods system was established in 1944. First of all, the SWFs allow national governments—preeminently those of Eurasia that are the major creditors—to profoundly influence subnational incentives, particularly those of corporations and their leadership. The SWFs can thereby substantially influence the bonuses and retirement pay of key figures in the political economies of investment target nations.

In the Anglo-Saxon countries, dominated by shareholder capital, that is exactly what the SWFs have done. They have made particularly heavy investments in financial institutions like Blackstone, Morgan Stanley, and Citicorp, whose leaders wield substantial national and international influence. Past actions like China's $3 billion equity investment in the Blackstone Group also create future expectations elsewhere in the business world,[40] which in turn magnify the political-economic leverage achieved by the original equity purchases.

The second major potential long-term political-economic impact of the SWFs and their relentless expansion affects the key currency role of the U.S. dollar. Surplus nations have traditionally invested their foreign exchange reserves in dollars through their national treasuries, allowing the United States to maintain financial stability despite huge deficit expenditures for security at the national level and housing at the household level. The rise of SWFs with narrower, profit-oriented incentive structures, powered in turn by the rising surpluses of East Asia and the Middle East that nourish them, have the potential to seriously disrupt this traditional foreign exchange equilibrium, and no macro-level incentive structure to prevent them from doing so. They want to make money, and supporting the U.S. dollar is only incidental at most.

The SWFs could also potentially undermine the dollar's key currency role by diverting investment away from American Treasury securities and from U.S. dollar assets more generally. This danger could be especially great when confidence in the dollar is otherwise eroded by American domestic financial problems and central bank reflationary efforts, as appeared increasingly possible during 2009 and thereafter. The rise of imported inflation in the Persian Gulf, related to American monetary policies over which Eurasian nations have little control, also threatens to erode the dollar-energy link and the dollar's related global key currency role.[41] Currency integration among the Gulf Cooperation Council (GCC) nations of the Persian Gulf could further undermine the dollar's long-term role, given the massive scale of the reserves and the SWFs of the member nations.[42]

Despite complex short-term political-economic cross-currents, the long-term logic of currency integration continues to be attractive. In addition to allowing the free movement of labor, capital, and goods, GCC monetary union could mitigate the inflationary pressure on the member states induced by a fluctuating dollar. Cross-border transactions within the Gulf would also be simplified while gaining impressive economies of scale. The global financial crisis of 2008–2009, although provoking an initial flight to safety benefiting the dollar, may indeed intensify longer-term prospects for GCC financial integration and for intensified interaction among financial surplus countries in East Asia and the Gulf, due to the massive structural deficits in the United States that resulted from it, as well as other lingering uncertainties in global trade and finance.[43]

A third potential impact of the SWFs on the global financial system could affect its transparency—a fundamental financial parameter, which the international community has struggled for many years to establish. Under prevailing legal norms, each country is supposed to supervise its firms domestically, monitoring their observance of international duties to disclose information. Government-owned SWFs are in a position to dispense with or short-circuit such regulations, even though they act in the same marketplace as private funds. The absence of appropriate information regarding SWFs makes it difficult to assess what kind of risk their counterpart companies, not to mention the nations with which they deal, could ultimately face.[44]

The Erosion of American Energy Independence

Another key American power resource—now also steadily eroding—has long been this country's relative energy independence and indeed, its ability to serve as an emergency supplier of last resort. The powerful leverage of the United States in the energy supply area was clearly manifest during World War II, when the United States fueled its entire wartime effort from domestic reserves and exported substantially to allies as well.[45] By the time the Korean

War broke out, the United States was beginning to sense its own vulnerability and encouraged the export of Saudi oil to Europe, to avoid excessively depleting American domestic reserves.[46]

U.S. energy dependence on the broader world has intensified substantially since 1970, and especially since the mid-1980s (Figure 8.5). In dollar terms, the increase has been especially steep, accelerated by the quadrupling of the world price of oil during the 1973 Yom Kippur War. American energy dependence on world markets rose sharply, in both quantitative and financial terms, during that period. Going forward, shale gas may well obviate the need for LNG imports, but will have less direct impact on the heavy U.S. dependence on imported oil.[47]

Compounding the global political-economic pressures promoting a long-term Eurasian transcontinental interdependence are significant changes in recent years within the energy distribution sector. Throughout the first century and more in the history of global petroleum, it was large, multinational firms based primarily in the United States and Britain that dominated trade in world energy.[48] As discussed in Chapter 3, all this changed radically amid the oil shocks of the 1970s. Western private-sector affiliates in major

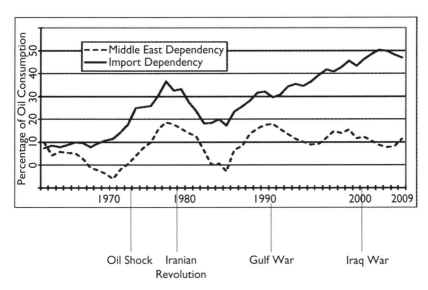

Figure 8.5: America's heavy oil import dependence.
Source: U.S. Department of Energy, *Annual Energy Review,* 2008 edition, http://www.eia/doe/gov/emeu/aer/contents.html.
Note: Figures are expressed in percentage of oil consumption.

oil-exporting countries, such as Aramco in Saudi Arabia, were nationalized, and national oil companies became suddenly dominant. Indeed, over three-quarters of global proven oil reserves are now in their hands.[49] Trans-Eurasian energy relationships, in short, are both steadily deepening in economic terms and increasingly mediated by local firms, without the involvement of the traditionally dominant Western multinationals, due to a key critical juncture in the early 1970s.

CHANGING EURASIAN GEOECONOMIC INCENTIVES

Since the early 1990s, Japan, South Korea, and increasingly China have been heavily dependent on the American market for both exports and ultimately economic growth itself. Indeed, by 2002 more than 22 percent of Chinese exports, generating over 8 percent of national GDP, flowed to the United States.[50] This ratio had been rising steadily for over two decades (Figure 8.6), with one single firm, Walmart, selling well over $20 billion in Chinese products to American consumers.[51]

This steadily rising dependence on the U.S. market, so crucial in past years to Chinese growth, now appears to have crested. Since its high-water mark in 2002, Chinese exports to the United States, as a share of total exports, have fallen from 22 to under 18 percent (Figure 8.7), as bilateral trade frictions intensify and the renminbi rises against the dollar. With alternative markets

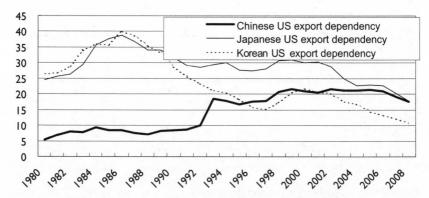

Figure 8.6: High Northeast Asian export dependence on the United States.
Source: International Monetary Fund, *Direction of Trade Statistics*, http://www.imfstatistics.org.

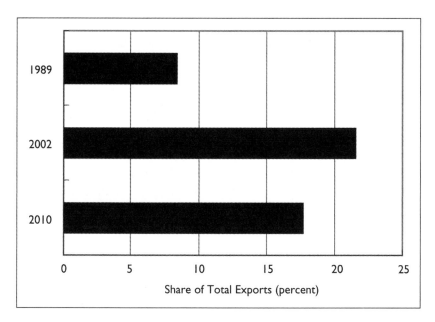

Figure 8.7: China's declining U.S. market reliance.
Source: International Monetary Fund, *Direction of Trade Statistics*, http://www
.imfstatistics.org.

expanding in the more rapidly growing nations of Asia and the Middle East, this declining trade dependence on America seems likely to continue and even accelerate.[52]

Meanwhile, other Asian nations traditionally dependent directly on the U.S. market are growing more dependent on China, either as an assembly way station or as a final market, hence increasing the PRC's centrality in the over-all Asian political economy. And as China grows more affluent, its role in the latter capacity inevitably rises. Since 2004, South Korea's exports to China, increasingly supplying final demand in the PRC, rather than components for exports to the United States, has exceeded those to the United States—by a margin of well over 2:1 in 2010.[53] A parallel, albeit less pronounced, dynamic prevails in triangular trade relations among the United States, Japan, and China, where Japan-China trade has exceeded U.S.-Japan trade by a steadily increasing amount since 2005, with the share of final consumption in China also rising.[54]

Some major nations of the New Silk Road, it should be noted, have never had the sort of deep economic ties with the United States that Northeast Asia has enjoyed, due to a different history of political-economic relations and the consequent weakness of transnational production and distribution networks linking them with the United States.[55] India and Russia—the two key potential members of a trans-Eurasian strategic coalition, apart from China—fall into this category. Their dependence on the U.S. market is strikingly lower than that of China or other Northeast Asian nations, arguably orienting their political-economic incentives in other directions (Figure 8.8). And that dependence on the United States is substantially lower, in both the Russian and the Indian cases, as a share of total exports than it was a decade ago. For India the drop has been precipitous—only 10.6 percent of Indian exports went to the United States in 2010, compared to 22.5 percent a decade earlier.[56] And Russian exports to the U.S., at 3.2 percent, were less than one-third the already low Indian ratio.

As China's traditionally high dependence on the American market, and that of its Northeast Asian neighbors, declines, and as Asian foreign exchange reserves steadily rise, the Washington-centric inhibitions on the PRC's foreign policy behavior are naturally reduced. Meanwhile, China's quest for energy and raw materials continues apace, fueled by explosive domestic growth. This quest impels Beijing and other rapidly growing Silk Road states to develop ties with a range of unsavory governments whose policies and values conflict sharply with American policy interests, as well as broader international

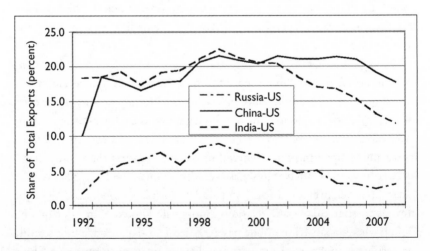

Figure 8.8: Chinese, Indian, and Russian trade dependence on the U.S. market (1992–2008)
Source: International Monetary Fund, *Direction of Trade Statistics,* http://www.imfstatistics.org.

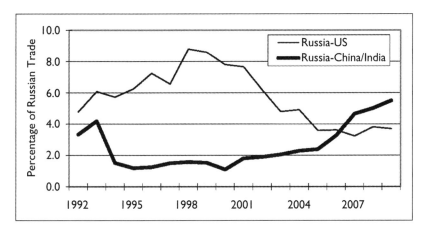

Figure 8.9: The historic post–Cold War continentalist shift in Russian trade (1992–2009).
Source: International Monetary Fund, *Direction of Trade Statistics,* http://www.imfstatistics.org.
Note: Unit is percentage of total Russian trade, with the heavier line indicating the combined share of China and India in Russian foreign trade.

norms. In these relationships, they frequently cooperate also with other members of the Eurasian strategic triangle and others significantly less dependent on the United States than China.

Both Russia and India are clear cases in point. Both have much lower dependence on the U.S. market than China (Figure 8.8)—and that dependence is, in both cases, sharply lower than it was at the end of 1999, when Vladimir Putin came to power in Moscow. Although limited competiveness may account in part for the low level, it hardly accounts for the decline, as Russian productivity has been improving, even as market dependence on the United States recedes. Conversely, in the Russian case at least, dependence on the strategic Eurasian triangle has—thanks to buoyant Russian energy exports to rapidly growing and energy-deficient China and India—rapidly eclipsed U.S.-Russian trade, with the gap widening steadily since 2006 (Figure 8.9).

Lack of Deference on Human Rights

Continental Eurasia, with limited and declining economic dependence on the United States, is, not surprisingly, also often disinclined to deference on other matters. The complications are evident in Darfur. There, well over 200,000 people are said to have been slaughtered over more than three years of unremitting genocide by northern Sudanese Arabs against the long-suffering blacks of the south. China supplied much of the weaponry used by Sudanese troops.

Despite the controversial nature of the Sudanese regime, a range of Eurasian firms, led by Chinese enterprises, have plunged into commercial involvements in the Sudan without hesitation. China's emerging oil major, CNPC, together with Malaysia's Petronas and India's Oil and Natural Gas Corporation (ONGC), have formed Greater Nile Petroleum Operating Company (GNPOC), a joint venture to exploit Sudanese oil, with ownership divided among CNPC (40 percent), Petronas (30 percent), ONGC (25 percent), and Sudapet (5 percent). GNPOC was producing an estimated 260,000 barrels per day as of January 2007.[57] Since 1998, this perverse Eurasian corporate alliance has been continuing to exploit Sudanese resources, little fazed by international condemnation. Japan too has been a major energy importer from the Sudan, especially from its southern segment, which became independent in mid-2011.[58]

Uzbekistan is another case in point. In mid-2005, hundreds of local citizens were killed at Andijan, in one of the largest massacres of unarmed civilians globally since Tiananmen Square in 1989. The number of fatalities is in dispute, with sharply contrasting assessments. The Uzbek government indicates that 169 were killed, although the Organization for Security and Cooperation in Europe estimates the number of fatalities at between 300 and 500, with some suggesting a toll as high as 700.[59]

The Uzbek government failed to investigate formally or to punish relevant parties and has reportedly intensified domestic repression in the wake of the incident. The government also retaliated against the West, which protested human rights violations, by expelling American military forces from Karshi-Khanabad Air Force Base as one consequence. Yet Eurasian nations such as China, Russia, Iran, or even India have failed to seriously question Uzbek governmental behavior, and several have deepened political-economic relations since Andijan.[60]

Myanmar follows the same pattern. In 1990 a bloody military coup nullified the unambiguous popular election victory of Aung San Suu Kyi, daughter of the martyred hero of the country's independence struggle and a future Nobel Peace Prize laureate. After years of persistently despotic rule, the military junta of General Than Shwe in 2007 brutally suppressed a broad-based rash of mass demonstrations, led by local monks, in which foreign journalists were killed, including a Japanese journalist who was brutally murdered. The West and Japan protested vehemently. Yet the Burmese military, supported by China, and by an India with deepened energy interests in northwestern Myanmar, basically ignored the international protests. In early 2008, following the junta's decision to block most foreign emergency assistance following massive cyclones in which 78,000 people died, international outrage exploded once again. As previously, the junta, backed by China and India, proved indifferent and immobile. Despite its perverse policies, energy relations with those giants deepened, including a major pipeline project from Yunnan across Myanmar to the Bay of Bengal.[61] Even a modest detente with the United States in late 2011 did not substantially change these underlying realities.

Destabilizing Implications of Rapid Eurasian Growth

Chronic political instability, as we have seen, has historically afflicted much of continental Eurasia, including the Middle East, China, and the former Soviet Union. Two of the key critical junctures that have reshaped Eurasian continental history—the Iranian Revolution (1979) and the collapse of the Soviet Union (1991)—exacerbated this problem. Classically, rapid economic growth is expected to moderate such instability and promote democracy by giving rise to a new middle class and generating resources to satisfy broad popular demands.[62] The fragility of public order, in the face of ethnic and religious ferment, continues to be manifest, as in Xinjiang and Kyrgyzstan during 2010–2011.

Multiple corrosive forces are at work. Urbanization and education bring rural dwellers to the cities and expose them to new perspectives. In virtually every nation of the New Silk Road, those new perspectives prominently include Islamic fundamentalism, since Muslims constitute either a majority or substantial minority in every major Eurasian nation except Japan and Korea.[63] Such fundamentalism was given fatefully enhanced prominence and support in 1979 by three related catalytic events, feeding on the inequality and the erosion of traditional institutions that are additional by-products of rapid growth: the critical juncture of the Iranian Revolution, the defensive Saudi response, and the Soviet invasion of Afghanistan. Its unsettling impact we see clearly in the "arc of crisis" surrounding the Persian Gulf today—including the ongoing instabilities in Iraq and Afghanistan.[64]

The prospects are strong that, in response to these destabilizing forces of socioeconomic transition, alternative streams of nationalism, autarky, and repression may well intensify. Certainly these tendencies have appeared in Russia, China, Central Asia, and Iran in recent years, inspired by the critical junctures of the past, especially the Iranian Revolution and Putin's soft authoritarianism. The governments of many Eurasian nations, as we have seen, demonstrate an aversion to the perverse uncertainties that prevail in a volatile world of neoliberal interdependence. Bolstered by energy revenues and the inherent attraction for others of their bountiful underlying reserves, the petrostates, in particular, are freed by the possession of energy resources from the need to conciliate the world community, and are increasingly prone to use energy as a geopolitical weapon. In the wake of the frustrating Iraq and Afghanistan ventures, as well as America's budget crisis, few ambitious outside powers are likely to venture again to forcefully compel or attempt to transform them, in accordance with either superpower interest or broader international norms.

Eurasia's emerging energy geopolitics thus do not herald the coming of a "world of liberty and law," as recent idealists have confidently proclaimed.[65] However salient that pattern might be in the legalistic societies of the West, it lacks the domestic cultural or institutional base to easily prevail across most New Silk Road nations, with their generally authoritarian traditions and often instrumental approach to human rights. Further, the West lacks leverage to impose such constraints from the outside, as the frustrating experience of Iranian sanctions suggests. These societies have limited Western trade dependence and often substantial energy resource buffers, not to mention like-minded regional allies. And the West, in the wake of Afghanistan and Iraq, lacks the financial and political wherewithal for sustained military involvement on the Eurasian continent, however technologically formidable its arsenal may be.

Rising global energy demand is thus leading us gradually toward an intra-Eurasian interdependence that—in the absence of creative new steps to alter the situation—has sobering future implications for international affairs. That grouping implies liberation from U.S.-made international rules and potentially the emergence of a lawless new region—a reversion to a Hobbesian "state of nature." That anarchic development has momentous implications at both the national and international levels.

Dangers of International Anarchy

Among the nations of the region, the absence of powerful outside dissuasion, combined with limited mutual economic interdependence and low transparency, has led to an ominous proliferation of weapons of mass destruction (WMD) across Southwest Asia. Few of the nations in the vicinity are members of the OECD. Many are not even members of the WTO. None ever had anything to do with the General Agreement on Tariffs and Trade. The inhabitants of this rough neighborhood are quintessentially people without rules— denizens of what Thomas Barnett calls the "non-integrated gap," devoid of stabilizing links to the key centers of global geopolitical power in Europe and North America.[66] For them, notions of constitutionalism, personal liberty, and the rule of international law are far-distant abstractions.

Yet the sojourners along the New Silk Road, who have never valued either Platonic rules or Kantian imperatives, do possess two resources that are potent broadly across international affairs—money and natural resources. Some in the region are also moderately advanced in technology. Being outsiders in an international system dominated by Europe and the United States, governed dramatically by parochial coalitions with limited reliance on international trade apart from energy, these nations have grown adept at cynically utilizing their resources as leverage to attain desired ends, however globally destabilizing such behavior might be.

Not surprisingly, nearly two-thirds of all the nations on earth possessing ballistic missiles are located along the New Silk Road, creating the extraordinary concentration revealed in Figure 8.10.[67] Eleven of these nations have only short-range missiles—with ranges of less than 1,000 kilometers.[68] Yet along the length of the road are also seven countries—China, India, Iran, Israel, North Korea, Pakistan, and Saudi Arabia—with intermediate-range ballistic missiles, possessing more substantial ranges of 1,000–3,000 kilometers. Indeed,

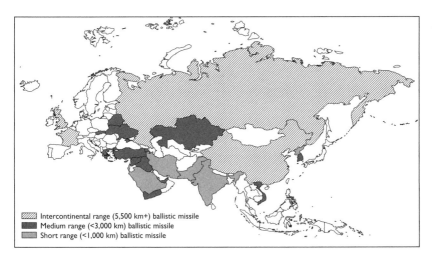

Figure 8.10: Ballistic missile deployments in Eurasia.
Source: Cirincione, Wolfstahl, and Rajkumar, *Deadly Arsenals,* 15.

Eurasian nations are the only countries in the world, apart from the conventional Great Powers, with such capabilities. Two of the countries involved, Russia and China, are also among the small, exclusive group of global powers possessing intercontinental ballistic missiles, with ranges exceeding 5,500 kilometers.

Eurasian continental powers also figure prominently among those retaining weapons of mass destruction, making their missile capabilities all the more dangerous and destabilizing. Indeed, there is a veritable swath of nations possessing chemical, biological, and nuclear weapons stretching across the Eurasian continent, without parallel anywhere else on earth (Figure 8.11). Five of the eight declared nuclear powers (Russia, China, India, Pakistan, and North Korea) are in the area, together with one undeclared nuclear power (Israel), and another clear aspirant (Iran). All of the seven nations suspected of retaining biological weapons or programs (China, Egypt, Iran, Israel, North Korea, Russia, and Syria) are likewise there.[69] So are all six of the nations (the "biological seven" minus Russia) that are suspected of retaining significant chemical weapons programs.[70] As in the case of missile capabilities, this configuration is unequaled anywhere on earth in the post–Cold War world. And Eurasia is also a turbulent region where terrorism, and the potential diffusion of weapons to terrorists, is a serious security problem.

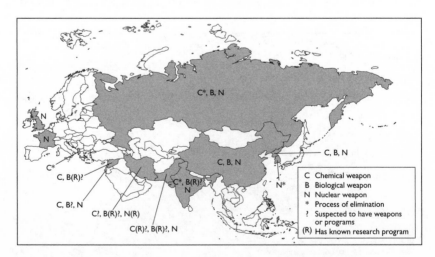

Figure 8.11: Chemical, biological, and nuclear weapons in Eurasia.
Source: Cirincione, Wolfstahl, and Rajkumar, *Deadly Arsenals*, 22.

Some wealthy, technologically advanced nations across the world, of course, have either forsworn or abandoned WMD programs. Prominent among those opting out of such deadly competition are Japan, Germany, Brazil, Argentina, South Africa, and several of the post-Soviet successor states, including Belarus, Kazakhstan, and Ukraine.[71] None of the New Silk Road nations, save Kazakhstan, however, is among them. And Kazakhstan was a WMD possessor only by accident, by virtue of being a successor state of the Soviet Union, with substantial Soviet nuclear forces already on its territory, when the USSR collapsed.

Domestic Instabilities

Apart from the perils of systemic anarchy at the international level, Southwest Asia clearly confronts serious challenges to public order at the domestic level as well. As noted earlier, profound challenges are evoked in any developing society by social transition in rapidly growing political economies—adjusting to urbanization, education, rising expectations, income inequality, and so on.[72] In addition, this region also confronts the pronounced specter of Islamic fundamentalism, exacerbated since the late 1970s by the Iranian Revolution and superpower intervention in the Islamic world (both in Iraq and in Afghanistan twice), as well as momentous dislocations surrounding the end of the Cold War.[73] The Soviet collapse and Putin's effort to reassert Russian dominance in the near abroad, in part through an unyielding attack on Muslim extremists in Chechnya and elsewhere, has made matters still more complex and volatile.

CAN EURASIA ENSURE ITS OWN STABILITY?

Beyond the realm of values lies the issue of capacity. Even if the Eurasian states wanted to uphold broader global norms, or to support systemic stability, and had the necessary resources, would they be institutionally or politically capable of doing so? Are they moving seriously in the direction of gaining such capacity? Clearly these nations are becoming a critical mass in the international system, and despite continuing tensions a more coherent transnational entity. Combined affluence and cohesion could well ultimately lead them to a more significant collective role in international affairs, albeit potentially under stronger Russian or Chinese geopolitical influence. Deepening Eurasian continental interaction could alternatively lead to chaotic intraregional balance-of-power struggles, with a potentially nuclear dimension, thus destabilizing one of the most economically vital regions on earth.

A crucial consideration, in thinking about the future of the Eurasian continent in world affairs, is the nature of governments and civil societies prevailing
in the countries concerned. How coherent are the administrative capabilities
of the states involved? How powerful and competent are their executives at
the cosmopolitan tasks of international affairs? And how effectively do the
civil societies of these nations alternately inform, nurture, and when necessary check the actions of the states within which they are embedded?

A casual review is not encouraging. None of the major nations of the
New Silk Road—not populous China or India, or affluent Japan—has a
powerful, unified executive branch. None have the requisite intelligence and
political-military operational capabilities, analogous to those that the United
States developed after World War II, required to play a smooth, transnational
coordinating role. None have the powerful, transcendent multinational firms
that Europe and the United States do, to informally coordinate across national
borders. And none has the vigorous civil society, to simultaneously inform and
constrain governmental action that the Western G7 nations possess.

To be sure, there are some important distinctions among them. East Asian
nations heavily dependent on manufactured export trade and enjoying strong
political-economic interdependence with the United States—notably Japan,
South Korea, and Singapore—are, for example, more subject to international norms than their less integrated counterparts elsewhere in the region.[74]
They have coherent domestic administrative structures, are combating terrorism efficiently, and have forsworn WMDs. They also have some capacity as
catalysts.

Most Eurasian nations are, for better or worse, however, top-heavy "reactive
states," devoid of consistent, systematic policy orientations.[75] Although there
is substantial cross-national variation with respect to details, most have large
and relatively powerful bureaucracies. The constituent ministries, however,
not to mention political actors, find it hard to coordinate with one another to
produce proactive national policies. And with the exception of Japan, South
Korea, Turkey, and India, few of these nations have a vigorous private sector
or middle class to sustain a market orientation and democratic values. Accordingly, foreign suasion often becomes a crucial catalyst for policy change.

These domestic deficiencies could potentially be offset by the enormous
dynamism and strategic coherence of powerful entrepôt microstates in their
midst, such as Singapore and Dubai. It is not inconceivable that such outposts
of cosmopolitanism could function like a modern-day Venice or Genoa, to
coordinate broader systemic functions that larger and more cumbersome

nations could not handle. Yet the rigidities of the major countries along the New Silk Road create a broader systemic problem—the danger of gridlock if left to self-governance. That bodes ill for both the stability of the region and its broader global role.

SILVER LININGS ON THE GLOBAL SCENE?

The picture I have painted here—rising interdependence within Eurasia, driven by energy, coupled with endemic intraregional tensions, particularly at the subnational level—is so unsettling that it naturally generates impulses to stabilize, both within Eurasia itself and further afield as well. Several of the nations of the region, such as India, have strengthened their relations with the United States, even as they have embraced Eurasia also. The United States itself has begun taking greater interest in the region since 9/11. And sustained economic growth has swelled the ranks of the local middle class in many nations, enhancing long-run prospects for stability and possibly even democracy. International NGOs beyond the region have also worked to sustain these trends.

History shows that dire challenges often provoke movement toward their positive resolution. It also shows, as in the case of nuclear weapons during the Cold War, that the prospect of total cataclysm itself can prove stabilizing. This may have relevance for rising global financial imbalances as well. Yet the prospect that American power, the rule of law, or the sheer scale of impending problems will produce stability is a slender reed on which to depend in coming years.

CONCLUSION: DUAL STRATEGIC CHALLENGES

Continental Eurasia is a contradictory world: one that paradoxically combines rising affluence with prospects of persistent political instability. In this sense the region is a prisoner of the past, through which it has been re-configured tumultuously, through critical junctures, over the past four decades. Incomes are rising across Eurasia, through the synergistic interaction of rapid East Asian industrial growth and rising energy revenues flowing to the Middle East, Russia, and Central Asia. As this interactive process moves forward, stimulated by the rising interdependence among these regions, Eurasia as a whole is gaining greater collective geostrategic weight in world affairs, even as many of its diverse nations become more volatile at home and at times capricious in their regional interactions.

One challenge, at the international level, is a "competitive security challenge," a strategic competition that pits nations against one another as rivals. The emergence of such competition could thus signal the end of a peaceful, Washington-centric era of clustering around a sole superpower, and the contrary reemergence of competitive balancing as a pervasive pattern in international affairs. Russia, with its substantial energy resources, relative trade and financial autonomy from the United States, and Cold War superpower heritage, clearly has the potential to become the linchpin for a balancing coalition in contradistinction to the United States.

Under President Vladimir Putin, Russia indeed began to play this role, although not in the overt Cold War fashion of previous years. Using energy and arms supplies as levers, the Kremlin has begun trying to forge loose ententes with other major regional powers, conspicuously India and China, to preempt deeper American political-military involvement in Asia and to encourage the United States to downsize its existing presence—in Central Asian military basing, for example. Should those Russian-inspired ententes cohere, linking populous, growing, and resource-rich Eurasian heartland powers in an energy embrace, they could pose more serious long-term global geostrategic difficulties as well.

The second strategic challenge posed by Eurasian continentalism, however, is a "cooperative security challenge"—one that can potentially unite nations of the world rather than divide them. It is the challenge provoked by the uncertainties of political transition that inevitably accompany economic growth, a syndrome especially prominent in the Eurasian nations due to their volatile energy and export-driven growth profiles. In the case of Eurasian nations, such instability is also unusually threatening to the broader world, because it tends to be increasingly entwined, especially since the Iranian Revolution critical juncture, with Islamic fundamentalism. And that Eurasia-bred fundamentalism—as the events of 9/11 and the London bombings so dramatically showed—can be motivated, organized to strike out at, and even incubated in, the very centers of power and culture of the Western industrialized world.[76]

As we have seen in this chapter, instability on the Eurasian continent threatens not only, or even predominantly, Western power centers. It also threatens Eurasian elites themselves. All of the major nations of Eurasia save Japan and Korea, as we saw in Chapter 3, have experienced major critical junctures in the past quarter century, which have often radically realigned local institutions and leadership. Many nations of the region, particularly in Central Asia and the Middle East, have conspicuously weak national consciousness, and some even lack clear boundaries. Transnational forces and ethnic consciousness are strong, making national elites themselves painfully vulnerable, as manifest in the Arab Spring and related turbulence across Eurasia in 2011.

Given their precarious domestic circumstances, local elites from China to Bahrain are naturally preoccupied with local stability and prone to cooperate with outside groups in sustaining it. Pervasive instability and weak human rights traditions incline most toward collaboration with authoritarians in the region, rather than with liberals farther afield. This self-protective impulse is the basis on which regional organizations, such as the SCO, are founded and sustained. It is the rationale for informal ententes, potentially such as that among Russia, China, and India, which supply weapons and energy to the developing nations of the region. International relations in Eurasia thus have a profoundly domestic basis, rooted in the tensions of transition that are endemic within the region. As Eurasian interdependence deepens, policymakers beyond Asia, not to mention those within it, must consider this stark yet promising reality—one opening cooperative prospects for mutual prosperity amid the dangers of energy geopolitics—in crafting options for the future.

Chapter 9 Prospects and Policy Implications

Energy and geopolitics, as we have seen in this volume, are coming into an increasingly intimate relationship with one another globally, with developments in Eurasia being the crucial nexus. That sprawling continent is growing explosively and will likely continue to grow rapidly for another generation, with China and India as the drivers. Their simultaneous expansion is provoking huge energy demand increases—likely to exceed half the increment in global consumption over the coming two decades. Given the immense magnitude of these prospective flows, they can only be supplied adequately in the end by the Middle East and the former Soviet Union. Sustained Asian growth, tighter energy markets, physical proximity of the major producers and consumers, and the catalytic effect of critical junctures like the Soviet collapse have given birth to a more continentally integrated Eurasia, and to a dynamic new era in Asian energy geopolitics.

This new interdependence across Eurasia, both via the traditional energy sea lanes and increasingly overland as well, is in no sense the comprehensive yet geographically confined integration that has already transpired in the European Union or North America. It is conspicuously more sector-specific, less institutionalized, less transparent, and less bound by legal strictures than regional integration in those other parts of the industrialized world. It is also, especially in energy, highly geopolitical. The partners are, by and large, petrostates and authoritarian capitalists, minimally dependent on the industrialized West and in many cases geographically isolated from it in landlocked locations, adjacent to inland seas. In no sense does this incipient trans-Eurasian phenomenon represent the coming of a "world of liberty and law," governed by common, enforceable standards, no matter how laudable those classic Western norms might be. If anything, the rise of Eurasian continental interdependence exerts a contradictory, antiglobalist pull, particularly as the Eurasian energy producers and consumers are structurally and often ideologically congenial to one another.

This nascent New Silk Road does, however, have concrete political-economic, as well as geopolitical, substance, with energy complementarities and aversion to the uncertainties of neoliberal interdependence in a volatile world at its core. Driven initially by the logic of energy markets but ultimately taking on a life of its own, this political-economic equation represents a sobering, protean new geoeconomic reality whose cohesion grows deeper in both good economic times and bad, even though regional tensions also stubbornly persist. Far beyond rhetoric, the emergence of an interactive, increasingly continentalist Eurasia is quietly transforming the nature of international affairs, reintroducing realist, geopolitical concerns in a postideological world that had fitfully tried for nearly two decades to transcend them.

WHAT WE HAVE FOUND

In this conclusion, before trying to explain causality or relate findings to theory and policy, it makes sense first to summarize what we have discovered empirically in the foregoing study, in three major areas.

Continentalism

We have found that the emerging Eurasia is profoundly shaped by globalization, but far from uniformly globalist in its character. Indeed, global forces have stirred Asian growth, provoking energy demand and social transformation that is drawing the West, East, and South of the continent much closer together, albeit in a halfway house short of globalism itself. Asia is indeed becoming, as Bill Emmott put it, "a continent created,"[1] with the former Soviet Union interacting with it in important new ways.

Trade and financial relationships among East Asia, South Asia, Russia, and the Middle East are substantial, and intensifying rapidly—especially in the trade category. In several cases, notably between China and Turkey on the one hand and Central Asia on the other, trade across old Cold War boundaries has become highly dynamic, in a Eurasian world unblemished by armed interstate conflict for more than a quarter century. Energy is in the vanguard of these flows, with two-thirds of the Middle East's oil and gas now flowing to Asia—a share that is rapidly rising in the wake of the global financial crisis.

While the most substantial energy flows—to Japan and Korea, in particular—still move by sea, significant overland energy flows, especially of natural gas, are beginning to emerge, especially between China and its neighbors, including Russia, Kazakhstan, Turkmenistan, and Myanmar. Indeed, land-based trade flows and related institutional developments, such as the creation and consolidation of the SCO and the CSTO, have been highly dynamic within Eurasia over the past decade, as has transcontinental diplomacy. CSTO has established a rapid-deployment force and has held joint exercises with SCO, whose member nations have also established the Joint Terrorism Center.

"Look East" policies are being vigorously pursued, not just by Malaysia but also by Saudi Arabia, Iran, and even Turkey. India pursues "Look West" policies toward Saudi Arabia. State visits among nations at the extremes of Eurasia are proliferating, giving increasing empirical substance to the phenomenon of continentalism, even as some geopolitical tensions—between China and Japan, for example—still persist. Defensive motives, especially since 9/11, in the face of terrorism, ethnic strife, and expanding American political-military presence, have reinforced the continentalist solidarity that is generated by energy complementarities.

Energy and Geopolitics

Market forces, of course, determine the short-term basics of energy supply and demand within Eurasia, as elsewhere. Yet we have found the continent's energy flows to be substantially and increasingly intertwined with geopolitics, partly due to its distinctive geography, with many energy reserves land-locked or inevitably passing through narrow straits en route to the broader world. The uniquely strategic nature of energy, so vital to both civilian and military life, coupled with the radical dependence of many consuming states on imports, intensifies this political linkage.

In contrast to previous decades, when Asia's primary energy consumers (Japan and Korea) lay on the periphery of the continent and sea lanes were the primary means of transport, the engines of demand today (China and India) lie in the heart of Eurasia, closer overland to potential suppliers. The Land of the Two Seas (Iran and its neighbors) is especially central. This increasing proximity of large supplier and consumer, coupled with rising producer dependence on energy for economic sustenance, the landlocked position of many new suppliers, and the disappearance of alternate foreign policy levers, has encouraged some producers, such as Russia and Iran, to subtly invoke the "energy weapon," further intensifying the geopolitical cast of energy itself.

Domestic Politics and Energy

Subnational politics within Asia, we have found, significantly influences international behavior, accelerating the emergence of Eurasian continentalism. In comparatively reviewing the approaches to energy policy and trade of the four largest Eurasian oil and gas exporter states, as well as the four largest Asian consumer nations, we found tremendous variation in national approaches—profoundly influenced, in each case, by domestic politics. Among the major producing nations, we found all to be growing increasingly dependent on energy exports, naturally enhancing their attraction to Asia, their largest and most rapidly growing market. We also found the countries with large populations, substantial military forces, and hence substantial domestic revenue needs to be destabilizing petrostates. They typically worked to force global hydrocarbon prices higher, often through erratic behavior, unless domestic institutions—as in Saudi Arabia, with its activist royal family and "islands of efficiency"—obviated that necessity. Conversely, we found petrostates with smaller populations and lower developmental needs to be stabilizing petrostates, with important roles in broader international system maintenance.

Domestic politics in major consuming nations also appear to vary crossnationally in matters of consequence, both to energy geopolitics and to Eurasian continental integration. Asian consuming nations, in particular, tend to be chronically energy insecure, given their chronic lack of hydrocarbons, their rapid growth, the relative weakness of their multinationals, and their limited political-military strength on the global scene. This insecurity naturally makes them increasingly conscious of neighboring Eurasian petrostates. These consumers also work intensely to improve energy efficiency, for both domestic and international reasons, and are also generally more open than Western nations to direct, politically inspired energy bargains with the petrostates. Unique local institutions like general trading companies and industrial groups, especially typical of Japan and Korea, facilitate such barter-oriented processes.

A final source of domestically inspired symbiosis between Eurasian producers and consumers, we have found, is a deepening common interest in energy efficiency. The energy producers, including Russia and Iran, have some of the highest rates of domestic energy consumption increase in the world, generating large and rising opportunity costs for their subsidy policies, as global energy prices rise. As the petrostates develop a middle class that purchases consumer electronics and automobiles in quantity, and as their downstream energy-processing sectors, like chemicals, steel, and fertilizers, begin to develop, their need for more efficient energy usage and for the technology that has made Asian consumers so proficient in these areas intensifies, producing a convergence of interest between producers and consumers that helps to stabilize the overall Eurasian petrostate-consumer relationship.

INTERPRETING THE EURASIAN CONTINENTALIST TENDENCY IN ENERGY GEOPOLITICS

As we have seen, Eurasia today is a very different political-economic entity from what it was a generation or two ago, at both the domestic and the international levels. And the continent occupies a very different place than previously in the dual worlds of energy and geopolitics, whose delicate intersection has been the focus of this volume. Forty years ago, in the early 1970s, when our story began, West Texas was the swing producer in global oil markets. The Texas Railroad Commission effectively set prices for the major consumers, concentrated on the two shores of the Atlantic, at the bidding of the Seven Sisters, which were overwhelmingly Anglo-American. Today, trends originating at the antipodes of Eurasia dominate both production and, increasingly, consumption as well, within a continent moving, however fitfully, toward deeper relationships at both the economic and political levels.

To explain the evolution of Eurasian energy geopolitics, and the related emergence of continentalism flowing from energy ties, I have employed four key concepts: resource complementarities, market dynamics, critical juncture, and interest convergence. Critical juncture, in particular, has been the central dynamic notion explaining structural change. It is time now to assess the utility of these ideas in accounting for the striking revival of Eurasian continentalism since the early 1970s—in answering succinctly the question *why*, with broader utility for social science theory as well. For the sake of simplicity,

I summarize my findings regarding causality, addressing hypotheses presented in the Introduction, in terms of these simple concepts:

- *Resource complementarities.* The Middle East and the former Soviet Union, as I have noted, hold roughly half of the proven oil as well as nearly three-quarters of the proven gas reserves on earth, and enjoy low marginal production costs. The consumers of rapidly growing East and South Asia are geographically close by. These circumstances create a pre-disposition for continental ties to emerge in Eurasian energy. The analytically interesting question is why the Eurasian petrostates have not always been the major suppliers of all the Asian consumers, at some uniform, stable level of mutual reliance. Resource complementarities alone cannot account for these differences, either cross-nationally or over time, although they of course create potentialities and generate expectations toward continentalism, as hypothesized earlier.

- *Interest convergence.* Political-economic changes at the domestic level, within both petrostates and consuming states, can have important implications for international relationships as well, as I suggested in Chapters 5 and 6. For example, rising hydrocarbon export reliance in the petrostates or changing demographics can provoke oil and gas exporters to become destabilizing petrostates. The rising domestic impact of energy inefficiencies, conversely, can gradually give both producers and efficient consumers like Japan and Korea new common interests and grounds for cooperation, promoting the sort of functionalist coordination hypothesized in the Introduction.

- *Market dynamics.* We have not argued that market forces are irrelevant to understanding the deepening energy ties prevailing along the New Silk Road. Asian consuming nations are becoming more affluent and need energy, while the petrostates of West Asia have energy in large quantities to supply. The analytical paradox comes, again, in the clear reality that mutual dependence between supplier and consumer at the antipodes of Eurasia frequently fails to correspond to price signals alone. Japan and Korea have been heavily and consistently dependent on the Middle East for many years, for example, yet have dealt little with Russia. China dealt first with the Middle East, but then reduced dependence and increased supply from both Africa and Central Asia. Such shifts are difficult to explain purely on the basis of market dynamics.

- *Critical juncture.* This concept helped crucially in understanding how the new Eurasian continentalist energy politics of the twenty-first century emerged and why the hypothesis that strong continental ties would emerge in energy was empirically verified. In Chapter 3, I described six episodes taking place in relatively short time frames that, I hypothesized, fatefully opened the way to post–Cold War transcontinental energy interdependence, and that then gave the New Silk Road its distinctive geopolitical character and its fateful future importance for world affairs. These episodes, transforming six of the eight large energy-producing and consuming nations of Eurasia, included (1) nationalization of Persian Gulf oil producers (1973–1975); (2) China's Four Modernizations (1978); (3) the Iranian Revolution (1979); (4) Indian economic reforms (1991–1992); (5) the collapse of the Soviet Union (1991); and (6) the advent of the Putin regime in post-Soviet Russia (1999). The 2011 Arab Spring, I concluded, did not have an equivalent degree of relevance for energy geopolitics and continentalism to the foregoing six CJs, however important in other dimensions. I have explored the long-term importance of these turning points by examining policy changes following the critical junctures, comparing the outcomes in each case to those in comparable nations (Japan and Korea) that did not experience critical junctures, as well as to other periods in the history of these nations that did not involve discontinuous policy change.

Comparative analysis of the CJs and their aftermath strongly suggests the heuristic value of the critical juncture concept. It provides a convincing explanation, first of all, for the expanding role of China and India in energy geopolitics—namely, their sudden economic reforms, which spurred economic growth and thus energy demand. The Chinese, Indian, and Russian CJs thus proved to be powerfully synergistic with one another, showing the utility of the concept. CJs (especially the collapse of the Soviet Union) also explain the erosion of some major Cold War barriers, allowing resource complementarity to stimulate trade flows, while also facilitating continental political-economic integration. CJs likewise provide insight into why hydrocarbon ententes and pipeline politics, discussed in Chapter 8, and fundamental to continentalism, have recently grown so salient across Eurasia, especially between China and Kazakhstan, Turkmenistan, and Uzbekistan. CJs also explain the new assertiveness of Eurasian national oil companies, why Islamic fundamentalism is intensifying, and why energy policy is assuming a more geostrategic cast across Eurasia as a whole, but especially in Russia.

Despite the considerable explanatory power of the critical juncture concept, especially in accounting for large structural changes in comparative political economy that facilitated continentalist energy interdependence, it remains underpredictive, especially in accounting for incremental details of regional integration, or situations where CJs were not present. CJs cannot explain, for example, variations in Japanese or Korean approaches to the New Silk Road, since such discontinuities have not recently occurred in either country. The concept fails to explain the roles of either the Western world or of globalization in provoking political-economic changes across Eurasia, or in accounting for the important phenomenon of globalized Islam, which featured so centrally in the 9/11 and London subway bombings.[2] Even though the Iranian Revolution, a critical juncture, did provoke Saudi as well as Iranian aid to fundamentalists, terrorist incidents in G-7 nations, such as the 2008 subway bombings in London, were by no means incited directly by either group. Similarly, critical junctures do not account for the broad binding dynamics in the global system, such as the establishment of WTO and more recently G20, that make narrower continentalist institutions, such as the SCO, less threatening to the globalist Western world.

Considering the Implications of Change

In the introduction I asked what implications the emergence of a new Eurasian continentalism might have for Asia and for the broader world. Now it is time to address that question. Once again, doing so by reviewing concepts employed in the analysis allows us both to review their utility and to answer more clearly the question at hand. Some of the key concepts employed were as follows.

ENTENTES AND CONTINENTALISM

As Eurasian continentalism, driven by deepening energy relationships, remains in the early stage of political economic evolution ("protocontinentalism," I contended), the transnational relationships now being formed exist at diverse levels of formality and institutionalization. In the introduction, as noted just above, I hypothesized that protocontinentalist relationships would develop readily in the energy area; that they would be strengthened by resource complementarities; and that they would also be enhanced by functional complementarities, as in energy efficiency. All three hypotheses, as suggested by data presented in Chapters 4 through 8, appear to be confirmed. Energy interdependence appears to be driving deeper transcontinental political-economic ties within Eurasia, in a broad range of areas, although both national and subnational tensions clearly persist.

The best way to capture the diversity in continentalist relationships within Eurasia, I concluded in Chapter 7, was with the notion of entente, by which I meant "an agreement between two or more governments or powers for cooperative action on policy." Although implying cooperation at the micro level, this concept does, of course, admit the possibility of tension or rivalry among ententes in more macro terms. I identified several varieties of ententes, including sectoral ententes, pariah ententes, hydrocarbon ententes (potentially intercorporate), and strategic triangles. Collectively, they capture the deepening reality of Eurasian continental interdependence, together with sociopolitical tensions that continue to persist, and that motivate authoritarian capitalist elites to intensify their illiberal policy-coordination efforts.

The Eurasian strategic triangle notion, which I identified empirically with the relationships among Russia, China, and India, deserves particular attention, not as an established reality but as a potential development with distinct global implications. I stressed that this trilateral relationship exists within the context of a multitiered international system, in which all those nations are interdependent with the West in other contexts, such as the UN, the WTO, and the G20. I did suggest, however, that the strategic Eurasian triangle could have perverse implications for the West if it grew too strong, to the exclusion of other ties. Russia does supply most of the armaments and a substantial portion of the energy that both China and India import, and their trade with Russia has been substantially more important for Russia than its trade with the United States since 2007, by a rising margin. The Russians thus do have powerful incentives to strengthen this strategic triangle with the emerging Asian continental giants, making countervailing steps by the United States and its allies—toward engagement with all three strategic triangle members—more urgent than would otherwise be apparent. U.S. diplomacy of the late 2000s undertook important early initiatives in this regard, to which the Russians, not surprisingly, responded with their own expanded overtures. From a heuristic point of view, this strategic triangle notion thus seems to be particularly useful, as a guide both to continentalist developments and as a basis for policy prescriptions to preempt or countervail it.

SYSTEM TRANSFORMATION

The origin of systemic change has been a classic issue for international relations theory since the early days of the discipline.[3] Recent and ongoing developments across the Eurasian continent do have important implications for this debate, in that they imply the emergence of a new, interactive continental entity with broader global significance. Hegemonic wars and functionalist incrementalism have been previously identified as two agents of systemic change. I suggest that domestic political-economic transformation, as in the case of China's recently deepening reliance for growth and energy supply on domestic sources and continental neighbors, can also be important. As the unipolar system of the post–Cold War years evolves in a more multipolar direction, alignments within Eurasia—and their domestic origins—provide an especially fertile field for analysis. Central Asia, in particular, adjoins Russia and China, far from the hegemonic United States, yet close to areas of substantial American and Chinese strategic interest, such as Afghanistan and Pakistan. The area's orientation is thus a geopolitical puzzle of major consequence for the global future.

INCIPIENT BALANCING

Research presented in Chapter 8 has suggested that Eurasian nations vary in their willingness to balance against, as opposed to allying with, the United States. Russia, Iran, and at times China have collaborated to offset American power in Central Asia, particularly since the color revolutions of 2005. The former two nations are the least dependent of the major Eurasian powers on the United States economically, the most partial to high energy prices, and the most conscious of potential political-military threats from Washington, and hence most prone to balance. Conversely, open, one-world globalism seems relatively more attractive to Japan, India, and China, in that order, for a mixture of economic and political-military reasons, including their energy-consumer status.

The continental Eurasian states have, in any event, taken some rejectionist steps toward U.S. presence that could suggest incipient balancing. In 2005, for example, the U.S. application for observer status at the SCO was formally rejected. The members of the SCO also strongly encouraged Uzbekistan to expel the United States from its base at Khanabad, in the face of harsh American criticism of the Karimov regime following the 2005 Andijan incident, which Uzbekistan did. In 2009 the SCO also encouraged Kyrgyzstan to expel the United States from its base at Manas, although President Bakiyev did not take the advice. As the U.S. presence in Afghanistan and its neighbors recedes, Eurasian incentives to balance against it could recede once again, but the imperative of local stability, and of balancing in the face of complex regional ethnic and geopolitical equations, will certainly remain.

ZONE OF AUTARKY

Although there is legitimate dispute as to whether the nations of continental Eurasia are as yet actively seeking to balance the United States in the heart of the continent, it seems clear that they desire a "zone of autarky" there. In such a sanctuary, they can aspire to handle matters of mutual concern, including domestic stabilization, without interference by either the United States or universalist global bodies, such as the United Nations. This aspiration seems to stem from defensive concerns of vulnerability in the face of American power, both hard and soft, and due to normative differences. As has been suggested, Eurasian continentalism appears to reject major Western legal and humanistic concepts, seeking refuge from such universalist notions in exclusivist nonglobal bodies like the SCO. Fears of ethnic unrest and Islamic fundamentalism intensify these defensive impulses for a zone of autarky.

LAND-BASED GEOPOLITICAL ACTIVITY

For nearly half a century from the Suez crisis of 1956–1957, maritime routes, particularly from Japan and Korea to the Gulf, were the heart of Asia's interaction with the Middle East, and Asian regionalism was configured in many ways along the seaways.[4] While that tendency has by no means disappeared,[5] this research suggests that "horizontal," land-based geopolitical relationships within Eurasia have become increasingly important within the past decade, following the collapse of the Soviet Union and the acceleration of Chinese and Indian growth. These emerging continentalist relationships also appear to be more dynamic, in many respects, than maritime transactions, although from a lower base, especially in the area of energy. The marked acceleration since 2008 of Eurasian pipeline, railway, and superhighway construction appears to be creating new continentalist economic realities. Their political-economic importance is clearly enhanced by the scale of the investments involved, and could be quite consequential to the regional future if the history of past infrastructural spending in developing nations is any guide. Those broader implications remain to be explored.

The simultaneous energy demands of China and India, coupled with an inland shift in China's political-economic center of gravity due to the Open Up the West initiative have intensified land-based geopolitical activity, especially between China and Central Asia, still further, this book has argued, and will continue to do so in the future.

ISSUES FOR FUTURE RESEARCH

Deepening energy interdependence between Northeast Asia and other Eurasian nations has given rise to deepening continental leadership networks, to soft institutionalism, and to deepened policy coordination that seems likely to intensify further in future years. How do deepening ties in one issue area influence those in other spheres? And what concrete, global role can emerging bodies such as AMED, the SCO, CAREC, and the CICA, as well as softer, more informal "Look East" personal elite networks, like those of Saudi Arabia's King Abdullah, play, and why? These are important issues in regional studies and international political economy that remain to be fully explored, but which have been raised and tentatively considered here.

This research has also contributed insights into the balance-of-power dynamics of international affairs. Clearly the emergence of a Eurasian energy entente with broader political-economic dimensions, including both interdependence and some enduring tensions, does not appear to presage a return to bipolarity in international relations, such as characterized the Cold War. Yet it does seem to indicate the reemergence in at least some sectors of balancing and containment dynamics and a resurgence of nation-state confrontations with a realist geopolitical cast, which have been unusual in international affairs for nearly a generation.

While the new continentalism does appear to presage more realism, as opposed to idealism, in international affairs, it generates rigidities as well. Pipelines, for example, tie nations together in structured new ways that reduce political-economic fluidity. Eurasian continentalism does open long-shuttered states to new relationships, but it does not necessarily render them liberal, democratic, or even fully capitalist. The domestic political-economic consequences of deepening continentalist ties clearly require further study.

This research has likewise contributed to understanding how energy supply and demand transactions influence international political economy—topics thus far largely neglected by serious analysts. We have explored the role of petrostates in international political economy from a comparative perspective and have identified key subnational determinants of their international behavior. We have found, for example, that intense interest group demands, especially common in large, populous nations at middle levels of development, lead nations to become destabilizing petrostates like Iran. We have also identified converse preconditions for stabilizing petrostates, such as contemporary Saudi Arabia, where pressure groups remain largely inchoate, and elite decision makers are largely shielded from those that exist. Clearly more research is needed on the connections among energy markets, geopolitics, and patterns of conflict in international affairs, as these associations are understudied theoretically and seem destined to grow more salient in the real world. These associations seem likely to be especially important in Eurasia, given that sprawling continent's high rates of economic growth and energy demand, as well as its unusual concentration of large, ambitious powers in close proximity overland to one another.

More work is also needed on the dynamics of systems transformation in international relations, since important incremental and sectoral changes are occurring, to which holistic explanations, such as hegemonic wars, do not pertain.[6] In particular, a better understanding is needed of how changes in resource markets and patterns of resource interdependence affect global governance in a multipolar world. Continentalism, such as that which we have seen in East and South Asian relations with the Middle East and Central Asia, could well play a substantial role in future world affairs, yet exactly how remains insufficiently conceptualized. The optimism of previous decades regarding the efficacy and inevitability of comprehensive global governance may well be misplaced.[7] Yet the heuristic value of conflict-oriented classical realist paradigms remains unclear as well, in a world of deepening political-economic interdependence, where stable patterns of trans-national interaction are fundamentally required.

The consequences for war and peace of classic configurations in international affairs, including bipolarity and multipolarity, need to be revisited as well. For the first time since the end of the Cold War, the shadow of multipolarity is deepening once again. Classically, as in Europe over three centuries between the Peace of Westphalia and the end of World War II, such a diffusion of power has often led to deepening balance-of-power struggles and turbulence in international relations. The ultimate consequence, in many cases, was war.

Europe's classical diplomatic history also showed, however, that although war was distinctly possible in a multipolar system, it was by no means inevitable. Nations could be dissuaded from violence. Institutional structures of understanding, such as the Concert of Vienna, could be painstakingly built. Outcomes were ultimately indeterminate, and dependent, in many cases, on the quality of diplomacy.[8] What the consequences of multipolarity might be, in a multitiered future system of rising resource competition, is clearly an important issue of both theoretical and practical relevance in the world now emerging.

This research also raises important conceptual issues at the interface of domestic politics and foreign policy—particularly regarding how cross-border energy transactions shape national political systems, and derivatively how those transformed energy-supplying and energy-consuming systems relate to one another. We have seen that Eurasian energy-exporting states, although not shuttered in the sense of being uninvolved in international trade, nevertheless are often soft-authoritarian, as in the case of Russia and Iran, and at best only semi-market-oriented. In interaction with authoritarian capitalist consumers such as China, these illiberal energy exporters hold the prospect of creating distinctive subsystems of the global political economy that lack the liberal attributes of the broad, globalist, Western-centric system as a whole. The prospective traits of the participants in Eurasian continentalist interaction, and the implications of their domestic politics for international behavior, are important topics for future research.

IMPLICATIONS FOR POLICY

The nations of Eurasia are coming into ever more intense continental interaction, driven by underlying complementarities, critical junctures, and deepening energy interdependence. These trends will likely intensify for at least another generation, with an increasingly seamless web of continental infrastructure, linking them in ever more substantial, enduring, and confining new ways. The quiet yet momentous transformation in global political economy that this deepening intra-Asian interaction implies is not yet well perceived in the United States, Western Europe, or Japan, but nevertheless holds major implications for the industrialized world. It mandates a persistent engagement with and intellectual attention to Eurasia that does not come naturally in the West.

The world of the New Silk Road now emerging will no doubt challenge any major nation's diplomacy, especially that of the United States. Despite Washington's continuing preponderance of military power, America will not, in the fluid world of volatile energy supply and demand looming before us, have the hegemonic leverage to impose its will so readily as it has since the Soviet collapse of the early 1990s. The complexities of commitments in South Asia, as those involvements wane, will be one constraint. The rising influence of energy producers like Russia and Iran, as well as emergent consumers like China and India, also generates an enhanced ability to counterbalance American influence, and to fill the vacuum left by its quiet erosion. Such ability on the part of indigenous Eurasian powers to balance is clearly leveraged by sustained growth in Asia and the Middle East, as well as by buoyant long-term energy prices. Sustained interest in intra-Eurasian cooperation is being enhanced, not only by rising energy interdependence and concerns for stability as U.S. presence wanes, but also, in a more structured, enduring fashion, by the recent proliferation of transcontinental pipelines and other permanent, heretofore lacking, infrastructure.

Global Regimes: Only a Partial Answer in a Realist World

The United States will likely find it harder to rely, in an increasingly multipolar world, on the power of global regimes that have so often in the past felicitously embedded America's own international influence and norms.[9] Globalism, after all, is in its essence antithetical to the parochialism and energy-centric mercantilism implicit in Eurasian continentalism, whose principal national and subnational adherents lack the broad interests and liberal values that would benefit from a globalist approach. Even should globalists be willing to subordinate their transformative interests to more pragmatic concerns, partisans of trans-Asian ties, with their more shuttered and parochial petrostate and authoritarian capitalist incentives, will be reluctant to meet the globalists halfway, particularly in the high-cost energy world that sustained Eurasian growth is bringing steadily into prospect.

Both the global nuclear nonproliferation regime—confronted with challenges from both Iran and North Korea—as well as the international human rights regime may thus well grow harder to sustain, should intra-Eurasian energy relationships gain broader political-economic coherence. Whatever the legitimacy of democracy as a global norm in the wake of the color revolutions of 2003–2005, American exposition of those values has since lost substantial international credibility, due both to contradictions between theory and practice, and to the waning of U.S. geopolitical power itself. Rising energy prices, which have both palpably enriched and emboldened shuttered petrostates such as Russia and Iran, have only intensified Washington's predicament.

In the world of deepening and increasingly structured Eurasian energy interdependence now emerging, Russia and other non-G7 powers will likely have more diplomatic options than they have traditionally had. It will be harder for the United States to impose its preferences than heretofore, although enduring tensions within the region will likely provide some potential entrée. Regional, cultural, and domestic-political understanding will be much more important tools of diplomacy than we have recently found, and America will need to actively employ them.

The difficulties that Western nations, including the United States, experience in shaping events across continental Eurasia and the Middle East are palpable, as demonstrated so clearly in the Sudan, Myanmar, and Georgian crises of 2007–2008, and more recently in Afghanistan, Iraq, and the Korean peninsula as well. Yet focused engagement is absolutely essential to prevent configurations adverse to Western interests, such as the potentially exclusivist Russia-India-China continental entente discussed in Chapter 7, from gaining critical momentum. Eurasian developments need to be priority topics of G7 and NATO policy attention, regardless of how cohesive the nations of continental Eurasia themselves ultimately prove to be. Their cohesion could, after all, prove perverse for the West, given their sheer population, resources, unmonitored weaponry, and geopolitical mass.

Conversely, globally consequential political-military dangers are implicit in Eurasian internal tensions that the nations of the continent also fear, and that can provide the basis for cooperation with countries beyond that part of the world. The ethnic complexities and concentration of chemical, biological, and nuclear weapons within that volatile region are extreme, as I have noted, and could potentially feed on one another. The energy dimension further magnifies this imperative of G7 attention, given the heavy dependence of Europe, Japan, and the United States on energy imports from the volatile nations of the Middle East and the former Soviet Union. Energy imperatives also mandate broad, strategic engagement with Eurasian nations—often multilateral—since engagement on such issues as energy efficiency helps to transform an otherwise exclusivist continental disposition, which tends to stand in defense of harsh, totalitarian values, into the acceptance of broader international frameworks and norms.

Creating Positive Incentives

The central imperative for American policy, in dealing with the energy producers and consumers of Eurasia, must be creating positive incentives, many of them multilaterally configured, for local adherence by such nations to global regimes, whose ambits range from nonproliferation to international finance. The prospect is disturbingly strong that Eurasian nations, particularly if Russia or Iran become a catalyst, will heed the siren's call of autarky, nationalist gratification, and armament, aligning with their continental neighbors increasingly against the interests of the G7 democracies, however subtle and hesitant they may be about direct confrontation with Washington and its allies. Engagement can moderate those isolationist impulses and thus thwart what could otherwise become for the United States and its allies a geopolitically dangerous, energy-based Third World balancing coalition.

Engagement would include centrally the largest energy producers in the world, including Russia and possibly a reliably non-nuclear Iran, if that were plausible, as well as large continental Asian consuming powers, like China and India. Russia would likely be, as it has been in the recent past, the catalytic agent of any balancing continentalist coalition, were it to materialize. U.S. receptivity to Moscow's WTO admission, like the recent START II agreement, is an appropriate form of preemptive strategic engagement, oriented toward inhibiting Moscow's balancing incentives through mutually beneficial U.S.-Russian globalist interdependence. Even more extensive American engagement of the emerging Eurasian continental giants, especially India, is also in order, as noted in a later section.

Involving Europe and Japan meaningfully in this co-optation process is especially crucial. They are, after all, key potential sources of technology and finance for many of the shuttered Eurasian states, including Iran. Their leverage is thus substantial, and their credibility often greater with the shuttered nations, like Iran and North Korea, than that of the United States alone. Their support for common allied objectives is critically needed.

Long-term, large-scale deployment of U.S. land forces in South Asia is neither financially nor politically sustainable, for reasons outlined in Chapter 8. Yet the Afghan conflict, ironically, could nevertheless be a short-term catalyst for the sort of Western engagement in network building and multilateral outreach to local groups in Eurasian nations that is very much needed from a long-term perspective. The Northern Distribution Network for supplies to Afghanistan, established by the 2009 Obama-Medvedev summit, to cite one positive example, is usefully helping to dismantle bureaucratic barriers and reduce border red tape, and well as creating transnational policy networks inside Eurasia involving Americans, across both the former Soviet Union and many Middle Eastern states.[10] The network could be powerfully complemented by the systematic expansion of regional transportation networks, especially between Central Asia and India, as well as potentially via Afghanistan.[11]

Area Expertise Crucial

To successfully engage with continental Eurasia, America and its allies also need to improve their own understanding of the New Silk Road nations themselves, while simultaneously aiding broader international efforts to do so. Traditionally, countries like Mongolia, Iran, Burma, and even China have been obscure to Western understanding, little known to all but a few area specialists. That clearly has to change.

Nowhere will enhancing local area expertise and cultural understanding be more crucial in furthering Western interests along the New Silk Road than in Iran, Afghanistan, Central Asia, and the Caucasus. That area, as we saw in the introduction, has enormous stores of natural resources, although poor infrastructure often makes access and mutual collaboration difficult. It has been growing remarkably rapidly, albeit in volatile fashion, due both to its own substantial energy resources and to proximity with the two Asian giants, China and India, not to mention Europe. Azerbaijan, in particular, grew more rapidly over the first decade after the Asian financial crisis than any other nation in the region, including China, although it, like others, suffered short-term setbacks in the 2008–2009 financial crisis. Kazakhstan and Uzbekistan, as well as Turkmenistan recently, have also been remarkably buoyant, their authoritarian politics notwithstanding, with a degree of continentalist financial isolation helping to shield them from broader global storms. And Georgia, like Afghanistan in another direction, is the strategic gateway of these nations to global markets.

Central Asia is also highly important in geopolitical terms, for reasons that far transcend its considerable recent value as a staging area for the Afghan conflict.[12] Situated almost perfectly on the opposite side of the globe from the continental United States, nestled next to Russia and China, Central Asia is in a near-perfect location for the deployment of Western military forces, especially for prospective antiterrorist operations. Its ability to maintain some autonomy from dominant Russian influence, in both pipeline diplomacy and in political-military terms, is also very much in the interest of Washington and its allies. Yet given Russia's direct proximity, as well as its embedded political-military role from the days of the former Soviet Union, Moscow's influence is only natural, and is difficult to marginalize without provocation.

Central Asia, like Afghanistan, is likewise important in the overall context of the more integrated continental Eurasia now emerging. A growing Central Asia has natural relationships, reinforced by classic history, with Russia, China, and Iran, but also incentives to balance those with broader ties, for the sake of national autonomy. It thus has natural interest in diverse relationships with Japan and Western Europe, not to mention the United States, although the region lacks the global knowledge or diplomatic expertise to nurture such cosmopolitan ties. An astute, multilaterally oriented American diplomacy, sensitive to local political circumstances, as well as the sentiments of allies in Europe and Northeast Asia, needs to provide that. One potential vehicle is "minilateral" diplomacy, including such configurations as U.S.–Japan trilateral dialogues with nations such as India and Kazakhstan.

All these considerations dictate a deft, multilateral Western diplomatic strategy for continental Eurasia, sensitive to local realities, culture, and politics, while also conscious of transnational realities now emerging. That approach also necessarily means better and more up-to-date area studies training for prospective government officials regarding the region than has been heretofore available, as well as closer coordination with allies. Presently there are virtually no Central Asia area studies institutes in the United States or Europe, apart from a pioneering venture at the SAIS/Johns Hopkins University, and there clearly need to be more.

Iran also clearly needs to be understood better. It has been more than three decades since Washington and Tehran broke diplomatic ties, amid the 1979–1981 hostage crisis, and expertise based on direct contact has atrophied badly on both sides. Regardless of its nuclear future, Iran will loom as the largest, most populous nation of the Persian Gulf for the foreseeable future, with both massive energy reserves and a commanding geopolitical position, central to the Land of the Two Seas. Responding to its challenge effectively will require a nuanced grasp of the country's history, society, economy, and politics, as well as military capacity and aspirations.

The Sea Lanes in a Continentalist World

The post–Cold War world, as we have seen throughout this book, has given rise to unprecedented new political-economic relationships within Eurasia—particularly among continental states, such as China, Iran, Turkey, Russia, and the nations of Central Asia. Since the global financial crisis of 2009, overland linkages such as pipelines and railroads have been growing with particular dynamism, but maritime ties remain important, especially for Northeast Asia and the Middle East.[13] For China, maritime dependence represents a security challenge, given the preeminence of the U.S. Navy in the energy sea lanes to the Gulf, prompting a variety of countervailing continentalist strategies. Japan and South Korea, conversely, are more comfortable with maritime linkages, and procure the overwhelming share of their oil and gas supplies by sea from the Persian Gulf, as we have seen.

Looking to the future, there is little question that the Indian Ocean and adjacent sea lanes will be of substantial and probably growing importance.

Their prominence is an integral piece of the deepening continentalist inter-dependence within Eurasia that is outlined here. The maritime routes are a part—but only a part—of the picture. They need to be seen in the context of the broader continental integration that is occurring, and the resistance of key parties, notably China and Russia, to reliance on them.

For outside powers like the United States, Australia, and Europe, however—not to mention Eurasian littoral states such as Japan, Korea, Singapore, and arguably India—the partial reliance of continental Eurasia on the energy sea lanes represents an important strategic opportunity. It represents a chance to countervail the growing power of the Eurasian continentalists, while enhancing their own energy security through preeminence in the energy sea lanes from Yokohama and Pusan to the Strait of Hormuz. Maintaining a substantial naval presence in these seaways should thus be an important strategic priority for the United States and its allies, in addition to the more direct engagement with continentalist powers described above.

Deterring and Engaging the Shuttered Petrostates

Recent and ongoing regional turbulence, including the conflict in Afghanistan, the August 2008 Russian invasion of Georgia, and the continuing Iranian nuclear program, have made it clear that American energy diplomacy needs a political-military dimension—and, conversely, that political-military programs like combating the Afghan insurgency badly need an economic component.[14] Some Eurasian petrostates, most conspicuously Russia and Iran, are major energy producers with large domestic financial requirements and strategic locations astride energy access routes. They stand to benefit by using political-military tools to manipulate energy markets and force hydrocarbon prices higher. Their domestic political systems are also so shuttered and domestically focused that denying them the benefits of global interdependence through economic sanctions has only marginal utility in influencing their behavior.

Indeed, such weapons may, as was evident in the case of North Korea during the early 2000s, create a vicious cycle of isolation and increasing truculence on both sides, strengthening hard-liners in their internal competition with more pragmatic moderates.[15] More promising is strategic engagement, on a range of issues, stretching from nonaggression guarantees, to shoring up failed states and antiterrorist measures, to missile defense. In this regard, it is crucial that the United States have credible interaction with the shuttered petrostates, both directly and through allies, providing such potentially destabilizing forces with tangible incentives to cooperate and disincentives to engage in disruptive behavior.

Co-opting Continental Powers, Especially India

Some might suggest that the emerging realities I have outlined in this volume mandate an emphatically realist, amoral foreign policy with little room for idealism. This is not the case. This work does indeed suggest the potential emergence of a potent and illiberal configuration, including China and Russia, as well as authoritarian regimes in the Middle East and Central Asia. This grouping has little use for human rights, democratization, or much of the conservative Wilsonian agenda that American neoconservatives have so fervently espoused since the days of Ronald Reagan and the fall of the Berlin Wall. Russia is the main foreign arms supplier of both China and India, while trade within this perverse triangle is growing rapidly also.

Whether this fragile alignment will deepen, and whether it will ultimately cohere, are by no means determined. India, in particular, is the uncertain link, with some powerful ideological, strategic, and economic reasons to prefer a globalist approach, even as it perceives continentalist attractions also. The broader world is capable of forestalling parochial continentalism— through deterrence, diplomacy, and engagement, combined with peaceful efforts at home, rather than by proactive military means. And we have a moral obligation to do so.

One consistent element of an engagement strategy with the emerging Eurasian nations must inevitably be energy itself, the very driver that has given trans-Asian relations their recently rising cohesion. The nations of Eurasia, after all, include both producers and consumers. Their interests cohere regarding the imperative of supply, but not necessarily with regard to price. Energy, after all, is a chessboard ultimately related to geopolitics, where policies in the energy realm can have profound ramifications for power politics, and vice versa. The United States and its allies need to work more actively to stabilize energy prices. That will help allow alternatives to the volatile, inefficient, hydrocarbon-dependent status quo to naturally emerge, as the private sector becomes more confident as to which alternative energy and resource-extraction projects, including shale gas, will be profitable.

At the level of global governance, it is, I argue, still possible in the world beyond Iraq to move closer to the rule of law, and to world order, than at present—the fitful emergence of Eurasian energy interdependence notwithstanding. Yet doing so will require much more complex, and more cosmopolitan, diplomacy than Americans are used to pursuing. It will require, in particular, dealing shrewdly with the pivotal, politically indeterminate elements in the New Silk Road coalition—China and especially India—with a special focus on energy. Energy is, after all, the principal basis for their nascent interdependence with petrostates of Eurasia, including the destabilizing ones.

The United States should also use the parochial self-interest of the Eurasian giants to encourage them to reject narrow, continentalist alignments driven by energy. Concretely, both China and India, as well as Russia, fear Islamic fundamentalism in Afghanistan and Central Asia and gain from infrastructural improvements and peaceful resource extraction. If presented subtly, they all have incentives to accept cooperative regional stabilization and transportation development schemes.

From a narrower geopolitical perspective, it is of particular importance for the United States to place high priority on deepened engagement with India. That country, after all, is the world's largest democracy and likely the world's most populous nation within a decade or two. It is also increasingly dynamic economically and possessed of substantial military forces—ground as well as naval—that have significant experience in multilateral peacekeeping. India shares NATO's broad geopolitical and antiterrorist concerns and could be an important guarantor of continental stability as the International Security Assistance Force presence in Afghanistan winds down, especially if tensions with Pakistan over Kashmir and other matters can be ameliorated. It is of particular importance to encourage all manner of infrastructural links between India and Central Asia via Afghanistan, including the TAPI pipeline, electric-power transmission networks, and transcontinental railway lines, as these sinews of interdependence enhance prospects for a substantial Indian geopolitical role in Central Asia that is not dependent on Iran. The Asian Development Bank, which leverages American financial assets with those of Japan and other allies, could be especially helpful in this regard.[16]

The emerging "Chindian" powers (China and India), as noted in Chapter 8, are both key drivers of Eurasian energy interdependence, due to their persistently high rates of economic growth. The "Chindians" are also themselves highly dependent for growth, however, on exports to the U.S. market—China in manufactures and India in services. Both are also, like the United States, Japan, and Europe, major energy importers. These multiple roles make "Chindia" uniquely influential in shaping the content and values orientation of trans-Asian policy outcomes and in determining the future cohesion of Eurasia itself.

China may well be tractable, provided the outside world vigilantly monitors its foreign policy behavior and pressure is judiciously applied. And India, with its democratic sentiments, is likewise susceptible to outside appeal. Both countries are globally trade dependent and growing energy consumers as well, who should be included systematically in global energy institutions, including the IEA. Both have some promising domestic energy reserves, such as shale gas, that could be more efficiently developed with adequately protected Western technology. International cooperation could also greatly improve their energy efficiency. Through complex transregional diplomacy, centering on American relations with these two developing giants, while coordinating with traditional allies like Japan and South Korea, it should still be possible to uphold liberal values and move closer to the rule of law and world order, particularly in the Pacific. Yet doing so will require effort, cultural understanding, and strategy—applied to both American relations with East Asia and to other, more volatile dimensions of the Eurasian energy relationship.

Reinforcing the U.S.-Japan-Korea Triangle

Japan and Korea are of course geographically part of Eurasia—Japan an island archipelago just off the east coast of the continent, and South Korea next door, on Eurasia's eastern tip. Yet both nations are democracies, allies of the United States, and economically advanced members of the OECD— more deeply embedded in the liberal world system than many of their continentalist neighbors to the West.

Japan and Korea, however, are, like the rest of Eurasia, also subject to the magnetic attraction of continentalism, especially in the energy sphere.[17] Should the DMZ standoff in Korea change, either through reunification or through broader relaxation of regional tensions, those continentalist attractions would grow still stronger. It is hence very much in the long-term American and globalist interest to see bilateral political-economic ties between Japan and South Korea strengthen and to support their mutual engagement with the broader world beyond continental Asia as well.

For many years the U.S.-Japan-Korea triangular relationship was badly complicated by historical animosity between Japan and South Korea. That bitterness has by no means disappeared but has grown markedly less pronounced than a decade ago—due both to the passing of generations and to political transition in both countries, especially since 2008. Today a vigorous and explicit trilateralism is increasingly welcome in all three capitals. To the extent that it includes collaborative nonmilitary approaches to continental

Eurasia, U.S.-Japan-Korea trilateral coopeation can also help brake the force of narrower, more parochial policies on the continent as well.

Freedom as the End, Energy Policy as an Important Means

Through complex transregional politics of its own, provided they are insightful, consumer-oriented, and capitalize on divergent interests across Eurasia, the United States and its democratic allies should thus be able to move closer to realizing their traditional values. Yet the struggle, given the geopolitical changes I have catalogued, will be a difficult one. Far easier—if only we had the self-discipline—would be unraveling, through domestic action, the perversely symbiotic combination of American consumption, East Asian manufacturing growth, energy price increases, and extraordinary Western lassitude in devising alternatives that has given rise to deepening energy-driven Eurasian continentalist geopolitical ties in the first place.

For precisely these reasons—because Americans overconsume, not least in the realm of hydrocarbons—energy efficiency needs to be one of our highest national security priorities. We need to move toward clean energy sources and to create a market for energy-efficient technology, beginning with household appliances and everyday transportation. Only by cutting America's energy consumption—the highest in the world and the most rapidly growing, in absolute terms, among the major nations—can we credibly reduce our reliance on Iran's Ahmadinejad, Uzbekistan's Karimov, and other autocratic arbiters of the Middle East's energy future. Related to energy efficiency, confronting the problem of climate change is also critical to America's security future, as specialists and politics of all political persuasions are belatedly coming to see. Likewise needed are supply-side incentives to encourage development of America's shale-gas and offshore energy resources.

Harnessing the Technological Strength of Allies

Cooperation with allies should be particularly fruitful and valuable in the energy technology area, for two crucial reasons. The publics of Europe and Northeast Asia see such issues, first of all, as fundamental to national security—indeed, more profoundly so than Americans have traditionally done. Stressing energy can thus significantly help strengthen both our trans-Atlantic and trans-Pacific alliances themselves. The allies, second, being even more energy deficient than the United States, have developed energy-saving technology of value throughout the G7, have persisted in such efforts even when energy prices were low, and are inclined to share the cost of furthering such cooperative ventures in the future.

Germany, for example, has some of the most pronounced pro-solar policies on earth, and advanced technology as well. As a result of its strong solar policy emphasis, half of the world's solar electricity is now produced in Germany, and its exports account for 15 percent of global sales of solar panels and other photovoltaic equipment.[18] Japan is preeminent in energy efficiency, having cut energy consumption per unit of GDP by 30 percent since 1973. The United States can productively cooperate with such technologically advanced allies, both to reduce reliance on hydrocarbons and simultaneously to reinforce alliance relationships.

The importance of active, eclectic American energy efficiency and energy-technology policies, as levers for building bridges to India, China, and other pivotal, consumption-sensitive members of a potential Eurasian energy entente, should not be underestimated. Given their large and rising energy imports, such nations are, or should be, vitally concerned about conservation and alternate sources of energy. For the United States to be persuasive in co-opting them, however, and thereby isolating more truculent petrostates like Iran, America needs to be much more active in pursuing energy-conserving and resource-development options itself. Collaboration with allies like Japan and Germany, which have pioneered in conservation, solar power, and energy-efficient mass transit, is one way to do this, using energy to strengthen alliances and to broaden the popular conception across the G7 of the very meaning of alliance itself.[19]

In the final analysis, Eurasian continentalist energy relationships, for all their seeming inevitability and the unsettling implications that their broader political-economic consolidation present are, after all, our own creation. Their prosperity flows from our own profligacy, lack of disciplined spending, and traditional view of a resource-unlimited future. The enemy, in short, is us. Only through hard work, saving, and more sensitive diplomacy can we prevent a nascent Eurasian energy-based entente from creating, in the world beyond Iraq and Afghanistan, a deepening threat to our values, not to mention our security. After all, the future, despite the increasing tensions of the new high-cost energy world that we ultimately confront, is, in the end, still for us to determine, if we have the foresight to see it, and the discipline to firmly grasp it.

Appendix A Profiles of
Eurasian Growth

Growth across Eurasia, that powerful stimulant of energy demand, economic interdependence, and geopolitical tension, has been a delicate, synergistic counterpoint between two pillars—the manufacturers and consumers of Asia, on the one hand, and the energy producers of the Middle East and the former Soviet Union, on the other. Growth across Eurasia originated first in the remarkable industrial and political-military successes of Meiji Japan during the late nineteenth century, resumed after an aggressive and disastrous interlude in the 1950s, and was later supplemented by the Four Tigers, China, and finally India as well. The dynamic expansion of industrial Asia led, over the past decade, to rising energy prices and a broadening swath of prosperity from Beijing to the Persian Gulf, which has sharply outstripped growth in the G7 nations, as indicated in Table A.1.

Some important nuances in Table A.1 are well worth noting. China and, since the early 1990s, India also have been consistent drivers of Asian continental growth, falling back only briefly in the face of crises like Tiananmen (1989–1990) and the Asian financial

Table A.1. A Broadening Quarter-Century Sweep of Eurasian Growth (1981–2010)

Country	1981	1982	1983	1984	1985	1986	1987	1988	1989	1990	1991	1992	1993	1994	1995	1996	1997	1998	1999	2000
China	5.2	9.1	10.9	15.2	13.5	8.8	11.6	11.3	4.1	3.8	9.2	14.2	14.0	13.1	10.9	10.0	9.3	7.8	7.6	8.4
India	6.0	3.5	7.3	3.8	5.2	4.8	4.0	9.6	6.0	5.5	1.1	5.3	4.8	6.7	7.6	7.6	4.1	6.2	7.4	4.0
Singapore	9.7	7.1	8.5	8.3	-1.4	2.1	9.8	11.5	10.0	9.2	6.6	6.3	11.7	11.6	8.2	7.8	8.3	-1.4	7.2	10.1
South Korea	6.2	7.3	10.8	8.1	6.8	10.6	11.1	10.6	6.7	9.2	9.4	5.9	6.1	8.5	9.2	7.0	4.7	-6.9	9.5	8.5
Iran	-5.2	13.0	12.6	-1.6	2.1	-9.2	-1.4	-6.3	6.2	13.7	12.6	4.3	-1.6	-0.4	2.7	7.1	3.4	2.7	1.9	5.1
Turkey	4.9	3.6	5.0	6.7	4.2	7.0	9.5	2.3	0.3	9.3	0.7	5.0	7.7	-4.7	7.9	7.4	7.6	2.3	-3.4	6.8
Saudi Arabia	4.7	-11.1	-8.2	-3.1	-4.3	5.1	-4.0	8.2	0.1	8.3	9.1	4.6	0.0	0.7	0.2	3.4	2.6	2.8	-0.7	4.9
UAE	2.8	-8.3	-5.4	4.6	-6.6	-18.8	6.3	-2.4	13.5	17.5	0.2	2.7	-0.9	7.3	7.9	6.2	6.7	4.3	3.9	5.0
Azerbaijan	—	—	—	—	—	—	—	—	—	—	-0.7	-22.6	-23.1	-19.7	-11.8	1.3	5.8	10.0	7.4	11.1
Kazakhstan	—	—	—	—	—	—	—	—	—	—	-11.0	-5.3	-9.2	-12.6	-8.2	0.5	1.7	-1.9	2.7	9.8
Uzbekistan	—	—	—	—	—	—	—	9.1	3.1	1.6	-0.5	-11.2	-2.3	-5.2	-0.9	1.7	5.2	4.3	4.3	3.8
Turkmenistan	—	—	—	—	—	—	—	11.0	-4.3	0.7	-4.7	-5.3	-10	-17	-7.2	-6.7	-11	6.7	16.5	18.6
Russia	—	—	—	—	—	—	—	—	—	-3.0	-5.0	-14.5	-8.7	-12.6	-4.1	-3.6	1.4	-5.3	6.4	10.0
Israel	5.1	1.8	3.5	0.9	3.4	4.8	7.2	2.0	0.9	6.8	7.7	5.6	5.6	6.9	6.7	5.6	2.9	4.3	3.3	9.2
Japan	2.9	2.8	1.6	3.1	5.1	3.0	3.8	6.8	5.3	5.2	3.4	1.0	0.2	1.1	2.0	2.7	1.6	-2.0	-0.1	2.9
United States	2.5	-2.0	4.5	7.2	4.1	3.4	3.3	4.1	3.5	1.9	-0.2	3.3	2.7	4.1	2.5	3.7	4.5	4.2	4.5	3.7
EU (15)	0.2	1.3	1.6	2.7	2.7	3.1	2.9	4.4	4.3	3.1	1.9	1.0	0.0	3.2	3.3	2.6	4.0	3.9	4.3	4.7

Country	2001	2002	2003	2004	2005	2006	2007	2008	2009	2010
China	**8.3**	**9.1**	**10.0**	**10.1**	**10.4**	**11.6**	**13.0**	**9.0**	**9.1**	**10.3**
India	**5.2**	3.8	**8.4**	**8.3**	**9.4**	**9.7**	**9.1**	**6.1**	**7.7**	**9.7**
Singapore	−2.4	4.2	3.5	**9.6**	**7.3**	**8.4**	**7.8**	1.1	−1.3	**14.5**
South Korea	4.0	**7.2**	2.8	4.6	4.0	**5.2**	**5.1**	2.2	0.2	**6.2**
Iran	3.7	**7.5**	**7.1**	**5.1**	4.6	**5.9**	**7.8**	2.3	1.8	3.0
Turkey	−5.7	**6.2**	**5.3**	**9.4**	**8.4**	**6.9**	4.7	0.9	−4.7	**8.9**
Saudi Arabia	0.5	0.1	**7.7**	**5.3**	**5.6**	3.2	3.3	4.4	0.1	3.9
UAE	1.7	2.6	**11.9**	**9.7**	**8.2**	**9.4**	**6.3**	**5.1**	−0.7	−2.5
Azerbaijan	**9.9**	**10.6**	**11.2**	**10.2**	**26.4**	**34.5**	**25.0**	**10.8**	**9.3**	**5.0**
Kazakhstan	**13.5**	**9.8**	**9.3**	**9.6**	**9.7**	**10.7**	**8.9**	3.2	1.2	**6.9**
Uzbekistan	4.2	4.0	4.2	**7.7**	**7.0**	**7.3**	**9.5**	**9.0**	**8.1**	**8.5**
Turkmenistan	**20.4**	**15.8**	**17.1**	**17.2**	**13.0**	**11.4**	**11.6**	**9.8**	**8.0**	**8.1**
Russia	**5.1**	4.7	**7.3**	**7.1**	**6.4**	**7.7**	**8.1**	**5.6**	−7.9	4.0
Israel	0.0	−0.7	1.5	**5.0**	**5.1**	**5.3**	**5.2**	4.0	0.8	4.7
Japan	0.2	0.3	1.4	2.7	1.9	2.0	2.4	−0.7	−5.2	2.9
United States	0.8	1.6	2.5	3.6	2.9	2.8	2.0	0.4	−2.6	2.9
EU (15)	1.9	1.9	1.6	3.0	2.6	3.6	3.2	0.4	−4.3	1.9

Source: World Bank, *World Development Indicators Online,* http://databank.worldbank.org/.

Note: Figures in bold denote economic growth of 5 percent or more.

turbulence of 1997–1999, although they passed through the global financial difficulties of 2008 with remarkable ease. A few entrepôt centers and facilitators like Singapore, South Korea, and recently the UAE have capitalized on their mediation skills to grow. Yet the general pattern has been for growth to gradually broaden from the developing "Chindian" giants toward the energy producers to their north and west, with the long-term growth trajectories of all these nations, including soft-authoritarian regimes in Russia and Central Asia, outstripping those of Israel, Japan, and the democratic West. Indeed, even Iran has been growing quite steadily, spurred by buoyant energy prices, despite international sanctions against its nuclear program.

Should Asian continentalism become a full-fledged reality, it could enhance the increasingly important global role of Russia, which finds itself more influential with most surrounding nations than a decade ago, when Vladimir Putin's regime was young. That sprawling nation is, after all, the only authentically Eurasian power in geographical terms, spanning nine time zones across the continental heartland. And Russia is simultaneously the only major G8 oil- and gas-exporting nation. It enjoys natural economic synergies with Asia's rapidly growing energy consumers. A Eurasian collaboration with authoritarian capitalist Russia could, however, easily undermine globalism and Western liberal values as we traditionally conceive them.

Other areas that have been growing vigorously, in periods of high global energy prices, include Central Asia and the Caucasus. Azerbaijan began its own hypergrowth in 1997, as the Baku-Tbilisi-Ceyhan pipeline was finalized. Kazakhstan began to grow rapidly around 1999, as crude oil production in the Tengiz oil fields at the head of the Caspian Sea began to soar, although it had more difficulties in the 2008 financial crisis than its neighbors. Uzbekistan began accelerating in 2003, as huge local gas fields such as Garbi and Shurtan entered production and the overall price of energy began to rise steadily worldwide. And Turkmenistan started its growth spurt in 2008, as its massive South Yolotan-Osman gas field began coming online.[1]

Appendix B Eurasian Continentalist Organizations

Title	Established
A. Eurasia/Asia-wide	
1. Asian Productivity Organization (APO)	1961
2. Center on Integrated Rural Development for Asia and the Pacific	1979
3. Economic Cooperation Organization (ECO)	1985
4. Collective Security Treaty Organization (CSTO)	1992
5. Conference on Interaction and Confidence Building Measures in Asia (CICA)	1992
6. Eurasia Patent Organization	1995
7. Eurasian Economic Community	1996
8. Shanghai Cooperation Organization (SCO)	2001
9. Asia Cooperation Dialogue (ACD)	2002
10. Eurasia Heritage Foundation	2004
11. Asia-Middle East Dialogue (AMED)	2005
12. Eurasian Development Bank	2006
13. Common Economic Space	2010

B. Regional

  1. League of Arab States   1945
  2. Confederation of Independent States (CIS)   1992
  3. ASEAN Plus Three (ASEAN+3)   1997
  4. Chiangmai Initiative   2000
  5. Regional Anti-Terrorist Structure (RATS)   2004
  6. East Asia Summit (EAS)   2005
  7. Comprehensive Economic Partnership in East Asia (CEPEA)   2006

C. Subregional

  1. Southeast Asian Ministers of Education Organization (SEAMEO)   1965
  2. Association of Southeast Asian Nations (ASEAN)   1967
  3. Central Asia Regional Economic Cooperation Program (CAREC)   1997
  4. Gulf Cooperation Council (GCC)   1981
  5. South Asian Association for Regional Cooperation (SAARC)   1985
  6. Tumen River Area Development Project (TRADP)   1991
  7. Northeast Asia Economic Forum   1991
  8. Greater Mekong Subregion (GMS)   1992
  9. Indonesia-Malaysia-Thailand Growth Triangle (IMT-GT)   1993
  10. Bay of Bengal Initiative for Multi-Sectoral Technical and Economic
Cooperation (BIMSTEC)   1997
  11. Greater Tumen Initiative   2001
  12. Northeast Asia Summit Secretariat   2011

D. Functional

  1. Organization of Petroleum Exporting Countries (OPEC)   1960
  2. Muslim World League   1962
  3. Organization of Arab Petroleum Exporting Countries (OAPEC)   1968
  4. Organization of the Islamic Conference   1969
  5. Islamic Development Bank   1973
  6. International Islamic Relief Organization   1979
  7. Gas Exporting Countries Forum (GECF)   2001
  8. Eurasian Group on Combatting Money Laundering and
Financing of Terrorism (EAG)   2004

Source: Asian Development Bank, *East Asian Regionalism: A Partnership of Shared Prosperity*; and Internet sources.
Note: This list is only illustrative and not comprehensive.

Notes

INTRODUCTION

1. The United States, for example, imported 61 percent of its total oil consumption in 2010, up from 9 percent in 1970 and 20.4 percent in 1985. See BP, *Statistical Review of World Energy,* 2011 edition; and Department of Energy, Energy Information Administration, http://www.eia.gov/dnav/pet/pet_snd_d_nus_mbbl_a_cur.htm.

2. BP, *Statistical Review of World Energy,* 2011 edition; and Department of Energy, Energy Information Administration, http://www.eia.gov/dnav/pet/pet_sum_snd_d _nus_mbbl_a_cur.htm.

3. On the importance of these networks, see Slaughter, "America's Edge."

4. "Eurasia" is used here to denote all the nations of the Asian continent, plus the territory of the former Soviet Union in its entirety, including all of the Russian Federation. "Asia" denotes the Asian continent, minus all the constituent parts of the former USSR.

5. Projected figures are 2010 estimates for the 2009–2030 period. See International Energy Agency, *World Energy Outlook,* 2011 edition, 81.

6. BP, *Statistical Review of World Energy,* 2011 edition, 6, 22.

7. Among recent works, see Simmons, *Twilight in the Desert*; Klare, *Rising Powers, Shrinking Planet*; and Friedman, *Hot, Flat, and Crowded.*

8. Calder, "Asia's Empty Tank"; Calder, *Pacific Defense*; Manning, *The Asian Energy Factor*; and Amy Myers Jaffe, "Beijing's Oil Diplomacy," *Survival* 44, no. 1 (Spring 2002): 115–134.

9. See, for example, Leonard Binder, James S. Coleman, Lucian W. Pye, Myron Weiner, Joseph Lapalombara, and Myron Verba (eds.), *Crises and Sequences in Political Development* (Princeton, NJ: Princeton University Press, 1971); Stephen Krasner, "Approaches to the State: Alternative Conceptions and Historical Dynamics," *Comparative Politics* 16, no. 2 (January 1984): 223–246; Gourevitch, *Politics in Hard Times*; Skowronek, *Building a New American State*; and Kent E. Calder, *Crisis and Compensation* (Princeton, NJ: Princeton University Press, 1988).

10. The term "New Silk Road" is employed here not as a precise geographical expression, but as a figurative expression for an alignment of Islamic-Confucian nations, together with Russia, that are geographically contiguous and have potential as an alternative geopolitical pole to the United States in post–Cold War international affairs. It is broadly synonymous, and used interchangeably here, with "Eurasia," and is a manifestation of the continentalism that the book takes up as a central analytic construct, discussed later in this chapter.

11. See, for example, Spykman and Nicholl, *The Geography of the Peace*.

12. See, for example, John Agnew, *Making Political Geography* (New York: Oxford University Press, 2002); Joe Painter and Alex Jeffrey, *Political Geography*, 2nd ed. (London: Sage, 2009); and Carolyn Gallaher, Carl T. Dahlman, and Mary Gilmartin, *Key Concepts in Political Geography* (London: Sage, 2009).

13. Turkish Foreign Minister Ahmet Davutoglu (2009–) is a conspicuous case in point. See Ahmet Davutoglu, *Civilizational Transformation and the Muslim World* (Kuala Lumpur: Mahir, 1994).

14. Friedman, *The World Is Flat*.

15. In Britain, "continentalism" was first used after 1714 by the Whig Cabinets of William Pitt the Elder and his successors, such as the first Duke of Newcastle, prime minister 1757–1762, to denote the school of thought advocating closer ties to the European continent, using the Crown's Hanoverian connection. In Canada, continentalism was espoused by those (especially nineteenth-century liberals and late-twentieth-century conservatives) who advocated closer ties with the United States and ultimately supported NAFTA. In the United States, continentalism was employed both in the mid-nineteenth century by manifest destiny supporters to validate expansion to the West Coast, and during the 1930s by isolationists such as Charles Beard, to keep the United States out of European wars. On these various historical applications, see Daniel A. Baugh, "Great Britain's 'Blue-Water' Policy, 1689–1815," *International History Review* 10, no. 1 (February 1988): 33–58; Goldwin Smith, *Canada and the Canadian Question* (1891); and Stephen J. Randall, "The New Continentalism: Canada, Mexico, and the U.S., 1943–1954," *American Review of Canadian Studies* 23, no. 2 (August 1, 1993): 267–281; as well as Charles A. Beard and Mary R. Beard, *America in Midpassage* (New York: Macmillan, 1939).

16. Continentalism can also be seen, from an analytical perspective, as "the processes of economic and political integration of continental nations." See "Continentalism," *Online Dictionary of the Social Sciences,* http://bitbucket.icaap.org.

17. See, for example, Benedict Anderson, *Imagined Communities: Reflections on the Origin and Spread of Nationalism* (London: Verso, 1983); Peter J. Katzenstein, "Regionalism

in Comparative Perspective," *Cooperation and Conflict* 31 (1996); Peter J. Katzenstein and Takashi Shiraishi (eds.), *Network Power* (New York: Cornell University Press, 1997); Lewis and Wigen, *The Myth of Continents*; Mattli, *The Logic of Regional Integration*; Schirm, *Globalization and the New Regionalism*; and T. J. Pempel (ed.), *Remapping East Asia: The Construction of a Region* (Ithaca, NY: Cornell University Press, 2005).

18. See, for example, Aggarwal, *Institutional Designs for a Complex World*; Vinod K. Aggarwal and Edward A. Fogarty, "Between Regionalism and Globalism: European Union Transregional and Inter-regional Trade Strateges," in Aggarwal and Fogarty, *European Union Trade Strategies*; Aggarwal and Morrison, *Asia-Pacific Crossroads*; and Ruland, Hanggi, and Roloff, *Interregionalism and International Relations*.

19. See Emmott, *Rivals*. Emmott speaks (pp. 25–47) of "a continent created." Robert Kaplan writes of a consolidated Eurasia in parallel fashion, although his strategic focus is maritime issues. See Kaplan, *Monsoon*.

20. See, for example, Acharya, *Singapore's Foreign Policy*.

21. For one early effort, see Christopher M. Dent, "From Inter-regionalism to Transregionalism? Future Challenges for ASEM," *Asia-Europe Journal* no. 1 (2003): 223–235.

22. Afghanistan, for example, apparently has $1.3 trillion in iron, copper, cobalt, gold, and critical-metal deposits like lithium, even though it lacks domestic oil and gas. See "U.S. Identifies Mineral Riches in Afghanistan," *New York Times,* June 14, 2010; and "World's Mining Companies Covet Afghan Riches," *New York Times,* June 18, 2010.

23. On the controversy in international relations theory over prospects for "balancing," as opposed to "bandwagoning," which largely fails to consider geoeconomic dimensions such as energy, see Walt, *The Origins of Alliances*; John Mearscheimer, "Back to the Future: Instability in Europe after the Cold War," *International Security* 15, no. 4 (Summer 1990): 5–56; and Kenneth Waltz, "Structural Realism after the Cold War," *International Security* 25, no. 1 (Summer 2000): 5–41.

CHAPTER 1. THE CHALLENGE OF A NEW WORLD EMERGING

1. See, for example, Huntington, *The Clash of Civilizations and the Remaking of World Order*. For a concise elaboration of the "Confucian-Islamic connection," see Samuel P. Huntington, "The Clash of Civilizations?" *Foreign Affairs* 72, no. 3 (1993): 45–48.

2. Precise per capita energy consumption figures for 2010 were 13.3 barrels for China, 3.2 for India, 28.8 for Japan, and 54.1 for the United States. See BP, *Statistical Review of World Energy*, 2011 edition, 44.

3. For export dependence figures, see World Trade Organization Statistics website: http://stat.wto.org/Home/WSDBHome.aspx. Note that Uzbekistan figures have not been included in the calculation.

4. See International Monetary Fund, *Direction of Trade Statistics,* annual.

5. In 1971, just before the Yom Kippur War and the two oil shocks of the 1970s, Europe's trade prominence for the Middle East was even more pronounced, with nearly 40 percent of Middle Eastern exports flowing there. See International Monetary Fund, *Direction of Trade Statistics.*

6. In November 2009, China outranked the United States as a Saudi oil export destination for the first time, although Japan remained the Saudis' largest overall customer. See Henry Meyer, "China and Saudi Arabia Form Stronger Trade Ties," *New York Times,* April 21, 2010. Saudi oil exports were 365 million barrels to China, 361 million to the United States, and 399 million to Japan in 2009. See "China's Rapid Growth Shifts the Geopolitics of Oil," *New York Times,* March 20, 2010; and Petroleum Association of Japan website, http://www.paj.gr.jp/statis/.

7. The IEA projects that Iraq will increase crude oil supply by 5 million barrels per day by 2035, with Saudi Arabia second at 4 million barrels per day. See International Energy Agency, *World Energy Outlook,* 2011 edition, Figure 3.17.

8. See Erica Downs, "China-Gulf Energy Relations" in Bryce Wakefield and Susan L. Levenstein, eds., *China and the Persian Gulf: Implications for the United States.* Washington, DC: Woodrow Wilson Center for Scholars, 2011, 62–78.

9. James Risen, "U.S. Identifies Vast Mineral Resources in Afghanistan," *New York Times,* June 13, 2010; "India, China in Line for Afghan Mine, Oil Contracts," Dawn .com, October 27, 2011; and Charles Wallace, "China, not U.S., Likely to Benefit from Afghanistan's Mineral Riches," *Daily Finance,* June 14, 2010.

10. The United States was the largest oil producer in the world from 1902, when it eclipsed Czarist Russia, until 1975, and then again in 1978, and 1982–1990, after which it ceded that position to Saudi Arabia and, intermittently, to Russia. In 2010 the United States imported an average of 11.7 million barrels per day, or over 61 percent of consumption, mostly from the Western Hemisphere and from West Africa. See Department of Energy, Energy Information Administration, http://tonto.eia.doe.gov /country/country_energy_data.cfm?fips=US.

11. On the embargo, see Zhang, *Economic Cold War.*

12. In 1960, for example, 43.7 percent of China's trade was with the USSR. That share declined to 9.6 percent by 1965, and to only 1.0 percent in 1970, and 1.3 percent in 1980. See Meng Xianzhang (ed.), *Zhongsu Maoyi Shi Ziliao* [Materials on the History of Sino-Soviet Trade] (Beijing: Chinese Foreign Trade Press, 1991), cited in Zhang, *Economic Cold War,* 282–283.

13. See Solingen, *Nuclear Logics.*

CHAPTER 2. WHERE GEOGRAPHY STILL MATTERS

Epigraph. Spykman, "Geography and Foreign Policy II," 236.

1. Friedman, *The World Is Flat.*

2. Kenichi Ohmae, *The Borderless World: Power and Strategy in the Inter-linked Economy,* rev. ed. (New York: Harper Collins, 1999).

3. Vernon, *Sovereignty at Bay.*

4. See Herodotus, *The History,* trans. David Grene (Chicago: University of Chicago Press, 1987).

5. See Dietrich Heinrich von Bulow, *The Spirit of the Modern System of War* (London: C. Mercier, 1806). The German original was published as *Vom Geist des Neuern Kriegssystem* in 1799.

6. Mahan, *The Influence of Sea Power upon History*; and Alfred Thayer Mahan, *The Influence of Sea Power upon the French Revolution and Empire, 1793–1812*, 2 vols. (Cambridge: Cambridge University Press, 1892).

7. Alfred Thayer Mahan, *The Life of Nelson: The Embodiment of the Sea Sower of Great Britain* (Boston: Little, Brown, 1897).

8. Mahan, *The Problem of Asia and Its Effect upon International Policies* (Boston: Little, Brown, 1900).

9. Mackinder, "The Geographical Pivot of History"; Mackinder, *Democratic Ideals and Reality*, 173–193; and Grygiel, *Great Powers and Geopolitical Change*, 6–7.

10. Mackinder, "The Geographical Pivot of History," 429.

11. Kaiser Wilhelm did avidly read Mahan's classic volume, *The Influence of Sea Power upon History*, embarking under its influence onto an aggressive naval expansion program. He relied of necessity, however, primarily on land-based power, in view of the Reich's underlying geopolitical position in Europe.

12. E. H. Carr, "From Munich to Moscow," part I, *Soviet Studies* 1, no. 1 (June 1949): 3–17, and part II, 1, no. 2 (October 1949): 93–105; Carr, *German-Soviet Relations between the Two World Wars*; and Kochan, *Russia and the Weimar Republic* (Cambridge: Bowes and Bowes, 1954).

13. Christian W. Spang, "Karl Haushofer Re-examined," in Spang and Wippich, *Japanese-German Relations, 1895–1945*, 143.

14. See Hopkirk, *Setting the East Ablaze*.

15. On early Soviet diplomacy toward Asia, particularly in China, see Allen S. Whiting, *Soviet Policies in China, 1917–1924* (New York: Columbia University Press, 1954).

16. William C. Wohlforth, "Heartland Dreams: Russian Geopolitics and Foreign Policy," in Danspeckgruber, *Perspectives on the Russian State in Transition*, 266.

17. Ziuganov, *Geografiia pobedy*; and Zhirinovskii, *Geopolitika I russkii vopros*.

18. Wohlforth, "Heartland Dreams," 268.

19. Goldman, *Petrostate*.

20. Grygiel, *Great Powers and Geopolitical Change*, xi.

21. Cemil Aydin, "From a 'Civilized' to an 'Islamic' Empire: Ottoman Grand Strategy during the Long 19th Century, 1815–1923." Presented at the American Historical Association Annual Convention, January 10, 2010.

22. Ahmet Davutoglu, *Strategik Derinlik, Turkiye'nin Uluslararasi Konomu* [Strategic Depth, Turkey's International Position] (Istanbul: Kure, 2001); and Joshua Walker, "Architect of Power," *Journal of International Security Affairs* no. 18 (Spring 2010): http://www.securityaffairs.org/issues/2010/18/walker.php.

23. Ahmet Davutoglu, *Civilizational Transformation and the Muslim World* (Kuala Lumpur: Mahir, 1994).

24. Walker, "Architect of Power."

25. In May 2010, Turkey signed an agreement with Russia to build a nuclear plant at Akkuyu. See "Turkey Building Nuclear Plant in Northern Peninsula of Sinop—Minister," BBC News, May 17, 2010.

26. John K. Fairbank, Edwin O. Reischauer, and Albert Craig, *East Asia: Tradition and Transformation* (Boston: Houghton Mifflin, 1978), 178.

27. Charles Hucker, *The Traditional Chinese State in Ming Times (1368–1644)* (Tucson: University of Arizona Press, 1961), 16.

28. See, for example, Sun-Tzu, *The Art of War*, trans. Ralph D. Sawyer (Boulder, CO: Westview Press, 1994).

29. Jonathan Spence, *The Memory Palace of Matteo Ricci* (New York: Viking Penguin, 1984), 54–55.

30. On the details of this early realist thinking and its twenty-first century relevance, see Yan Xuetong. *Ancient Chinese Thought, Modern Chinese Power*. Princeton: Princeton University Press, 2011.

31. Henry Kissinger. *On China*. New York: Penguin Press, 2011.

32. Dai Bingguo, "Persisting with Taking the Path of Peaceful Development." Beijing: Ministry of Foreign Affairs of the PRC, December 6, 2010, cited in Henry Kissinger. *On China*, 564.

33. Kissinger. *On China*, p. 512.

34. Grygiel, *Great Powers and Geopolitical Change*, 123–163.

35. Spang, "Karl Haushofer Re-examined," 146.

36. For details, see Kawanishi, *Tōa Chiseigaku no Kōsō* [The Concept of Oriental Geo-politics].

37. Asano, *Nichidokuso Tairiku Burokku Ron*[On the Japanese-German-Soviet Conti-nental Bloc], 297–298.

38. See Bassin, "Race Contra Space."

39. Kennan, *Memoires*; Kissinger, *Diplomacy*; and Brzezinski, *The Grand Chessboard*.

40. Particularly influential in the policy world were Spykman's two major books: *Ameri-can Strategy in World Politics*; and *The Geography of the Peace*. The latter was edited by Helen R. Nicholl and published soon after Spykman's untimely death.

41. Spykman, *The Geography of the Peace*.

42. See, for example, Kenneth Waltz, *Theory of International Politics* (Reading, PA: Addison-Wesley, 1979); Albert Wohlstetter, "Illusions of Distance," *Foreign Affairs* 45, no. 2 (1968): 242–255; and Grygiel, *Great Powers and Geopolitical Change*, 13–15.

43. Grygiel, *Great Powers and Geopolitical Change*, 3.

44. See Rosecrance, *The Rise of the Virtual State*.

45. The University of Paris, for example, in 1989 established a program in geopolitical studies, while a new review of geopolitics, *Limes*, began publishing in Italy in 1991. See Grygiel, *Great Powers and Geopolitical Change*, 179–180.

46. See, for example, O'Tuathail, *Critical Geopolitics*; and Agnew, *Geopolitics*.

47. See the work of O'Tuathail, in particular, in this regard.

48. In 2010 Japanese consumption was 3.9 tons of oil equivalent annually, and Germa-ny's was 3.9. See BP, *Statistical Review of World Energy*, 2011 edition, 44.

49. U.S. per capita energy consumption is around 7.4 tons of oil equivalent per year, compared to 1.8 for China and 0.4 for India. Ibid.

50. Major newly confirmed Turkmenistan reserves, reported in 2009, are included in this figure. See BP, *Statistical Review of World Energy*, 2011 edition, http://www.bp .com/productlanding.do?categoryId=6929&contentId=7044622.

51. On the potential of shale gas as a major energy supply option for the United States domestically, see "An Unconventional Glut," *The Economist,* March 11, 2010, http://www.economist.com/business-finance/displaystorm.cfm?story. Within Eurasia, the one nation with major potential may be China.

52. President Jimmy Carter's national security advisor, Zbigniew Brzezinski, was the recognized originator of this concept, amid the Iranian Revolution. See, for example, "The Crescent of Crisis," *Time,* January 15, 1979; and Lenczowski, "The Arc of Crisis."

53. Goldman, *Petrostate.*

54. Oil prices almost quadrupled following the 1973 oil shockand nearly doubled following the 1979 shock.

55. "International: Japan Port Aid Offer for Gwadar," *Lloyd's List*, March 8, 2000.

56. See Energy Information Agency, http://www.eia.doe.gov/emeu/cabs/China/Natural Gas.html.

57. Ibid. The Tarim Basin is reportedly scheduled to feed gas to the fourth pipeline.

58. See Saitō, *Central Asia's Oil and Gas Sector since the 2008 Financial Crisis.*

59. "International: Japan Port Aid Offer for Gwadar."

60. "China Suspected in Port Deal; Beijing Naval Vessels Expected to Dock at Pakistani Site," *Washington Times,* May 31, 2001.

61. "City of Fishermen in Pakistan Becomes Strategic Port," *New York Times*, September 28, 2009.

62. "Bomb Kills Three Chinese in Pakistan; 11 Injured in Blast at Seaport Construction Site," *Washington Post,* May 4, 2004.

63. "Loan Paves Way for Key Pakistan Link," *Lloyd's List*, December 5, 2008. The road improvement was to cut the travel time between Karachi and Peshawar in half, from seventy-two hours to thirty-six.

64. "Iran: Turkish State Gas Company Says Gas Pipeline to Iran Complete," BBC News, July 26, 2001.

65. "Iraq to Allow Iranian Natural Gas Transit," *Platts Oilgram News,* August 11, 2010.

66. Turkey and China have exchanged high-level state visits annually since 2010; 2011 was "China Year in Turkey," and 2012 is "Turkey Year in China." Turkey has established a new Consulate General in Guangzhou, a community itself increasingly active in trans-continental Eurasian relations. Turkey has expanded bilateral airline linkages with China, agreed to high-speed rail cooperation, and established a Turkish industrial zone in Xinjiang. See Burak Ege Bekdil, "Turkey, China in Exercises," *Defense News,* October 17, 2010; and "Turkey, China move for 'new cooperation paradigm'", *Sunday's Zalman,* November 3, 2010.

67. In 2008 Gazprom's import price from Central Asia into Russia averaged $140–$160 per thousand cubic meters, while the export price to Europe averaged $400, or nearly three times as much. See Damila Bochkarev, "European Gas Prices: Implications of Gazprom's Strategic Engagement with Central Asia," *Pipeline and Gas Journal* 236, no. 6 (June 2009); Gazprom, "Gazprom in Figures 2004–2008," http://www.gazprom.com/f/posts/71/879403/3se.pdf; "Europe May Face New Year's Gas Crisis; Russia Could Pass on Huge Price Increases to Ukraine, Triggering a Repeat of 2006

Showdown," *Globe and Mail* (Canada), July 9, 2008; and Internal Revenue Service, http://www.irs.gov/businesses/small/international/article/0,,id=206089,00.html.

68. Russian domestic wholesale prices for natural gas in 2008 averaged $52 per thousand cubic meters for households, and $68 per thousand cubic meters for industrial use, both substantially lower than Russian import prices from Central Asia and export prices to Europe. See Gazprom, "Gazprom in Figures 2004–2008 Factbook", at: http://gazprom.com/f/posts/71/879403/3se.pdf and Internal Revenue Service, at: http://www.irs.gov/businesses/small/international/article/O,,id=206089,00.html.

69. See, for example, Garver, Leverett, and Leverett, *Moving (Slightly) Closer to Iran.*

70. Henry Kissinger also adds that a geopolitical approach pays attention to the requirements of equilibrium. See Everett C. Dolman, "Understanding Critical Geopolitics: Geopolitics and Risk Security," in Colin S. Gray and G. R. Sloan, *Geopolitics, Geography, and Strategy* (Portland: Frank Cass, 1999), 107–124.

71. In Japan, these prohibitions on ocean-going travel were universal, and continued for over two centuries (1639–1854), despite some limited visits from China, Korea, and the Netherlands. In China, controls on overseas voyages were intermittent, and dependent on imperial edict. The Jiaqing Ming emperor (1522–1566), for example, banned foreign trade. See Jansen, *The Making of Modern Japan* (Cambridge, MA: Harvard University Press, 2000); Wang, *Yaou Dalu Jiaoliushi*, 252–260; and Cohen, *East Asia at the Center*, 190–191.

CHAPTER 3. SIX CRITICAL JUNCTURES AND EURASIA'S TRANSFORMATION

1. See, for example, Emmott, *Rivals.*

2. Walter Mattli's 1999 book, for example, reviewed two major explanations for European integration: neofunctionalism, which stresses the spillover effect of supranational agencies; and intergovernmentalism, which focuses on bargaining among state leaders. See Mattli, *The Logic of Regional Integration.*

3. On the notion of institutionalized norms and culture, see Katzenstein, *The Culture of National Security*; and Krasner, *International Regimes.*

4. Mattli. *The Logic of Regional Integration*, 11–12.

5. For additional explication of the critical juncture framework, and its rationale in the analysis of regional integration, see Kent E. Calder and Min Ye, "Critical Junctures and East Asian Integration", *Journal of East Asian Studies* 4, No. 2, (2004): 181–226; as well as Kent E. Calder and Min Ye. *The Making of Northeast Asia*. Stanford: Stanford University Press, 2010.

6. Theda Skocpol and Paul Pierson, "Historical Institutionalism on Contemporary Political Science", in Ira Katznelson and Helen Milner (eds.) *Political Science: State of the Discipline.* New York: W.W. Norton and Company, 2002, 720.

7. See Binder et al. *Crises and Sequences in Political Development*; Krasner, "Approaches to the State: Alternative Conceptions and Historical Dynamics", *Comparative Politics* 16, No. 2 (1984): 223–246; Nelson Polsby, *Political Innovation in America: The Politics of Policy Innovation.* New Haven: Yale University Press, 1984; Peter Gourevitch,

Politics in Hard Times. Ithaca: Cornell University Press, 1986; and Kent E. Calder, *Crisis and Compensation.* Princeton: Princeton University Press, 1988.

8. Binder et al., *Crises and Sequences,* 308.

9. Krasner, "Approaches to the State", *Comparative Politics,* January, 1984: 223–246.

10. Stephen Skowronek, *Building a New American State: The Expansion of National Administrative Capacities, 1877–1920.* Cambridge: Cambridge University Press, 1982.

11. Skowronek. *Building a New American State,* 10.

12. Gourevitch, *Politics in Hard Times,* 35.

13. Calder, *Crisis and Compensation,* 28.

14. Graham Allison and Philip Zelikow, *Essence of Decision,* 2nd ed. New York: Longman, 1999.

15. The operational definition of crisis implied here is that which I employed in *Crisis and Compensation,* 37, 39–42—namely, "prospect of major loss or unwanted change that threatens the established order."

16. Aggarwal and Morrison, *Asia-Pacific Crossroads,* 36.

17. Allison and Zelikow, *Essence of Decision.*

18. Ibid., 295.

19. Aggarwal and Morrison, *Asia-Pacific Crossroads,* 26.

20. On the logic of two-level foreign-policy games, see Putnam, "Diplomacy and Domestic Politics."

21. See Calder and Ye, *The Making of Northeast Asia,* 94–95.

22. In 2011 China and India together accounted for 36 percent of the world's population. See World Bank, World Development Indicators Online, http://databank.world bank.org/.

23. Yergin, *The Prize,* 509.

24. Ibid., 291.

25. Interestingly, U.S. Commerce Secretary Harold Ickes came to realize the strategic and commercial importance of Aramco very early, amid World War II, and convinced President Franklin D. Roosevelt to set up the Petroleum Reserve Corporation, which attempted to buy Aramco. SoCal and Texaco flatly refused. See Krasner, *Defending the National Interest,* 192–193.

26. "Oil: Shadow over Aramco," *Time,* March 4, 1974.

27. The Ras Tanura petrochemical complex, based on feedstock from the long-standing Aramco refinery, is a joint venture with Dow Chemical, to produce 4 million tons per year of upstream and 7 million tons per year of downstream petrochemical products by 2013. See Chemicals-Technology.com, "Ras Tanura Integrated Petrochemical Complex," http://www.chemicals-technology.com/projects/rastanura/.

28. AGIP offered a 75–25 split to the Iranians in 1957, which was accepted. See Yergin, *The Prize,* 503–505. Japan's Arabian Oil Company negotiated 57–43 agreements with the Saudis and the Kuwaitis, leading to discovery of the Khafji oil field in Saudi Arabia, Japan's first equity oil in the Middle East, in 1960. See ibid., 505–506.

29. Tariki, who spent a dozen years studying in Nasser's Cairo, strongly pressed for greater Saudi influence in oil markets, through control over prices, production, and ownership,

thereby gaining his nickname of the Red Sheikh. See ibid., 513–514. For nationalization, see Brown, *Oil, God, and Gold*, 248.

30. "Saudi Arabia Bars Oil Nationalization," *New York Times*, November 8, 1963.

31. Krasner, *Defending the National Interest*, 249.

32. Item 229: "Memorandum for the Record," Washington, May 24, 1967, *Foreign Relations of the United States*, Vol. 34, quoted in Amy Myers Jaffe, *Saudi Aramco: National Flagship with Global Responsibilities* (Houston: Rice University Baker Institute for Public Policy, 2007), 34.

33. Ibid., 36.

34. Marcel, *Oil Titans*, 27; and Yergin, *The Prize*.

35. Krasner, *Defending the National Interest*, 250; Yergin, *The Prize*, 647; and Marcel, *Oil Titans*, 29.

36. Ibid.

37. Yergin, *The Prize*, 652.

38. In 2006, for example, nine of the ten largest corporate petroleum reserve holdings in the world were in the hands of national oil companies, eight of which were in the Middle East. The only even nominally private firm in the top ten was Russia's Lukoil, which also has a substantial government "golden share" through the Russian state bank, and top executives both personally and professionally close to the Kremlin. See Lukoil, http://www.lukoil.com/static_6_5id_213_html; and "Russian State Bank Takes Minority Interest in Lukoil," *Platts Oilgram News*, June 16, 2009; and Ian Nathan (editor), "The Energy Intelligence Top 100: Ranking the World's Oil Companies," *Energy Intelligence Research*, 2007 edition.

39. Yergin, *The Prize*, 588–589. Egypt's assault across the Suez Canal came, surprisingly, at 2 P.M. in the afternoon.

40. See ibid., 593–597.

41. Faisal ultimately agreed, in the early fall of 1973, to interviews with the *Washington Post*, *Christian Science Monitor*, *Newsweek*, and NBC Television, regarding the urgent need for changes in U.S. Middle East policy. See ibid., 596.

42. Ibid., 597.

43. Elizabeth Stephens, *U.S. Policy toward Israel: The Role of Political Culture in Defining the Special Relationship* (Portland, OR: Sussex Academic Press, 2006), 147.

44. Oil prices were raised from $3.01 a barrel for Arabian Light to $5.11. See Krasner, *Defending the National Interest*, 253.

45. Brown, *Oil, God, and Gold*, 294.

46. Robert Pirog, *The Role of National Oil Companies in the International Oil Market* (Washington, DC: Congressional Research Service, 2007), 3. These national oil companies, incidentally, have been prone to subsidize domestic consumption. The price of gasoline in Saudi Arabia in 2010 was $0.61 per gallon in Saudi Arabia, $0.38 in Iran, and $0.08 in Venezuela, for example, compared to $8.03 in Norway.

47. Ian Nathan (editor). "The Energy Intelligence Top 100: Ranking the World's Oil Companies," 2007 edition.

48. Kenneth Juster, "Japanese Foreign Policy Making during the Oil Crisis," *Japan Interpreter*, 11 (Winter 1977): 293–312.

49. Tanaka was particularly concerned with uranium and tar sands development, as well as natural gas. For details, see Yamaoka, *Tanaka Kakuei: Fūjirareta Shigen Senryaku*.

50. For the classic study of Deng Xiaoping and his key role in making Chinese political-economic history, see Ezra F. Vogel, *Deng Xiaoping and the Transformation of China*. Cambridge, MA: Harvard University Press, 2011.

51. On the early genesis of the Four Modernizations, see Immaneul C. Y. Hu, *China without Mao: The Search for a New Order* (New York: Oxford University Press, 1990); and Vogel, *Deng Xiaoping*, 184–248.

52. Hu, *China without Mao* 94.

53. On the differences in the Hua and Deng approaches to Chinese economic development, see Edwin Moise, *Modern China: A History* (New York: Longman, 1994), 194.

54. Hua thus, in Vogel's view, deserves more credit for China's opening than conventionally given, especially for instituting the SEZ concept. See Vogel, *Deng Xiaoping*, 185, 190.

55. World Bank, World Development Indicators Online, http://databank.worldbank.org.

56. World Trade Organization, http://www.wto.org.

57. Keith Bradsher, "Security Issues Top the Environment in China's Energy Plan," *New York Times*, June 18, 2010.

58. Shirk, *How China Opened Its Door*, 6.

59. Ibid.

60. Encarnation, *Dislodging Multinationals*.

61. Government of India Ministry of Finance, *Economic Survey*, 2001–2002 edition, http://indiabudget.nic.in/es2000–01/welcome.html.

62. "RBI Buys 200 Tonnes of Gold from IMF," *Hindu Business Line*, November 4, 2009, http://www.thehindubusinessline.com.

63. International Monetary Fund, *International Financial Statistics*, http://www.imfstatistics.org. By the end of September 2010, India's foreign exchange reserves had risen to $265.2 billion.

64. "Half Yearly Report on Management of Foreign Exchange Reserves, April–September, 2009," Reserve Bank of India Department of External Investment and Operations Reports, http://rbidocs.rbi.org.in/rdocs/Publications/PDRs/HYRMF190810.pdf.

65. Jha, *The Perilous Road to the Market*, 171.

66. Ibid., 172.

67. Gourevitch, "Second Image Reversed."

68. Min Ye, *Embedded States: The Politics of Economic Transitions in China and India*, doctoral dissertation, Department of Politics, Princeton University, 2007.

69. See Montek S. Ahluwalia, "Economic Reforms in India since 1991: Has Gradualism Worked?" *Journal of Economic Perspectives* 16, no. 3 (Summer 2002): 67–88.

70. Arvind Panagariya, *India: The Emerging Giant* (Oxford: Oxford University Press, 2008), 103.

71. Montek S. Ahluwalia, "Economic Reforms in India since 1991," in K. R. Gupta (ed.), *Studies in Indian Economy,* Vol. 2 (New Delhi: Gupta.Atlantic, 2007), 33–63.

72. Boulnois, *Silk Road*, 422–423.

73. On the Soviet decline, see Remnick, *Lenin's Tomb*.

74. Soviet-bloc hard-currency debts, contracted in a futile effort to modernize and catch the West, were also a debilitating factor. See Stephen Kotkin, "The Kiss of Debt," in Ferguson et al. (eds.), *The Shock of the Global*, 80–93.

75. Fatalities included 11,321 Red Army, 548 KGB, and 28 Ministry of Internal Affairs combat deaths. See G. F. Krivosheev, *Soviet Casualties and Combat Losses in the Twentieth Century* (London: Greenhill, 1997), 287.

76. Neil Robinson, "The Global Economy, Reform and Crisis in Russia," *Review of International Political Economy* 6, no. 4 (Winter 1999), 531–564.

77. "Russia: Foreign Investment," Encyclopedia of the Nations, http://country-data.com /cgi-bin/query/r-11472.html.

78. Karrar, *The New Silk Road Diplomacy*, 57.

79. Ibid.

80. Ibid., 60.

81. On the expanding export-processing activities in Urumqi Special Economic and Export Zone, see "Urumqi Economic and Technological Development Zone," at: http://rightsite .asia/en/industrial-zone/ulumuqi-economic-technology-development-zone.

82. Hiro, *Inside Central Asia*, 98.

83. Ibid., 383.

84. See Joshi, *Reconnecting India and Central Asia*.

85. ONGC in 2010 held a 20 percent interest in the Sakhalin I project, unaffected by Russian reduction of foreign shares in Sakhalin II. See "India Said Looking to Sakhalin 1 for LNG; Would Compete with China for Supply, Report Says," *Platts Oilgram News,* December 14, 2006. For the 2008 acquisition, see "India's ONGC Buys into Russian Oil Sector with Takeover of British Energy Company," *Nikkei Weekly*, February 2, 2009; "Energy: Indian Suitor Wins £1.4bn Bid Battle for Imperial Oil," *Guardian*, August 27, 2008.

86. On the genesis of the Tengiz and Kashagan projects, see Levine, *The Oil and the Glory*, 82–101, 327–344.

87. Only Egypt, with 82 million, and Turkey, with 79 million, have more people, in the Middle East as a whole. See CIA, *The World Factbook*, https://www.cia.gov/library /publications/the-world-factbook/index.html.

88. Only Saudi Arabia is larger, by about 30 percent, although much of the Saudi Kingdom, including the so-called Empty Quarter, is virtually uninhabited desert. See ibid.

89. Shiites do enjoy majority standing in Bahrain and Azerbaijan, as well as Iran and Iraq, but their political power is limited in the former countries. Shiites also are important in Lebanon, where they lead the Hezbollah (Party of God), and also make up 40 percent of the population in the strategic oil-producing Eastern Province of Saudi Arabia. See Sherifa Zuhur, *Saudi Arabia: Islamic Threat, Political Reform, and the Global War on Terror* (Carlisle, PA: U.S. Army War College, March, 2005), http:// www.carlisle.army.mil/ssi.

90. Shiites believe that Mohammed's son-in-law Ali was the rightful successor to the Prophet, reject the first three Muslim caliphs, and bemoan Ali's assassination, after only five years as caliph, in 661. Strongly opposed to dominant Sunni doctrine, and

with only 10–15 percent of total Muslim population, they have been widely persecuted in Sunni-dominated lands as apostates. On details, see Nasr, *The Shia Revival*.

91. Iran's third largest import supplier (since 2008) is Germany. See International Monetary Fund, *Direction of Trade Statistics*.

92. International Monetary Fund. *Direction of Trade Statistics*.

93. On the early machinations in Iran of the AIOC and its predecessor, the Anglo-Persian Oil Company, see Yergin, *The Prize*, 134–149, 473–474.

94. On the 1953 coup and its longer-term implications for U.S.-Iranian relations, see Kinzer, *All the Shah's Men*.

95. Michael Axworthy, *Empire of the Mind: A History of Iran* (New York: Basic Books, 2008), 248.

96. Ibid.

97. Ibid., 158.

98. See Sasiorowski and Byrne, *Mohammed Mosaddeq and the 1953 Coup in Iran*. Mossadegh had strongly opposed the Anglo-Persian Agreement of 1919, which established AIOC's original presence, and also Reza Shah's accession to power, for which he was imprisoned.

99. On these classic cases, see Crane Brinton, *The Anatomy of Revolution* (New York: Prentice-Hall, 1952); Skocpol, *States and Social Revolutions*; and Huntington, *Political Order in Changing Societies*.

100. See Kurzman, *The Unthinkable Revolution in Iran*, 99.

101. Charles Tustin Kamps, "Operation Eagle Claw: The Iran Hostage Rescue Mission," *Air and Space Power Journal* (Fall 2006): http://www.airpower.maxwell.af.mil.

102. M. Parvizi Amineh (ed.), *The Greater Middle East in Global Politics: Social Science Perspectives on the Changing Geography of World Politics* (Leiden: Brill, 2007), 79.

103. Garver, *China and Iran*, 166–167.

104. Deng's China enjoyed very positive relations with the shah in his last days on Iran's Peacock Throne, with Hua Guofeng actually visiting him formally in Tehran during August 1978, even as the revolution was brewing. See ibid., 48–56.

105. Ibid., 72.

106. R. Jeffrey Smith, "Dozens of U.S. Items Used in Iraq Arms", *Washington Post,* July 22, 2002.

107. Esposito, *The Iranian Revolution*, 108.

108. Ayatollah Khomeini, "Message of Revolution," *Journal of the Islamic Revolutionary Guards* 2, no. 6 (1981): 35–36.

109. Apart from turbulence in Saudi Arabia, there were two abortive Iranian-inspired coups in Bahrain, with its Shiite majority, in the early 1980s, and assorted Iran-inspired violence, including attacks on the French and U.S. embassies, as well as two airplane hijackings, in Kuwait. See Esposito, *The Iranian Revolution*, 110.

110. Vassiliev, *The History of Saudi Arabia*, 396.

111. Putin's paternal grandfather, Spiridon Ivanovich Putin, had worked at Vladimir Lenin's dacha in Gorki as a cook. After Lenin's death, he continued to serve Nadezhda Krupskaya, Lenin's widow, and later had occasion also to cook for Joseph Stalin at one of his dachas.

112. See World Bank, *Transition*, 4.

113. World Bank, World Development Indicators Online, http://databank.worldbank.org/.

114. P. L. Dash, "Perils of Putin's Russia," *Economic and Political Weekly* 36, no. 4; and *Money, Banking and Finance* (January 27–February 2, 2001): 288–291.

115. For details, see Olcott, *The Energy Dimension in Russian Global Strategy*, 15–23. De-Beers, Hewlett Packard, and Analytik Jena were among the Western corporate partners of the State Mining Institute.

116. On how Putin transformed the Russian political economy to make energy a major tool of Russian national influence, see Goldman, *Petrostate*; and Kimura, *Pūtin no Enerugī Senryaku*.

117. Lucas, *The New Cold War*, 87–100, 163–188.

118. Ibid., 52–53.

119. The Valdai International Discussion Club, established in 2004 by the Russian news agency Novosti and other Russian sponsors, brings foreign experts and journalists to Russia annually for dialogue with top Russian leaders and professional counterparts, including on occasion Putin. For details, see "Valdai Discussion Club," http://en.rian.ru/valdai.

120. On Putin's Russia and its relationship to the GECF, see Lucas, *The New Cold War*, 181–182.

121. Ibid., 182.

122. On Russian Euroasianism, see Laruelle, *Russian Eurasianism*.

123. Rangsimaporn, "Interpreting Eurasianism."

124. Ibid.

125. Turkey bought 64 percent of its natural gas and 40 percent of its oil from Russia in 2010. See Turkey's PM goes to Russia with gas in mind", *Sabah*, March 15, 2011, at: http://www.sabahenglish.com/Economy/2011/03/15/turkeys_pm_goes_to_russia_with_gas_in_mind. The Blue Stream pipeline, through which gas from Russia was supplied, is a remarkable feat of deepwater seabed engineering, but currently uses only one-third of its capacity, giving Turkey economic incentives to exploit Blue Stream more fully rather than build additional pipelines like Nabucco, which the West has been encouraging it to construct.

126. Real GDP growth averaged 7 percent annually during the years of Putin's first presidency, as opposed to a sharp decline during the previous Yeltsin administration. Putin's popularity never fell below 65 percent during his two initial terms as president of Russia. See "Putin's Performance in Office—Trends," *Russia Votes*, http://www.russiavotes.org/president/putin_performance_trends.php.

127. See, for example, Scott Peterson, "Egypt's revolution redefines what's possible in the Arab world", *Christian Science Monitor*, February 11, 2011; Brad Nelson, "The Role Social Media in the Middle East Uprisings", *Ahramonline*, April 1, 2011d, at: http://www.english.ahram.org.eng/NewsContentP/4/9021/Opinion/The-Role-of-Social-Media-in-the-Middle-East-Uprisi.aspx. ; and Mary Kaldor, "What the Arab Spring, Europe Protests have in Common", *Voice of America*, August 19, 2011, at: http://www.voanews/com/home/world/What-the-Arab-Spring-Europe-Protests-Have-in-Common/128O9994.

128. I am endebted for this observation to Ryan Calder, Ph.D. candidate in Sociology at the University of California, Berkeley.

129. Rashid Khalidi, "The Arab Spring", *The Nation*, March 21, 2011, at: http://www .thenation.com/article/158991/arab-spring.

130. In Libya, Moammar Qaddafi was finally overthrown in August, 2011, after five bloody months of struggle, with outside military support, but institutions supporting coherent democratic government and administration remained weak.

131. See Lisa Anderson, "Demystifying the Arab Spring", *Foreign Affairs* 90, No. 3, 4–6.

132. Most protests occurred in Qatif and smaller cities in the Eastern Province, calling for release of prisoners, equal representation in key offices, and withdrawal of the Peninsula Shield Force from Bahrain. See Brian Whitaker, "Saudi Arabia's Subtle Protests are Serious", *The Guardian*, March 2, 2011.

133. On the Saudi stabilization policies, which involved both controversial military intervention in Bahrain and $130 billion in incremental domestic spending over the ensuing five years, see Bernard Haykel, "Saudi Arabia vs. the Arab Spring", *Project Syndicate*, August 16, 2011, at: http://www.project.syndicate.org/NorthAfrica.commentary/haykel4/English.

134. For a comprehensive assessment of the sociopolitical implications worldwide of the Iranian Revolution, see Esposito, *The Iranian Revolution*. Also Maloney, *Iran's Long Reach*.

135. Nasr, *The Shia Revival*, especially 185–210 and 234–236. Iran has also, of course, enhanced the influence and capabilities of Hezbollah in Lebanon.

CHAPTER 4. COMPARATIVE ENERGY PRODUCER PROFILES

1. Gabon terminated its membership in 1995, and Indonesia in 2009. See http://www .opec.org/open_web/en/about_us/25.htm.

2. Palmer, *Guardians of the Gulf*.

3. China, the second largest oil importer, brought in almost 6 million barrels per day from abroad in 2010. See BP, *Statistical Review of World Energy,* 2011 edition, 18.

4. International Energy Agency, *World Energy Outlook,* 2011 edition, 137.

5. In 2010 Saudi Arabia's share was 19.1 percent, Iran's was 9.9 percent, and Iraq's was 8.3 percent.

6. BP, *Statistical Review of World Energy,* 2011 edition, 6.

7. Nunn, Schlesinger, and Ebel, *The Geopolitics of Energy into the Twenty-First Century*.

8. The 2009 IEA forecast suggests that the Middle East share of global oil exports will rise from 53.4 percent in 2008 to 58.3 percent in 2025, even as Russia's share declines from 19.0 to 13.3 percent. See International Energy Agency, *World Energy Outlook,* 2011 edition, 137.

9. See, for example, Broadman, *Africa's Silk Road*. Nonresource ties between "Chindia" and Africa, however, do seem promising over the long run, as Broadman suggests.

10. BP, *Statistical Review of World Energy,* 2011 edition, 6.

11. "Oil Discovery Rocks Brazil," at http://www.cnn.com/world, November 9, 2007.

12. Among the formidable technical difficulties are the enormous depth and pressures involved, especially with deep production under the sea bed. See Department of Energy Country Analysis Brief, Brazil, http://www.eia.doegov.emeu/cabs/Brazil/Oil.html.

13. BP, *Statistical Review of World Energy,* 2011 edition, 8.

14. OPEC, *OPEC Annual Statistical Bulletin,* 2008 edition. Qatar's gas exports are somewhat more diversified.

15. See Energy Information Agency, U.S. Department of Energy, http://tonto.eia.doe.gov/. In 2010 49 percent of net U.S. petroleum imports came from the Western Hemisphere, and only 18 percent from the Persian Gulf.

16. Africa provides 10 percent more oil to Europe than does the Middle East. This calculation includes both North Africa, which provided Europe with 1,677,000 barrels per day in 2010, and West Africa, which provided an additional 920,000 barrels per day. East and South Africa provided an additional 2,000. See BP, *Statistical Review of World Energy,* 2011 edition, 18.

17. Europe in 2010 obtained 18.7 percent of its oil imports from the Middle East, compared to 14.7 percent for the United States. Ibid., 18.

18. Over 77 percent of Middle East oil exports flowed to Asia in 2010. The category "Middle East" included minor Syrian, Yemeni, and Omani production, but was otherwise entirely Persian Gulf. Ibid.

19. Goldman, *Petrostate,* Table 2.1, 35–37.

20. World Bank, *World Development Indicators,* http://devdata.worldbank.org; and EuroStat, http://epp.eurostat.ec.europa.eu.

21. Predictably buoyant prices could be an important precondition, as the Central Asian nations are landlocked, their resources are thus relatively inaccessible, and their exploitation inevitably involves costly infrastructural investment that would not be required to source reserves in other competitive locations such as the Persian Gulf.

22. Kashagan is not expected to begin production until at least 2013, some eight years after the original scheduled startup date of 2005. Peak production of 1.5 million barrels per day is not expected to be attained, however, until at least 2019, increasing prospects that Kazakhstan as a whole will be increasing production for many years to come. See Department of Energy Country Analysis Brief, Kazakhstan, http://www.eia.doe.gov/emeu/cabs.Kazakhstan/Oil.html.

23. BP, *Statistical Review of World Energy,* 2011 edition, 20.

24. Ibid.

25. The Kashagan field, discovered in 2000 at the northern end of the Caspian Sea, is estimated to have commercial oil reserves of 9–16 billion barrels, although unfortunately located two and a half miles beneath the seabed, amid high concentrations of poisonous hydrogen-sulfide gas. Kashagan is the world's largest oil find in the past three decades since Alaska's North Slope discoveries. See Guy Chazan, "In Caspian, Big Oil Fights Ice, Fumes, Kazakhs", *Wall Street Journal,* August 28, 2007. For Azerbaijan, see BP, *Statistical Review of World Energy,* 2011 edition, 20.

26. China and India appear to have some shale-gas reserves, but currently lack needed technology, and appear unlikely to provide adequate incentives to multinationals. On

the shale-gas factor in global energy markets, and why its largest impact will likely be in the U.S. and Europe, see John Deutch, "The Good News about Gas", *Foreign Affairs* (January/February 2011): 82–93.

27. Shale gas doubled as a share of U.S. natural gas supply, between 2008 and 2010, from 5 to around 10 percent, due to production costs between one-third and one-half of conventional gas wells, and future recoverable reserves are estimated at around one fourth those of conventional natural gas. See Deutch, "The Good News about Gas", *Foreign Affairs* (January-February 2011): 84–85.

CHAPTER 5. THE COMPARATIVE POLITICAL ECONOMY OF EURASIAN PETROSTATES

1. See, for example, Jeffrey D. Sachs and Andrew M. Warner, "Natural Resource Abundance and Economic Growth," Development Discussion Paper No. 517a (Cambridge, MA: Harvard Institute for International Development, 1995); as well as Michael L. Ross, "The Political Economy of the Resource Curse," *World Politics* 51 (January 1999); and R. M. Auty, *Resource Abundance and Economic Development* (Oxford: Oxford University Press, 2001).
2. Karl, *The Paradox of Plenty*; Yates, *The Rentier State in Africa*; Crystal, *Oil and Politics in the Gulf*; and Goldman, *Petrostate*.
3. Friedman, "The First Law of Petropolitics."
4. Coronil, *The Magical State*. Marshall Goldman's volume has further popularized the term and has provided important insights into how the Russian petrostate operates, but he failed to define explicitly what he meant by it. See Goldman, *Petrostate*.
5. Ross, "Does Oil Hinder Democracy?"
6. The GCC includes Saudi Arabia, Kuwait, Qatar, Bahrain, the United Arab Emirates, and Oman.
7. On the concept of a "world of liberty and law," see Ikenberry and Slaughter, "A World of Liberty under Law."
8. Iran's reliance on oil and gas exports as a share of total exports was 88 percent in 2004 and 87 percent in 2005, only declining thereafter, under the impact of sanctions, to an estimated 80 percent in 2010, according to International Monetary Fund and World Trade Organization figures. See WTO and IMF websites.
9. The Russian Federation consolidated from eleven to nine time zones in March 2010.
10. Russia in 2008 exported $308.6 billion in oil and gas, as compared to $29.5 billion in 1998. See World Trade Organization, http://stat.wto.org/Home/WSDBHome.aspx?Language=E.
11. "Mortality rate" denotes the percentage of individuals age fifteen years or older who do not survive to the age of sixty. In 2006 the Russian male mortality rate was 42.9 percent, much higher than in the United States (14.1); Germany (10.7); Britain (10.0); or Japan (9.0). See *World Bank Development Indicators*. http://data.worldbank.org/data-catalog/world-development-indicators.
12. U.S. Energy Information Administration data, http://www.eia.gov/countries/country-data.cfm?fips=RS. See also BP. *Statistical Review of World Energy,* 2011 edition.

13. Goldman, *Petrostate*, 14, 202. In contrast, Russia supplied only 0.3 percent of the world's machinery exports in 2006.

14. Oil and gas revenues together constituted 46 percent of Russian federal government revenue in 2010. See Russia CEIC Database Team, "Russia's oil and gas revenues," May 16, 2011, at: http:blog.securities.com/2011/05/russias-oil-and-gas-revenues-federal-budget-dilemma/.

15. "Supply of Uranium," World Nuclear Association. http://www.world-nuclear.org/info/info/inf75.html.

16. For a detailed, strongly positive view of Nazarbayev, see Aitken, *Nazarbayev and the Making of Kazakhstan*.

17. Freedom House ranks Kazakhstan as a "not free" country, together with Iran, Russia, and other Central Asian countries. With 7 being the lowest score for domestic progress, in 2010 Kazakhstan's democracy score was 6.43, having been downgraded from 5.96 in 2002. See Freedom House rankings, http://www.freedomhouse.eu/images/nit2011/kazakhstan.pdf. Kazakhstan also ranked 120 out of 180 in Transparency International's Corruption Perceptions Index in 2009; see http://www.transparency.org/policy_research/surveys?indices/cpi/2009/cpi_2009_table.

18. In 2010 Kazakhstan produced over 1.7 million barrels of oil per day, making it the nineteenth largest producer in the world. It exported around 88 percent of that total, or around 1.35 million barrels per day, ranking nineteenth in that category as well. See CIA, *The World Factbook*, https://www.cia.gov.library/publications/the-world-factbook/geos.kz.html.

19. BP. *Statistical Review of World Energy*, 2011 edition, 6.

20. On the Tengiz negotiations, see Levine, *The Oil and the Glory*, 82–143; and Aitken, *Nazarbayev and the Making of Kazakhstan*, 173–175.

21. Aitken, *Nazarbayev and the Making of Kazakhstan*, 179–183.

22. Ibid., 129–148.

23. Kazakhstan has, for example, frequently hosted the Congress of World Religions and Traditions—at Astana in 2003, 2006, and 2009. Ibid., 205.

24. News "Kazakh Paper Slams Western Oil Consortium for Production Delay, High Costs," BBC, September 18, 2010.

25. These figures include Alaska. See Daniel Johnston, *International Exploration Economics, Risk, and Contract Analysis* (Tulsa, OK: Penn Well Corporation, 2003), 199.

26. Guy Chazan, "In Caspian, Big Oil Fights Ice, Fumes, Kazakhs," *Wall Street Journal*, August 28, 2007, http://www.rigzone.com/news/article.asp?a_id=49533.

27. "Change of Guard at Kashagan Helm," *Upstream*, January 23, 2009, http://www.upstreamonline.com/live/article170381.ece.

28. The consortium members are ENI, Exxon Mobil, Total, ConocoPhillips, Inpex, and KazMunaiGaz. Shell left the group in May, 2011. See Stratfor, "Royal Dutch Shell Leaves Major Kazakh Energy Project", *Forbes*, May 31, 2011.

29. On these critical uncertainties and possible long-term outcomes, see Olcott, *Kazakhstan*, 214–244.

30. See Gaye Christofferson, "China's Intentions for Russian and Central Asian Oil and Gas," *NBR Analysis* 9, no. 2 (March 1998).

31. In 2010, around 19 percent of all the oil produced in Kazakhstan wa PRC equity oil. See Saitō, *Central Asia's Oil and Gas Sector since the 2008 Financial Crisis.*

32. "Turkmen Leader, Chinese Official Discuss Boosting Cooperation," BBC, June 19, 2010.

33. Roman Muzalevsky, "Race on for Kazakh uranium," *Asia Times*, April 19, 2011. http://www.atimes.com/atimes/Central_Asia/MD19Ag01.html.

34. Actual production was 10.007 million barrels. See BP, *Statistical Review of World Energy*, 2011 edition, 8.

35. Carola Hoyos, "Expansion into Lead Position", *Financial Times,* Saudi Arabia Special Report, September 23, 2009, 2. Around the end of 2010, Saudi Arabia reportedly held 4 million bbl/day of surplus oil-production capacity. See "Saudi Minister: OPEC nations have capacity to produce surplus oil", CNN World, February 23, 2011. http://articles.cnn.com/2011-03-23/wpr;d/libya.saudi.arabia.oil_1_swing.producer.oil-peter-beutel?_s=PM:WORLD.

36. BP, *Statistical Review of World Energy,* 2011 edition, 18.

37. BP, *Statistical Review of World Energy*, 2011 edition, 6. These figures exclude Canadian oil sands, but not Venezuelan Heavy oil, which Venezuela declares as part of its oil reserves.

38. The Ghawar field, the world's largest, has been pumping up to 5.5 million barrels per day since shortly after its discovery in 1948. The Safaniya field, Saudi Arabia's largest offshore, is located 265 km north of Dhahran. Discovered in 1951, it is 50 km by 15 km with a producing capability of more than 1.2 million barrels per day. For details, see Saudi Aramco website, http://www.saudiaramco.com/irj/portal/anonymous?favlnk=%2FSaudiAramcoPublic%2Fdocs%2FOur+Business%2FOil+Operations%2FOil+Fields+%26+Reserves%2FSafaniya&ln=en.

39. Freedom House rates Bahrain, Oman, Qatar, Saudi Arabia, and the UAE as not free, and Kuwait as partly free. See Freedom House, *Freedom in the World 2010*, http://www.freedomhouse.org/uploads/fiw10/FIW_2010_Tables_and_Graphs.pdf.

40. See, for example, Palmer, *Guardians of the Gulf*; and Bronson, *Thicker Than Oil.*

41. Palmer, *Guardians of the Gulf,* 41–42.

42. Ibid., 43–35.

43. Saudi Arabia's massive Ras Tanura refinery was built to supply the United States with aviation fuel for the Pacific conflict, late in World War II. During the Korean War, for example, the U.S. military obtained as much as half of its fuel supply from the Persian Gulf, and preeminently from Saudi Arabia. See ibid., 44–51; and "A Billion Barrels Ago," *Aramco World,* May 1962, 3–6.

44. Obaid, *The Oil Kingdom at 100*, 99–100.

45. In August 1985, for example, the Saudis linked their oil price to the spot market for crude, and by early 1986 increased production from 2 million barrels per day to 5 million. Crude oil prices plummeted below $10 a barrel, putting extreme pressure on Soviet exporters at a critical juncture in the Cold War. See WTRG Economics, "Oil Price History and Analysis," http://www.wtrg.com/prices.htm.

46. On American basing in Saudi Arabia, see Calder, *Embattled Garrisons*, 154–159.

47. Prince Saud Al Faisal Bin Abdulaziz Al Saud, *Saudi Arabia and the International Oil Market* (Houston: Baker Institute for Public Policy, September 21, 2005), 4.

48. From 1990 to 1997, for example, world oil consumption increased 6.2 million barrels per day, with Asian consumption accounting for all but 300,000 barrels of that gain. See WTRG Economics, *Oil Price History and Analysis*, http://www.wtrg.com/princes.htm.

49. Carola Hoyos, "Expansion into Lead Position," *Financial Times,* September 23, 2009.

50. At the opening ceremony in Riyadh for the International Energy Forum's headquarters building, King Abdullah declared, "The oil policy of Saudi Arabia is based on two main factors: achieving a reasonable and fair price for oil; and ensuring adequate supplies to all consumers." See "King Abdullah Address at Opening of IEF Headquarters," November 19, 2005, http://www.saudiembassy.net/archive/2005/speeches/page2.aspx.

51. See, for example, Simmons, *Twilight in the Desert*.

52. Carola Hoyos, "Expansion into Lead Position, *Financial Times*, Saudi Arabia Special Report, September 23, 2009, 2.

53. Al-Saud, *Saudi Arabia and the International Oil Market*, 7. For details on the organization, see "Energy Security Through Dialogue," the International Energy Forum's online brochure, at http://www.ief.org/Documents/International%20Energy%20Forum%20brochure.pdf.

54. International Energy Forum, "Energy Security Through Dialogue."

55. Palmer, *Guardians of the Gulf*, 27–28.

56. Rachel Bronson, "Understanding US-Saudi Relations," in Parl Aarts and Gerd Nonneman (eds.), *Saudi Arabia in the Balance: Political Economy, Society, and Foreign Affairs* (London: Hurst, 2005), 385.

57. Steffen Hertog. *Princes, Brokers, and Bureaucrats*, 5.

58. Ibid., 5, 37, 98–101.

59. Ibid., 128. On the early history of Aramco under U.S. ownership, see Lebkicker, Rentz, and Steinecke, *Aramco Handbook*, 131–224; Brown, *Oil, God, and Gold*; and Vitalis, *America's Kingdom*.

60. Obaid, *The Oil Kingdom at 100*, xii.

61. Wawwab, Speers, and Hoye, *Saudi Aramco and Its World*, 223. Saudi Arabia took 60 percent ownership in 1974 and 100 percent in 1980.

62. "Saudi Arabia to Strengthen China Relations: Naimi," *Platts Oilgram News*, November 13, 2009; "China's Rapid Growth Shifts the Geopolitics of Oil," *New York Times*, March 20, 2010; "China: A Strategic Partner of Saudi Arabia", *China Online*, http://www.china.or.cn/opinion/2010-12/31-content_21655145.htm; and "Looking east: The Saudis are hedging their bets", *The Economist*, December 12, 2010.

63. "Saudi Aramco to Maintain Investments Amid Downturn," *Chemical Week*, March 30, 2009.

64. "Looking east: The Saudis are hedging their bets", *The Economist*, December 9, 2010.

65. For details, see Arabian Oil Company, http://www.aoc.co.jp/e/his/history.html.

66. Obaid, *The Oil Kingdom at 100*, xiii.

67. Ibid., 21.

68. Ibid., 29–30. Ali al-Naimi, a technocrat rather than a political appointee, served as president of Saudi Aramco 1983–1995, before becoming minister of petroleum and

mineral resources. He is a graduate of Lehigh University in Pennsylvania, with an MA in geology from Stanford University.

69. Among the members of the Supreme Council in 2000, for example, the minister of foreign affairs was a Princeton graduate in economics; the minister of petroleum was a Lehigh graduate and a Stanford MA in geology; the minister of finance was a PhD in economics from Colorado State; and the minister of industry and electricity was a Harvard PhD in Physics, while the secretary general of the council had a doctoral degree from Harvard Law School in comparative legal systems. See ibid., 22–27.

70. See Saudi Arabia National Industrial Clusters Development Program, http://www.saudiclusters.com/aboutnicd.html.

71. Hertog, *Princes, Brokers, and Bureaucrats*, 100.

72. Ibid.

73. Obaid, *The Oil Kingdom at 100*.

74. "When kings and princes grow old", *The Economist*, July 15, 2010.

75. Robert Lacey, *Inside the Kingdom: Kings, Clerics, Modernists, Terrorists, and the Struggle for Saudi Arabia* (New York: Viking, 2009), 38.

76. "The House of Saud," *New Internationalist*, August 2000, http://www.thirdworldtraveler.com/Zeroes/House_Saud.html.

77. Between 1982 and 1999 the Saudi gross national income per capita fell from $14,600 to $6,556, before rising back to $16,190 in 2009. See World Bank, World Development Indicators Online, http://devdata.worldbank.org

78. Mordechai Abir, "Saudi Arabia, Iraq, and the War on Terrorism," *Jerusalem Issue Brief* 2, no. 11 (November 26, 2002).

79. Steffen Hertog, "Segmented Clientelism: The Political Economy of Saudi Economic Reform Efforts," in Paul Aarts and Gerd Nonneman (eds.), *Saudi Arabia in the Balance: Political Economy, Society, Foreign Affairs* (London: Hurst, 2005), 127.

80. Hertog. *Princes, Brokers, and Bureaucrats*, 84–136.

81. King Faisal was especially vigorous in this effort, from the mid-1960s. Ibid., 78–81.

82. Cordesman and Obaid, *National Security in Saudi Arabia*, 265.

83. Daryl Champion, *The Paradoxical Kingdom: Saudi Arabia and the Momentum of Reform* (London: Hurst, 2003), 132–133.

84. Robin Wright, *Sacred Rage: The Crusade of Modern Islam* (London: A. Deutsch, 1986), 148.

85. Lacey, *Inside the Kingdom*, 40.

86. Ibid., 14–45.

87. Sixty-three of the fundamentalists who occupied the Grand Mosque, including the leader Juhaiman, forty other Saudis, ten Egyptians, seven Yemenis, three Kuwaitis, one Sudanese, and one Iraqi, were tried secretly and then beheaded publicly. The condemned were dispersed for their executions to eight different cities across Saudi Arabia, to make clear the kingdom's harsh response. Against the Shia in the Eastern Province, authorities launched major security sweeps, detaining hundreds. See Wright, *Sacred Rage*, 155.

88. Rachel Bronson, "Rethinking Religion: The Legacy of the U.S.-Saudi Relationship," *Washington Quarterly* 24, no. 4 (Autumn 2005), 127.

89. These religious charities include the World Muslim League, International Islamic Relief Organization, Islamic Development Bank, Organization of the Islamic Conference, Saudi Red Crescent, and so on. See Obaid, *The Oil Kingdom at 100*, 110.

90. The Muslim World League, for example, reportedly received more than $1 billion in contributions from the Saudi royal family alone, from its establishment by King Faisal himself in 1962 until 2003. See Steven Emerson, "Terrorism Financing: Origination, Organization, and Prevention: Saudi Arabia, Terrorist Financing, and the War on Terror," testimony before the U.S. Senate Committee on Government Affairs, July 31, 2003, http://hsgac.senate.gov.

91. Bronson, "Rethinking Religion."

92. Huntington, *Political Order in Changing Societies* (New Haven, CT: Yale University Press, 1968).

93. Henry Meyer, "China and Saudi Arabia Form Stronger Trade Ties," *New York Times*, April 20, 2010.

94. See Harsh V. Pant, "Saudi Arabia Woos China and India," *Middle East Quarterly*, (Fall 2006), http://www.meforum.org/article/1019.

95. In 2010 over half of Saudi oil flowed to Asia, and only 14 percent to the United States. See "The Saudis Hedge Their Bets", *The Economist*, December 9, 2010. Saudi oil exports were 365 million barrels to China, 361 million to the United States, and 399 million to Japan in 2009. See "China's Rapid Growth Shifts the Geopolitics of Oil," *New York Times*, March 20, 2010; and Petroleum Association of Japan, http://www.paj.gr.jp/statis/.

96. Michael Vatikiotis, "Oil Supply 1: The Arabs Look to the East," *International Herald Tribune*, November 17, 2004.

97. The King Abdullah Economic City, focused on the steel, plastic, and aluminum industries and under construction near Jeddah, will be the size of Washington, DC, and will house 50,000 Saudis by 2012. The Knowledge Economic City, being built near Medina, will house 150,000 residents, in addition to research centers and schools. See *Financial Times*, September 23, 2009.

98. In late 2011, Indonesia had over 211 million Muslims, 86 percent of its population. India was second with 159 million. In the Middle East, the largest Muslim populations were in Turkey (78 million), Iran (76 million), Egypt (73 million), Iraq (29 million), and Saudi Arabia (26 million). See CIA, *World Factbook*.

99. Pant, "Saudi Arabia Woos China and India."

100. Venezuela has recently included its substantial heavy oil reserves in its declaration of proven reserves, leading to its being ranked second, ahead of Iran, but there is little short-term prospect of their exploitation. See BP, *Statistical Review of World Energy*, 2011 edition, p. 6, http://bp.com/statisticalreview.

101. Ibid., p. 20.

102. Department of Energy, Energy Information Administration, http://www.eia.doe.gov/emeu/cabs/Iran/Oil.html.

103. Figures are for July 2011. See CIA, *World Factbook*.

104. M. Massarrat, "Iran's Energy Policy: Current Dilemmas and Perspective for a Sustainable Energy Policy," *International Journal of Environmental Science and Technology* 1, no. 3 (Autumn 2004), 237.

105. Iranian per capita GDP in 1988 was $2,241, rising to $4,624 in 2010. World Bank, World Development Indicator, http://devdata.worldbank.org.; and CIA, *World Factbook*.

106. For analyses of Taishō Japan with relevance for contemporary Iranian politics, see Peter Duus, *Party Rivalry and Political Change in Taishō Japan* (Cambridge, MA: Harvard University Press, 1968); Robert Scalapino, *Democracy and the Party Movement in Prewar Japan* (Berkeley: University of California Press, 1953); and David Titus, *Palace and Politics in Prewar Japan* (New York: Columbia University Press, 1974).

107. Massarrat, "Iran's Energy Policy," 238.

108. Ibid.

109. Subsidies for food, as well as fuel, comprise around 20 percent of Iranian GDP. See Takeyh, *Hidden Iran*, 38.

110. In January 2005, for example, the Majlis decided to freeze domestic prices of all fuels, including gasoline, at 2003 levels. In January 2010, the Majlis enacted energy price reforms that dismantled the subsidies, with 50 percent of the government revenue thus generated returned to consumers, with 30 percent going to business and 20 percent to government. Actual implementation and economic impact, however, remain unclear, as the program was to be introduced over five years. See "Iran to Cut Oil Subsidies in Energy Reform," *IMF Survey Online*, September 28, 2010, http://www.imf.org.

111. Esfahani and Taheripour, "Hidden Public Expenditures and the Economy in Iran."

112. International Energy Agency, *World Energy Outlook*, 2010 edition.

113. Askari, "Iran's Economic Policy Dilemma."

114. "In Iran, a Fight over Slashing Subsidies: The President Has Demanded $40 Billion in Cuts. Lawmakers Say OK to $20 billion," *Los Angeles Times*, March 23, 2010.

115. Cyrus Bina, "Petroleum and Energy Policy in Iran," *Economic and Political Weekly*, January 3, 2009, http://mrzine.monthlyreview.org/2009/bina070809.html; and Statistical, Economic and Social Research and Training Centre for Islamic Countries, http://www.sesric.org/databases-index.php.

116. "Iran Plans to Cut Gas Imports, Subsidies: Move Targets Fuel Smuggling," *Washington Times*, July 3, 2006.

117. "Pressure Intensifies on Iran's Oil Sector," *Platts Oilgram Price Report*, April 14, 2010; "Iran Sees $60–$80/Barrel Oil Price in 2010," *Platts Oilgram Price Report*, March 2, 2010.

118. Massarrat, "Iran's Energy Policy," 234.

119. Ibid.

120. Ibid., 236.

121. Bina, "Petroleum and Energy Policy in Iran," 23.

122. Ibid.

123. "Angry Protests Flare in Iran over Petrol Rationing," *Turkish Press*, http://www.turkish press.com/news.asp?.

124. Department of State Foreign Press Center, http://fpc.state.gov/documents/organi zation/23591.pdf.

125. Edward Yeranian, "Iranian Police on Alert as Government Cutbacks Begin," Global Security.org, December 19, 2010.

126. CIA, *World Factbook*.

127. "Iran, Pakistan Sign Gas Deal without India," *Platts Oilgram News,* May 27, 2009.

128. "India Invites Iran for Resumption of Gas Pipeline Talks," BBC, May 15, 2010.

129. See, for example, Nilofor Suhrawady, "Iran and India True Friends: Ahmedinejad," *Arab News*, May 1, 2008.

130. "Work on Iran-Pakistan gas pipeline to bein in six months", *People's Daily Online*, July 6, 2011. http://english.peoplesdaily.com.cn/90001/90777/90851/7430725.html.

131. "World Briefing Asia: Tajikistan: Iran's Leader Visits," *New York Times*, July 26, 2006. "South Asia Rolls Out Red Carpet for Iran's Leader: Energy Deals the High-light of Ahmadinejad's Trip to India, Pakistan and Sri Lanka," *Straits Times*, April 30, 2008. "China: Iran's President to Visit Pavilion at Shanghai Expo," *New York Times*, June 9, 2010. "New Turkmenistan-Iran Gas Link Starts Up," *Platts Oilgram News*, January 7, 2010.

132. "President of Iran Calls for Unity against West: Ahmadinejad Tells Shanghai Coop-eration Organization It Can Grow Stronger and Stop Interference by Domineering States," *South China Morning Post*, June 16, 2006; "At Asian Security Meeting, Putin and Iranian Criticize the U.S.," *New York Times*, August 17, 2007. "Asia-Pacific Bali Meeting Muslim Nations Back Hardline Leader; Don't Threaten Us: Iran," *Advertiser* (Australia), May 15, 2006. Formally known as the Conference on Interaction and Confidence Building Measures in Asia, the Asian security summit brings together leaders of Asian nations every two years. See *Tehran Times*, June 7, 2010.

133. "Putin Heads Alliance to Defend Iran," *Times of London*, October 17, 2007. "Iran, Indonesia Sign Deal to Build Banten Refinery," *Platts Oilgram News*, March 12, 2008. "Malaysia's Abdullah Arrives in Iran for Ahmadinejad Talks," BBC, December 22, 2008.

134. For bilateral trade figures between Iran and various nations, see IMF, *Direction of Trade Statistics*.

135. See Garver, Leverett, and Leverett, *Moving (Slightly) Closer to Iran*. China did not, for example, veto the UN Security Council resolution imposing a series of sanctions against Iran on June 9, 2010. See "Special Report: Iran: Tehran Defiant as UN Agrees New Wave of Sanctions: Resolution Fails to Win Unanimous Support Obama Hails Toughest Ever Package of Measures," *Guardian*, June 10, 2010.

136. "Energy Wastage Criticized," *Iran Daily*, April 15, 2009, http://www.iran-daily.com /1388/3374/html/economy.htm.

137. Zhu Yinghuang and Wang Hao, "Made in China Subway Fulfills Iranian Dream," *China Daily*, June 12, 2004. Sections of the Tehran subway, built by China, have been running since February 2000 and transport over 700,000 passengers per day.

138. See, for example, Goldman, *Petrostate*.

139. See, for example, Karl, *The Paradox of Plenty*; and, at a more popular level, Friedman, "The First Law of Petropolitics."

140. China has invested $120 billion in Iran's energy sector over the past five years, and in 2011 purchased 14 percent of its imported oil from Iran. See "China's Growing Energy Apetite and Strategy," *Eurasian Energy Analysis*, June 29, 2011.

CHAPTER 6. ENERGY-INSECURE ASIAN CAPITALIST CONSUMERS

1. The United States in 2009 was the largest net oil importer in the world (9.6 million barrels per day), followed by Japan (4.23), China (4.22), Germany (2.3), India (2.2), and South Korea (2.1), while Taiwan (0.9) ranked as tenth largest. See U.S. Department of Energy, Country Energy Profiles, http://tonto.eia.doe.gov/country/index.cfm.

2. For more detailed examples, particularly relating to Japan, see Calder, "Japan's Energy Angst and the Caspian Great Game," 12–18.

3. In 2007, the Chinese consumed 1,484 kilograms of oil-equivalent energy per capita, compared to 7,766 kilograms for Americans, 4,730 kilograms for Russians, and 4,019 kilograms for Japanese. See World Bank, *World Development Indicators on Energy Use*, http://data.worldbank.org/indicator/EG.USE.PCAP.KG.OE.

4. U.S. Energy Information Administration, *International Energy Outlook*, 2010 edition, Appendix F, Table F13, http://www.eia.doe.gov/oiaf/ieo/pdf/ieoenduse.pdf.

5. On this point, see Robert Kaplan, "China's Grand Map: How Far Will Beijing Reach on Land and at Sea?" *Foreign Affairs* 89, no. 3 (May/June 2010): 23.

6. On Chinese soft power, its limits, and its implications, see Joshua Kurlantzick, *Charm Offensive: How China's Soft Power Is Transforming the World* (New Haven, CT: Yale University Press, 2007); and David M. Lampton, *The Three Faces of Chinese Power: Might, Money, and Minds* (Berkeley: University of California Press, 2008).

7. John K. Fairbank, *The United States and China*, 4th ed. (Cambridge, MA: Harvard University Press, 1979).

8. David Barboza, "China Plans $586 Billion Economic Stimulus," *International Herald Tribune*, November 9, 2008, http://www.iht.com/articles/2008/11/09/business/yuan.php.

9. Quoted in David Kerr, "Central Asian and Russian Perspectives on China's Strategic Emergence," *International Affairs* 86, no. 1 (2010): 127.

10. National Statistical Bureau of China, *Xinjiang Statistical Yearbook*, 2009 edition.

11. In late July, 2011, for example, at least 14 people were killed and nearly 40 wounded in weekend incidents in Kashgar, in which a truck driver was stabbed, his truck used to run down pedestrians, and separately a police station was bombed and four suspects shot and killed. These incidents followed another serious 2008 terrorist incident, just outside Kashgar. See "Weekend violence in Uyghur region kills 14", *CNN World*, July 31, 2011, http://articles.cnn.com.2011-07-31/world/china.violence_1_week end_violence-knifing-spre.

12. Millward, *Eurasian Crossroads*, 97. On the Open Up the West campaign, see Goodman, *China's Campaign to Open Up the West*, especially p. 21 on Jiang's initial address.

13. The stimulus plan included, for example, $88 billion for intercity rail lines, the highest priority in the plan, with the preponderant share building inland from the eastern seaboard. All stimulus funds were to be spent by the end of fiscal 2010. See Keith Bradsher, "China's Route Forward," *New York Times*, January 23, 2009.

14. Michael Wines, "Spending for Stability in China's Far West," *New York Times*, July 8, 2010.

15. China has aggressively promoted UHV transmission which provides large amounts of power over long distances efficiently when volume is large, becaue its power demand is growing rapidly, and energy resources are far from load centers. UHV can potentially be applied across national border, thus enhancing continentalism. On UHV transmission, see David Winning, "Going the Distance", *Wall Street Journal*, April 27, 2009; and Jerry Li, "From Strong to Smart: The Chinese Smart Grid and its Relation with the Globe," *Asian Energy Platform*, September, 2009, http://www.aepfm .org/ufiles/pdf/Smart%20Grid%20%20Sept.pdf.

16. Sun Yat-sen, *The International Development of China* (New York: G.P. Putnam's Sons, 1922).

17. Goodman, *China's Campaign to Open Up the West*, 22.

18. On Hu Angang's arguments in favor of the Open Up the West strategy, see ibid., 24–27.

19. See, for example, Hu, Kang, and Wang, *The Political Economy of Uneven Development*.

20. Ibid., 28.

21. Gao Zhengang et al., *The Path Towards Opening Up the West*, 2–3, cited in Goodman, *China's Campaign to Open Up the West,* 29.

22. Ibid., 35. The Desert Petroleum Highway was built between 1993 and 1995, at an investment of RMB 785 million. See Chinese Embassy, http://china-embassy-org/eng/ zt/zfbps/t36551.htm.

23. Goodman, *China's Campaign to Open Up the West,* 31.

24. For example, in 2003, the average wage of staff members and workers in Shanghai was nearly three times that of inner regions like Jiangxi. See National Bureau of Statistics of China, *China Statistical Yearbook,* 2004 edition.

25. Goodman, *China's Campaign to Open Up the West,* 40.

26. Ibid., 41–42.

27. See ibid., 44–64; and Millward, *Eurasian Crossroads*, 235–254. The Xinjiang Production and Construction Corps, for example, was closely affiliated with the CCP, and played a central role in Xinjiang development during the 1950s, securing the territory with a string of cities, farm complexes, and industries, as well as attracting demobilized soldiers to settle in Xinjiang, with a force of close to 2.5 million.

28. Yao Bin, "Xinjiang Takes Off", *Beijing Review*, August 11, 2011, 2.

29. Ding Ying, "Partnering for Development", *Beijing Review*, August 11, 2011, 24.

30. Ibid. Trade through Alanshankou Port on the China-Kazakh border, one of Xinjiang's largest of 29 open border-trading posts, grew 23 percent in 2010, for example, to over $17 billion, while that through Horgos, also on the Kazakh border exceeded $3 billion. See Ding Ying, "Prosperous Xinjiang", *Beijing Review*, August 11, 2011, 18–20.

31. The China-Eurasia Expo was co-organized by 29 Chinese government departments, co-hosted by 22 provinces and municipalities, and co-sponsored by 11 government agencies of Xinjiang. It was accompanied by a broad range of Track II activities involving over 20 Eurasian nations, including Kazakhstan, Russia, Iran, and Pakistan, as well as China. See Xiao Ding, "Gateway to Eurasia", *Beijing Review*, August 11, 2011, 27.

32. Both Shanghai and Kashgar are cooperating to fund $250 million of projects in Kashgar, many with an international dimension. Cooperative local-level projects are providing as much as a quarter of Kashgar's total revenue, and equivalent amounts Xinjiang-wide. See Yuan Yuan, "More Help, More Prosperity", *Beijing Review*, August 11, 2011, 26.

33. In 2000 Tibet's population of only 2.6 million was 94.1 percent non-Han Chinese. See Goodman, *China's Campaign to Open Up the West*, 8–9.

34. For a vivid description of the railway and its construction process, see Lustgarten, *China's Great Train*.

35. *China Daily*, July 1, 2006, http://www.chinadaily.com/cn/home/index.html.

36. Sino-Indian trade was $2.9 billion in 2000, and reached $61.7 billion in 2010. See International Monetary Fund, *Direction of Trade Statistics*.

37. Saibal Dasgupta,"Tibet rail to connect China with Nepal", *Times of India,* August 29, 2006, http://articles.timesofindia.indiatimes.com/2006-08-29/rest-of-world/27824741 _1_tibet-rail-dalai-lama-railway-line.

38. Xin Dingding, "Qinghai-Tibet railway to get six new lines", *China Daily*, August 17, 2008.

39. "China Begins Building Tibet-Nepal Rail Link: Official," *AFP*, April 26, 2008.

40. International Monetary Fund. *Direction of Trade Statistics*.

41. See Bo Kong, "The Geopolitics of the Myanmar-China Oil and Gas Pipelines," in Edward C. Chow, ed. *Pipeline Politics in Asia: Energy, Markets, and Supply Routes*. Seattle: National Bureau of Asian Research Special Report 23, September, 2010, 55–66.

42. Lan Xinzhen, "Nanning-Singapore Economic Corridor", *Beijing Review*, August 26, 2010, http://www.bjreview.com/cn/quotes/txt/2010-08/24/content_293425_2.htm.

43. Ibid.

44. This latter project, 5000 kilometers long, is expected to be completed by 2015. Construction began in April, 2011. For details, see "Kunming-Singapore High-Speed Railway begins construction," *People's Daily Online*, April 25, 2011, http://english .peopledaily.com.cn/90001/90776/90882/7360790.html.

45. B.P. *Statistical Review of World Energy*, 2011 edition, 18.

46. In 2007 China imported nearly 140 billion cubic feet of LNG, its first year as a net gas importer, and in 2009 began importing piped natural gas from Turkmenistan's mammoth South Yolotan gas field. Gas imports of 350 billion cubic feet in 2009 were expected to rise to over 1 trillion cubic feet by 2011. See U.S. Department of Energy, Energy Information Administration, "Country Analysis Briefs: China," http://www .eia.doe.gov.

47. See Kong, *China's International Petroleum Policy*, 33–94.

48. These firms are heavily state owned: CNPC, 90 percent; Sinopec, 75 percent; and CNOOC, 70 percent. They also receive substantial government loans and case-by-case subsidies. See Charles E. Ziegler, "Competing for Markets and Influence: Asian National Oil Companies in Eurasia," *Asian Perspectives* 32, no. 1 (2008): 132.

49. Ibid.

50. Ibid.

51. "ExxonMobil, Aramco's China Refinery Starts," Reuters, May 19, 2009, http://www.reuters.com/article/idUSPEK25382720090519.

52. "A World-Class Collaboration," ExxonMobil, March 31, 2010, http://www.exxonmobil.com/corporate/news_features_20100331_worldclass.aspx.

53. "ExxonMobil Celebrates China's Fujian Facility Completion," ExxonMobil, November 11, 2009, http://www.businesswire.com/portal/site/home/permalink/?ndmViewId=news_view&newsId=20091110006688&newsLang=en.

54. Tang Fuchun, "Phase II Oil Reserve Candidate Sites Chosen," China.org, February 15, 2007, http://www.china.org.cn/english/BAT/200243.htm.

55. Ibid.

56. In March 2009, CNPC and Myanmar Oil and Gas Enterprises signed a $2.9 billion agreement to build parallel oil and gas pipelines from Mandalay Island port on the Burmese coast into Yunnan Province, to carry oil supplies from the Middle East and Africa to southern China. The Myanmar pipelines, to be completed by late 2012, are expected to carry 22 million tons of crude oil annually, as well as 12 billion cubic meters of natural gas. See "Burma, China Complete First Phase of Joint Oil, Gas Project," BBC, November 11, 2010. Also, Bo Kong, "The Geopolitics of the Myanmar-China Oil and Gas Pipelines", in Edward C. Chow (editor), *Pipeline Politics in Asia: Energy, Markets, and Supply Routes.* Seattle: NBAR Special Report 23, September, 2010d, 55–65. China is building pipelines from Gwadar, on the Baluchistan coast, and only a few hundred miles from the Persian Gulf, across Pakistan and into Xinjiang. Late in 2009 Beijing temporarily suspended the gas pipeline project, although that effort retains long-term logic. Financial conditions and global recession were cited as the ostensible reason, but terrorism may also have been a factor in this particularly restive province. See Robert M. Cutler, "India Seeks to Re-enter New Iran-Pakistan Gas Deal," Central Asia Caucus Institute, April 28, 2010, http://www.cacianalyst.org/?q=node/5314.

57. "CNPC Opens New Leg of Second West-East Pipeline," *Platts Oilgram News*, November 24, 2010. The entire West-East pipeline, including one trunk and eight branches, is scheduled for completion by December 31, 2012.

58. "China's 2nd west-east gas pipeline can start operation at June end," *Xinhuanet*, June 29, 2011, http://news.xinhuanet.com/english2010/China/2011-06/29/c_13957221.htm.

59. "Chinese President Returns from 'Fruitful' Central Asian Visits," BBC, December 15, 2009.

60. Ibid. The first Sino-Russian pipeline would connect Russia's massive Kovykta gas field to China's Xinjiang, while the second would connect Sakhalin to northeastern China, likely terminating near Beijing.

61. "High Speed Rail: New Silk Road," xinhuanet.com, March 12, 2010, 49.

62. Melinda Liu, Anna Nemtsova, and Owen Matthews, "The New Silk Road," *Newsweek,* May 10, 2010. The high-speed rail portion is to link seventeen countries with over 8,000 kilometers of railway. China's first major domestic high-speed trunk line was introduced between Wuhan and Guangzhou in December 2009.

63. The national high-speed project as a whole will involve investments of $300 billion by 2020, including two major east-west routes: Xuzhou-Lanzhou and Shanghai-Kunming. See "China Speeds Up Railway Building in Its Vast West Regions," BBC, November 23, 2009.

64. IBM will, in this context, be building its Global Rail Innovation Center in Beijing. See Peter Fairley, "China's High-Speed Rail Revolution," *Technology Review*, January 11, 2010, http://www.technologyreview.com.

65. Anthony Bubalo and Malcolm Cook, "Horizontal Asia," *American Interest* 5, no. 5 (May/June 2010): 17.

66. "China Uses Railway Lines to Extend Trade and Influence," *Daily Telegraph*, October 18, 2008.

67. "Freight Mobility and Intermodal Connectivity in China," *China's Transportation System and Plans for the Future*. Federal Highway Administration, U.S. Department of Transportation. http://international.fhwa.dot.gov/pubs/pl08020/fmic_08_03.cfm.

68. Gaël Raballand and Agnès Andrésy, "Why Should Trade between Central Asia and China Continue to Expand?" *Asia Europe Journal* 5, no. 2 (June 2007): 235–252.

69. "Mitsubishi, Exxon, China Firm Sign Natural-Gas Pipeline Deal," *Daily Yomiuri*, August 24, 1995.

70. Chinese reluctance to share profits with foreign firms was also a factor. See "PetroChina Cuts Pipeline's Foreign Ties; Negotiations with Shell and ExxonMobil End Amid Talk the Energy Giant Has Sufficient Finances to Complete the Project," *South China Morning Post*, August 4, 2004.

71. In mid-2010, for example, China announced strategic plans for Xinjiang's "leapfrog development," involving a doubling of fixed-asset investment in the region by 2015, and targeted sister-city support totaling over 10 billion RMB from nineteen provinces and cities elsewhere in China to counterparts in Xinjiang. Shenzhen in Guangdong, for example, was paired with Kashgar in southwestern Xinjiang. See "China Outlines Strategic Plans for Xinjiang's 'Leapfrog Development,'" BBC, May 20, 2010; and "Beijing Sets Out 10-Year Strategy to End Poverty in Xinjiang," *South China Morning Post*, May 21, 2010.

72. India's population passed 1.2 billion in early 2012. See Central Intelligence Agency, *The World Factbook*, http://www.cia.gov/library/publications/the-world-factbook/geos/in.html.

73. United Nations Secretariat, Department of Economic and Social Affairs, Population Division, *World Population Prospects: The 2008 Revision,* http://esa.un.org/unpp.

74. Indians consumed an average of 510 kg of oil-equivalent energy in 2006, compared to a world average of 1,818 kilos, or 7,778 kg in the United States. See http://worldbank.org.

75. India's birth rate in 2011 was estimated at 20.97 per thousand, compared to China's 12.29 per thousand. See CIA, *World Factbook*.

76. Eric Beinhocker, Diana Farrell, and Adil Zainubhai, "Tracking the Growth of India's Middle Class," *McKinsey Quarterly*, August 2007, https://www.mckinsey quarterly.com. There is no official definition of the middle class in India, which makes quantification highly subjective. McKinsey estimated the middle class at 50 million in 2005, using a definition of disposable household income of from 200,000 to one million rupees. At the other end of the spectrum, the World Bank estimated the middle class at 264 million, using the median poverty line of seventy countries as a lower bound, and the U.S. poverty line as an upper bound. CNN-IBN estimated the middle class at 20 percent of the population, or just over 200 million people, by using car, scooter, color TV, or telephone ownership as the key criterion. On this statistical issue, see Deutsche Bank Research, "The Middle Class in India: Issues and Opportunities," February 15, 2010, http://www.dbresearch.com.

77. Deutsche Bank Research, "The Middle Class in India."

78. Kemp, *The East Moves West*, 35.

79. Ibid.

80 International Energy Agency, *World Energy Outlook*, 2009 edition, 646.

81. International Energy Agency, *World Energy Outlook*, 2011 edition, 596.

82. Joshi, *Reconnecting India and Central Asia*, 21–22.

83. Muslims of India, http://www.faqs.org/minorities/South-Asia/Muslims-of-India.html. Muslims constituted 14.6 percent of India's population in 2010.

84. Joshi, *Reconnecting India and Central Asia*, 23.

85. Ibid.

86. Kemp, *The East Moves West*, 23. The Raj was located in Calcutta until 1912, and then in New Delhi.

87. See Curzon, *Persia and the Persian Question*; George N. Curzon, "Frontiers," delivered as the Romanes Lecture, Oxford University, October 7, 1907; Gilmour, *Curzon*; and Mohan, *Crossing the Rubicon*, 204–207. Lord George Curzon served as viceroy of India from 1898 to 1905, before also serving as chancellor of Oxford University and British foreign secretary.

88. Kemp, *The East Moves West*, 23–24. Literally "soldier" in Persian, the term *sepoy* commonly refers to Indians in the service of a European power. In the modern Indian, Pakistani, and Bangladeshi armed forces, the term refers to those with a rank analogous to that of private in Western armies.

89. John Eckhouse, "Migrant Workers' Economic Impact," *San Francisco Chronicle*, July 1, 1991, cited in Kemp, *The East Moves West*, 251.

90. Indian migrant workers comprise a remarkably large proportion of the local population in the GCC countries of the Persian Gulf, as follows: UAE (46 percent), Bahrain (27 percent), Qatar (18 percent), Oman (11 percent), Kuwait (8 percent), and Saudi Arabia (4 percent). See Kemp, *The East Moves West*, 26.

91. "Russia's Putin in India to Sign Arms Deals Worth Crores," *Economic Times*, , March 12, 2010, http://articles.economictimes.indiatimes.com/2010-03-12/news/28450280_1 _russia-s-putin-admiral-gorshkov-russian-military-equipment.

92. Mark Magnier, "India Embraces Russia Arms," *Los Angeles Times*, March 13, 2010, http://articles.latimes.com/2010/mar/13/world/la-fg-russia-india13-2010mar13.

93. "Putin in Deal to Build Nuclear Reactors for India," *Guardian*, March 12, 2010, http://www.guardian.co.uk/world/2010/mar/12/russia-india-nuclear-reactor-deal.

94. "India, Russia Sign Deals," Chinadaily.com.cn, December 22, 2010.

95. Starr and Kuchins, *The Key to Success in Afghanistan*.

96. U.S. Department of Energy, Energy Information Administration, "Country Analysis Briefs: India," http://www.eai.doe.gov.

97. India has bought six nuclear reactors from Areva of France, and four from Rosatom of Russia, adding 11,000 megawatts of electric capacity. Ibid.

98. Ibid.

99. The 2011 International Energy Agency projection was for India's oil imports to rise from 2.2 million barrels per day in 2008 to 6.8 million barrels per day in 2035, and for natural gas consumption to rise from 59 billion cubic feet in 2009 to 150 billion cubic feet in 2030. See International Energy Agency, *World Energy Outlook*, 2011 edition, 159.

100. *Middle East Business Intelligence*, April 13, 2008.

101. Ibid., 40.

102. "Tracing the Terror Route," *Indian Express*, December 10, 2008.

103. Lashkar-e-Taiba was founded in 1990 in the Kunar Province of Afghanistan, but is now based in Pakistan. Its declared objective is jihad against the Indian government and the liberation of Kashmir. See Joshi, *Reconnecting India and Central Asia*, 89.

104. Ibid., 58.

105. CIA, *World Factbook*. In 2010 Japan had a nominal GDP of $5.46 trillion, compared to $14.66 trillion for the United States, and $5.88 trillion for China.

106. In April 2010, Japan had $1.047 trillion in official reserve assets. See International Monetary Fund, "Japan: International Reserves and Foreign Currency Liquidity," http://www.imf.org.

107. CIA, *World Factbook*.

108. Ibid.

109. Japanese natural gas proven reserves at the beginning of 2009 were 20.9 billion cubic meters, while annual consumption in 2008 was around 101.1 billion cubic meters. Ibid.

110. See Manning, *The Asian Energy Factor*.

111. See, for example, Yergin, *The Prize*, especially 305–327, 351–367; and Ekonomisuto, *Sengo Sangyō Shi e no Shōgen* [Testimony to Postwar Industrial History].

112. For more on the concept of energy angst and its historical expression, see Calder, "Japan's Energy Angst and the Caspian Great Game"; and Calder, "Japan's Energy Angst."

113. U.S. Department of Energy, Energy Information Administration, "Country Analysis Brief: Japan," http://www.eia.doe.gov.

114. Johnson, *MITI and the Japanese Miracle*; and Kent E. Calder, *Crisis and Compensation* (Princeton, NJ: Princeton University Press, 1988), 127–155.

115. Martin Fackler, "Japan Sees a Chance to Promote Its Energy-Frugal Ways, *New York Times*, July 4, 2008, http://www.nytimes.com/2008/07/04/world/asia/04japan.html.

116. Japan has spent $45 billion on steel sector energy saving since 1973. Twenty-one percent of all autos on Japanese highways were low emission even by early 2006. For such details on Japanese energy efficiency efforts, see *Washington Post*, February 16, 2006.

117. For an outline of these measures, see Devin T. Stewart and Warren Wilczewski, "How Japan Became an Efficiency Superpower: Lessons for U.S. Energy Policy under Obama," in *Policy Innovations: The Central Address for a Fairer Globalization* (New York: Carnegie Council, 2009), http://www.policyinnovations.org/ideas/briefings/data/000102/:pf_printable?.

118. This approach was proposed for broader trilateral emulation at the 2008 Tōyako G8 summit, hosted by Fukuda Yasuo in northern Japan. See Ministry of Foreign Affairs, "G8 Hokkaido Toyako Summit Tackles Climate Change," June 2008, http://www.mofa.go.jp/policy/environment/warm/coolearth50/initiative.pdf.

119. In the steel industry, Japan invested about $45 billion in developing energy-saving technologies between 1972 and 2006. See Martin Fackler, "Japan Sees a Chance to Promote Its Energy-Frugal Ways," *New York Times*, July 4, 2008.

120. Amelia Timbers, "Learning from Japan's Energy Efficiency," Matter Network, August 7, 2008, http://www.matternetwork.com/2008/8/7/g-8-learn-from-japans.cfm.

121. James Brooke, "Japan Squeezes to Get the Most out of Costly Fuel," *New York Times*, June 4, 2005.

122. Ibid.

123. Stewart and Wilczewski, "How Japan Became an Efficiency Superpower."

124. Between 1994 and 2005, for example, the Japanese tax code subsidized the introduction of photovoltaic systems by Japanese households, through subsidies. NEDO also supported solar power until 2002, provoking economies of scale that halved the price of photovoltaics and led to Japanese industrial leadership in thin-film solar technology. The expiration of the subsidies, combined with Germany's adoption of a feed-in tariff, however, led to Japan's ceding leadership in the solar power sector to Germany during the Koizumi years (2001–2006). Ibid.

125. See, for example, Kazuhito Suwa, "'Smart' Electric Power Grid Moving Toward Fruition," *Asahi Shimbun*, February 27, 2010, http://www.asahi.com/english/TKY201002260442.html.

126. Ibid. More than twenty Japanese companies, including Tokyo and Kansai Power, Toshiba, Fujitsu, and Sekisui House, joined hands in January 2010 to create an original smart-grid format, supported by METI.

127. Kitamura Yojirō, *Isuramu Manē no Honryū: Nihon ni Oshiyoseru 1000chō en no Tsunami* [Torrent of Islamic Money: A Quintillion Yen Tsunami Flooding into Japan] (Tokyo: Kōdansha, 2009), 190–286.

128. See Yergin, *The Prize*, 305–327.

129. In purchasing-power parity terms, the South Korean economy was one-third the scale of Japan in 2010, although in nominal terms it was only one fifth as large. See Central Intelligence Agency, *The World Factbook*.

130. For more detail on the energy challenges that Korea confronts, see Calder, *Korea's Energy Insecurities*, especially 7–27.

131. International Energy Agency, *Energy Balances of OECD Countries*, 2010 edition.

132. "South Korea's Oil Dependence on Middle East Hits 84.2 Percent in 1Q of 2010," Qatar News Agency, May 21, 2010, http://www.qnaol.net.

133. International Energy Agency, *Oil Information: Crude and Product Imports*, 2010 edition. Paris: International Energy Agency, 2011.

134. Jong Sung Hwang and Sang-Hyun Park, "Review of Individual Economies: Republic of Korea," in Shahid Akhtar and Patricia Arinto (eds.), *Digital Review of Asia Pacific 2009–2010* (Singapore: International Development Research Centre, 2009), 234–240.

135. National Information Society Agency, *2009 Informatization White Paper* (Seoul: National Information Society Agency, 2009), 34–54.

136. See Calder, *Korea's Energy Insecurities*, 44–48.

137. Song Jung-a, "South Korea's Nuclear Ambitions," *Financial Times*, March 29, 2010, http://www.ft.com.

138. U.S. Department of Energy, Energy Information Administration, "Country Brief: South Korea," http://www.eia.doe.gov.

139. While the government began privatizing the electric power sector generally in 2001, it has explicitly indicated plans to retain control of one element—the Korea Hydro and Nuclear Power Company, which operates the country's nuclear and hydroelectric power stations.

140. David Adam Stott, "South Korea's Global Nuclear Ambitions," *Asia-Pacific Journal*, 12-1-10, March 22, 2010.

141. Department of Energy, Energy Information Administration, http://www.eia.gov /countries/country-data.cfm?fips=KS.

142. On the prospects, see Stott, "South Korea's Global Nuclear Ambitions."

143. Ibid.

144. Myra P. Saefong, "Asia Powers Up Its Nuclear Ambitions," *Market Watch*, May 20, 2010, http://www.marketwatch.com.

145. Lee became president of Hyundai Construction in 1977 at age thirty-five, the youngest CEO in the firm's history. During twenty-seven years with the Hyundai Group, he served as CEO of eight businesses, and earned the name "The Bulldozer," for the drive with which he managed difficult projects. See *The Columbia Encyclopedia*, 6th ed., http://www.encyclopedia.com/doc/1E1-LeeMyungBk.html.

146. Stott, "South Korea's Global Nuclear Ambitions."

147. Ibid.

148. Ibid.

149. Saban Kardas, "Turkey Signs Nuclear Deal with South Korea," *Asia Times*, March 10, 2010, http://www.atimes.com.

150. In March 2010, for example, the ROK struck a 150-billion won ($133 million) deal to export a research-purpose nuclear reactor to Jordan. See "Korea to Export Nuke Research Reactor to Jordan," *Korea Times*, March 30, 2010.

151. "Korean Air Plans Silk Road in Air," *New Europe*, April 25, 2010, http://www .neurope.eu.

152. "Korea Launches Collaborative Medical Tourism Initiative in ME," *Khaleej Times*, May 22, 2010, http://www.menafn.com.

153. Moon Ihlwan, "Russia's Ties with South Korea Deepen," *Bloomberg Businessweek*, April 26, 2010, http://www.businessweek.com.

154. Friedman, *The World Is Flat.*
155. See Fareed Zakaria, *The Rise of the Rest* (New York: W.W. Norton, 2008).

CHAPTER 7. EMERGING ENTENTES AMID COMPLEX CONTINENTALISM

1. By "entente," I mean a cooperative agreement or understanding between or among political-economic powers.
2. By "complex continentalism," I mean the continental political-economic interdependence marked by both conflict and cooperation at the continental level.
3. See Emmott, *Rivals*, 25–47.
4. Edward Hallett Carr, *A History of Soviet Russia*, vol. 1, *The Bolshevik Revolution, 1917–1923*; vol. 2, *The Interregnum, 1923–1924* (New York: Macmillan, 1951).
5. On the significant early Bolshevik efforts on the East, see Hopkirk, *Setting the East Ablaze.*
6. Jian Chen, *Mao's China and the Cold War* (Chapel Hill: University of North Carolina Press, 2001); and Thomas Christensen, *Useful Adversary: Grand Strategy, Domestic Mobilization, and Sino-American Conflict, 1947–1958* (Princeton, NJ: Princeton University Press, 1996).
7. Zhang, *Economic Cold War.*
8. See Chen, *Mao's China and the Cold War*; Lorenz M. Luthi, *The Sino-Soviet Split: Cold War in the Communist World* (Princeton, NJ: Princeton University Press, 2008); and Lowell Dittmer, *Sino-Soviet Normalization and Its International Implications, 1945–1990* (Seattle: University of Washington Press, 1992).
9. The Chinese ambushed the Soviets, who suffered almost fifty casualties. See William Burr (ed.), "The Sino-Soviet Border Conflict, 1969: U.S. Reactions and Diplomatic Maneuvers", 1969, National Security Archive, June 12, 2001, http://www.gwu.edu/nsarchiv/NSAEBB/NSAEBB49/.
10. On this "San Francisco system" political-economic structure, so called because it was embedded in the 1951 San Francisco peace treaty resolution to the Pacific War, see Calder, "Securing Security through Prosperity."
11. Fravel, "Regime Insecurity and International Cooperation: Explaining China's Compromises in Territorial Disputes."
12. National Portal of India, http://india.gov.in/knowindia/india_at_a_glance.php.
13. See, for example, Michael Schwartz, "Ethnic Rioting Ravages Kyrgyzstan," *New York Times*, June 14, 2010; and "Weekend violence in Uyghur region kills 14", *CNN World*, July 31, 2011, http://articles.cnn.com/2011-07-31/world/china/violence_1_weekend-violence-kinfing-spre.
14. "Can China Bridge the Great Ethnic Divide in Xinjiang?" *Globe and Mail* (Canada), July 9, 2009.
15. By 2011, for example, Xinjiang had 29 land ports affording access to neighboring countries, including an elaborate new cooperation center at Horgos, on the Sino-Kazakh border, that served as a free trade zone focusing on agricultural-processing trade, manufacturing, financial services, and tourism. All four of China's major state-owned banks had branches at the center, which provided free convertibility

among the U.S. dollar, Chinese renmenbi, and Kazakh tenge. See Ding Ying, "Prosperous Xinjiang," *Beijing Review*, August 11, 2011, 19.

16. Uyghurs in Central Asia, many of whose ancestors arrived with the Mongols, number 500,000, of whom 200,000 live in Kazakhstan. See Chien-Peng Chung, "The Defense of Xinjiang, Politics, Economics, and Security in Central Asia," *Harvard International Review* 25, no. 2 (Summer 2003): http://www.harvardir.org/index.php ?page=article&id=1124&p=.

17. According to the PRC's State Council Information Office, Uyghur separatists had been responsible for over two hundred terrorist incidents in Xinjiang, as of early 2002. Amnesty International, however, claims that Beijing justifies broader suppression of Uyghurs under such claims of terrorism. See Chung, "The Defense of Xinjiang," 59; and Amnesty International, *Amnesty Report*, 2008 edition, http://thereport .amnesty.org/eng/regions/asia-pacific/china.

18. Harry Harding (ed.), *China's Foreign Relations in the 1980s* (New Haven, CT: Yale University Press, 1984); Goldstein, *Rising to the Challenge*, 119–120; Alastair Iain Johnston, "Socialization in International Institutions: The ASEAN Way and International Relations Theory," in G. John Ikenberry and Michael Mastanduno (eds.), *International Relations Theory and the Asia-Pacific* (New York: Columbia University Press, 2003), 127; and Rosemary Foot, "China's Regional Activism: Leadership, Leverage and Protection," *Global Change, Peace and Security* 17, no. 2 (2005): 144.

19. This terminology originated around 2001 with President Jiang Zemin. See Jim Nichol, "Central Asia's Security: Issues and Implications for U.S. Interests." Washington, DC: Congressional Research Service, March 11, 2010.

20. Dru C. Gladney, "China's 'Uyghur Problem' and the Shanghai Cooperation Organization," presented at the U.S.-China Economic and Security Review Commission Hearings, Washington, DC, August 3, 2006, 7.

21. Ibid.

22. In late July 2008, for example, an Uyghur truck driver and an accomplice killed sixteen border policemen in Kashgar, Xinjiang, just before the Beijing Olympics, by ramming them with a dump truck as they were out jogging, and then attacking the survivors with knives. See *Yomiuri Shimbun*, July 31, 2008. In 2009, there were serious riots in Urumchi and further violence in Kashgar. See "Nothing Can Excuse the Violence in Xinjiang," *South China Morning Post*, July 7, 2009; and "156 Dead in Chinese Riots; Conflict between Uighur, Han: 1,434 Arrested as Police Sweep Tenements in Muslim Uighur Districts," *Montreal Gazette*, July 7, 2009. In the summer of 2011 there was further ethnic violence in Kashgar and Khotan, as noted elsewhere, despite substantial efforts by the Chinese government to stimulate economic development in Uyghur-majority areas.

23. International Monetary Fund, *Direction of Trade Statistics,* annual..

24. China's arms supplies to Iran—over half of Tehran's nominal imported total—are one significant exception, to be detailed later. See Garver, *China and Iran*.

25. There are roughly 4 million ethnic Russians in Kazakhstan alone, and a further 1.4 million in Uzbekistan as well. See BBC Country Profile, http://news.bbc.co .uk/2/hi/asia-pacific/country_profiles/; Embassy of Uzbekistan in the USA,

http://www.uzbekistan.org/uzbekistan/people/; and Embassy of Ukraine in the USA, http://www.mfa.gov.ua/usa/en/publication/content/377.htm.

26. During 2005–2008, Russia was the second-largest arms exporter worldwide, exporting $21 billion in weapons, compared to $51.3 billion for the United States. Russia exported $16 billion of weapons to Asia, however, representing 76.1 percent of its global exports. This figure was substantially greater than U.S. weapons exports to Asia during the 2005–2008 period, which totaled only $12 billion. See Richard F. Grimmett, *Conventional Arms Transfers to Developing Nations, 2001–2008* (Washington, DC: Congressional Research Service, September 4, 2009).

27. Calculation from Stockholm International Peace Research Institute arms transfer database, http://www.sipri.org/databases/armstransfers/armstransfers.

28. "Asia's Changing Balance of Power", *Wall Street Journal*, December 10, 2010.

29. "India, Russia Sign Deals," Chinadaily.com.cn, December 22, 2010. India plans to induct up to 300 of the new fighters being developed into its air force.

30. The sale of ten Boeing C-17 cargo planes, worth $5 billion, was, for example, announced during the Obama visit. See "Wealthy and Worried, India Is Rich Arms Market," *New York Times*, November 4, 2010.

31. See International Institute for Strategic Studies, *The Military Balance*, 2011 edition, 338.

32. International Monetary Fund, *Direction of Trade Statistics,* 1999, 2010. http://elibrary-data.imf.org/.

33. IMF. *Direction of Trade Statistics.*

34. See Calder and Ye, *The Making of Northeast Asia.*

35. The shares of native-born Russian inhabitants in the various near abroad republics in 1990 were: Kazakhstan (67 percent), Azerbaijan (66 percent), and over 50 percent in Uzbekistan, Kyrgyzstan, and Turkmenistan. See Vladimir Shlapentokh, Munir Sendich, and Emil Payin (eds.), *The New Russian Diaspora: Russian Minorities in the Former USSR* (Armonk, NY: M.E. Sharpe, 1994), 37–38.

36. Maria Levitov, "Putin Woos Former Republics as Russia Competes with BRIC Peers," *Bloomberg Businessweek*, May 18, 2010, http://www.businessweek.com.

37. Russia, for example, recently supplied twenty MiG-31 upgrades and forty S-300 air-defense missiles to the Kazakh Air Force, which is supplied exclusively by Russia. See International Institute for Strategic Studies, *The Military Balance*, 2010 edition, 376.

38. Levitov, "Putin Woos Former Republics."

39. Ibid.

40. U.S. defense outlays for fiscal year 2010 were 712.8 billion. See International Institute for Strategic Studies, *The Military Balance*, 2011 edition, 56.

41. See, for example, Emmott, *Rivals*, 222–231.

42. "Russia's Primakov Urges 'Strategic Triangle' with China, India," http://www.pacificnet.net/jue/chinanews/archives/docs/981221.html; and "Russia Favours 'Strategic Triangle' among India, Russia and China," Rediff on the Net, December 21, 1998, http://www.rediff.com/news/1998/dec/21rus.htm.

43. "China Refuses Russia's Call to Form Strategic Triangle with India," at: http://www.arabicnews.com/ansub/Daily/Day/981223/1998122320.html.

44. On the June 2005 Vladivostok meeting among foreign ministers Sergey Lavrov, Natvar Singh, and Li Zhaoxing, see http://www.kommersant.com/page/asp?id= 582650.

45. On the November, 2010 Wuhan trilateral Foreign Ministers' meeting among China, Russia, and India, indicating an agreement on the next session during the last half of 2011 in Russia, see "Joint Communique of the Tenth Meeting of the Foreign Ministers of the People's Republic of China, and Russian Federation, and the Republic of India", *The Hindu*, November 15, 2010.

46. "Hu Jintao at the Brazilia BRIC Summit," BBC, April 17, 2010.

47. President George W. Bush, "Remarks by the President at 2002 Graduation Exercise of the U.S. Military Academy, West Point, New York," Whitehouse.gov, http://www .whitehouse.gov/news/releases/2002/06/print/20020601–3.html.

48. Sultan Shahin, "Three of a Kind: India, China, and Russia," *Asia Times*, September 27, 2003, http://www.atimes.com.

49. Joshi, *Reconnecting India and Central Asia*, 33–80.

50. "Uzbek Move to Remove Military Hardware from Enclave to Thaw Kyrgyz Ties," BBC, June 8, 2010.

51. "Islamic 'Foreigners' Join War against the Infidel along the Afghan Border; Pakistan," *The Times*, March 20, 2010.

52. "One Decision, Many Messages," *New York Times*, November 25, 2009.

53. One major reason for this favorable view of Russia, and of balancing, has been the pivotal role in domestic politics of the Communist Party of India, a sometime coalition partner of the ruling Congress Party and a periodic ruling power at the state level in its own right. On the communist political role, see M. V. S. Koteswara Rao, *Communist Parties and the United Front Experience in Kerala and West Bengal* (Hyderabad: Prajasakti Book House, 2003).

54. For example, see Breslin, "Understanding China's Regional Rise."

55. Statistics from the Indian Department of Commerce Export-Import Data Bank, http://commerce.nic.in/eid/default.asp. The UAE did nominally exceed China in trade volume with India during 2008, but it functioned significantly as an entrepôt center for the trade of third countries, particularly Iran. In 2009 China surpassed the UAE as well.

56. "Chinese Minister on Achievements of Premier Wen's Visits to India, Pakistan," BBC, December 20, 2010. Premier Wen was accompanied by over 500 ranking Chinese businessmen on his visit to New Delhi.

57. Ibid.

58. See Solingen, *Nuclear Logics*, 164–186 and 213–228, on the shuttered state concept. Pakistan, in particular, has significant nonenergy trade with the broader world, including a free trade agreement with the United States.

59. Mark Landler, "U.N. Official Sees a "Wal-Mart"in Nuclear Trafficking", *New York Times,* January 23, 2004.

60. Cirincione, Wolfsthal, and Rajkumar, *Deadly Arsenals*, 248; and Corera, *Shopping for Bombs*, especially 176–194.

61. Corera, *Shopping for Bombs*, 106–126.

62. Khan was placed under house arrest, which continued for five years, after which he was freed by a Pakistani court, reportedly with the tacit political support of President Asif Ali Zardari. See Salman Masood and David E. Sanger, "Pakistan Frees Nuclear Dealer in Snub to U.S.," *New York Times*, February 7, 2009, 1.

63. Huntington, *The Clash of Civilizations*, 188.

64. North Korea reportedly earned over $4 billion from these sales during 1981–1989. See Jasper Becker, *Rogue Regime: Kim Jong-il and the Looming Threat of North Korea* (New York: Oxford University Press, 2005), 159; and Garver, *China and Iran*, 80–82.

65. In 1990 China sold $2 billion worth of arms (in current U.S. dollars). By 1995, however, China's arms exports had declined to $600 million, and by 1998 this number had further decreased to $500 million. Thus, over the course of eight years, Chinese arms exports declined by 75 percent. For more details, see Medeiros and Gill, *Chinese Arms Exports*, 6; Grimmett, *Conventional Arms Transfers to Developing Nations, 1991–1998* (Washington, DC: Library of Congress, August 4, 1999); and Richard F. Grimmett, *Conventional Arms Transfers to Developing Nations, 1990–1997* (Washington, DC: Library of Congress, July 31, 1998).

66. See Huntington, *Clash of Civilizations*, 189, on this deepening relationship.

67. Ibid.

68. Stockholm International Peace Research Institute, *SIPRI Yearbook*, 1981–2002 editions. Stockholm International Peace Research Institute, Arms Transfers Database, http://www.sipri.org/databases/armstransfers/armstransfers; and Garver, *China and Iran*, 166. The PRC supplied over $2.1 billion in weapons to Iran during the war. Its total supplies were, at least nominally, more than double the total for North Korea, the next largest supplier, and seven times that of Russia, in third place.

69. Garver, *China and Iran*, 170–194.

70. Cited in Huntington, *Clash of Civilizations*, 188.

71. Ibid.

72. Ibid., 139–155; Huntington, *Clash of Civilizations*, 190.

73. See Kenneth Katzman, *Iran: Arms and Technology Acquisitions* (Washington, DC: Library of Congress Congressional Research Service, June 22, 1998), 5.

74. Becker, *Rogue Regime*, 159.

75. Cirincione, Wolfsthal, and Rajkumar, *Deadly Arsenals*, 289. Also see Fitzpatrick, "Iran and North Korea."

76. Fitzpatrick, "Iran and North Korea," 62.

77. Ibid., 63.

78. In November 2005, *Der Spiegel* reported an Iranian deal with North Korea to exchange Iranian oil and gas supplies for North Korean assistance in developing missiles suitable for delivering nuclear warheads. See "Mullas helfen Stainsten [Mullahs Helping Stalinists]," *Der Spiegel*, November 28, 2005.

79. David E. Sanger and William J. Broad, "US Concludes North Korea Has More Nuclear Sites," *New York Times*, December 15, 2010.

80. Fitzpatrick, "Iran and North Korea," 64.

81. Braun and Chyba, "Proliferation Rings."

82. Chestnut, "Illicit Activity and Proliferation."

83. Cirincione, Wolfsthal, and Rajkumar, *Deadly Arsenals*, 290.
84. Some observers speculated that North Korea was looking to liquidate a covert highly enriched uranium program it had allegedly acquired from A. Q. Khan's Pakistan, by off-loading centrifuges to Syria. See *New York Times*, September 17, 2007; *Los Angeles Times*, January 17, 2008; and *Wall Street Journal*, June 30, 2008.
85. For a brief summary, see Andrew Scobell, *North Korea's Strategic Intentions* (Washington, DC: Strategic Studies Institute Monograph, July 2005), 64. For a summary of North Korea's provocations, see Dick K. Nanto, *North Korea: Chronology of Provocations* (Washington, DC: Library of Congress Congressional Research Service, March 18, 2003).
86. See *New York Times*, December 20, 1987.
87. "With Russian Prodding, CSTO Begins Taking Shape," *Faster Times*, October 30, 2009, http://thefastertimes.com.
88. "Iran Invited to Join CSTO," http://www.globalresearc.ca.index.php.
89. Sino-Russian relations appear to have been given momentum not only by Putin's proactive foreign-policy orientation, but also by Jiang Zemin's pro-Russian orientation. Jiang, a Russian speaker from a stint at Moscow's Stalin Auto Works in the 1950s, reportedly serenaded Putin with songs in Russian and played the piano during breaks in the initial summit session. See *Wall Street Journal*, June 18, 2001.
90. John Daly, "'Shanghai Five' Expands to Combat Islamic Radicals," *Jane's Terrorism and Security Monitor*, July 19, 2001, 2.
91. Pepe Escobar, "Beijing and Moscow beyond the SCO summit", *Al Jazeera*, June 22, 2011.
92. "Uzbekistan: Shanghai Body Countries Step Up Terror Fight Cooperation," BBC, April 29, 2010.
93. Timothy Craig, *The Shanghai Cooperation Organization: Origins and Implications* (Monterey, CA: Naval Postgraduate School, 2003), 43.
94. "Shanghai Cooperation Organization Eyes Economic, Security Cooperation," *Eurasia Daily Monitor* 2, no. 202 (October 31, 2005).
95. Xinhuanet.com, July 18, 2009.
96. "Chinese Premier Calls for Expansion of Energy Cooperation within Shanghai Body," BBC, November 25, 2010.
97. Pepe Escobar, "Beijing and Moscow beyond the SCO summit", *Al Jazeera*, June, 22, 2011, http://english.aljazeera.net/indepth/opinion/2011/06/20115216348413.html.
98. See Calder and Ye, *The Making of Northeast Asia*, 149–151.
99. CICA is an intergovernmental forum for enhancing stability across Asia, first proposed by Kazakh President Nazarbayev in 1992. It has held three major summits, including Istanbul in June 2010, which drew leaders from twenty-eight nations, including Russia's Putin, Afghanistan's Karzai, Kazakhstan's Nazarbayev, and Iran's Ahmadinejad, hosted by Turkey's Erdogan. For details, see the CICA website, http://www.s-cica.org.
100. "Russia Vows Improved Oil-Sector Tax Regime," *Platts' Oilgram News*, November 1, 2010.

101. These are especially well developed in Southeast and Northeast Asia, but such stabilizing sociopolitical networks are beginning to spread across the continent. On the Northeast Asian paradigm, see Calder and Ye, *The Making of Northeast Asia*.

102. For details, see, for example, International Energy Agency, *World Energy Outlook*, 2007 edition, which focuses specifically on the energy challenges of China and India.

103. Japan accounted for 31.4 percent and South Korea for 14.9 percent of world LNG trade in 2010. See BP, *Statistical Review of World Energy*, June 2011 edition, 28.

104. The large and expanding flows to the PRC from Turkmenistan were moving through the Turkmenistan-Uzbekistan-Kazakhstan pipeline to China. See Roman Muzalevsky, "Turkmen-Chinese Cooperation: Key to Turkmenistan's Diversification Strategy," *Eurasia Daily Monitor* 7, no. 92 (May 12, 2010): http://www.jamestown.org/programs/edm/single/?tx_ttnews[tt_news]=36369&tx_ttnews[backPid]=484&no_cache=1.

105. State Statistics Bureau of the People's Republic of China, *China Statistical Yearbook*, various editions (Beijing: China Statistical Information and Consultancy Service Center).

106. David Kerr, "Central Asian and Russian Perspectives on China's Strategic Emergence," *International Affairs* 86, no. 1 (January 2010): 127–152.

107. In 2007, Russia supplied 66.8 percent of Turkey's natural gas. See U.S. Department of Energy, Energy Information Administration, http://www.eai.doe.gov/emeu/cabs/Russia/NaturalGas.html; BP, *Statistical Review of World Energy*, 2011 edition.

108. Bhaskar Balakrishnan, "IPI: A Pipeline of Risks," *Hindu Business Line*, December 10, 2008, http://www.thehindubusinessline.com/2008/12/10/stories/2008121050010800.htm.

109. "Pakistan Keen to Import Gas from Iran," BBC, October 2, 2010.

110. "Pakistan Invites China to Join Iran-Pakistan-India Gas Pipeline," *Pakistan Daily*, October 18, 2008, http://www.daily.pk/business/businessnews/7834-pakistan-invites-china-to-join-iran-pakistan-india-gas-pipeline.html.

111. The Yadaravan field reportedly has 3.2 billion barrels of recoverable oil reserves, and 80 billion cubic meters of natural gas. The cost of the Yadaravan project was estimated by Iranian authorities at $2 billion, borne mainly by China. See "China's Sinopec, Iran ink Yadaravan deal", Chinamining.org, December 11, 2007, http://www.chinamining.org/investment/2007-12-11/1197342545d8153.html.

112. Janue Perlez, "Pakistan gives China 50 Fighter Jets", *New York Times*, May 19, 2011; and Pepe Escober, "Do the China-Pakistan pipeline shuffle", *Al Jazeera*, May 27, 2011, http://www.english.aljazeera.net/indepth/opinion/2011/05/11/2011/527194451497291.html.

113. Aditi Malhotra, "Revisiting the early years of China-Pakistan Relations", *Centre for Land Warfare Studies*, August 23, 2011, http//www.claws.in/index.php?action=master+task=933+u_id=119.

114. Ahmad Ahmadani, "China offered engineering pact for Iran pipeline, *The Nation*, August 27, 2011.

115. On the genesis of the TAPI option, see John Foster, "Afghanistan, the TAPI Pipeline, and Energy Geopolitics," *Journal of Energy Security*, April 2010, http://www.ensec.org.

116. "India inks framework pact for TAPI gas pipeline", *Hindustan Times*, September 20, 2010.

117. On the broader economic and geopolitical logic of infrastructure in Central Asia as a catalyst for peace building and economic development in Afghanistan and its environs, see Starr and Kuchins, *The Key to Success in Afghanistan*. Estimate is from the Asian Development Bank.

118. "Moscow backs TAPI gas pipeline", United Press International, January 24, 2011, http://www.upi.com/Business_News/Energy-Resources/2011/01/24/Moscow-backs -TAPI-gas-pipeline/UPI-35131295873509/.

119. Although Exxon and SODECO have not lost their combined 60 percent interest, the Russian government under Putin denied them their contractual option to extend their share an additional 20 percent once the consortium finished its investing period. Russia insisted, instead, that the 20 percent go to India, which had had nothing to do with Sakhalin I until then, as part of a 2001 deal to sell Russian aircraft to India. See "India Buys into Sakhalin Project," *Moscow Times*, January 25, 2001. Additionally, Exxon cut a deal with China to sell the non-Russian share of the gas to China, giving SODECO 30 percent of profits from sales to China, so the arrangement has imperfections from the Japanese perspective also. See "Exxon-Mobil, Gazprom Deny Sakhalin Sales Deal," *Platts Oilgram News*, May 7, 2009.

120. "Putin Opens Russian Section of ESPO Oil Line to China," *Platts Oilgram News*, August 31, 2010.

121. "Rosneft Starts Oil Deliveries to ESPO Pipeline to China," *Eurasia Review*, November 3, 2010, http://eurasiareview.com.

122. Robert Morley, "How Russia Is About to Dramatically Change the World," The Trumpet.com, http://www.thetrumpet.com.

123. "Putin Launches First Phase of ESPO Oil Line," *Oil and Gas Journal,* January 11, 2010.

124. "Purchasers Lining Up for Russia's New ESPO Blend," *Oil and Gas Journal*, March 1, 2010.

125. On these tensions, see O. B. Borisov and B. T. Koloskov, *Sino-Chinese Relations, 1945–1970* (Bloomington: Indiana University Press, 1975), 159. Forty-five percent of these advisors worked in industry, transport, and communications. Also see Deborah A. Kaples, "Soviet Advisors in China in the 1950s," in Anne Westad (ed.), *Brothers in Arms: The Rise and Fall of the Sino-Soviet Alliance, 1945–1963* (Washington, DC: Woodrow Wilson Center Press, 1998), 121.

126. Chow et al., "Pipeline Projects in Asia," 58.

127. Calder and Ye, *The Making of Northeast Asia.*

128. Slaughter, "America's Edge."

129. Urumqi, for example, has a rapidly expanding Export Processing Zone, situated next to its also rapidly expanding international airport, which China Southern uses as a hub, in direct flights to Dubai, Istanbul, Teheran, Novosibirsk, and many other Eurasian destinations. In September, 2011 it also inaugurated an annual China-Eurasia Expo, drawing participants from over 20 countries. See Xiao Ding, "Gateway to Asia", *Beijing Review*, August 11, 2011, 27.

130. Saudi Arabia's SABIC, for example, has located its Far East headquarters in Singapore.

131. See, for example, Davidson, *Dubai*, 137–176; and Preston, *Singapore in the Global System*.

132. Of the 6 million, around 890,000 are Emirati citizens. Indians (1.75 million), Pakistanis (1.25 million), and Bangladeshis (500,000) are among the other major communities. See the State Department website, http://www.state.gov/r/pa/ei/bgn/5444.htm#one.

133. Rosecrance, *The Rise of the Virtual State*.

134. Lee Kuan Yew, quoted in Morrison and Suhrke, *Strategies of Survival*, 187.

135. Leifer, *Singapore's Foreign Policy*, 157–162.

136. Ibid., 91–95, 100–108.

137. Ibid., 70–91.

138. Davidson, *Dubai*, 184–185.

139. See, for example, Moravcsik, *The Choice for Europe*.

140. On the summit, see Kahin, *The Asian-African Conference*; Wright, *The Color Curtain*; and Mackie, *Bandung 1955*.

141. Anand Giridharadas, "Saudi Arabia Pursues a 'Look-East Policy,'" *International Herald Tribune*, January 26, 2006. On Malaysia and its neighbors, see Michael D. Barr, *Cultural Politics and Asian Values: The Tepid War* (London: Routledge, 2002), especially 30–46.

142. See, for example, Simon Tisall, "Does Turkey Look East?" March 26, 2007, http://www.turkishpolitix.com.

143. Kaveh L. Afrasiabi, "Iran Steps into Enemy Territory," *Asia Times*, April 29, 2008; and Manouchehr Mottaki, "How Can Anybody Be Persian?" *Le Monde*, October 27, 2007.

144. "Russia Studies Creation of Gas Cartel," *International Herald Tribune*, February 12, 2007.

145. Apart from his Silk Road promotion activities, Goh was also central to the creation of ASEM in 1996, and the Forum for East Asia-Latin America Cooperation in 1998. See Acharya, *Singapore's Foreign Policy*, 76.

146. See "Asia-Middle East Dialogue," http://www.amed.sq/english. AMED II was held on April 5–6, 2008, at Sharm El-Sheikh, Egypt, involving fifty member countries.

147. A clear example was Putin's January 2008 state visit to Bulgaria, during which that country's participation in the $10 billion South Stream pipeline from Russia to Bulgaria under the Black Sea was confirmed. See *International Herald Tribune*, January 14, 2008.

148. *Hindu Business Line*, February 15, 2005, http://www.thehindubusinessline.com/2005/02/15/stories/2005021526903000.htm. Aiyar served as petroleum and natural gas minister from May 2004 until January 2006.

149. Shwe Gas Movement, November 2, 2006, http://www.shwe.org/docs/aiyar-proposes-iran-india-gas-pipeline-extension-to-china-via-myanmar.

150. "Remarks by HE President Kim Dae-Jung of the Republic of Korea," at the ASEM 4 Summit, September 23–24, 2002, Copenhagen, http://www.umdken; and Korea

Railroad Research Institute, *ASEM Symposium on an Iron Silk Road: Overcoming the Land Divide between Asia and Europe* (Seoul: Korea Railroad Research Institute, 2004). For North Korea, see Ministry of Unification, ROK, "Sunshine Policy for Peace and Cooperation," May 28, 2002, http://www.unikorea.go.kr/eng/.

151. The group presented its final report to the November 2001 Brunei Asean Plus Three Summit. See *Asian Economic News*, November 12, 2001.

152. *Korea Times*, March 20, 2008.

153. Len, "Japan's Central Asian Diplomacy."

154. Calder and Ye, *The Making of Northeast Asia*.

CHAPTER 8. STRATEGIC IMPLICATIONS

1. On this point, see Altman, "The Great Crash, 2008." Altman sees the United States and Europe as much more seriously impacted by the crisis than China, in particular.

2. Frieden, *Global Capitalism*; as well as Ferguson et al., *The Shock of the Global*.

3. American productivity growth has been over 2.5 percent for over a decade, more than 1 percent higher than the European average. According to the World Economic Forum, the United States ranks first in the world in innovation and second in company spending on research and development, as well as quality of research institutions. See Zakaria, *The Post-American World*, 41.

4. In 2010, U.S. defense expenditures were around $692.8 billion, or around 46 percent of the global total. See International Institute for Strategic Studies, *The Military Balance*, 2011 edition, 477.

5. In the case of Japan, this support reached well over $4.2 billion annually. See U.S. Department of Defense, *Allied Contributions to the Common Defense*, annual.

6. Calder, *Embattled Garrisons*, 4–63; Robert E. Harkavy, *Bases Abroad: The Global Foreign Military Presence* (Oxford: Oxford University Press, 1989); and Christopher Sandars, *America's Overseas Garrisons* (Oxford: Oxford University Press, 2000).

7. See Ikenberry, *Liberal Order and Imperial Ambition*.

8. In the second quarter of 2011, the U.S. dollar accounted for 32.5 percent of global reserves, while the runner-up, the euro, accounted for 14.4 percent. Figures calculated from the International Monetary Fund's Currency Composition of Official Foreign Exchange Reserves, http://www.imf.org/external/np/sta/cofer/eng/cofer.pdf.

9. The U.S. trade deficit in 2010 was $645.9 billion, while the current account deficit was $470.9 billion. Data from the Bureau of Economic Analysis. See http://bea.gov/international/index.htm.

10. Nye, *Soft Power*; Nye, *The Powers to Lead*; and Slaughter, "America's Edge."

11. Between fiscal years 2001 and 2010, the U.S. government authorized over $1.12 trillion in wartime funding, principally for Iraq and Afghanistan, with the total rising from $33.8 billion in fiscal year 2001–2002 to $171 billion in 2010. Veterans Administration medical costs rose to $2 billion in fiscal 2010 and are expected to rise steadily, together with veterans' pension costs, in future years. Continuing residual antiterrorist troop presence of 60,000 in these countries or elsewhere would add around $588

billion up to the year 2020, according to Congressional Budget Office 2010 estimates. See Belasco, *The Cost of Iraq, Afghanistan, and Other Global War on Terror Operations since 9/11*, CRS-6, and 7.

12. See, for example, Andrew Kohut (ed.), *What the World Thinks in 2002* (Washington,
DC: Pew Research Center for the People and the Press, 2002); and "Anti-Americanism
Is One 'Ism' That Thrives; Globalist," *International Herald Tribune*, November 26, 2005.

13. U.S. Department of the Treasury, http://www.treasurydirect.gov/govt/reports/pd
/histdebt/histdebt.htm.

14. Debt was also rising more rapidly, on an annual basis. In 1990 the U.S. annual current account deficit was $79 billion, roughly one-tenth that of 2005. See http://bea
.gov/bea/di/table1.xls, which provides data on the balance on the current account
from 1960–2005.

15. Mandelbaum, *The Frugal Superpower*, 18.

16. Ibid., 9–34.

17. Ibid., 13; and Office of Management and Budget, *Budget of the U.S. Government*, Fiscal
Year 2011, 146.

18. Mandelbaum, *The Frugal Superpower*, 146.

19. 2010 U.S. Government unfunded obligations were $61.6 trillion, and U.S. GDP for
2010 was around $14.5 trillion. See Dennis Cauchon, US Funding for Future Prom-
ises lags by Trillions", *USA Today*, June 13, 2011.

20. Mandelbaum, *The Frugan Superpower,* 20.

21. Russian foreign exchange reserves, for example, grew more than sixteen-fold between
2000 and 2011, from $24.2 billion to $449.5 billion—the painful 2008 global financial
crisis notwithstanding. See International Monetary Fund, *International Financial
Statistics*, annual.

22. China's share of global foreign exchange reserves in 2009 was 46.2 percent, including Hong Kong, and Japan's was 19.2 percent, bringing their combined share to 65.3
percent. See ibid.

23. Ibid., figures for second quarter, 2010.

24. Ibid. The unallocated share of LDC reserves rose, meanwhile, from 36.1 percent to
44.7 percent, and the share held in euros rose from 12.2 percent to 14.4 percent.

25. Iran took the additional step of ending all oil sales in dollars at the end of March
2007. See Jerome R. Corsi, "Iran Leads Attack against the U.S. Dollar," *Global Policy
Forum*, April 12, 2007.

26. As of the first quarter of 2010, India was the top official purchaser of gold (747.7 tons),
followed by China (472.3 tons). See "Ad Campaign Spurring China's Big Gold Rush,"
Globe and Mail (Canada), July 2, 2010.

27. Investopedia, http://www.investopedia.com/terms/sovereign_wealth_fund.asp.

28. Council on Foreign Relations, "Sovereign Wealth Funds," http://www.cfr.org/
publication/15251. Nations also hold sovereign wealth through international reserves,
public pension funds, and state-owned enterprises.

29. "Has Anything Changed in the Industry?" *Business Times Singapore*, June 2, 2010.

30. Anders Åslund, "The Truth about Sovereign Wealth Funds," *Foreign Policy*, December 2007, http://www.foreignpolicy.com/story/cms.php?story_id=4056.

31. See Sovereign Wealth Fund Institute. *Fund Rankings*, www.swfinstitute.org/fund-rankings/.

32. As of November, 2010, 58 percent of sovereign-wealth fund inflow was oil and gas related, according to the Sovereign Wealth Fund Institute. See www.swfinstitute.org/fud-rankings/.

33. Of UAE oil exports, 1.58 million barrels per day, or 67 percent, went to Japan in 2007, which also took 2.21 barrels per day from Saudi Arabia, or 32 percent of Saudi exports, compared to 26 percent for the rest of Asia, 22 percent for the United States, and 12 percent for Europe. Data are from OPEC. See gulfnews.com, July 11, 2008.

34. Embassy of UAE to the USA, http://www.uae-embassy.org/node/149.

35. China's foreign exchange reserves were $3.2 trillion as of September, 2011, not including Hong Kong. See PRC State Administration of Foreign Exchange, September, 2011.

36. World Trade Organization, http://stat.wto.org/.

37. The China Investment Corporation is the second largest of three major Chinese SWFs. See Daniel Gross, "Exec Desperately Seeks SWF," *Newsweek*, January 7, 2008.

38. Patrick Hosking, "World Order Is Changing as Old Captains Bow to the New Kings," *Times*, December 22, 2007; and "Dubai Fund Scoops Up a 'Significant Stake' in Sony," *Independent*, November 27, 2007. Dubai International Capital is believed to have held around 3 percent of Sony shares, worth around $1.5 billion.

39. "Japanese Firms Go Door to Door to Woo Middle Eastern Investors," *Nikkei Weekly*, January 21, 2008.

40. *Wall Street Journal*, May 19, 2008.

41. "The Rise of the Gulf," *Economist*, April 26, 2008, 38. Iran, for example, has already elected to denominate its oil exports in euros.

42. In 2011 the GCC included six nations—Saudi Arabia, the UAE, Bahrain, Qatar, Kuwait, and Oman.

43. The 2008–2009 U.S. financial crisis and the subsequent 2010 euro crisis do appear to have stimulated renewed discussion in the Gulf of GCC currency integration, and the creation of a common unit, dubbed the "Gulfo," although substantial issues remain such as location of a potential central bank, which the Saudis and some others expect to be in Riyadh. A GCC currency unit, if achieved, could have substantial credibility as a pricing unit, given the combined $1.2 billion GDP of the Gulf nations and their massive proven oil reserves, amounting to 40 percent of the global total. See "How Much Is That Barrel in 'Gulfos'? Dollar at Risk of Being Displaced as Pricing Currency for Oil Contracts," *Daily Telegraph*, December 16, 2009.

44. "Rapid Growth of Asian SWFs Creates Concern," *Nikkei Weekly*, February 18, 2008.

45. In World War I, the United States actually provided, from its domestic reserves, 90 percent of the entire consumption of the Allied war effort, once it had entered the war. See Palmer, *Guardians of the Gulf*, 14.

46. Ibid., 15–19, 52–59.

47. John Deutch, "The Good News about Gas", *Foreign Affairs*, January/February, 2011, 82–93.

48. See Yergin, *The Prize*; and Krasner, *Defending the National Interest.*
49. In 2010, global proven oil reserves were 1.38 trillion barrels, with national oil companies that allowed no equity participation by foreign firms controlling over 80 percent of the total. Partially or fully privatized Russian oil companies controlled another 6 percent. By comparison, prominent Western multinational oil companies— Exxon Mobil, BP, Chevron, and the Royal Dutch Shell Group—ranked 14th, 17th, 19th, and 25th, respectively, and now control less than 10 percent of the world's oil and gas resource base. See Rice University James A. Baker III Institute for Public Policy, *The Changing Role of National Oil in International Energy Markets* (Houston: Baker Institute Policy Report No. 35, April, 2007), 1, http://bakerinstitute.org/Pubs/BI%20Rep 35.pdf; and BP, *Statistical Review of World Energy*, 2011 edition.
50. International Monetary Fund, *Direction of Trade Statistics*, http://www.imfstatistics.org.
51. See Robert E. Scott, "The Walmart Effect," *Economic Policy Institute Issue Brief* 235, June 26, 2007, http://www.epi.org/content/cfm.ib235.
52. Anoop Singh, director of the IMF's Asia and Pacific Department, maintains that, based on expected trends, within five years Asia's economy will be about 50 percent larger than it is today (in terms of purchasing power parity), account for more than a third of global output, and be comparable in size to the economies of the United States and Europe. By 2030, Asian GDP will exceed that of the Group of Seven industrialized countries. See Anoop Singh, "Asia Leading the Way," *Finance and Development* 47, no. 2 (June 2010): 4, http://www.imf.org/external/pubs/ft/fandd/2010/06/pdf/fd0610.pdf.
53. In 2010, Korean exports to China reached $138.0 billion, while Korean exports to the United States was only $50.6 billion. See International Monetary Fund, *Direction of Trade Statistics*, http://www.imfstatistics.org.
54. Ibid.
55. Japan and South Korea have been charter members, as noted earlier, of the San Francisco system of political-economic relations between the United States and its allies in the Pacific, established following the San Francisco peace treaty of 1951 ending World War II in the Pacific, enjoying preferential access to the U.S. market. China became a de facto member following Nixon's visit there in 1972, and Sino-American cross-recognition in 1979. See Calder, "Securing Security through Prosperity."
56. International Monetary Fund, *Direction of Trade Statistics.* The comparison is between 2009 and 1999.
57. U.S. Department of Energy, Energy Information Administration, http://www.eia.doe.gov/emeu/cabs/Sudan/Oil.html.
58. In 2008, Japan, with 102,000 barrels per day, was the second-largest importer of Sudanese oil, after China, which imported 214,000 barrels per day. See *Sudan Tribune*, September 18, 2009, http://sudantribune.com.
59. "Uzbek Troops Reclaim Town from Rebels," AP, May 19, 2005, http://www.msnbc.msn.com/id/7883837/. "Preliminary Findings on the Events in Andijan, Uzbekistan, 13 May 2005," Organization for Security and Cooperation in Europe and Office

of Democratic Institutions and Human Rights, June 20, 2005, http://www.osce.org /documents/odihr/2005/06/15233_en.pdf.

60. "The Dragon and the Tyrant; Uzbekistan and China," *Economist*, June 4, 2005; and Jeremy Page, "Mayhem Follows Uzbek Massacre," *Times*, May 16, 2005.

61. On the details, see Bo Kong, "The Geopolitics of the Myanmar-China Oil and Gas Pipelines," in Edward Chow (ed.), *Pipeline Politics in Asia: The Intersection of Demand, Energy Markets, and Supply Routes*. Seattle: National Bureau of Asian Research Special Report 23, September, 2010, 55–65.

62. See, for example, Huntington, *The Third Wave*.

63. In the three most populous nations of continental Asia—India, China, and Russia— Muslim populations number 150, 20, and 15 million people respectively, while most of the others feature Islamic majorities.

64. See Ahmed Rashid, *Taliban* (New Haven, CT: Yale University Press, 2000); Rashid, *Jihad*; Nasr, *The Shia Revival*; and Charles Allen, *God's Terrorists: The Wahhabi Cult and the Hidden Roots of Modern Jihad* (New York: Da Capo, 2006).

65. Ikenberry and Slaughter, "A World of Liberty under Law."

66. Barnett, *The Pentagon's New Map*.

67. Nineteen of twenty-nine ballistic missile-producing nations are located in this area. See Cirincione, Wolfstahl, and Rajkumar, *Deadly Arsenals*, 15.

68. Several, such as Syria, South Korea, and Taiwan, are, however, in geographical locations where even such short-range missiles can be deadly and destabilizing, and several also have sympathetic ties with radical nongovernmental groups. Any missiles of over 300-kilometer range, capable of carrying 500-kilogram payloads, are subject to the Missile Technology Control Regime, however, http://www.mtcr.info.html.

69. Ibid., 11.

70. Ibid., 13.

71. Campbell, Einhorn, and Reiss, *The Nuclear Tipping Point*.

72. For the classic statement of this problem, see Huntington, *Political Order in Changing Societies*.

73. Nasr, *The Shia Revival*; and Dilip Hiro, *After Empire: The Birth of a Multipolar World* (New York: Nation Books, 2010).

74. To that extent, Solingen's distinction between the strategic proclivities of shuttered and nonshuttered states is tenable. See Solingen, *Nuclear Logics*.

75. On the concept of the reactive state, see Calder, "Japanese Foreign Economic Policy Formation."

76. Roy, *Globalized Islam*.

CHAPTER 9. PROSPECTS AND POLICY IMPLICATIONS

1. Emmott, *Rivals*, 25.

2. Roy, *Globalized Islam*.

3. For useful reviews, see Gilpin, *War and Change in International Politics*; and Gilpin, *The Political Economy of International Relations*.

4. Frost, *Asia's New Regionalism*.

5. Kaplan, *Monsoon*.

6. On the classic explanations, see Gilpin, *War and Change in International Relations*; and Gilpin, *The Political Economy of International Relations*.

7. Keohane, *After Hegemony*; Nye and Donahue, *Governance in a Globalizing World*; and Ikenberry and Slaughter, "A World of Liberty under Law."

8. Kissinger, *A World Restored*; and Kissinger, *Diplomacy*.

9. Ikenberry, *After Victory*.

10. Andrew C. Kuchins and Thomas Sanderson, "Central Asia's Northern Exposure," *New York Times*, August 5, 2009.

11. Starr and Kuchins, *The Key to Success in Afghanistan*.

12. NATO forces deployed in connection with the Afghan conflict in mid-2010, for example, required 300 percent more supplies in 2010 than three years previously. See Center for Strategic and International Studies, Central Asia and Afghanistan podcast, June 22, 2010.

13. On the strategic importance of those maritime ties, see Kent E. Calder. *Pacific Defense*; and Robert D. Kaplan. *Monsoon*.

14. See, for example, Richard Weitz, "Afghanistan: New Approaches Needed to Defeat Insurgency," Eurasianet.org, April 16, 2008; and John J. Kruzel, "Iraq Counterinsurgency Lessons Apply to Afghanistan, Petraeus Says," http://www.defense.gov/news/articleraspx?id=54746.

15. On this problem, see Sigal, *Disarming Strangers*.

16. The Asian Development Bank is especially strategic as a vehicle for multilateral policymaking in Eurasia as the United States and Japan together have majority voting rights. It serves, importantly, as secretariat for the Central Asian Regional Economic Cooperation (CAREC) Program, which has been instrumental in infrastructure feasibility studies, and in streamlining border-clearance procedures. On the ADB's assessment and aspirations, see Asian Development Bank, *Infrastructure for a Seamless Asia*.

17. Calder and Ye, *The Making of Northeast Asia*.

18. Craig Whitlock, "Cloudy Germany a Powerhouse in Solar Energy," *Washington Post*, May 5, 2007.

19. On the importance of broadening the definition of alliance to generate common socioeconomic equities with allies, see Calder, *Pacific Alliance*, especially 216–238.

APPENDIX A

1. The South Yolotan-Osman field is reputedly the fifth largest on earth, with between 4 and 14 trillion cubic meters of reserves. See Guy Chazan, "Turkmenistan Gas Field Is One of World's Largest," *Wall Street Journal*, October 16, 2008.

Bibliography

Acharya, Amitav. *Singapore's Foreign Policy: The Search for Regional Order.* Singapore: World Scientific Publishing, 2008.

Acharya, Amitav, and Alastair Iain Johnston (eds.). *Crafting Cooperation: Regional International Institutions in Comparative Perspective.* Cambridge: Cambridge University Press, 2007.

Acheson, Dean. *Present at the Creation: My Years at the State Department.* New York: Norton, 1969.

Agnew, John A. *Geopolitics: Re-visioning World Politics.* London: Routledge, 1998.

Aggarwal, Vinod K. (ed.). *Institutional Designs for a Complex World: Bargaining, Linkages, and Nesting.* Ithaca: Cornell University Press, 1998.

Aggarwal, Vinod K., and Edward A. Fogarty (eds.). *European Union Trade Strategies: Between Globalism and Regionalism.* London: Palgrave, 2004.

Aggarwal, Vinod K., and Charles E. Morrison. *Asia-Pacific Crossroads.* New York: St. Martin's, 1998.

Aitken, Jonathan. *Nazarbayev and the Making of Kazakhstan.* London: Continuum, 2009.

Allison, Graham, and Philip Zelikow. *Essence of Decision* (second edition). New York: Longman, 1999.

Altman, Roger C. "The Great Crash, 2008: A Geopolitical Setback for the West." *Foreign Affairs* 88, no. 1 (2009): 2–14.

Amsden, Alice. *Asia's Next Giant: South Korea and Late Industrialization.* Oxford: Oxford University Press, 1989.

Asano Risaburō. *Nichidokuso Tairiku Burokku Ron: Sono Chiseigakuteki Kōsatsu* (On the Japanese-German-Soviet Continental Bloc: Geopolitical Observations). Tokyo: Tokaidō, 1941.

Asian Development Bank. *Emerging Asian Regionalism: A Partnership for Shared Prosperity.* Manila: Asian Development Bank Institute, 2008.

———. *Infrastructure for a Seamless Asia.* Manila: Asian Development Bank Institute, 2009.

Askari, Hossein. "Iran's Economic Policy Dilemma." *International Journal* 59, no. 3 (Summer 2004): 655–668.

Aydin, Cemil. *The Politics of Anti-Westernism in Asia: Visions of World Order in Pan-Islamic and Pan-Asian Thought.* New York: Columbia University Press, 2007.

Barnett, Thomas P. M. *The Pentagon's New Map: War and Peace in the Twenty-First Century.* New York: G.P. Putnam's Sons, 2004.

Barnhardt, Michael. *Japan Prepares for Total War: The Search for Economic Security, 1919–1941.* Ithaca, NY: Cornell University Press, 1987.

Bassin, Mark. "Race Contra Space: The Conflict between German 'Geopolitik' and National Socialism." *Political Geography Quarterly* 6, no. 2 (1987): 115–134.

Beckwith, Christopher I. *The Tibetan Empire in Central Asia.* Princeton, NJ: Princeton University Press, 1987.

Belasco, Amy. *The Cost of Iraq, Afghanistan, and Other Global War on Terror Operations since 9/11.* Washington, DC: Congressional Research Service, 2010.

Bix, Herbert B. *Hirohito and the Making of Modern Japan.* New York: Harper Perennial, 2001.

Bobrick, Benson. *East of the Sun: The Epic Conquest and Tragic History of Siberia.* New York: Poseidon Press, 1992.

Bose, Sisir K., and Sugata Bose (eds.). *The Essential Writings of Netaji Subjas Chandra Bose.* Delhi: Oxford University Press, 1998.

Boulnois, Luce. *Silk Road: Monks, Warriors, and Merchants.* Hong Kong: Odyssey Books, 2004.

BP. *Statistical Review of World Energy.* London: BP, annual.

Braun, Chaim, and Christopher F. Chyba. "Proliferation Rings: New Challenges to the Nuclear Nonproliferation Regime." *International Security* 29, no. 2 (Autumn 2004): 5–49.

Breslin, Shaun. "Understanding China's Regional Rise: Interpretations, Identities, and Implications." *International Affairs* 85, no. 4 (July 2009): 817–835.

Broadman, Harry G. *Africa's Silk Road: China and India's Economic Frontier.* Washington, DC: World Bank, 2007.

Bronson, Rachel. "Rethinking Religion: The Legacy of the U.S.-Saudi Relationship." *Washington Quarterly* 24, no. 4 (Autumn 2005): 121–137.

———. *Thicker Than Oil: America's Uneasy Partnership with Saudi Arabia.* Oxford: Oxford University Press, 2006.

Brown, Anthony C. *Oil, God, and Gold: The Story of Aramco and the Saudi Kings.* New York: Houghton Mifflin, 1999.

Brzezinski, Zbigniew. "A Geo-strategy for Eurasia." *Foreign Affairs* 76, no. 5 (September/October 1997): 50–64.

———. *The Grand Chessboard: American Primacy and Its Geostrategic Imperatives.* New York: Basic Books, 1997.

Calder, Kent E. "Asia's Empty Tank." *Foreign Affairs* 75, no. 2 (March/April 1996): 55–68.

———. *China's Energy Diplomacy and Its Geopolitical Implications.* Washington, DC: Reischauer Center for East Asian Studies Asia-Pacific Policy Papers, No. 3, 2006.

———. *Embattled Garrisons: Comparative Base Politics and American Globalism.* Princeton, NJ: Princeton University Press, 2007.

———. "Japanese Foreign Economic Policy: Explaining the Reactive State." *World Politics* 40, no. 4 (July 1988): 517–541.

———. "Japan's Energy Angst and the Caspian Great Game." *NBR Analysis* 12, no. 1 (March 2001).

———. "Japan's Energy Angst: Asia's Changing Energy Prospects and the View from Tokyo." *Strategic Analysis* 32, no. 1 (January 2008): 123–129.

———. *Korea's Energy Insecurities: Comparative and Regional Perspectives.* Washington, DC: Korea Economic Institute Special Studies Series, Number 3, 2005.

———. *Pacific Alliance: Reviving U.S.-Japan Relations.* New Haven, CT: Yale University Press, 2009.

———. *Pacific Defense.* New York: William Morrow, 1996.

———. "Securing Security through Prosperity: The San Francisco System in Comparative Perspective." *Pacific Review* 17, no. 1 (January 2004): 135–157.

———. *Strategic Capitalism: Private Business and Public Purpose in Japanese Industrial Finance.* Princeton, NJ: Princeton University Press, 1993.

Calder, Kent E., and Roy Hofheinz Jr. *The Eastasia Edge.* New York: Basic Books, 1982.

Calder, Kent E., and Min Ye. *The Making of Northeast Asia.* Stanford, CA: Stanford University Press, 2010.

———. "Regionalism and Critical Junctures: Explaining the 'Organization Gap' in Northeast Asia." *Journal of East Asian Studies* 4, no. 2 (May–August 2004): 191–226.

Campbell, Kurt M., Robert J. Einhorn, and Mitchell B. Reiss (eds.). *The Nuclear Tipping Point.* Washington, DC: Brookings Institution, 2004.

Carr, Edward Hallet. *German-Soviet Relations between the Two World Wars.* Baltimore: Johns Hopkins University Press, 1951.

Chamberlin, William Henry. *Japan over Asia.* Boston: Little, Brown, 1937.

Chestnut, Sheena. "Illicit Activity and Proliferation: North Korean Smuggling Networks." *International Security* 32, no. 1 (Summer 2007): 80–111.

Chow, Edward C., Leigh E. Hendrix, Mikkal E. Herberg, Shoichi Itoh, Bo Kong, Marie Lall, and Paul Stevens. "Pipeline Politics in Asia: The Intersection of Demand, Energy Markets, and Supply Routes." *NBR Special Report* 23 (September 2010).

Cirincione, Joseph, Jon B. Wolfsthal, and Miriam Rajkumar. *Deadly Arsenals: Nuclear, Biological, and Chemical Threats* (second edition). Washington, DC: Carnegie Endowment for International Peace, 2005.

Cohen, Warren I. *East Asia at the Center: Four Thousand Years of Engagement with the World.* New York: Columbia University Press, 2000.

Cohen-Tanugi, Laurent. *The Shape of the World to Come: Charting the Geopolitics of a New Century*. New York: Columbia University Press, 2008.

Collins, John M. *Military Geography*. Washington, DC: National Defense University Press, 1998.

Cordesman, Anthony H., and Nawaf E. Obaid. *National Security in Saudi Arabia: Threats, Responses, and Challenges*. Washington, DC: Center for Strategic and International Studies, 2005.

Corera, Gordon. *Shopping for Bombs: Nuclear Proliferation, Global Insecurity, and the Rise and Fall of the A.Q. Khan Network*. Oxford: Oxford University Press, 2006.

Coronil, Fernando. *The Magical State: Nature, Money, and Modernity in Venezuela*. Chicago: University of Chicago Press, 1997.

Crystal, Jill. *Oil and Politics in the Gulf: Rulers and Merchants in Kuwait and Qatar*. New York: Cambridge University Press, 1990.

Curzon, George N. *Persia and the Persian Question*. London: Longmans, Green, 1892.

Danspeckgruber, Wolfgang (ed.). *Perspectives on the Russian State in Transition*. Princeton,NJ: Liechtenstein Institute on Self-Determination, 2006.

Davidson, Christopher M. *Dubai: The Vulnerability of Success*. New York: Columbia University Press, 2008.

De Blij, Harm. *The Power of Place: Geography, Destiny, and Globalization's Rough Landscape*. New York: Oxford University Press, 2009.

Dorpalen, Andreas. *The World of General Haushofer*. New York: Farrar and Rinehart, 1984.

Dower, John. *Embracing Defeat*. New York: W.W. Norton, 1999.

Dual, R. P. *The Impact of the Russo-Japanese War on Indian Politics*. Delhi: S. Chand, 1966.

Duara, Prasenjit. "Transnationalism and the Predicament of Sovereignity: China, 1900–1945." *American Historical Review* 102, no. 4 (1997): 1030–1051.

Eckert, Carter J. *Offspring of Empire: The Koch'ang Kims and the Colonial Origins of Korean Capitalism, 1876–1945*. Seattle: University of Washington Press, 1991.

Economy, Elizabeth. *The River Runs Black: The Environmental Challenge to China's Future*. Ithaca, NY: Cornell University Press, 2004.

Ekonomisuto Henshū bu (ed.). *Sengo Sangyō Shi e no Shōgen: Energī Kakumei to Bōei Seisan no Kiseki* (Testimony to Postwar Industrial History: Tracing Energy Revolution and Defense Production). Tokyo: Mainichi Shimbun Sha, 1978.

Emmott, Bill. *Rivals: How the Power Struggle between China, India, and Japan Will Shape Our Next Decade*. Orlando, FL: Harcourt, 2008.

Encarnation, Dennis. *Dislodging Multinationals: India's Strategy in Comparative Perspective*. Ithaca, NY: Cornell University Press, 1989.

Esenbel, Selcuk. "Japan's Global Claim to Asia and the World of Islam: Transnational Nationalism and World Power, 1900–1945." *American Historical Review* 109, no. 4 (October 2004): 1140–1170.

Esfahani, Hadi Salehi, and Farzad Taheripour. "Hidden Public Expenditures and the Economy in Iran." *International Journal of Middle East Studies* 34, no. 4 (November 2002): 691–718.

Esposito, John L. (ed.). *The Iranian Revolution: Its Global Impact.* Miami: Florida International University Press, 1990.

Ewans, Martin. *Afghanistan: A Short History of Its People and Politics.* New York: Harper Collins, 2002.

Ferguson, Niall. *Empire: The Rise and Demise of the British World Order and the Lessons for Global Power.* New York: Basic Books, 2002.

Ferguson, Niall, Charles S. Maier, Erez Manela, and Daniel J. Sargent (eds.). *The Shock of the Global: The 1970s in Perspective.* Cambridge, MA: Harvard University Press, 2010.

Fitzpatrick, Mark. "Iran and North Korea: The Proliferation Nexus." *Survival* 48, no. 1 (2006): 61–80.

Frank, Andre Gunder. *Re-Orient: Global Economy in the Asian Age.* Berkeley: University of California Press, 1998.

Fravel, M. Taylor. "Regime Insecurity and International Cooperation: Explaining China's Compromises in Territorial Disputes." *International Security* 30, no. 2 (Autumn 2005): 46–83.

Frieden, Jeffrey A. *Global Capitalism: Its Fall and Rise in the Twentieth Century.* New York: W.W. Norton, 2006.

Friedman, Thomas L. "The First Law of Petropolitics." *Foreign Policy,* May/June 2006, 28–34.

———. *Hot, Flat, and Crowded: Why We Need a Green Revolution and How It Can Renew America.* New York: Farrar, Straus, and Giroux, 2008.

———. *The World Is Flat: A Brief History of the 21st Century.* New York: Farrar, Straus, and Giroux, 2005.

Frost, Ellen L. *Asia's New Regionalism.* Boulder, CO: Lynne Rienner, 2008.

Frye, Richard N. *The Heritage of Central Asia: From Antiquity to the Turkish Expansion.* Princeton, NJ: Markus Wiener, 1996.

Gaddis, John Lewis. *Strategies of Containment: A Critical Appraisal of American National Security Policy during the Cold War* (revised edition). Oxford: Oxford University Press, 2005.

Garver, John W. *China and Iran: Ancient Partners in a Post-imperial World.* Seattle: University of Washington Press, 2006.

———. "Development of China's Overland Transportation Links with Central, Southwest, and South Asia." *China Quarterly,* March 2006, 1–22.

Garver, John W., Flynt Leverett, and Hillary Leverett. *Moving (Slightly) Closer to Iran: China's Shifting Calculus for Managing Its Persian Gulf Dilemma.* Washington, DC: Reischauer Center for East Asian Studies, 2009.

Gasiorowski, Mark J., and Malcolm Byrne (eds.). *Mohammad Mosaddeq and the 1953 Coup in Iran.* Syracuse, NY: Syracuse University Press, 2004.

Gilmour, David. *Curzon: Imperial Statesman.* New York: Farrar, Straus, and Giroux, 1994.

Gilpin, Robert. *The Political Economy of International Relations.* Princeton, NJ: Princeton University Press, 1987.

———. *War and Change in World Politics.* Cambridge: Cambridge University Press, 1981.

Goldman, Marshall I. *Petrostate: Putin, Power, and the New Russia.* Oxford: Oxford University Press, 2008.

Goldstein, Avery. *Rising to the Challenge: China's Grand Strategy and International Security*. Stanford, CA: Stanford University Press, 2005.

Goncharov, Sergei, John Lewis, and Xue Litai. *Uncertain Partners: Stalin, Mao, and the Korean War*. Stanford, CA: Stanford University Press, 2005.

Goodman, David S. G. (ed.). *China's Campaign to Open Up the West: National, Provincial, and Local Perspectives*. Cambridge: Cambridge University Press, 2004.

Gourevitch, Peter. *Politics in Hard Times: Comparative Responses to International Economic Crisis*. Ithaca, NY: Cornell University Press, 1993.

———. "Second Image Reversed: The International Sources of Domestic Politics." *International Organization* 32, no. 4 (Autumn 1978): 881–912.

Grousset, Rene. *The Empire of the Steppes: A History of Central Asia*. New Brunswick, NJ: Rutgers University Press, 1970.

Grygiel, Jakub J. *Great Powers and Geopolitical Change*. Baltimore: Johns Hopkins University Press, 2006.

Harrison, Selig S. *Seabed Petroleum in Northeast Asia: Conflict or Cooperation?* Washington, DC: Woodrow Wilson International Center for Scholars Asia Program, 2005.

Hay, Stephen. *Asian Ideas of East and West: Tagore and His Critics in Japan, China, and India*. Cambridge, MA: Harvard University Press, 1970.

Hayashi, Ryoichi. *The Silk Road and the Shoso-in*. New York: Weatherhill, 1975.

Held, David, Anthony McGrew, David Goldblatt, and Jonathan Perraton. *Global Transformations: Politics, Economics, and Culture*. Stanford, CA: Stanford University Press, 1999.

Hertog, Steffen. *Princes, Brokers, and Bureaucrats: Oil and the State in Saudi Arabia*. Ithaca, NY: Cornell University Press, 2010.

Hiro, Dilip. *Inside Central Asia*. New York: Peter Mayer, 2009.

Hopkirk, Peter. *The Great Game: The Struggle for Empire in Central Asia*. New York: Kodansha International, 1994.

———. *Setting the East Ablaze: Lenin's Dream of an Empire in Asia*. New London: J. Murray, 1984.

Hotta, Eri. *Pan-Asianism and Japan's War, 1931–1945*. New York: Palgrave Macmillan, 2007.

Hu Angang, Kang Xiaoguang, and Wang Shaoguang. *The Political Economy of Uneven Development: The Case of China*. New York: Eastgate Books, 2000.

Huntington, Samuel P. *The Clash of Civilizations and the Remaking of World Order*. New York: Simon and Schuster, 1996.

———. *Political Order in Changing Societies*. New Haven: Yale University Press, 1968.

———. *The Third Wave: Democratization in the Late Twentieth Century*. Norman: University of Oklahoma Press, 1992.

Ikenberry, G. John. *After Victory*. Princeton, NJ: Princeton University Press, 2001.

———. *Liberal Order and Imperial Ambition: Essays on American Power and International Order*. Malden, MA: Polity, 2006.

Ikenberry, G. John, and Anne-Marie Slaughter. "A World of Liberty under Law." *Global Asia* 2, no. 1 (April 2007): 112–118.

Inoguchi, Takashi. *Global Change: A Japanese Perspective*. New York: Palgrave, 2001.

International Energy Agency. *Energy Balances of OECD Countries*. Paris: International Energy Agency, annual.

————. *World Energy Outlook*. Paris: International Energy Agency, 2007–2011.

International Institute for Strategic Studies. *The Military Balance*. London: International Institute for Strategic Studies, annual.

International Monetary Fund. *Direction of Trade Statistics*. Washington, DC: International Monetary Fund, annual, 1980–2010.

————. *International Financial Statistics*. Washington, DC: International Monetary Fund, annual.

Jansen, Marius B. *The Japanese and Sun Yat-sen*. Stanford, CA: Stanford University Press, 1954.

————. *The Making of Modern Japan*. Cambridge, MA: Harvard University Press, 2000.

Jha, Prem Shankar. *The Perilous Road to the Market: The Political Economy of Reform in Russia, India, and China*. London: Pluto Press, 2002.

Johnson, Chalmers. *An Instance of Treason: Ozaki Hotsumi and the Sorge Spy Ring*. Stanford, CA: Stanford University Press, 1990.

————. *Japan's Public Policy Companies*. Washington, DC: American Enterprise Institute of Public Policy Research, 1978.

————. *MITI and the Japanese Miracle*. Stanford, CA: Stanford University Press, 1982.

Johnson, Rob. *Oil, Islam, and Conflict: Central Asia since 1945*. Trowbridge, Wiltshire: Cromwell Press, 2007.

Joshi, Nirmala (ed.). *Reconnecting India and Central Asia: Emerging Security and Economic Dimensions*. Washington, DC: Central Asia–Caucasus Institute Silk Road Studies Program, 2010.

Kahin, George McTurnan. *The Asian-African Conference: Bandung, Indonesia, April 1955*. Ithaca, NY: Cornell University Press, 1956.

Kaplan, Robert D. *Monsoon: The Indian Ocean and the Future of American Power*. New York: Random House, 2010.

Karl, Terry Lynn. *The Paradox of Plenty: Oil Booms and Petro-states*. Berkeley: University of California Press, 1997.

Karrar, Hasan H. *The New Silk Road Diplomacy: China's Central Asian Foreign Policy since the Cold War*. Vancouver: UBC Press, 2009.

Katzenstein, Peter J. *The Culture of National Security*. New York: Columbia University Press, 1996.

Katznelson, Ira, and Helen Milner (eds.). *Political Science: State of the Discipline*. New York: W.W. Norton, 2002.

Kawanishi, Masaaki. *Toa Chiseigaku no Kōsō* (Structural Oriental Geopolitics). Tokyo: Jitsugyō no Nihonsha, 1942.

Keddie, Nikki R. *Modern Iran: Roots and Results of Revolution* (updated edition). New Haven, CT: Yale University Press, 2006.

Kemp, Geoffrey. *The East Moves West: India, China, and Asia's Growing Presence in the Middle East*. Washington, DC: Brookings Institution, 2010.

Kennan, George F. *Memoires*. Boston: Little, Brown, 1962.

Kennedy, Paul (ed.). *Grand Strategies in War and Peace*. New Haven, CT: Yale University Press, 1991.

————. *The Rise and Fall of the Great Powers*. New York: Random House, 1987.

Keohane, Robert. *After Hegemony: Cooperation and Discord in the World Political Economy*. Princeton, NJ: Princeton University Press, 1984.

Keohane, Robert, and Joseph Nye. *Power and Interdependence*. Glenview, IL: Scott, Foresman, 1989.

Kimura, Hiroshi. *Pūtin no Enerugī Senryaku* (Putin's Energy Strategy). Tokyo: Hokusei-dō, 2008.

Kinzer, Stephen. *All the Shah's Men: An American Coup and the Roots of Middle East Terror*. New York: John Wiley, 2003.

———. *Reset: Iran, Turkey, and America's Future*. New York: Times Books, 2010.

Kissinger, Henry. *On China*. New York: The Penguin Press, 2011.

———. *Diplomacy*. New York: Simon and Schuster, 1994.

———. *A World Restored*. Gloucester, MA: Peter Smith, 1973.

Klare, Michael T. *Rising Powers, Shrinking Planet: The New Geopolitics of Energy*. New York: Henry Holt, 2008.

Kochan, Lionel. *Russia and the Weimar Republic*. Cambridge: Bowes and Bowes, 1954.

Kohut, Andrew, and Bruce Stokes. *America against the World: How We Are Different and How We Are Disliked*. New York: Times Books, 2006.

Kong, Bo. *China's International Petroleum Policy*. Santa Barbara, CA: ABC-Clio, 2010.

Krasner, Stephen. *Defending the National Interest: Raw Materials Investments and U.S. Foreign Policy*. Princeton, NJ: Princeton University Press, 1978.

——— (ed.). *International Regimes*. Ithaca, NY: Cornell University Press, 1983.

Kupchan, Charles A. *How Enemies Become Friends: The Sources of Stable Peace*. Princeton, NJ: Princeton University Press, 2010.

———. *The Persian Gulf and the West: The Dilemmas of Security*. Boston: Allen and Unwin, 1987.

Kurzman, Charles. *The Unthinkable Revolution in Iran*. Cambridge, MA: Harvard University Press, 2004.

Larner, John. *Marco Polo and the Discovery of the World*. New Haven, CT: Yale University Press, 1999.

Larrabee, F. Stephen. "Turkey Rediscovers the Middle East." *Foreign Affairs* 86, no. 4 (2007): 103–114.

Larrabee, F. Stephen, and Ian O. Lesser. *Turkish Foreign Policy in an Age of Uncertainty*. Santa Monica, CA: Rand Center for Middle East Public Policy, 2003.

Laruelle, Marlene. *Russian Eurasianism: An Ideology of Empire*. Baltimore: Johns Hopkins University Press, 2008.

Latif, Asad-ul Iqbal. *Between Rising Powers: China, Singapore, and India*. Singapore: Institute of Southeast Asian Studies, 2007.

Layne, Christopher. "From Preponderance to Offshore Balancing: America's Future Grand Strategy." *International Security* 22, no. 1 (Summer 1997): 86–124.

Lebkicker, Roy, George Rentz, and Max Steinecke. *Aramco Handbook*. Dhahran: Arabian American Oil Company, 1960.

Lechner, Frank J., and John Boli (eds.). *The Globalization Reader* (second edition). Oxford: Blackwell, 2004.

Legvold, Robert (ed.). *Thinking Strategically: The Major Powers, Kazakhstan, and the Central Asian Nexus.* Cambridge, MA: MIT Press, 2003.

Leifer, Michael. *Singapore's Foreign Policy: Coping with Vulnerability.* London: Routledge, 2000.

Len, Christopher. "Japan's Central Asian Diplomacy: Motivations, Implications, and Prospects for the Region." *China and Eurasia Forum Quarterly* 3, no. 3 (November 2005): 127–149.

Lenczowski, George. "The Arc of Crisis: Its Central Sector." *Foreign Affairs,* Spring 1979, 796–820.

Lenin, Vladimir. *Imperialism: The Highest State of Capitalism.* New York: International Publishers, 1939.

Levine, Steve. *The Oil and the Glory: The Pursuit of Empire and Fortune on the Caspian Sea.* New York: Random House, 2007.

Lewis, Bernard. *What Went Wrong? Western Impact and Middle Eastern Response.* Oxford: Oxford University Press, 2002.

Lewis, David Levering. *God's Crucible: Islam and the Making of Europe, 570–1215.* New York: W.W. Norton, 2008.

Lewis, Martin W., and Karen E. Wigen. *The Myth of Continents: A Critique of Metageography.* Berkeley: University of California Press, 1997.

Lim, Robyn. *The Geopolitics of East Asia: The Search for Equilibrium.* London: Routledge, 2003.

Lo, Bobo. *Axis of Convenience: Moscow, Beijing, and the New Geopolitics.* London: Chatham House, 2008.

Lucas, Edward. *The New Cold War: Putin's Russia and the Threat to the West.* London: Palgrave Macmillan, 2008.

Luft, Gal, and Anne Korin (eds.). *Energy Security Challenges for the 21st Century.* Santa Barbara, CA: ABC-Clio, 2009.

Lustgarten, Abraham. *China's Great Train: Beijing's Drive West and the Campaign to Remake Tibet.* New York: Times Books, 2008.

Mackie, Jamie. *Bandung 1955: Non-alignment and Afro-Asian Solidarity.* Singapore: Editions Didier Millet, 2005.

Mackinder, Halford J. *Democratic Ideals and Reality: A Study in the Politics of Reconstruction.* Washington, DC: National Defense University Press, 1996.

———. "The Geographical Pivot of History." *Geographical Journal* 23, no. 4 (April 1904): 421–437.

———. "The Round World and the Winning of Peace." *Foreign Affairs* 21, no. 4 (July 1943): 595–605.

Mahan, Alfred Thayer. *The Influence of Sea Power upon History, 1660–1783.* Boston: Little, Brown, 1890.

———. *The Problem of Asia and Its Effect upon International Policies.* Boston: Little, Brown, 1900.

Maloney, Suzanne. *Iran's Long Reach: Iran as a Pivotal State in the Muslim World.* Washington, DC: United States Institute of Peace, 2008.

Mandelbaum, Michael. *The Case for Goliath.* New York: Perseus, 2005.

―――. *The Frugal Superpower: America's Global Leadership in a Cash-Strapped Era.* New York: Perseus, 2010.

Manning, Robert. *The Asian Energy Factor: Myths and Dilemmas of Energy, Security and the Pacific Future.* New York: Palgrave, 2000.

Marcel, Valerie. *Oil Titans: National Oil Companies in the Middle East.* London: Royal Institute of International Affairs, 2006.

Marozzi, Justin. *Tamerlane: Sword of Islam, Conqueror of the World.* London: Harper Perennial, 2005.

Mattli, Walter. *The Logic of Regional Integration: Europe and Beyond.* Cambridge: Cambridge University Press, 1999.

Medeiros, Evan S., and Bates Gill. *Chinese Arms Exports: Policy, Players and Process.* Carlisle, PA: U.S. Army Strategic Studies Institute, 2000.

Millward, James. *Eurasian Crossroads: A History of Xinjiang.* New York: Columbia University Press, 2007.

―――. *Violent Separatism in Xinjiang: A Critical Assessment.* Washington, DC: East-West Center, 2004.

Ministry of Economy, Trade, and Industry Agency for Natural Resources and Energy. *Energy White Paper.* Tokyo: Government Publication Office, annual.

Miyata, Osamu. *Chūō Ajia Shigen Gaikō* (Central Asian Resource Diplomacy). Tokyo: Jiji Tsūshin Sha, 1999.

Mohan, C. Raja. *Crossing the Rubicon: The Shaping of India's New Foreign Policy.* New Delhi: Penguin, 2003.

Moravcsik, Andrew. *The Choice for Europe: Social Purpose and State Power from Messina to Maastricht.* Ithaca, NY: Cornell University Press, 1998.

Morrison, Charles E., and Astri Suhrke. *Strategies of Survival: The Foreign Policy Dilemmas of Smaller Asian States.* Brisbane: University of Queensland Press, 1978.

Murobuse, Kōshin. *Nanshin-ron* (On Southern Advance). Tokyo: Nihon Hyōron Sha, 1937.

Murphy, David Thomas. *The Heroic Earth: Geopolitical Thought in Weimar Germany, 1918–1933.* Kent, OH: Kent State University Press, 1997.

Nasr, Vali. *The Shia Revival: How Conflicts within Islam Will Shape the Future.* New York: W.W. Norton, 2006.

Nebenzhal, Kenneth. *Mapping the Silk Road and Beyond: 2000 Years of Exploring the East.* London: Phaidon, 2004.

Nehru, Jawaharlal. *An Autobiography.* Delhi: Oxford University Press, 1969.

Nunn, Sam, James Schlesinger, and Robert E. Ebel. *The Geopolitics of Energy into the Twenty-First Century.* Washington, DC: CSIS Press, 2000.

Nye, Joseph. *The Powers to Lead.* Oxford: Oxford University Press, 2008.

―――. *Soft Power: The Means to Success in World Politics.* New York: Public Affairs, 2004.

Nye, Joseph, and John D. Donahue (eds.). *Governance in a Globalizing World.* Washington, DC: Brookings Institution Press, 2000.

Obaid, Nawaf E. *The Oil Kingdom at 100.* Washington, DC: Washington Institute for Near East Policy, 2000.

Odom, William E., and Robert Dujarric. *America's Inadvertent Empire*. New Haven, CT: Yale University Press, 2004.

Okakura, Tenshin. *The Awakening of Japan*. New York: Century, 1904.

———. *The Book of Tea*. New York: Putnam, 1906.

———. *The Ideals of the East*. Tokyo: Heibonsha, 1983.

Ōkawa, Shūmei. *Fukkō Azia no Sho Mondai* (Some Issues in Reemerging Asia). Tokyo: Meiji Shobō, 1939.

Olcott, Martha Brill. *Central Asia's Second Chance*. Washington, DC: Carnegie Endowment for International Peace, 2005.

———. *The Energy Dimension in Russian Global Strategy: Vladimir Putin and the Geopolitics of Oil*. Houston: Rice University Baker Institute for Public Policy, 2004.

———. *Kazakhstan: Unfulfilled Promise*. Washington, DC: Carnegie Endowment for International Peace, 2002.

Olson, Mancur, and Richard Zeckhauser. "An Economic Theory of Alliances." *Review of Economics and Statistics* 48, no. 3 (1966): 266–279.

Organization of Petroleum Exporting Countries. *OPEC Annual Statistical Bulletin*. Vienna: Organization of Petroleum Exporting Countries, annual.

O'Tuathail, G. O. *Critical Geopolitics*. Minneapolis: University of Minnesota Press, 1996.

Palmer, Michael A. *Guardians of the Gulf: A History of America's Expanding Role in the Persian Gulf, 1833–1992*. New York: Free Press, 1992.

Pan, Esther. *China, Africa, and Oil*. New York: Council on Foreign Relations, 2007.

Peattie, Mark R. *Ishiwara Kanji and Japan's Confrontation with the West*. Princeton, NJ: Princeton University Press, 1975.

Pickering, Jeffrey. *Britain's Withdrawal from East of Suez*. Hampshire: Macmillan, 1998.

Polo, Marco. *The Travels*. London: Penguin, 1958.

Preston, Peter. *Singapore in the Global System: Relationship, Structure, and Change*. London: Routledge, 2007.

Putnam, Robert D. "Diplomacy and Domestic Politics: The Logic of Two-Level Games." *International Organization* 42 (Summer 1988): 427–460.

Rangsimaporn, Paradorn. "Interpreting Eurasianism: Justifying Russia's Role in East Asia." *Euro-Asian Studies* 58, no. 3 (May 2006): 271–289.

Rashid, Ahmed. *Jihad: The Rise of Militant Islam in Central Asia*. New York: Penguin Books, 2002.

Remnick, David. *Lenin's Tomb: The Last Days of the Soviet Empire*. New York: Vintage Books, 1994.

Rosecrance, Richard. *The Rise of the Virtual State: Wealth and Power in the Coming Century*. New York: Basic Books, 1999.

Rosenau, James. *Along the Domestic-Foreign Frontier*. Cambridge: Cambridge University Press, 1997.

Ross, Michael L. "Does Oil Hinder Democracy?" *World Politics* 53 (April 2001): 325–361.

———. "The Political Economy of the Resource Curse." *World Politics* 51 (January 1999) 297–322.

Roy, Olivier. *Globalized Islam: The Search for a New Ummah*. New York: Columbia University Press, 2004.

————. *The New Central Asia: The Creation of Nations.* New York: New York University Press, 2000.

Ruland, Jurgen, Heiner Hanggi, and Ralf Roloff (eds.). *Interregionalism and International Relations: A Stepping Stone to Global Governance?* London: Routledge, 2008.

Rumer, Boris (ed.). *Central Asia: The Gathering Storm.* Armonk, NY: M.E. Sharpe, 2002.

Saitō, Hirokazu. *Central Asia's Oil and Gas Sector since the 2008 Financial Crisis: The Rising Role of China.* Washington, DC: SAIS Reischauer Center for East Asian Studies, 2010.

Sasiorowski, Mark J., and Malcolm Byrne (eds.). *Mohammed Mosaddeq and the 1953 Coup in Iran.* Syracuse: Syracuse University Press, 2004.

Saunders, J. J. *The History of the Mongol Conquests.* Philadelphia: University of Pennsylvania Press, 1971.

Schafer, Edward H. *The Golden Peach of Samarkand: A Study of T'ang Exotics.* Berkeley: University of California Press, 1963.

Schirm, Stefan. *Globalization and the New Regionalism.* Cambridge: Cambridge University Press, 2002.

Schwartz, Stephen. *The Two Faces of Islam: The House of Sa'ud from Tradition to Terror.* New York: Doubleday, 2002.

Shirk, Susan L. *How China Opened Its Door: The Political Success of the PRC's Foreign Trade and Investment Reforms.* Washington, DC: Brookings Institution, 1994.

Sigal, Leon V. *Disarming Strangers: Nuclear Diplomacy with North Korea.* Princeton, NJ: Princeton University Press, 1998.

Simmons, Matthew R. *Twilight in the Desert: The Coming Saudi Oil Shock and the World Economy.* New York: John Wiley, 2005.

Skocpol, Theda. *States and Social Revolutions: A Comparative Analysis of France, Russia, and China.* Cambridge: Cambridge University Press, 1979.

Skowronek, Stephen. *Building a New American State.* Cambridge: Cambridge University Press, 1982.

Slaughter, Anne-Marie. "America's Edge: Power in the Networked Century." *Foreign Affairs* 88, no. 1 (January/February 2009): 94–113.

Sohrabi, Nader. "Historicizing Revolutions: Constitutional Revisions in the Ottoman Empire, Iran, and Russia, 1905–1908." *American Journal of Sociology* 100, no. 6 (July 1995): 1385–1447.

Solingen, Etel. *Nuclear Logics: Contrasting Paths in East Asia and the Middle East.* Princeton, NJ: Princeton University Press, 2007.

Spang, Christian W., and Rolf-Harald Wippich (eds.). *Japanese-German Relations, 1895–1945: War, Diplomacy, and Public Opinion.* London: Routledge, 2006.

Spykman, Nicholas John. *America's Strategy in World Politics: The United States and the Balance of Power.* New York: Harcourt, Brace, 1942.

————. "Geography and Foreign Policy II." *American Political Science Review* 32, no. 2 (April 1938): 213–236.

Spykman, Nicholas John, and Helen R. Nicholl (eds.). *The Geography of the Peace.* New York: Harcourt, Brace, 1944.

Spykman, Nicholas John, and Abbie A. Rollins. "Geographic Objectives in Foreign Policy." *American Political Science Review* 33, no. 3 (June 1939): 391–410.

Starr, S. Frederick (ed.). *Xinjiang: China's Muslim Borderland.* Armonk, NY: M.E. Sharpe, 2004.

Starr, S. Frederick, and Andrew C. Kuchins. *The Key to Success in Afghanistan: A Modern Silk Road Strategy.* Washington, DC: Central Asia-Caucasus Institute, 2010.

Stiglitz, Joseph E. *Globalization and Its Discontents.* New York: W.W. Norton, 2003.

Stockholm International Peace Research Institute. *SIPRI Yearbook.* Oxford: Oxford University Press, 1981–2010 editions.

Stulberg, Adam N. *Well-Oiled Diplomacy: Strategic Manipulation and Russia's Energy Statecraft in Eurasia.* Albany: State University of New York Press, 2007.

Sugiyama, Masaaki. *Mongoru Teikoku no Kōbō* (The Rise and Fall of the Mongol Empire). Tokyo: Kōdansha, 1996.

Sun Yat-sen. *China and Japan: Natural Friends—Unnatural Enemies: A Guide for China's Foreign Policy.* Shanghai: China United Press, 1941.

Takeyh, Ray. *Guardians of the Revolution: Iran and the World in the Age of the Ayatollahs.* Oxford: Oxford University Press, 2009.

———. *Hidden Iran: Paradox and Power in the Islamic Republic.* New York: Times Books, 2006.

Tanaka, Akihiko. *The New Middle Ages.* Tokyo: International House of Japan, 2002.

Tanaka, Yōji (ed.). *Roshiya Shi* (A History of Russia). Tokyo: Yamakawa Shuppan Sha, 1995.

Tanner, Stephen. *Afghanistan: A Military History from Alexander the Great to the Fall of the Taliban.* Cambridge, MA: Da Capo, 2002.

Tilly, Charles. *State Formation in Western Europe.* Princeton, NJ: Princeton University Press, 1975.

U.S. Department of Defense. *Allied Contributions to the Common Defense: Report to the United States Congress by the Secretary of Defense.* Washington, DC: U.S. Department of Defense, March 2001.

———. *Base Structure Report.* Washington, DC: U.S. Department of Defense, biannual.

———. *World Manpower Distribution by Geographical Area* (Fall 2008).

U.S. Department of Energy. *International Energy Outlook.* Washington, DC: U.S. Department of Energy, 2006–2010 editions.

———. *International Petroleum Monthly.* Washington, DC: U.S. Department of Energy, 2006–2010 monthly editions.

U.S. Department of Energy, Energy Information Administration. *Country Briefs,* including periodic issues for China, Japan, Korea, India, Russia, Iran, Saudi Arabia, and Kazakhstan.

U.S. Department of State. *Foreign Relations of the United States.* http://www.state.gov/r/pa/ho/frus/c4035.htm

Vassiliev, Alexei. *The History of Saudi Arabia.* London: Sagi, 2000.

Vayrynen, Raimo (ed.). *Globalization and Global Governance.* Lanham, MD: Rowman and Littlefield, 1999.

Vernon, Raymond. *Sovereignty at Bay: The Multinational Spread of U.S. Enterprises.* New York: Basic Books, 1971.

Vitalis, Robert. *America's Kingdom: Mythmaking on the Saudi Oil Frontier.* London: Verso, 2009.

Vogel, Ezra F. *Deng Xiaoping and the Transformation of China.* Cambridge, MA: Harvard University Press, 2011.

Walt, Stephen. *The Origins of Alliances.* Ithaca, NY: Cornell University Press, 1987.

Wang Yue. *Yaou Dalu Jiaoliu Shi* (A Comprehensive History of the Silk Road). Tokyo: Chūō Kōron Shinsha, 2002.

Wawwab, Ismail A., Peter C. Speers, and Paul F. Hoye. *Saudi Aramco and Its World.* Dhahran: Saudi Arabian Oil Company, 1995.

Westad, Anne (ed.). *Brothers in Arms: The Rise and Fall of the Sino-Soviet Alliance, 1945–1963.* Washington, DC: Woodrow Wilson Center Press, 1998.

Woo, Jung-en. *Race to the Swift.* New York: Columbia University Press, 1991.

World Bank. *Transition: The First Ten Years—Analysis and Lessons for Eastern Europe and the Former Soviet Union.* Washington, DC: World Bank, 2002.

Wright, Richard. *The Color Curtain: A Report on the Bandung Conference.* New York: World, 1956.

Wu, Kang, and Fereidun Fesharaki (eds.). *Asia's Energy Future: Regional Dynamics and Global Implications.* Honolulu: East-West Center, 2007.

Yamaoka Junichirō. *Tanaka Kakuei: Fūjirareta Shigen Senryaku* (Tanaka Kakuei: Constrained Resource Strategy). Tokyo: Sōshisha, 2009.

Yates, Douglas A. *The Rentier State in Africa: Oil Rent Dependency and Neocolonialism in the Republic of Gabon.* Trenton, NJ: Africa World Press, 1996.

Yergin, Daniel. *The Quest: Energy, Security, and the Remaking of the Modern World.* New York: The Penguin Press, 2011.

———. "Ensuring Energy Security." *Foreign Affairs,* March/April 2006, 69–82.

———. *The Prize: The Epic Quest for Oil, Money, and Power.* New York: Touchstone, 1991.

Yoshikawa, Yukie. *Japan's Asianism, 1868–1945: Dilemmas of Japanese Modernization.* Washington, DC: Reischauer Center for East Asian Studies, 2010.

Yoshino, Sakuzō. *Yoshino Sakuzō Zenshū* (The Collected Works of Yoshino Sakuzō). Tokyo: Iwanami, 1996.

Zagoria, Donald S. *The Sino-Soviet Conflict, 1956–1961.* Princeton, NJ: Princeton University Press, 1962.

Zakaria, Fareed. *The Post-American World.* New York: W.W. Norton, 2008.

Zhang, Shu Guang. *Economic Cold War: American's Embargo against China and the Sino-Soviet Alliance, 1949–1963.* Stanford, CA: Stanford University Press, 2001.

Zhirinovskii, Vladimir. *Geopolitika I russkii vopros* (Geopolitics and the Russian Question). Moscow: Galeriia, 1998.

Ziuganov, Gennadii. *Geografiia pobedy: osnovy rossiskoigeopolitiki* (The Geography of Victory: Foundations of Russian Geopolitics). Moscow: G. Ziuganov, 1997.

Index